SEATTLE

3RD EDITION

Where to Stay and Eat
for All Budgets

Must-See Sights
and Local Secrets

Ratings You Can Trust

Portions of this book appear in *Fodor's Pacific Northwest*

Fodor's Travel Publications   New York, Toronto, London, Sydney, Auckland
www.fodors.com

FODOR'S SEATTLE

Editors: Laura M. Kidder, senior editor; Jane Onstott

Editorial Production: Ira-Neil Dittersdorf

Editorial Contributors: Shelley Arenas, Gina Bacon, John Doerper, Julie Fay, Satu Hummasti, Vanessa Lazo Greaves, Holly S. Smith

Maps: David Lindroth *cartographer;* Bob Blake and Rebecca Baer, *map editors*

Design: Fabrizio La Rocca, *creative director;* Guido Caroti, *art director;* Melanie Marin, *senior picture editor*

Production/Manufacturing: Angela L. McLean

Cover Photo (Spinning amusement ride and Space Needle): Paul Souders/ WorldFoto

Third Edition

ISBN 1–4000–1330–5

ISSN 1531–3417

SPECIAL SALES

This book is available for special discounts for bulk purchases for sales promotions or premiums. Special editions, including personalized covers, excerpts of existing books, and corporate imprints, can be created in large quantities for special needs. For more information, write to Special Markets/Premium Sales, 1745 Broadway, MD 6-2, New York, New York, 10019 or e-mail specialmarkets@ randomhouse.com.

AN IMPORTANT TIP & AN INVITATION

Although all prices, opening times, and other details in this book are based on information supplied to us at press time, changes occur all the time in the travel world, and Fodor's cannot accept responsibility for facts that become outdated or for inadvertent errors or omissions. So **always confirm information when it matters,** especially if you're making a detour to visit a specific place. Your experiences—positive and negative—matter to us. If we have missed or misstated something, **please write to us.** We follow up on all suggestions. Contact the Seattle editors at editors@fodors.com or c/o Fodor's at 1745 Broadway, New York, New York 10019.

PRINTED IN THE UNITED STATES OF AMERICA

10 9 8 7 6 5 4 3 2 1

DESTINATION SEATTLE

Seattle may be a technology capital, but its links to the primeval landscape are ever present. The city's office towers rise from the blue-gray saltwater inlets and freshwater lakes like the battlements of a fortress. These skyscrapers, however, are easily dwarfed by the serrated crests of the North Cascades; the imposing, snow-capped volcanic crater of Mt. Rainier south of the city; and the jagged Olympic Mountains to the west. Several million people live in the metropolitan environs, but nature is as close as an urban creek where salmon spawn; a wooded ravine that shelters coyotes and deer; or shoreside alders and blackberry tangles that hide goldfinches, wrens, and sharp-shinned hawks. Beavers gnaw on shade trees; seals and otters frolic beside the ferry docks; great blue herons, ducks, and Canada geese hang out in marshy fringes; orca pods sometimes swim along the waterfront; and cougars and black bears occasionally show up in the suburbs. Sometimes, people from outside Seattle—and even Washington State—have also been spotted in town and around. Ready to join them? Have a great trip!

Karen Cure

Karen Cure, Editorial Director

CONTENTS

Maps

CloseUps

ABOUT THIS BOOK

There's no doubt that the best source for travel advice is a like-minded friend who's just been where you're headed. But with or without that friend, you'll have a better trip with a Fodor's guide in hand. Once you've learned to find your way around its pages, you'll be in great shape to find your way around your destination.

SELECTION Our goal is to cover the best properties, sights, and activities, as well as the most interesting communities. We make a point of including local food-lovers' hot spots as well as neighborhood options, and we avoid all that's touristy unless it's worth your time. Everything you read about in this book is recommended wholeheartedly by our writers and editors. Flip to **On the Road with Fodor's** to learn more about who they are. It goes without saying that no property in the book has paid to be included.

RATINGS Orange stars ★ denote sights and properties that our editors and writers consider the very best in the area covered by the entire book. These, the best of the best, are listed in the **Fodor's Choice** section in the front of the book. Black stars ★ highlight the sights and properties we deem **Highly Recommended,** the don't-miss sights within any region. Fodor's Choice and Highly Recommended options in each region are usually listed on the title page of the chapter covering that region. Use the index to find complete descriptions. In cities, sights pinpointed with numbered map bullets ❶ in the margins tend to be more important than those without bullets.

SPECIAL SPOTS **Pleasures & Pastimes** focuses on types of experiences that reveal the spirit of the destination. Watch for **Off the Beaten Path** sights. Some are out of the way, some are quirky, and all are worth your while. If the munchies hit while you're exploring, look for **Need a Break?** suggestions.

TIME IT RIGHT Wondering when to go? Check **On the Calendar** up front and chapters' **Timing** sections for weather and crowd overviews and best days and times to visit.

SEE IT ALL Use Fodor's exclusive **Great Itineraries** as a model for your trip. (For a good overview, follow those that begin the book.) In cities, **Good Walks** guide you to important sights in each neighborhood; ☛ indicates the starting points of walks and itineraries in the text and on the map.

BUDGET WELL Hotel and restaurant price categories from ¢ to $$$$ are defined in the opening pages of each chapter—expect to find a balanced selection for every budget. For attractions, we always give standard adult admission fees; reductions are usually available for children, students, and senior citizens. Look in **Discounts & Deals** in Smart Travel Tips for information on destination-wide ticket schemes. Want to pay with plastic? **AE, D, DC, MC, V** following restaurant and hotel listings indicate whether American Express, Discover, Diners Club, MasterCard, or Visa are accepted.

BASIC INFO **Smart Travel Tips** lists travel essentials for the entire area covered by the book; city- and region-specific basics end each chapter. To find the best way to get around, see the transportation section; see individual modes of travel ("Car Travel," "Train Travel") for details. We assume you'll check Web sites or call for particulars.

ON THE MAPS	**Maps** throughout the book show you what's where and help you find your way around. Black and orange numbered bullets ❶ ❶ in the text correlate to bullets on maps.
BACKGROUND	In general, we give background information within the chapters in the course of explaining sights as well as in **CloseUp** boxes.
FIND IT FAST	Within the Exploring chapter, sights are grouped by neighborhood. Where to Eat and Where to Stay are also organized by neighborhood. The Nightlife & the Arts and Sports & the Outdoors chapters are arranged alphabetically by type of entertainment or sport. Within Shopping, reviews are grouped according to neighborhood and to their focus. The Side Trips chapter explores Puget Sound, the San Juan Islands, and the national parks. Heads at the top of each page help you find what you need within a chapter.
DON'T FORGET	**Restaurants** are open for lunch and dinner daily unless we state otherwise; we mention dress only when there's a specific requirement and reservations only when they're essential or not accepted—it's always best to book ahead. **Hotels** have private baths, phone, TVs, and air-conditioning and operate on the European Plan (a.k.a. EP, meaning without meals), unless we state otherwise. We always list facilities but not whether you'll be charged extra to use them, so when pricing accommodations, find out what's included.

SYMBOLS

Many Listings
- ★ Fodor's Choice
- ★ Highly recommended
- ✉ Physical address
- ✛ Directions
- ⌖ Mailing address
- ☎ Telephone
- 🖷 Fax
- ⊕ On the Web
- ✎ E-mail
- 💷 Admission fee
- ☻ Open/closed times
- ► Start of walk/itinerary
- ⊟ Credit cards

Outdoors
- ⚠ Camping

Hotels & Restaurants
- 🏨 Hotel
- ⤺ Number of rooms
- ⌂ Facilities
- ❍ Meal plans
- ✕ Restaurant
- ⛉ Reservations
- 👗 Dress code
- ↘ Smoking
- ⚇ BYOB
- ✕🏨 Hotel with restaurant that warrants a visit

Other
- ☾ Family-friendly
- 🛈 Contact information
- ⇨ See also
- ✉ Branch address
- ☞ Take note

ON THE ROAD WITH FODOR'S

A trip takes you out of yourself. Concerns of life at home completely disappear, driven away by more immediate thoughts—about, say, what marvels will beguile the next day, or where you'll have dinner. That's where Fodor's comes in. We make sure that you know all your options, so that you don't miss something that's around the next bend just because you didn't know it was there. Because the best memories of your trip might well have nothing to do with what you came to Seattle to see, we guide you to sights large and small all over the city. You might set out to shop in Pike Place Market and see the Space Needle, but back at home you find yourself unable to forget lingering in a coffeehouse or brew pub or browsing in a neighborhood bookstore. With Fodor's at your side, serendipitous discoveries are never far away.

Our success in showing you every corner of Seattle is a credit to our extraordinary writers. Although there's no substitute for travel advice from a good friend who knows your style, our contributors are the next best thing—the kind of people you would poll for travel advice if you knew them.

Shelley Arenas is coauthor of *Lobster Kids Guide to Exploring Seattle* and directs ParentCafe.org, a nonprofit parenting resources Web site. She has contributed to numerous guidebooks, including Fodor's *CityGuide Seattle, Away From It All, Pacific Northwest,* and *Great American Drives of the West.* She was born in Seattle, grew up in eastern Washington, spent summers at a lake in northern Idaho, and has lived in Seattle all her adult life.

Gina Bacon, who covered Mt. Rainier and Mt. St. Helens, is a Pacific Northwest native and freelance writer based in Camas, WA, which is along the Lewis and Clark Trail. She has written for *Portland Up-Close, Portrait of Puget Sound, Garden Showcase,* and *The Columbian* newspaper, among other publications.

Veteran writer and Washington resident **John Doerper,** who covered North Cascades National Park and environs, has explored the Pacific Northwest for more than 25 years and has written extensively about this fascinating region. He is also the author of several guidebooks.

A champion of great service, great food, and comfortable beds, freelance writer **Julie Fay** updated the Where to Eat and Where to Stay chapters. The Seattle native has been contributing to Fodor's guides since 1997. She also works as a development associate for the House of Dames Productions theater group and is on the board of directors for Cinema Seattle, which presents the Seattle International Film Festival. Julie is a fifth-generation Washingtonian who keeps in touch with her pioneer roots by spending summers at a cabin built by her great-grandparents on the shores of Bellingham Bay.

After too many seasons leading adventure tours through the western United States, **Vanessa Lazo Greaves,** who updated the Shopping chapter, traded her hiking boots for high heels and set out to explore fashion publishing. During a business trip to Seattle for *W* magazine, she fell madly in love with the city and decided to experience the next decade as a resident. Now raising a son and restoring an old house and garden with her husband, Vanessa writes about food for an online site, dispenses fashion advice, and still stops to help lost tourists.

After covering parts of Indonesia, Australia, Peru, and Oregon for Fodor's, western Washington resident **Holly S. Smith** enjoyed working on something closer to home. Her young children, ages five, three, and one, also had a great time tagging along on explorations of local attractions and activities in the Seattle and its environs, the San Juan Islands, and the Olympic Peninsula. Holly, who is a regular Fodor's updater and editor, has also written several travel and cultural books, including *Adventuring in Indonesia, Aceh: Art & Culture,* and *How to Bounce Back Quickly After Losing Your Job.*

Seattle is basically a strip of land boxed in and cut in half by water: On the west is Puget Sound. On the east is Lake Washington. In the middle—the city. As Seattle has developed, the lines between its neighborhoods and suburbs have blurred so much that boundaries are often set more by local opinion than anything else. The city's neighborhoods generally break down as follows.

Downtown & Environs

Downtown & the Waterfront. Seattle's business and government core is also the center for upscale shopping, international entertainment, and such popular tourist spots as Pike Place Market. Downtown's 8- by 10-block area is bounded on the west by Elliott Bay and the waterfront, on the south by Pioneer Square and the International District (its southern border is Columbia Street), on the north by Belltown and Queen Anne (Virginia Street is the cutoff), and on the east by I–5 and the convention center. Traffic is a mess on weekdays and during major events, so park your car in a garage or lot and explore on foot. Buses are free in the city center; there are also a waterfront trolley that runs to Pioneer Square and the International District and a mile-long monorail that connects Westlake Mall to the Seattle Center. There are steep climbs from the waterfront to the midtown shops and museums.

The waterfront stretches south from the old Downtown near Pioneer Square, past the sports stadiums and through the industrial regions of Harbor Island around Duwamish Head, to the bluffs and beaches of West Seattle. To the north the waterfront follows Elliott Bay around the Magnolia Bluffs to Shilshole Bay and beyond. In the latter half of the 20th century, the Port of Seattle and the city developed the Downtown waterfront into a promenade, whose surviving docks house shops, restaurants, marinas, the Seattle Aquarium, the Maritime Discovery Center, and the Bell Harbor International Conference Center. Tour-company and private boats dock at piers 54 to 70, Washington State ferries depart from Pier 52, and cruise ships anchor at Pier 66.

Belltown. Just north of Pike Place Market is Belltown, a formerly nondescript commercial and low-rent residential area that has turned trendy. Condominiums have risen, old storefronts and union halls have been converted into restaurants, and upscale shops have moved in. Belltown is now alive late into the night, and parking spots are hard to find—go early for a cheap lot and explore on foot. Walking is also the best way to enjoy the shops and the views of Puget Sound and the Olympic Mountains. The district's boundaries are, roughly, from Elliott Bay east to Sixth Avenue, and north from Virginia Street to Denny Way.

Queen Anne. Queen Anne Hill rises between Belltown and Denny Way to the south and the Lake Washington Ship Canal to the north. To the west (after 15th Avenue West) is the Magnolia district; to the east, Aurora Avenue and Lake Union. This rolling neighborhood has two parts, each with its own personality. Upper Queen Anne, atop Queen Anne Hill, has upscale houses, fashionable restaurants, and trendy businesses. Lower Queen Anne, at the foot of the hill, has seen some gentrification but remains more a working-class neighborhood of small homes, apartments, and shops. It's also home to the Seattle Center, the Space Needle, the Experience Music Project, and the Pacific Science Center. Stores and restaurants predominate along Mercer and Roy streets, at the foot of the hill, and on Queen Anne Avenue atop the hill. Many of the tree-lined streets have great panoramas of Puget Sound and the Olympic or Cascade mountains.

Pioneer Square. Seattle's oldest neighborhood is always a hub of activity, with a multitude of restaurants, shops, and art galleries. Streets lined with massive redbrick and sandstone buildings provide a glimpse of how Seattle appeared when it was rebuilt after the Great Fire of 1889. At the corner of Yesler Way and Second Avenue stands the 42-story Smith Tower, the tallest building west of the Mississippi when it was completed in 1914. Yesler Way was once called Skid Road, a term born when timber was slid down the street to a steam-powered waterfront mill. At night this historic district drapes itself with party attire, when tourists and locals alike head to its many rock clubs, sports bars, and taverns. The famous Elliott Bay Bookstore and Pioneer Park are two well-known local attractions. Pioneer Square is bordered by Alaskan Way South, Columbia Street, Fourth Avenue South, and South King Street.

International District. Once called Chinatown, the International District has expanded its roots to include Japanese, Vietnamese, Cambodian, Malaysian, and Filipino traditions. Known locally as the "I.D.," the neighborhood is southeast of Downtown, between Yesler Way to the north, Dearborn Street to the south, 5th Avenue South to the west, and 12th Avenue to the east. Small produce markets thrive here, making it a great place to shop for exotic ingredients and to enjoy authentic Asian food. Don't miss the sprawling, two-story Uwajimaya supermarket.

Sodo. This rapidly expanding commercial area is southwest of the former Kingdome sports stadium (famously demolished by dynamite), from which the neighborhood's "South of the Dome" nickname is derived. Wedged in the corner between Pioneer Square and the I.D., Sodo stretches approximately from Fourth Avenue to the waterfront along First Avenue South, Highway 99, and Alaskan Way, between South King Street to the north and Spokane Street to the south. The area includes both Safeco Field baseball stadium and the Seahawks football stadium, as well as an increasing number of brewpubs, restaurants, sports memorabilia stores, and art galleries.

First Hill. This compact neighborhood is sandwiched between Downtown and Capitol Hill, bordered by Pine Street to the north and I–5 to the west. Referred to as "Pill Hill" for its abundance of hospitals and medical offices, it runs roughly south past Madison to James Street and east nearly to Broadway—although many Seattleites consider the former to be part of Downtown and the latter all Capitol Hill. During the day you'll see mostly working professionals—doctors, nurses, and patients hurrying to appointments, and the thirtysomethings who live here in posh condos and studio apartments strolling briskly to and from their Downtown jobs. After dark and on weekends it's dead.

Central Area. The hub of the African-American community is also referred to as the Central District. It lies east of Downtown, adjacent to Capitol Hill and First Hill, and it's bordered by I–90, Martin Luther King Jr. Way, East Madison Street, and 12th Avenue. In the 1940s, this part of town nurtured a dynamic jazz scene, but the area also has suffered from neglect and economic blight. Although its high school (Garfield High) educated such legends as Jimi Hendrix and Quincy Jones, gang activity has also plagued its streets. It's a proud neighborhood of beautiful and beloved churches, creative street art, and some of the city's best home-style restaurants.

North & East of Downtown

Lake Union & Environs. Lake Union is in the heart of Seattle, bordered by Queen Anne to the west, Wallingford to the north, Eastlake and Capitol Hill to the east, and the commercial and industrial flats of the Denny Regrade to the south. The natural freshwater lake was once a center of maritime industry, but underwent a transformation in the 1980s and 1990s, when condominiums, parks, and restaurants began to replace shipyards, gasworks, and mills. The eastern and western shores are lined with houseboats; a pretty paved footpath runs along the southern waterfront past yacht docks and restaurants with decks—great spots to relax and watch sailboats, floatplanes, gulls, and the occasional bald eagle. Gasworks Park, which juts into the lake's northern end, has views of the water and Downtown. In summer, throngs head here for Fourth of July fireworks, concerts, and Shakespearean plays.

Capitol Hill. Northeast of Downtown and east of I-5 is Capitol Hill, the center of Seattle's youth culture. Yet it's also an elegant neighborhood, with tree-lined streets; 19th-century mansions; Lakeview Cemetery, where many of the city's notables are buried; and Frederick Law Olmsted's Volunteer Park, where you'll find the Asian Art Museum. The Broadway district, south of St. Mark's Cathedral, is home to Seattle's most diverse population: the city's gay community, grunge rockers, multiethnic store and restaurant owners, and multiracial Generation Xers. Young people are not only attracted by the neighborhood's many shops, theaters, bars, and cafés, but also by the many educational institutions crowning the ridge: Seattle University, Central Seattle Community College, and Cornish College of the Arts. To the north and east lies the Montlake neighborhood, bordering the southern bank of the Lake Washington Ship Canal and the eastern edge of the Washington Park Arboretum. The Pike–Pine street corridor dividing Capitol Hill from First Hill has some of the city's most edgy shops, clubs, and cafés.

University District. Northeast of Lake Union, this area encircles the University of Washington, whose vast campus stretches from Portage Bay to Union Bay. Dubbed the "U-District," this is a lively, eclectic neighborhood of shops, restaurants, apartments, and older homes, many of which have been converted to student flats. The district is bisected by two main arteries: Northeast 45th Street, site of the University Village shopping area, and University Way Northeast, the heart of the UW campus known locally as "The Ave." Crafts and bookstores, funky clothes shops, cheap ethnic restaurants, and pubs line this street, and there's a popular Saturday farmers market where it intersects with Northeast 50th Street. The ship canal's Montlake Cut, which runs from Lake Union to Lake Washington, is dotted mostly with university facilities and marine-related businesses.

Ravenna. This unpretentious neighborhood just north of the U-District was named after a seaside district in northeast Italy. There's nothing flashy or quirky about these quiet shaded streets, home to many middle-class single-family homes. And that's just fine by those who live here. They're proud of this residential neighborhood's "down-to-earth" feel, with its family restaurants and homey shops. The district's boundaries are Northeast 75th Street, I-5, 43rd Avenue Northeast, and Ravenna Boulevard/Northeast 55th Street.

Mercer Island. Microsoft cofounder and all-around rich guy Paul Allen keeps a house on this island between Seattle and the Eastside communities. Elite country clubs and palatial estates, as well as numerous parks and protected wetlands, are the norm. The median price for a home is $575,000—pocket change for the city notables who live here. Lots of old money lines these tidy streets, which are not, as one might expect, paved in gold. Several public lakeside parks are around the island's edges, so you don't have to be rich and famous to enjoy Mercer's beauty.

Bellevue. Three-quarters of a century ago, Bellevue was a pleasant little town in the country, with rows of shops along Main Street serving the farmers who grew strawberries. After the first floating bridge across Lake Union was built in the 1940s, suburban homes began to replace the strawberry fields. Then came the huge Bellevue Mall, the Meydenbauer convention center, and more suburban sprawl. Even though Main Street and a few other corners of old Bellevue remain, this Eastside city's main focus is its mercantile core. However, with the Theater at Meydenbauer and many first-class performance groups and galleries, the local arts scene is garnering followers as well.

Kirkland. A small town on Lake Washington's east shore, Kirkland has the most lively downtown of any Eastside community. Its business district, along the Lake Street waterfront, is lined with shops, restaurants, pubs, and parks. Best of all, there are convenient parking (if you arrive early enough) and easy pedestrian access to the lake. The heart of downtown is known as Moss Bay—although the actual bay vanished when the Lake Union Ship Canal lowered the water level by 8.8 feet.

Issaquah. This developing area southeast of Bellevue was once the home of the Snoqualmie Indian tribe, which lived off the area's abundant fish and game and named the place Squak for the sound of migrating fowl. From this, later settlers called the town Issaquah, which became a timber and coal mining hub through the 1920s. Today, nestled up to the southeast nub of Lake Sammamish, Issaquah is a great place to hike, boat, or horseback ride. The surrounding Cougar, Tiger, and Squak mountain foothills—dubbed the Issaquah Alps—are older than the Cascade range.

Redmond. A string of pretty parks makes Redmond an inviting place to experience the outdoors, whether by foot along the 13-mi (21-km) Sammamish River Trail, by horse at Farrel–McWhirter Park, by bicycle at the Marymoor Park Velodrome track, by water on Lake Sammamish, or by hot-air balloon over the whole scene. You can picnic at Idylwood Park; play tennis at Marymoor Park; or mountain-bike the gravel, 3-mi (5-km) Puget Power–Redmond Trail.

North & West of Downtown

Wallingford. "Eclectic" is the word to describe this neighborhood of small, close-set shops and restaurants centered on North 45th Street, between Green Lake to the north, Fremont to the south and west, and I–5 and the U-District to the east. Part post-college crowd, part modest yuppie, part foreign transplant, part struggling family, Wallingford's residents and business owners have turned it into a fun, friendly place that's full of color and energy.

Fremont. Fremont is an artsy district north of Lake Union and the Lake Washington Ship Canal, east of Ballard, south and west of Wallingford, and south of Woodland Park. The compact neighborhood of 14,000 residents is made for walking, so park your car (preferably along the ship canal's north bank, south of the Fremont Bridge), and explore. You can peer into galleries, browse vintage clothing and housewares shops, pause in a café for a latte, or enjoy a meal in one of Seattle's best restaurants. You also can soak up this neighborhood's independent spirit, highlighted on First Saturday artwalks, the warm-weather Sunday market, and the Summer Solstice Parade.

Ballard. Northwest of Lake Union, Ballard is at the mouth of Shishole Bay and the fun-to-tour Chittenden Locks, which connect Lake Washington to Puget Sound. This community has the Pacific Northwest's largest fishing harbor and is the winter home for the Alaskan fishing fleet, which includes vessels that range from tiny salmon trollers to large factory trawlers. Once an independent village of Scandinavian fishermen, this marine-oriented community of small houses and cottage gardens is also the site of the Nordic Heritage Museum. The compact commercial district along Market Street, near 15th Avenue West, has small, modern shops, and many cafés are clustered between the boatyards and ship chandleries of the canal and harborfront.

Magnolia. West of Queen Anne, Magnolia is a quiet residential neighborhood rising among the bluffs between Elliott Bay and the Ship Canal. The area's expensive, precariously perched homes are surrounded by gardens; there are no native magnolias, but you'll see plenty of exotic ones in bloom. Magnolia got its name from an early Vancouver expedition that mistook the native madronas for magnolias. On the bluffs above the bay are great views across Puget Sound to the Olympic Mountains from the neighborhood's many parks. The 534-acre Discovery Park is a refuge for urban wildlife as well as a stopover for migrating birds. Spectacular cliff-top views take in the Olympic and Cascade ranges. The park also has quiet dells, meadows, streams, and 2 mi (3 km) of protected tidal beaches with sand dunes.

West Seattle. South of the city and on a peninsula just across Elliott Bay lies West Seattle. It was here, in 1851, that a group of settlers known as the Denny Party staked their claim to the land that would become Seattle. Today the neighborhood is a mix of rich and poor; as prices have skyrocketed in Seattle proper, many people have fled to West Seattle in search of affordable housing. On a drive through it you'll pass miles of beautiful beaches, cute shops and restaurants, and cozy single-family homes. Its center, called the Junction, is home to a shopping area as well as 10 of the neighborhood's 11 murals. Gorgeous Alki Beach sweeps around the area's perimeter, offering views of Puget Sound and the Seattle skyline. Lincoln Park, a sprawling, forested tract of land near the Fauntleroy ferry terminal, is a fine place to hike, bike, blade, and relax on the beach.

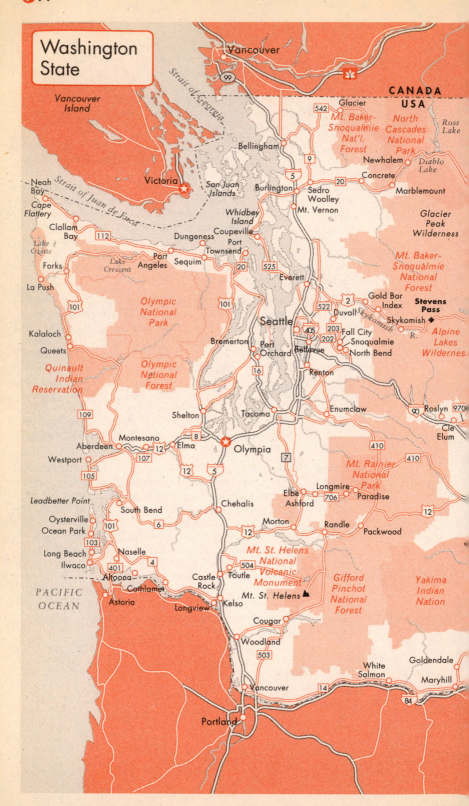

Washington State

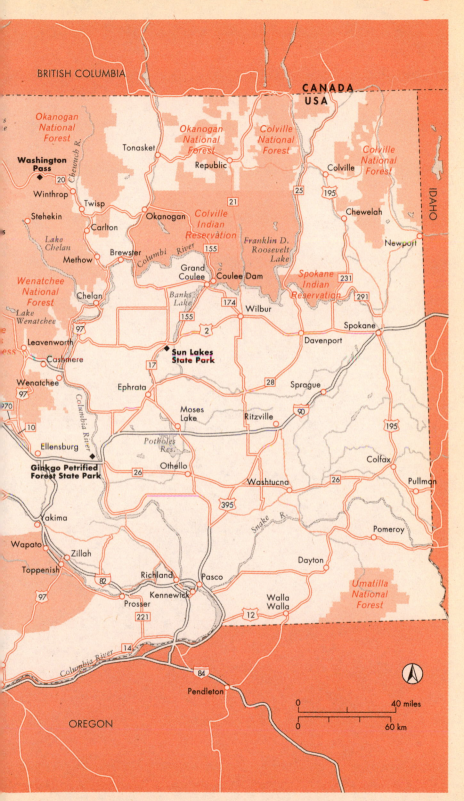

BRITISH COLUMBIA

Okanogan National Forest

Tonasket

Okanogan National Forest

Colville National Forest

Republic

Colville

Colville National Forest

Washington Pass ◆

Chewuch R.

20

Winthrop

Twisp

25

195

Chewelah

Stehekin

Carlton

Okanogan

21

Colville Indian Reservation

Newport

Lake Chelan

Methow

Brewster

Columbia River

155

Franklin D. Roosevelt Lake

Wenatchee National Forest

Chelan

Grand Coulee

Coulee Dam

Spokane Indian Reservation

231

291

Lake Wenatchee

97

Banks Lake

174

Wilbur

Spokane

Leavenworth

155

Davenport

Cashmere

2

Wenatchee

97

Sun Lakes State Park ◆

97

970

17

28

Sprague

10

Ellensburg

Ephrata

Columbia River

Moses Lake

90

Ritzville

195

Colfax

Ginkgo Petrified Forest State Park ■

Potholes Res.

Othello

26

26

Pullman

26

395

Washtucna

Snake R.

Pomeroy

Yakima

Wapato

Zillah

Dayton

Toppenish

82

Richland

Pasco

Umatilla National Forest

97

Prosser

Kennewick

Walla Walla

221

12

14

Columbia River

84

Pendleton

OREGON

CANADA
USA

IDAHO

0 _____ 40 miles

0 _____ 60 km

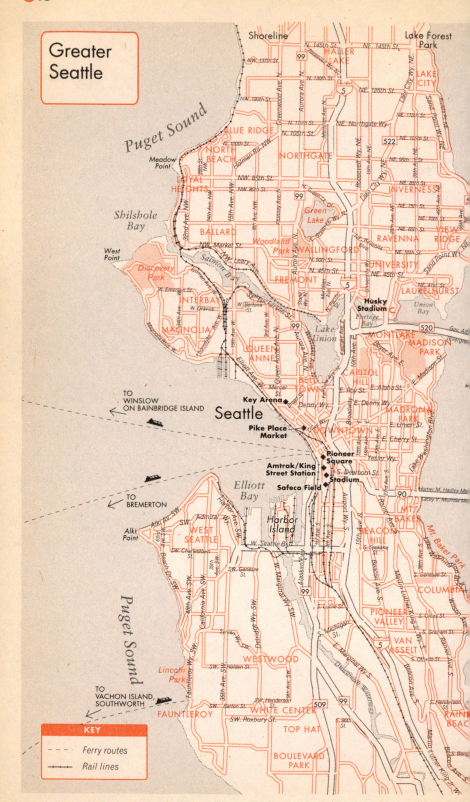

Greater Seattle

Puget Sound

Shoreline

Lake Forest
Park

NW. 137th St.

99

HALLER
LAKE

NE. 145th St.

N. 145th St.

Roosevelt Wy. NE.

NE. 145th St.

NW. 120th St.

N. 130th St.

5

NE. 125th St.

LAKE
CITY

Greenwood Ave. N.

Aurora Ave. N.

N. 110th St.

NE. Northgate Wy.

NE. 115th St.

Lake City Wy. NE.

Sand Point Wy. NE.

BLUE RIDGE

Meridian Ave. N.

N. 105th St.

Holman Rd. NW.

N. 100th St.

522

NE. 105th St.

NORTH
BEACH

Roosevelt Wy. NE.

NE. 96th St.

Meadow
Point

NW. 85th St.

NW. 85th St.

NORTHGATE

8th Ave. NW.

NE. 85th St.

INVERNESS

NW. 80th St.

N. Green Lake Dr.

NE. 75th St.

LOYAL
HEIGHTS

15th Ave. NW.

24th Ave. NW.

Green
Lake

Lake City Wy. NE.

NE. 70th St.

VIEW
RIDGE

99

Green Lake Dr. N.

NE. 65th St.

Sand Point Wy. NE.

Shilshole
Bay

BALLARD

NW. Market St.

Woodland
Park

NE. Ravenna

RAVENNA

NE. 55th St.

West
Point

NW. Leary Wy.

WALLINGFORD

N. 50th St.

UNIVERSITY

NE. 50th St.

Discovery
Park

Salmon Bay

Gilman Ave. W.

FREMONT

N. 45th St.

5

NE. 45th St.

LAURELHURST

W. Emerson St.

W. Nickerson St.

N. 41st St.

INTERBAY

W. Bertona
St.

Stone Wy. N.

Husky
Stadium

Union
Bay

W. Dravus

Husky
Stadium

Portage
Bay

MONTLAKE

520

Gov. Atb

MAGNOLIA

Magnolia Blvd. W.

34th Ave. W.

15th Ave. W.

99

Lake
Union

MADISON
PARK

Evergreen

QUEEN
ANNE

Queen Anne Ave. N.

Aurora Ave. N.

Boyer Ave. E.

CAPITOL
HILL

E. Madison St.

Elliott Ave. W.

Mercer St.

BELL
TOWN

Broadway

E. Aloha St.

E. Roy St.

MADRONA
PARK

TO WINSLOW
ON BAINBRIDGE ISLAND

Key Arena

Denny Wy.

E. Denny Wy.

E. Union St.

Seattle

Pike Place
Market

DOWNTOWN

E. Cherry St.

Lake Washington Blvd.

Pioneer
Square

Yesler Wy.

Amtrak/King
Street Station

S. Dearborn St.

90

Homer M. Hadley Mem.

Stadium

TO
BREMERTON

Safeco Field

Lacey V. Murrow Me.

Elliott
Bay

Harbor
Island

MT.
BAKER

Alki Ave. SW.

Harbor Ave. SW.

S. Spokane St.

BEACON
HILL

Mt. Baker Blvd.

Alki
Point

W. Seattle Bridge

Alaskan Wy. S.

15th Ave. S.

Mt. Baker Park

WEST
SEATTLE

SW.
Admiral Wy.

W. Seattle Bridge

E. Marginal Wy. S.

S. Spokane St.

S. Genesee St.

Beach Dr. SW.

61st Ave. SW.

SW. Charlestown
St.

39th Ave. SW.

SW. Genesee
St.

99

COLUMBIA

California Ave. SW.

Delridge Wy. SW.

S. Lucile St.

PIONEER
VALLEY

S. Graham St.

S. Orcas St.

Sylvan Wy. SW.

35th Ave. SW.

S. Michigan
St.

VAN
ASSELT

S. Othello St.

Puget Sound

Lincoln
Park

Fauntleroy Wy. SW.

WESTWOOD

SW. Holden St.

Duwamish Waterway

509

Martin Luther King Jr. Wy. S.

RAIN
BEAC

TO
VACHON ISLAND,
SOUTHWORTH

36th Ave. SW.

SW. Barton St.

SW. Henderson St.

99

S. Henderson
St.

FAUNTLEROY

WHITE CENTER

SW. Roxbury St.

TOP HAT

S. 96th
St.

Beacon Ave. S.

BOULEVARD
PARK

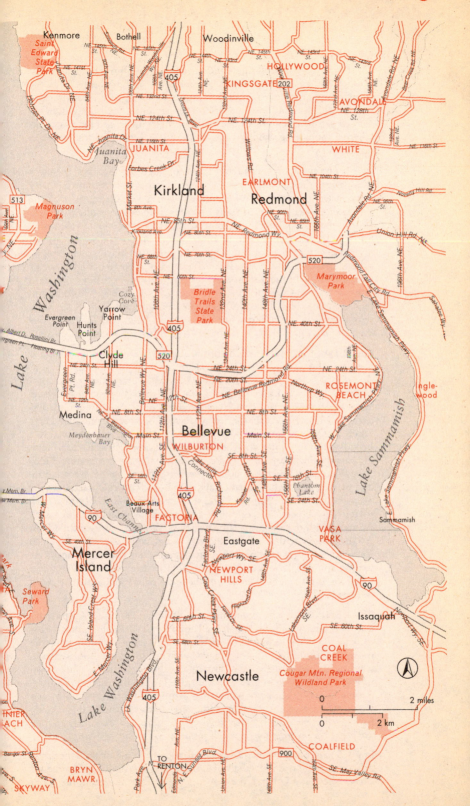

Seattle in 6 Days

Most of Seattle's central sights and activities are within walking distance of one another, and you can easily reach those in the suburbs by public transportation. Before you explore, though, you'll need three things—comfortable walking shoes, layered clothing, and a flexible mindset. It's easy to get off-track in this fascinating city, to linger too long in an intriguing shop, or to stumble onto a local festival that you don't want to leave. Enjoy!

Day 1: Get up with the sun and stroll to Pike Place Market, the sight that defines the city's world-savvy spirit. Grab a latte or have a hearty breakfast at a market café. Spend the morning wandering through the fish, fruit, flower, and crafts stalls, and then head underground to browse stores selling knickknacks and books. Take the steps down to the docks and visit the Odyssey Maritime Discovery Center or the Seattle Aquarium. Stop at a waterfront eatery for a classic Seattle lunch: cedar-smoked salmon on a sourdough roll, steamed clams, or a bread bowl of chunky clam chowder. In the afternoon take a cruise on Elliott Bay or shop in Downtown's cosmopolitan shops. Return to Pike Place Market and have dinner at one of the city's esteemed restaurants. Top off the night with a concert, a play, or a little clubbing in Belltown. *Take this tour any day; the market and waterfront attractions are open daily all year.*

Day 2: Take the two-minute monorail ride from Downtown's Westlake Center mall to the Seattle Center. Head up the Space Needle for 360-degree city views; a drink from the SkyCity coffee bar is the perfect complement. Afterward take in one of Seattle Center's many ground-level attractions: the Pacific Science Center, the Children's Museum, the Experience Music Project, or the Science Fiction Experience museum. Have lunch in Queen Anne or Belltown, and then walk southwest down Broadway to the water and the Olympic Sculpture Park. Ride the trolley past the docks and through Pioneer Square to the International District. Wander around the slim shaded streets, absorbing the Asian culture and picking up goodies at fruit stalls, tea shops, and knickknack stores. Tour the Wing Luke Museum, and then head up to Kobe Terrace Park for a look at Elliott Bay. For dinner, try a neighborhood joint along 12th Avenue South or dine at Uwajimaya, the Asian superstore with a Pan-Asian food court that will enable you to eat your way from Japan to Vietnam. See what's happening at the Nippon Kan Theater, or head east to the Capitol Hill shops and bars. *Not on Monday, when the Wing Luke Museum is closed, or Sunday, when local shops are closed or have shorter hours.*

Day 3: Start the day by exploring art galleries and antiques shops in Pioneer Square. Wander through the Klondike Gold Rush National Historical Park, then grab a latte at the corner Starbucks before you take the Seattle Underground Tour. Have lunch at Elliott Bay Books' downstairs café, then stay awhile to browse the shelves upstairs. Walk down to Pier 52 and catch a ferry to Bainbridge Island, then spend the afternoon exploring the quaint shops of Winslow on foot. Have dinner at a waterfront restaurant, then catch the ferry back to Seattle. If you're up for nightlife, head back south to Pioneer Square. *Have a camera handy during the ferry ride, when you'll see amazing views of Seattle.*

Day 4: Since you've covered Downtown, today you can explore the vastly differing neighborhoods just outside the city. Grab a quick coffee (or carrot juice) at a Green Lake café, then take a stroll around the water to watch Seattleites—and their dogs—waking up with a jog. Visitors of all ages find both the Woodland Park Zoo and the Ballard Locks captivating, so consider rounding out the morning with a visit to one or the other. Have lunch in Wallingford, then head down to Fremont for a little shopping. Cross over to the University District and the University of Washington's Waterfront Activities Center, where you can rent a kayak to enjoy views from the water—or head to the Kenmore Air terminal for a seaplane flight over the city. Try one of the UW's inexpensive little ethnic restaurants for dinner, then spend the evening shopping at University Village or bar-hopping the Avenue. *Stick to weekdays for this tour, as weekends are packed around the lake and at the zoo and the locks.*

Day 5: Today is for culture, so plan to spend the morning at the Frye Art Museum, the Burke Museum of Natural History and Culture, the Henry Art Gallery, or the Museum of History & Industry. Afterward, drive northeast to the Woodinville vineyards. Take a Chateau Ste. Michelle Winery tour, which includes tastings, then head across the street to the Columbia Winery to sample the vintages. For the gourmet lunch, book (months) ahead to dine at the Northwest's famous, Victorian-inspired Herbfarm. There are also lots of inexpensive Italian, Mexican, and American restaurants in and around Woodinville. Or wait to eat until after you've toured the Redhook Brewery, where the portions are large and the wood-beamed bar is spacious. Complete your Woodinville experience with a visit to Molbak's extensive nursery and gardens, a local landmark. Drive back through Kirkland, pausing to wander along the docks and the beach and to browse in waterfront shops. End the day in Bellevue with a little shopping at the glitzy malls and dinner at a trendy restaurant. *Although the wineries, nursery, and shops are open daily, the museums are closed on Monday.*

Day 6: Drive to Capitol Hill, park the car, and set out on a late morning stroll through Volunteer Park, then tour the Seattle Asian Art Museum and the conservatory. Have lunch on Broadway, with its ethnic restaurants and funky boutiques; do a little shopping here and along 12th Avenue. Afterward, drive south to the Museum of Flight in Renton to explore local aviation history in a hangar full of airplanes from every era. Drive to West Seattle's Alki Beach for the afternoon, and then have dinner at a beachside restaurant. *The Asian Art Museum is closed Monday, but you can take the rest of this tour any day.*

If You Have More Time
You can easily reach the Olympic Peninsula in a few hours, then spend a couple of summer days hiking and wildlife-watching in Olympic National Park. For coastal views, you can also relax or beachcomb along the gorgeous west coast sands around Long Beach and Ocean Shores. If you enjoy skiing and snowboarding excursions, head an hour northeast into Cascade ranges, or on to Canada, just a three-hour drive north of Seattle. Take a Victoria Clipper cruise northwest of Seattle for a day of whale-watching and sightseeing in the San Juan Islands; from here, it's easy to connect by ferry to Victoria, Canada. Driving a few hours due east of Seattle, you can explore the beautiful central Washington orchards and Lake Chelan. It's just three hours south of Seattle to the Mt. St. Helens volcano crater, the Columbia River and gorge, and Portland, Oregon.

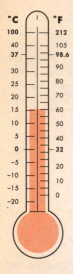

°C		°F
100		212
40		105
37		98.6
30		90
25		80
20		70
15		60
10		50
5		40
0		32
−5		20
−10		10
−15		0
−20		

The Pacific Northwest climate is most enjoyable from May through October. July through September there's nary a drop of rain, with pleasantly warm days reaching into the mid-70s and 80s. Although the weather can be dodgy, spring and fall are also excellent times to visit, as accommodation, transport, and tour costs are usually much lower (and the crowds much thinner). If you want snow, head for the nearby mountains, as temperatures rarely dip below the low 40s here, even in winter. When it does snow in Seattle (usually in December or January), everything grinds to a halt.

Climate

Seattle residents are very friendly, but they fudge when it comes to the weather: it's rarely as cold and rainy as the natives claim. Indeed, Seattle's climate is surprisingly benign for a city that's farther north then Québec City. The coastal regions are uniformly mild, and inland regions are protected against the ocean's blustery winter winds by the Olympic mountain range. The Cascades stand guard on Seattle's opposite side, keeping the bitter temperatures of eastern Washington from reaching the coast.

Seattle has an average of only 36 inches of rainfall a year—less than New York, Chicago, or Miami. The wetness, however, is concentrated in winter, when cloudy skies and drizzly weather persist. More than 75% of Seattle's annual precipitation occurs from October through March.

Because the climate is moist but mild, flowering shrubs and perennials flourish. Blossoms appear in every season: plum, cherry, magnolia, and daffodils in early spring, followed by tulips, rhododendrons, and peonies; roses, foxglove, and lilies in summer; pink and red camellia blossoms in autumn; sweet-scented heather in winter. The city's many parks and public gardens show off a variety of colorful international blooms, topiary, and trees—even palm and bamboo species—and are enthralling to walk through at any time of year.

Forecasts Weather Channel Connection ☎ 900/932–8437, 95¢ per minute from a Touch-Tone phone ⊕ www.weather.com.

SEATTLE TEMPERATURES

Jan.	45F	7C	May	66F	19C	Sept.	69F	20C
	35	2		47	8		52	11
Feb.	50F	10C	June	70F	21C	Oct.	62F	16C
	37	3		52	11		47	8
Mar.	53F	12C	July	76F	24C	Nov.	51F	10C
	38	3		56	13		40	4
Apr.	59F	13C	Aug.	75F	24C	Dec.	47F	8C
	42	5		55	13		37	3

ON THE CALENDAR

WINTER

Dec. 31

New Year's Eve is famously celebrated at the Seattle Center's Space Needle, from where a spectacular fireworks show is staged at midnight.

February

Fat Tuesday has major festivities around Pioneer Square, including a parade, Cajun food, and lively music from the bayou. The **Lunar New Year Celebration,** including a Lion Dance Parade in the International District, marks the Chinese New Year. Asian-theme song and dance performances, food samples, arts and crafts vendors, and hands-on activities take place at the Seattle Center.

SPRING

Late Mar.– mid-Apr.

The **Skagit Valley Tulip Festival** enchants visitors to the Mount Vernon and La Conner areas with more than 1,000 acres of tulips in full bloom. Music, a crafts market, and parades take place in Mount Vernon, about 1½ hours north of Seattle. **Seattle Cherry Blossom Festival** celebrates Japanese arts and family traditions with costumes, music, crafts, ceremonies, and the famous Taiko drummers. **Opening Day** for the Seattle Mariners is a huge celebration of the city's baseball traditions—but beware of traffic snarls at all hours, especially around the stadium.

May–mid-June

Cinco de Mayo, celebrating the defeat of the French occupation in Mexico, is a fun event throughout the city. The **University District Street Fair** begins with a parade that merges into an avenue lined with crafts booths, food stalls, the well-known produce market, and stages for local bands and performance artists. The **Seattle International Children's Festival** at the Seattle Center brings international music, dance, and theater to young audiences. The **Seattle International Film Festival** presents more than 200 features in three weeks at various locations around town. Highlights include the New Directors Showcase, the Children's Film Fest, and the Secret Festival.

Late May

Northwest Folklife Festival lures musicians and artists to Seattle for one of the largest such fests in the United States. **Ski to Sea Race** is a multidiscipline race (skiing, running, biking, boating) from Mt. Baker down to Bellingham Bay. The **Pike Place Market Festival** celebrates the famed Downtown gathering of produce, food, and crafts stalls and shops, and includes free children's activities and entertainment.

SUMMER

June

The **Pioneer Square Fire Festival** highlights the city's firefighting history, beginning with the Great Fire of 1889, with contests and lots of music and food. **Pagdiriwang** celebrates the joy of Philippine traditions at the Seattle Center. **Edmonds Art Festival,** along the Edmonds waterfront north of Seattle, is one of the region's biggest arts events. The classic **Fremont Street Fair** celebrates the unique, unusual, and truly bizarre performance and visual artists who live and work in the neighborhood. It's kicked off by the famous Summer Solstice Parade (and its naked bicyclists).

July 4	**Independence Day** in Seattle means two spectacular celebrations. Gasworks Park is the site of a day of entertainment, culminating in orchestral music (usually provided by the Seattle Symphony) and a fireworks display over Lake Union. A full slate of activities unwinds on the other side of Queen Anne Hill at the Fourth of Jul-Ivar Celebration—named for Ivar's seafood restaurant, a Seattle institution—before the skies light up over Elliott Bay.
July	The **Wooden Boat Festival** on Lake Union combines tours of amazing nautical structures with local sea lore and related crafts. **The Bite of Seattle** serves up sumptuous specialties from the city's finest restaurants. **WOMAD** (World of Music, Arts, and Dance), a touring festival of international artists, wows Seattle at Marymoor Park for a weekend of music, dance, and workshops. Seattle's **King County Fair** offers loads of old-fashioned fun with carnival rides, agricultural displays, country music, and child-oriented activities.
Mid-July–Aug.	**Seafair,** Seattle's biggest festival of the year (really a collection of smaller regional events), kicks off with a torchlight parade through Downtown and culminates in hydroplane races on Lake Washington. **Pista Sa Nayon** is a street fair that celebrates Seattle's Filipino community. The **International District Summer Festival** brings Asian traditions together through crafts, music, games, and performances in the I.D. The **Ballard Seafood Fest** rates as one of the best neighborhood feasts, with its salmon back, lutefisk-eating contest, and creative activities. **Belltown UnCorked!** unites local restaurants for a day of wine tasting and food samplings. **Bon Odori** is a festival of Japanese traditions with a parade, folk dancing, and lots of food.
Early Sept.	**Bumbershoot,** a Seattle arts festival held during Labor Day weekend, presents more than 400 performers in music, dance, theater, comedy, and the visual and literary arts. The **Puyallup Fair**—with its endless "Do the Puyallup!" musical slogan—draws locals southeast for livestock and produce shows and competitions, food and drink tastings, and carnival rides.
FALL	
Late Sept.– early Oct.	Nearly 100 local, national, and international theater companies perform at the 10-day **Seattle Fringe Festival. Festa Italia** is a week-long celebration of Seattle's Italian community at the Seattle Center and Seward Park.
October	**Issaquah Salmon Days** honors the return of the salmon to area waters with festivities, crafts booths, live entertainment, and, well, lots of grilled salmon.
November	Seattle's **Thanksgiving Day Parade,** sponsored by the Bon-Macy's department store, kicks off the city's shopping season with an hour-long march of majorettes, brass bands, law enforcement vehicles, and performance artists. The event, which occurs the Friday after Thanksgiving, is topped off by the lighting of the Christmas tree at Westlake Center and a fireworks display.

PLEASURES & PASTIMES

Outdoor Adventures Outdoor experiences are what this region is all about, and Seattle makes a perfect base from which to do it all. Head north to hike in the Cascade range, or travel south to climb Mt. Rainier or explore Mt. St. Helens. Visit the San Juan and Gulf islands—on foot or by ferry, canoe, or kayak. Head southwest to camp, hike, and spot wildlife in Olympic National Park's fern-filled rain forests, snow-topped mountains, surf-swept coastline. Wildflower meadows, glistening lakes, roiling waterfalls, and untouched snowfields abound. Modern highways easily take you to base points, where there are numerous historical attractions and places to stay and eat.

Savory Cuisine A quick scan of Pike Place Market's stalls shows you what's on restaurant plates every season: strawberries in June, Walla Walla onions in July, wild blackberries in August, and apples in autumn. Such ingredients fused with European and Asian cooking techniques define the heart of Pacific Northwest cuisine. Seafood also stars on most of the city's menus, including meaty grilled salmon; fresh shellfish; thick, milky clam chowder; or *cioppino* (seafood stew in a tomato base). An amazing variety of ethnic restaurants—particularly in the International District, Wallingford, and the University District—serve up authentic dishes from countries on nearly every continent. Washington's wineries produce many award-winning labels; ask your server what's best to pair with your meal. Local brews come in a range of flavors, which you can often try in sample sizes.

The Art of the Matter The best way to view the works in Seattle's museums and galleries is on the First Thursday art walk, when admission is free and artists are often out with their displays. Western Washington is particularly known for its excellent glass art, the red-hot molten glass more easily fashioned in the region's temperate climate. Books are also big here, and most bookstores host readings, workshops, and other events. Music is a regular part of life in this city, too, so look for up-and-coming artists at local festivals and summertime venues. Benaroya Hall, with its perfect acoustics, is home to Seattle's award-winning symphony orchestra, while the beautiful McCaw Hall at the Seattle Center houses the city's renowned opera and ballet companies. Many historic theaters run first-rate performances with local casts.

Life After Dark Although Seattle was the birthplace of grunge rock, today a variety of music overshadows the rumpled memories of the '90s. Clubs showcase the passionate musical stylings of everything from tinny garage bands to the biggest international names in Top 40 rock, country, and jazz and blues. Key Arena at the Seattle Center and Downtown's Paramount Theater are the two top indoor concert sites; in summer, outdoor music echoes from parks and at Pier 62. You can also catch a movie, see a stand-up comedian, or have a drink while watching the lights flicker on the water of Elliott Bay or one of the lakes. If you want to dance, head to a club in Downtown, Belltown, Capitol Hill, or the U-District.

All in the Family There's no better place to find something for everyone in your family than at the Pike Place Market, overlooking Elliott Bay. On the bay itself are the Seattle Aquarium and the Maritime Discovery Center; the half-hour ferry ride to Bainbridge Island from the busy waterfront terminal is entertaining. Hands-on museums, IMAX theaters, the Space Needle, and the Woodland Park Zoo are also perfect for families. Waterfront activities centers offer the chance to kayak, sail, or cruise on Seattle's lakes and bays, and just about every neighborhood has a park with a playground, picnic areas, and other facilities.

Playing It Up

The classy Seahawks Stadium is home to the Seattle Seahawks football team. A block or so away is Safeco Field, another fine stadium and one that's home to the Seattle Mariners baseball team. The Seattle Supersonics shoot their hoops at Key Arena. Also look for Seafair's summer hydroplane races on Lake Washington, horseracing at Emerald Downs, cycling at the Marymoor Park Velodrome, and boating and fishing in the Sound and on the lakes. Hiking, horseback riding, rock climbing, and mountaineering potential abounds through the Cascade and Olympic mountain peaks and foothills. Two uniquely Northwest pursuits, clamming and crabbing, are also popular.

FODOR'S CHOICE

The sights, restaurants, hotels, and other travel experiences on these pages are our editors' top picks—our Fodor's Choices. They're the best of their type in the area covered by the book—not to be missed and always worth your time. In the chapters that follow, you will find all the details.

LODGING

$$$$ **Fairmont Olympic Hotel,** Downtown. An estimable dame adorned with marble and draped with textiles.

$$$–$$$$ **Alexis Hotel,** Downtown. French and Italian fabrics? Free wine in the early evening? Why, it's a little bit of Europe in the middle of Seattle.

$$$–$$$$ **Inn at Langley,** Langley (Whidbey Island). Sleek lines, modern furniture, and big windows allow your eyes to focus on what's really important: the sea and mountain views.

$$$–$$$$ **Inn at the Market,** Downtown. Just because the furniture is contemporary doesn't mean that such noble traditions as fresh flowers and free morning newspapers must become obsolete.

$$$–$$$$ **W Seattle,** Downtown. The "W" stands for "welcoming," not to mention "wicked comfortable," and "way cool."

$$–$$$ **Colette's Bed & Breakfast,** near Port Angeles. The excellent service is rivaled only by the Olympic Peninsula location and the way-cool amenities—CD and DVD players, Jacuzzis, fireplaces.

$$–$$$ **Inn at Harbor Steps,** Downtown. Public areas are low-key, guest rooms are commodious, and breakfast is a buffet.

BUDGET LODGING

¢–$$ **Gaslight Inn,** Capitol Hill. No two spaces are alike thanks to eclectic paint effects, fabrics, and fittings. You're as likely to find a glass chandelier as you are log furniture.

RESTAURANTS

$$$$ **Lampreia,** Belltown. The dishes, like the beige-and-gold color scheme, are classic with a little sparkle: pheasant is paired with apples, champagne, and sauerkraut; lamb is served with pesto.

$$$$ **Rover's,** Madison Valley. It's French blended with the Pacific Northwest—in terms of the food, the service, and the feel of the place.

$$$–$$$$ **Christina's,** Eastsound (Orcas Island). The seafood is fresh and well prepared, and the sea views are fine.

$$$–$$$$ **Le Gourmand,** Phinney. The chef grows his own poppies and harvests the seeds for his homemade crackers. Enough said.

$$–$$$$ **Ray's Boathouse,** Ballard. Puget Sound views complement the impeccably fresh and well-prepared seafood.

$$–$$$ **Cafe Juanita,** Kirkland. Eastsiders love the northern Italian dishes, some of which are made with produce from the restaurant's own garden.

$$-$$$	**Dahlia Lounge,** Downtown. There's romance—think low lights and the color red. There's good food—think crab cakes, seared ahi tuna, and coconut-cream pie.
$$-$$$	**Duck Soup Inn,** San Juan Island. Outside it's all about cedar shingles and flowering vines. Inside it's all about up-to-date dishes with a smidge of the Asian here and a dash of the Latin American there.
$$-$$$	**Le Pichet,** Downtown. It's all French brasserie, from the earthenware wine vessels to the crusty baguettes for your ham and cheese, er, *jambon et fromage*.
$-$$$	**Oceanaire,** Downtown. This place is about retro. Your clams casino or oysters Rockefeller or baked Alaska is served in a room that evokes a supper club circa 1930.

BUDGET RESTAURANTS

$$	**Restaurant Zoë,** Belltown. Is it only the inspired dishes that make the place so popular? After all, a charming waitstaff and a lively bar can be just as fetching as house-smoked hangar steak or pan-seared scallops on herbed rissotto.
$-$$	**Marco's Supper Club,** Belltown. None of the flatware matches, which seems in keeping with the eclectic menu. When was the last time you had to choose between pork in a mole sauce and jerk chicken?
$	**Hing Loon,** International District. Rumor has it that the city's Chinese chefs head here when they crave noodles.
¢-$	**Salumi,** Pioneer Square. It's a terrific, tiny, Italian lunch spot. The chef hands out samples while you wait for a table—prepare to sit with complete strangers.

AFTER HOURS

Bada Lounge, Belltown. Try saying this 10 times fast (and after a few drinks): "A slick crowd slinks around a sleek spot."

Dimitriou's Jazz Alley, Downtown. Smooth, silky jazz minus all the cigarette smoke. Dinner shows are a possibility.

BEACHES

Alki Beach, West Seattle. If the water weren't so cold, you'd swear you were on a California beach—complete with singles flirting and families building sand castles.

Sand Point Magnuson Park, Sand Point. There's a swimming beach, it's true, but this Lake Washington park also has 200 acres of space for cycling, running, in-line skating, and many other sports amenities.

FEATS OF ENGINEERING

Ballard Locks, Ballard. Each year, thousands of boats and millions of salmon travel through the locks from Puget Sound to Lake Washington and Lake Union.

Space Needle, Queen Anne. It takes 42 seconds to ride the elevator up to the observation deck of this Seattle icon.

GARDEN

Washington Park Arboretum, Capitol Hill. Stroll through the greenhouse or the immaculate Japanese garden, both highlights of the park's 200 acres.

MUSEUMS

Seattle Asian Art Museum, Capitol Hill. Pick an Asian country—any Asian country—and you're likely to find art or artifacts from it here.

Wing Luke Museum, International District. Costumes, crafts, and photographs of immigrants from Asia and the Pacific islands all under one roof.

OUTDOOR ACTIVITIES

Center for Wooden Boats, Lake Union. The vessels rented out by the hour at this museum are wooden classics—rowboats, catboats, sloops.

Crystal Mountain Ski Area, near Mt. Rainier National Park. Many swear that the state's biggest ski area is also its best.

Harbour Pointe Golf Club, Mukilteo. It has 18 hilly championship holes and Puget Sound views—all about 30 minutes north of Seattle.

Hoh Valley Trail, Olympic National Park. The scenery is like a mantra: valley, river, meadow. Watch for elk in winter.

Whistler, British Columbia, Canada, ski area. It's massive and magnificent—mecca, really. You can't call yourself a skier if you visit Seattle in winter and don't hit the slopes here.

Wonderland Trail, Mt. Rainier National Park. It's 93 mi long and takes in every possible type of mountain scenery. No other Rainier route can possibly compare.

PERFORMING ARTS

5th Avenue Theater, Downtown. A chinoiserie landmark in operation since the 1920s. Look for lavish productions for half the year, and a variety of offerings the other half.

Marion Oliver McCaw Hall, Queen Anne. Glass is put to good use in the home of the Seattle Opera and the Pacific Northwest Ballet.

Seattle Symphony, Downtown. The Grammy-nominated symphony performs in Benaroya Hall, a fitting place thanks to its exceptional acoustics.

QUINTESSENTIAL SEATTLE

Pike Place Market, Downtown. There's nothing quite like this market when it's in full swing. Try to visit on a Saturday afternoon for a robust experience.

Pioneer Square District, Downtown. A 24/7 district: shop and gallery hop by day, wine and dine by night.

Vivace Roasteria, Capitol Hill. It's easy to while away an afternoon or evening here, sipping what may well be the city's best espresso.

SHOPPING

Elliott Bay Book Company, Pioneer Square. An enormous independent bookseller that keeps Seattle's literary heart beating clear and strong.

Recreational Equipment, Inc., Downtown. It's so much more than just a sporting-goods store, and it has a 65-foot climbing wall to prove it.

Stonington Gallery, Pioneer Square. This is *the* place to find contemporary works by members of Northwest Coast tribes.

Sur La Table, Downtown. If you like to cook, there are some 12,500 reasons to shop here.

Uwajimaya, International District. Do Shiseido and Hello Kitty have a place in your heart? What about Korean art, Vietnamese ceramics, Chinese pastries, or other foods and goods from Asia? This market has it all and then some.

SMART TRAVEL TIPS

Finding out about your destination before you leave home means you won't squander time organizing everyday minutiae once you've arrived. You'll be more streetwise when you hit the ground as well, and better prepared to explore the aspects of Seattle that drew you here in the first place. The organizations in this section can provide information to supplement this guide; contact them for up-to-the-minute details. Happy landings!

ADDRESSES

Streets in the Seattle area generally run north–south, whereas avenues run east–west. Downtown roads are straightforward, numbered west to east and named north to south. Suburbs are designated with directionals attached to the street names. N (north) is for lower Queen Anne, around the Seattle Center, and Fremont, Wallingford, and Green Lake. NE (northeast) is for the University District, and NW (northwest) designates Ballard. S (south) marks Downtown streets around Pioneer Square and the International District, as well as neighborhoods south of the city—although SW (southwest) means West Seattle. E (east) designates Capitol Hill; W (west) means upper Queen Anne and Magnolia.

Directionals are noted as prefixes to streets and suffixes to avenues; thus, if someone says "NW 67th," it is safe to assume they are referring to Northwest 67th *Street,* not avenue. Conversely, if someone says a destination is on "33rd E," they are referring to 33rd *Avenue* East. Another local trick is a mnemonic device for remembering the sequence of Downtown streets. Beginning with Jefferson Street and working north, there are two streets for the first letter of each of the following words: "Jesus Christ Made Seattle Under Protest" (i.e., Jefferson and James, Columbia and Cherry, Marion and Madison, Spring and Seneca, University and Union, Pike and Pine).

AIR TRAVEL

Seattle is a hub for regional air service as well as that to Canada and Asia. It's also a convenient North American gateway for flights originating in Australia, New Zealand, and the South Pacific. But it's a long westbound flight to Seattle from Europe. Such flights usually stop in New

York; Washington, D.C.; Boston; or Chicago after crossing the Atlantic.

AIRPORT

The major gateway is Seattle–Tacoma (Sea-Tac) International Airport.

Airport Information Seattle-Tacoma International Airport ⊠ Pacific Hwy. S (Hwy. 99) ☎ 206/431-4444 ⊕ www.portseattle.org/seatac.

AIRPORT TRANSFERS

Sea-Tac is about 15 mi south of Downtown on I–5 (from the airport, follow the signs to I–5 North, and take the Seneca Street Exit for Downtown). Although it can take as little as 30 minutes to ride between Downtown and the airport, it's best to **allow 1½ hours for the trip** in case of traffic snarls.

Metered cabs cost $25–$30 between the airport and Downtown, though some taxi companies offer a flat rate to Sea-Tac from select Downtown hotels. Shuttle Express has the only 24-hour door-to-door service, a flat $20 from the airport to Downtown. You can make arrangements at the Shuttle Express counter upon arrival. For trips to the airport, make reservations at least 24 hours in advance. Express Car and Atlas Towncar have limo service to and from the airport. The fare is $45 to Downtown and can be shared by up to four passengers.

Gray Line Airport Express provides service to Downtown hotels for $8.50. Your least expensive transportation option ($2; cash only) is a Metro Transit city bus. You can catch one outside the baggage claim areas for the 45-minute ride into town. **Take Express Tunnel Bus 194 or regular Buses 174 or 184.**

Taxis & Shuttles Atlas Towncar ☎ 206/860-7777 or 888/646-0606 ⊕ www.atlastowncar.com. **Gray Line Airport Express** ☎ 206/626-6088 ⊕ www.graylineseattle.com. **Metro Transit** ☎ 206/553-3000. **Shuttle Express/Express Car** ☎ 206/622-1424, 800/487-7433 in WA ⊕ www.shuttleexpress.com.

BOOKING

When you book, look for nonstop flights and remember that "direct" flights stop at least once. Try to avoid connecting flights, which require a change of plane. Two airlines may operate a connecting flight jointly, so ask whether your airline operates every segment of the trip; you may find that the carrier you prefer flies you only part of the way. To find more booking tips and to check prices and make online flight reservations, log on to www.fodors.com.

CARRIERS

American, Continental, Delta, Northwest, United, and U.S. Airways are among the domestic airlines that fly to Seattle. Asiana and EVA have direct flights across the Pacific to Seattle. British Airways, KLM, Lufthansa, and Scandinavian Airlines have daily flights, via the east coast, from London, Paris, and other European capitals. Air Canada, Asiana, British Airways, and United Airlines all fly weekly to Seattle from Sydney, Australia. Although Qantas has the most connections from Australia and Air New Zealand has the most flights from New Zealand, you must fly into Vancouver, B.C., and connect with code-sharing airlines to reach Seattle.

Alaska Airlines, America West, Big Sky, Frontier Airlines, Horizon Air, JetBlue, Sun Country, and United Express provide frequent service to Seattle from cities in Washington, Oregon, Idaho, Montana, and California. Alaska Airlines has the most extensive schedule from the 49th state to Seattle; Hawaiian Airlines and Northwest make several weekly flights from the 50th state.

Air Canada flies between Seattle and Victoria, B.C. Helijet Airways provides jet helicopter service from Seattle's Boeing Field to Vancouver and Victoria, B.C. Kenmore Air has scheduled floatplane flights from Seattle's Lake Union to the San Juan Islands, Victoria, and the Gulf Islands of British Columbia. The company also provides fly-in service to fishing resorts in coastal British Columbia.

Major Airlines Air Canada ☎ 888/247-2262 ⊕ www.aircanada.ca. **Air New Zealand** ☎ 800/663-0921 ⊕ www.airnewzealand.com. **Alaska Airlines** ☎ 800/252-7522 ⊕ www.alaskaairlines.com. **American** ☎ 800/433-7300 ⊕ www.im.aa.com. **Asiana** ☎ 206/516-0301 or 800/227-4262 ⊕ www.us.flyasiana.com. **British Airways** ☎ 800/247-9297 ⊕ www.britishairways.com. **Continental** ☎ 800/523-3273 ⊕ www.continental.com. **Delta** ☎ 800/221-1212 ⊕ www.delta.com. **EVA** ☎ 800/695-1188 ⊕ www.evaair.com. **Hawaiian Airlines** ☎ 800/367-5320 ⊕ www.hawaiianair.com. **Lufthansa** ☎ 800/563-5954 ⊕ www.lufthansa.com. **Northwest/KLM** ☎ 800/225-2525 ⊕ www.nwa.com. **Qantas** ☎ 800/227-4500 ⊕ www.qantas.com.

Scandinavian Airlines ☏ 800/221-2350 ⊕ www. scandinavian.net. **United/United Express** ☏ 800/241-6522 ⊕ www.ual.com. **US Airways/US Airways Express** ☏ 800/428-4322 ⊕ www.usair.com.

⚡ Smaller Airlines America West ☏ 800/235-9292 ⊕ www.americawest.com. **Big Sky** ☏ 800/237-7788. **Frontier** ☏ 800/432-1359, ⊕ www.frontierairlines.com. **Helijet** ☏ 800/665-4354, 604/273-1414 in Vancouver ⊕ www.helijet.com. **Horizon Air** ☏ 800/547-9308 ⊕ www.alaskaairlines.com. **JetBlue** ☏ 800/JET-BLUE ⊕ www.jetblue.com. **Kenmore Air** ☏ 800/543-9595 ⊕ www. kenmoreair.com. **Skywest** ☏ 800/453-9417 ⊕ www.skywest.com. **Sun Country** ☏ 800/359-6786. **United Express** ☏ 800/241-6522.

CHECK-IN & BOARDING

Always **find out your carrier's check-in policy.** Plan to arrive at the airport about two hours before your scheduled departure time for domestic flights and 2½ to 3 hours before international flights. You may need to arrive earlier if you're flying from one of the busier airports or during peak air-traffic times. To avoid delays at airport-security checkpoints, try not to wear any metal. Jewelry, belt and other buckles, steel-toe shoes, barrettes, and underwire bras are among the items that can set off detectors.

Assuming that not everyone with a ticket will show up, airlines routinely overbook planes. When everyone does, airlines ask for volunteers to give up their seats. In return, these volunteers usually get a several-hundred-dollar flight voucher, which can be used toward the purchase of another ticket, and are rebooked on the next flight out. If there are not enough volunteers, the airline must choose who will be denied boarding. The first to get bumped are passengers who checked in late and those flying on discounted tickets, so get to the gate and check in as early as possible, especially during peak periods.

Always **bring a government-issued photo ID** to the airport; even when it's not required, a passport is best.

CUTTING COSTS

The least expensive airfares to Seattle are priced for round-trip travel and must usually be purchased in advance. Airlines generally allow you to change your return date for a fee; most low-fare tickets, however, are nonrefundable. It's smart to call a number of airlines and check the Internet;

when you are quoted a good price, book it on the spot—the same fare may not be available the next day, or even the next hour. Always check different routings and look into using alternate airports. Also, price off-peak flights, which may be significantly less expensive than others. Travel agents, especially low-fare specialists (⇨ Discounts and Deals), are helpful.

Consolidators are another good source. They buy tickets for scheduled flights at reduced rates from the airlines, then sell them at prices that beat the best fare available directly from the airlines. Sometimes you can even get your money back if you need to return the ticket. Carefully read the fine print detailing penalties for changes and cancellations, purchase the ticket with a credit card, and confirm your consolidator reservation with the airline.

⚡ Consolidators AirlineConsolidator.com ☏ 888/468-5385 ⊕ www.airlineconsolidator.com; for international tickets. **Best Fares** ☏ 800/576-8255 or 800/576-1600 ⊕ www.bestfares.com; $59.90 annual membership. **Cheap Tickets** ☏ 800/377-1000 or 888/922-8849 ⊕ www.cheaptickets.com. **Expedia** ☏ 800/397-3342 or 404/728-8787 ⊕ www.expedia. com. **Hotwire** ☏ 866/468-9473 or 920/330-9418 ⊕ www.hotwire.com. **Now Voyager Travel** ✉ 45 W. 21st St., 5th fl., New York, NY 10010 ☏ 212/459-1616 ⧖ 212/243-2711 ⊕ www.nowvoyagertravel. com. **Onetravel.com** ⊕ www.onetravel.com. **Orbitz** ☏ 888/656-4546 ⊕ www.orbitz.com. **Priceline. com** ⊕ www.priceline.com. **Travelocity** ☏ 888/709-5983, 877/282-2925 in Canada, 0870/111-7060 in the U.K. ⊕ www.travelocity.com.

ENJOYING THE FLIGHT

State your seat preference when purchasing your ticket, and then repeat it when you confirm and when you check in. For more legroom, you can request one of the few emergency-aisle seats at check-in, if you are capable of lifting at least 50 pounds—a Federal Aviation Administration requirement of passengers in these seats. Seats behind a bulkhead also offer more legroom, but they don't have underseat storage. Don't sit in the row in front of the emergency aisle or in front of a bulkhead, where seats may not recline.

Ask the airline whether a snack or meal is served on the flight. If you have dietary concerns, request special meals when booking. These can be vegetarian, low-cholesterol, or kosher, for example. It's a good idea to pack some healthful snacks and a small (plastic) bottle of water in your carry-on bag. On long flights, try to maintain a normal routine, to help fight jet lag. At night, get some sleep. By day, eat light meals, drink water (not alcohol), and **move around the cabin** to stretch your legs. For additional jet-lag tips consult *Fodor's FYI: Travel Fit & Healthy* (available at bookstores everywhere).

FLYING TIMES

Nonstop flying time from New York to Seattle is approximately 5 hours; flights from Chicago are about 4–4½ hours; flights between Los Angeles and Seattle take 2½ hours; flights between London and Seattle are about 9½ hours.

HOW TO COMPLAIN

If your baggage goes astray or your flight goes awry, complain right away. Most carriers require that you **file a claim immediately.** The Aviation Consumer Protection Division of the Department of Transportation publishes *Fly-Rights*, which discusses airlines and consumer issues and is available online. You can also find articles and information on mytravelrights.com, the Web site of the nonprofit Consumer Travel Rights Center.

7 Airline Complaints Aviation Consumer Protection Division ⊠ U.S. Department of Transportation, C-75, Room 4107, 400 7th St. SW, Washington, DC 20590 ☎ 202/366-2220 ⊕ airconsumer.ost.dot.gov. Federal Aviation Administration Consumer Hotline ⊠ for inquiries: FAA, 800 Independence Ave. SW, Washington, DC 20591 ☎ 800/322-7873 ⊕ www.faa.gov.

RECONFIRMING

Check the status of your flight before you leave for the airport. You can do this on your carrier's Web site, by linking to a flight-status checker (many Web booking services offer these), or by calling your carrier or travel agent.

BOAT & FERRY TRAVEL

Ferries are a major part of Seattle's transportation network, and they're the only way to reach such points as Vashon Island and the San Juans. Ferries also transport thousands of commuters a day from Bainbridge Island, Bremerton, and other outer towns to their jobs in the city. For visitors, ferries are one of the best ways to get a feel for the region and its ties to the sea.

Passenger-only speedboats depart from Seattle's Pier 50 weekdays on runs to Vashon Island. It's $7.40 from Seattle; the return trip is free. A $1 surcharge is collected in both directions on the Bremerton route. Late spring through fall, the Elliott Bay Water Taxi makes a quick, eight-minute journey from Pier 54 to Seacrest Park in West Seattle for $2 each way. Clipper Navigation operates the passenger-only *Victoria Clipper* jet catamaran service between Seattle, the San Juan Islands, and Victoria.

The Washington State Ferry system serves the Puget Sound and San Juan Islands area. Peak-season fares are charged the first Sunday in May through the second Saturday in October. However, ferry schedules change quarterly, with the summer schedule running mid-June through mid-September. Ferries around Seattle are especially crowded during the city's weekday rush hours and holiday events, while San Juan Islands ferries can be jammed on weekends, holidays, and all of mid-June through September. **Be at the ferry, or have your car in line, at least 20 minutes before departure**—and prepare to wait several hours during heavily traveled times. Walk-on space is always available; **if possible, leave your car behind.** ⋅

FARES & SCHEDULES

You can pick up sailing schedules and tickets on board the ferries or at the terminals, and schedules are usually posted in local businesses around the docks. The Washington State Ferry (WSF) automated hotline also provides travel details, including weekly departure and arrival times, wait times, cancellations, and seasonal fare changes. To ask questions or make international reservations for journeys to Sidney, British Columbia, call the regular WSF hotline. Note that schedules often differ from weekdays to weekends and holidays, and departure times may be altered due to ferry or dock maintenance, severe weather or tides, and high traffic volume.

Peak-season round-trip walk-on fares from Seattle are $5.40 to Bainbridge and Bremerton, and from Edmonds to Kingston; $4.20 from Fauntleroy in West Seattle to Southworth; $3.50 from Fauntleroy or Southworth to Vashon Island; $3.20 from Mukilteo to Clinton, on Whidbey Island; and $2.08 each way between Port

Townsend and Keystone. It's $10.60 from Anacortes to any point in the San Juan Islands, or $13.10–$17.85 to Sidney, B.C., depending on the ferry; tolls are collected on westbound routes only. Seniors (age 65 and over) and those with disabilities pay half fare; children 5–18 get a 30% discount, and those under age five ride free.

Peak-season vehicle fares (including one adult driver) are $12 from Seattle to Bainbridge and Bremerton, and from Edmonds to Kingston; $15.50 from Fauntleroy, Southworth, and Point Defiance in Tacoma to Vashon; $9.50 from Port Townsend to Keystone, and from Fauntleroy to Southworth; and $7.25 from Mukilteo to Clinton. From Anacortes, vehicle and driver fares through the San Juans are $29.50 to Lopez Island, $35.25 to Orcas and Shaw islands, $39.50 to Friday Harbor, and $44.25–$66.75 to Sidney, B.C.

Note that on some routes you only pay for one portion of each round-trip journey— for example, you pay the entire $12 car and driver fee when traveling *from* Seattle to Bainbridge or Bremerton; going *to* the city from these points is *free*. You can pay with cash, major credit cards, debit cards with MasterCard or Visa logos, traveler's checks, or personal checks drawn on Washington State banks.

🚩 **Boat & Ferry Information** **Clipper Navigation** ☎ 250/382-8100 in Victoria, 206/448-5000 in Seattle, 800/888-2535 in the U.S. ⊕ www.victoriaclipper.com. **Elliott Bay Water Taxi** ✉ Pier 54, Downtown ☎ 206/553-3000. **Washington State Ferries** ✉ Colman Dock, Pier 52, Downtown ☎ 206/464-6400, 888/808-7977, or 800/843-3779 (automated line) in WA and BC ⊕ www.wsdot.wa.gov/ferries.

BUS TRAVEL

The Metropolitan Transit's transportation network is inexpensive and fairly comprehensive. Most buses, which are wheelchair accessible, run until around midnight or 1 AM; some run all night. The visitor center at the Washington State Convention and Trade Center has maps and schedules or you can call Metro Transit directly.

Greyhound Lines and Northwest Trailways have regular service to points throughout the Pacific Northwest and the United States. The regional Greyhound/Trailways bus terminal at Ninth Avenue

and Stewart Street is convenient to all Downtown destinations.

FARES & SCHEDULES

Between 6 AM and 7 PM, all public transportation is free within the Metro Bus Ride Free Area, bounded by Battery Street to the north, Sixth Avenue to the east (and over to Ninth Avenue near the convention center), South Jackson Street to the south, and the waterfront to the west; you'll pay as you disembark if you ride out of this area. Throughout King County, one-zone fares are $1.50; two-zone fares are $2. Onboard fare collection boxes have prices posted on them. The $5 King County Visitor Pass is a bargain if you're doing a lot of touring. Valid for one day, it includes rides on King, Pierce, and Snohomish county buses, the waterfront trolley, and the Elliott Bay Water Taxi. You can purchase passes online or at Metro offices.

Greyhound buses travel several times daily to major towns along I–5 and I–90. Main routes head south from Seattle through Tacoma (45 minutes, $5), Olympia (1 hour and 45 minutes, $7.75), and Portland (3–5 hours, $20.75), all the way to San Francisco (20–25 hours, $66.75) and Los Angeles (26–29 hours, $86). Buses going north from Seattle pass through Mt. Vernon (1½ hours, $7.75), Everett (1 hour and 45 minutes, $6), and Bellingham (2 hours, $13.75), close to the Canadian border. Eastern routes head to Yakima (3 hours and 20 minutes, $22.75), Spokane (6–8 hours, $27.75), and many points in between and beyond. Fares are slightly less on weekdays and for round-trip tickets. Ask about companion rates, advance purchase savings, and seasonal discounts.

Northwestern Trailways also has daily buses within Washington, including from Seattle south through Tacoma ($6), north through Everett ($6), and east through Spokane ($29). Although tickets aren't discounted for advance purchase or seasonal sales, senior travelers receive 10% off the fare.

PAYING

Fares for city buses are collected in cash or by prepaid tickets *as you board* the bus heading into Downtown, and *as you exit the bus* on the way out of Downtown. You can only buy bus passes at Metro offices or online, not on the vehicle; cash, debit cards, MasterCard, and Visa are accepted. Greyhound Lines accepts American Express, MasterCard, and Visa.

RESERVATIONS

Long-distance bus lines don't accept reservations. One-way and round-trip tickets on Greyhound and Trailways guarantee seating at the time listed; tickets aren't disbursed if a date or time is sold out. Reservations aren't accepted for travel on bus passes, either, so call ahead to check availability and get to the terminal at least an hour before departure time. You can purchase tickets for immediate departure, as well as for up to one year in advance.

🔢 **Bus Information** **Greyhound Lines** ⊠ 811 Stewart St., Downtown ☎ 800/231-2222 or 206/628-5526 ⊕ www.greyhound.com. **Metropolitan Transit** ☎ 206/553-3000 or 206/287-8463 for automated schedule line ⊕ transit.metrokc.gov/bus. **Northwest Trailways** ⊠ 811 Stewart St., Downtown ☎ 800/366-3830 ⊕ www.trailways.com.

BUSINESS HOURS

BANKS & OFFICES

Normal banking and office hours are weekdays from 9 to 6; some bank branches are also open on Saturday morning.

GAS STATIONS

The majority of gas stations in Seattle and immediately off I–5 in rural areas are open 24 hours.

MUSEUMS & SIGHTS

Museums are generally open from 10 to 5 Tuesday through Saturday, with longer hours on first Thursdays and shorter hours on Sunday. Most major sites are open daily from 9 to 5 or later except on Christmas, New Year's Day, and Easter Sunday. Woodland Park Zoo and the Seattle Aquarium are open every day of the year.

PHARMACIES

There are a handful of 24-hour pharmacies in the Seattle area; others generally operate from 9 AM to 9 PM.

SHOPS

Most shops and department stores in Downtown Seattle are open 10 to 6 daily. Stores in Bellevue are open 10 to 9 daily except Sunday, when things close around 6. Malls in other suburbs also stay open late, although smaller shops may vary their hours and days each week. Watch for department store sales around major holidays, when doors open as early as 6 AM, and "Moonlight Sales," when stores stay open until 9 or later.

CAMERAS & PHOTOGRAPHY

The natural splendor of the Pacific Northwest will call out to your camera lens. The water and islands, along with the urban centers and small villages, are all worthy of your attention. Seize the sunny times of day for the clearest shots. The *Kodak Guide to Shooting Great Travel Pictures* (available at bookstores everywhere) is loaded with tips.

🔢 **Photo Help** **Kodak Information Center** ☎ 800/242-2424 ⊕ www.kodak.com.

EQUIPMENT PRECAUTIONS

Don't pack film or equipment in checked luggage, where it is much more susceptible to damage. X-ray machines used to view checked luggage are extremely powerful and therefore are likely to ruin your film. Try to ask for hand inspection of film, which becomes clouded after repeated exposure to airport X-ray machines, and keep videotapes and computer disks away from metal detectors. Always keep film, tape, and computer disks out of the sun. Carry an extra supply of batteries, and be prepared to turn on your camera, camcorder, or laptop to prove to airport security personnel that the device is real.

CAR RENTAL

Rates in Seattle begin at $21 a day and $110 a week for an economy car with air-conditioning, automatic transmission, and unlimited mileage. This does not include the car-rental tax of 18.5%. Try to **avoid renting a car from a major agency at the airport** where rental fees are higher and an additional 10% airport tax is charged. Several local agencies at the airport, or within a mile vicinity of it along Highway 99/Pacific Highway South, do have low rates, however.

🔢 **Major Agencies** **Alamo** ☎ 800/327-9633 ⊕ www.alamo.com. **Avis** ☎ 800/331-1212, 800/879-2847 or 800/272-5871 in Canada, 0870/606-0100 in the U.K., 02/9353-9000 in Australia, 09/526-2847 in New Zealand ⊕ www.avis.com. **Budget** ☎ 800/527-0700, 0870/156-5656 in the U.K.

⊕ www.budget.com. **Dollar** ☎ 800/800-4000, 0124/622-0111 in the U.K., where it's affiliated with Sixt, 02/9223-1444 in Australia ⊕ www.dollar.com. **Hertz** ☎ 800/654-3131, 800/263-0600 in Canada, 0870/844-8844 in the U.K., 02/9669-2444 in Australia, 09/256-8690 in New Zealand ⊕ www.hertz.com. **National Car Rental** ☎ 800/227-7368, 0870/600-6666 in the U.K. ⊕ www.nationalcar.com.

CUTTING COSTS

For a good deal, book through a travel agent who will shop around. Also, price local car-rental companies—whose prices may be lower still, although their service and maintenance may not be as good as those of major rental agencies—and research rates on the Internet. Remember to ask about required deposits, cancellation penalties, and drop-off charges if you're planning to pick up the car in one city and leave it in another. If you're traveling during a holiday period, also make sure that a confirmed reservation guarantees you a car.

Ace ExtraCar has the lowest rates for area car rentals, with discounts for Web bookings. Advantage has online coupons for double category upgrades on weekends. Express Rent-A-Car, located behind the airport, offers 10% online discount coupons. Park Place Rentals has a luxury fleet of vehicles and offers 15% discount coupons online.

Local Agencies **Ace ExtraCar** ⊠ 16300 Pacific Hwy. S, Sea-Tac ☎ 206/246-7844 or 800/227-5397 ⊕ www.bnm.com. **Advantage** ⊠ Sea-Tac Airport, ground fl., Sea-Tac ☎ 800/777-5500 ⊕ www.bnm.com. **Best Rent-a-Car** ⊠ 6501 Aurora Ave. N, Green Lake ☎ 206/784-2378 ⊕ www.bestrent-a-car.com. **Chuck Olson Auto Rentals** ⊠ 17037 Aurora Ave. N, Edmonds ☎ 206/522-7661 ⊕ www.chuckolsonchev.com. **Express Rent-A-Car** ⊠ 18451 Des Moines Memorial Dr., Sea-Tac ☎ 866/443-6825 ⊕ www.bnm.com. **Park Place Rentals** ⊠ 13824 Northup Way, Bellevue ☎ 866/687-7200 ⊕ www.bnm.com.

INSURANCE

When driving a rented car you are generally responsible for any damage to or loss of the vehicle. You also may be liable for any property damage or personal injury that you may cause while driving. Before you rent, see what coverage you already have under the terms of your personal auto-insurance policy and credit cards.

For about $9 to $25 a day, rental companies sell protection, known as a collision- or loss-damage waiver (CDW or LDW), that eliminates your liability for damage to the car; it's always optional and should never be automatically added to your bill. In most states you don't need a CDW if you have personal auto insurance or other liability insurance. However, **make sure you have enough coverage to pay for the car.** If you do not have auto insurance or an umbrella policy that covers damage to third parties, purchasing liability insurance and a CDW or LDW is highly recommended.

REQUIREMENTS & RESTRICTIONS

In Washington State you must be 21 and hold a major credit card to rent a car. Rates may be higher if you're under 25. You'll pay about $3 per day per child seat for children under age 4 or 40 pounds, or per booster seat for children ages 4 to 6 or under 60 pounds, both of which are compulsory in Washington state.

SURCHARGES

Before you pick up a car in one city and leave it in another, ask about drop-off charges or one-way service fees, which can be substantial. Note, too, that some rental agencies charge extra if you return the car before the time specified in your contract. To avoid a hefty refueling fee, fill the tank just before you turn in the car, but be aware that gas stations near the rental outlet may overcharge. Some companies will allow you to purchase a tank of gas in advance when you rent the car, so that you may return the car on empty—but this is almost never a good deal. Surcharges may apply if you're under 25 or if you take the car outside the area approved by the rental agency. You'll pay extra for child seats (about $3 a day), which are compulsory for children under six, and usually for additional drivers (about $10 per day).

CAR TRAVEL

If you aren't staying in a central location, you may find Seattle's transit system inadequate for getting around quickly and easily. Access to a car is *almost* a necessity. Predictably, there is congestion on the highway and surface streets that extends well past traditional rush hours.

I–5, Seattle's major highway, runs right through the middle of the city and acts as the main north–south arterial. Highway 99 (often referred to as Aurora Avenue) runs parallel to I–5 and is another main north–south throughway. Denny Way is an important east–west route within Seattle, especially for those trying to get from the waterfront or Lower Queen Anne to Capitol Hill. I–405 is the major highway that runs east of Lake Washington, beginning in South Center to connect Renton, Bellevue, Kirkland, and Woodinville.

With many of the tech companies headquartered in the smaller cities east of Lake Washington, there's a whole lot of traffic between Seattle and the Eastside. I–90 is the major east–west state highway linking Seattle with south Bellevue, Issaquah, and cities east of the Cascades; Highway 520 branches off from I–5 near Montlake and connects Seattle to north Bellevue and Redmond. The Lake Washington Floating Bridge (part of I–90) and the Evergreen Point Floating Bridge (part of Highway 520) are the only routes across Lake Washington.

EMERGENCY SERVICES

Seattle AAA is a full-service travel agency that offers maps and roadside service for an enrollment fee.

7 Auto Impound Hotline ☎ 206/684–5444. Emergency Resource Center ☎ 206/684–3355. Emergency Roadside Assistance ☎ 800/ AAA–HELP national number. **Seattle AAA** ☎ 206/ 448–5353.

GASOLINE

Gas stations are conveniently located throughout Seattle. If you are looking for gas Downtown, you'll find stations around Safeco stadium, on Dearborn in the International District, on Denny in north Belltown, and on Broadway in Capitol Hill. Self-serve stations are most common, and major credit and debit cards are widely accepted. Prices get much cheaper as you head south toward Tacoma, and are about the same in the city as in its suburbs. Gas is much more expensive on islands and the closer you get to Canada.

PARKING

Metered street parking exists in Downtown Seattle, but consider yourself lucky if you manage to snag a spot during a weekday or peak evening dining hours. Meters are $1 per hour and take quarters or dimes. Parking is free on Sunday, holidays, and after 6

PM weekdays. **Be vigilant about keeping your meter running.** Parking enforcement officers are notoriously efficient; you will get ticketed if the meter runs out. The maximum meter time is two hours, so if you plan to be Downtown longer, find a parking lot or garage. The Washington State Convention and Visitors Bureau publishes a brochure mapping the city's parking areas and listing discounted spaces.

Most Downtown malls and high-rises have garages; pay lots are more common to the north and south of the core. The cheapest places to park are in the International District, Belltown, and First Hill—if you're lucky enough to find a space. Lot and garage rates begin at $3 an hour and cap off between $15 and $25 for the day. Park before 9 AM to take advantage of early-bird specials, which typically run $12 to $15.

Garages take credit and debit cards, but lots only take cash, so bring the right denominations. Since most open lots are unattended, you push your money through a hole on a numbered metal cabinet—and it usually takes a couple of minutes to roll up the bills and stuff them into the impossibly tiny slot. Make sure to stuff your bills into the same number slot as your parking space, and don't forget to lock up your car.

About two dozen major Downtown stores participate in the CityPark program, in which shoppers who spend at least $20 at their location get a $1 discount token for use at participating CityPark garages and lots. Tokens may also be used on King County Metro, Community Transit, and Sound Transit buses. A CityPark logo designates shops that are part of the program; garages and lots include those in the Ampco, CPS, Diamond, Imperial, Key Park, Republic, Standard, and U-Park systems. In the International District, look for the dragon parking sign in shop windows; these stores also provide discount parking tokens that can be used in specific neighborhood lots.

Evening and weekend parking rates are usually less than those on weekdays, around $5 for parking between 6 and midnight and $5–$12 for parking all day on weekends. After 5 PM, it's just $3 to park at Pacific Place for up to four hours.

7 **Parking Garages Bon Marchè** ⊠ 3rd Ave. and Pine St., Downtown ☎ 206/506–2000. **Pacific**

Place Shopping Center ⊠ 600 Pine St., Downtown ☎ 206/405-2655. **Rainier Square** ⊠ 409 Union St., Downtown ☎ 206/373-7119. **Washington State Convention Center** ⊠ 800 Convention Pl., Downtown ☎ 206/694-5000. **Westlake Center** ⊠ Olive Way, between 4th and 5th Aves., Downtown ☎ 206/467-3044.

🛈 **CityPark Sites** Ampco ☎ 206/624-1870. CPS ☎ 206/624-0882. Diamond ☎ 206/284-6303. Imperial ☎ 206/381-1789. Key ☎ 206/284-4300. Republic ☎ 206/783-4144. Standard ☎ 206/521-5984. U-Park ☎ 206/284-9797.

ROAD CONDITIONS

In coastal areas, the mild, damp climate contributes to roadways that are frequently wet. Winter snowfalls are not common (generally only once or twice a year), but when snow does fall, traffic grinds to a halt and the roadways become treacherous and stay that way until the snow melts.

Tire chains, studs, or snow tires are essential equipment for winter travel in mountain areas such as Leavenworth, Washington, or Mt. Rainier. If you're planning to drive to high elevations, be sure to check the weather forecast beforehand. Even the main highway mountain passes can be forced to close because of snow conditions. In winter months, state and provincial highway departments operate snow advisory telephone lines that give pass conditions.

🛈 **Winter Road-Condition Reports** Washington State Road Condition Reports ☎ 888/766-4636 ⊕ traffic.wsdot.wa.gov.

RULES OF THE ROAD

Speed limits in Seattle vary between 25 and 35 mph. Right turns are allowed on most red lights after you've come to a full stop, and left turns are allowed on adjoining one-way streets. Passengers are required to wear seat belts. The speed limits on the U.S. interstate highways in Washington State are 65 mph in rural areas and 60 mph in urban zones; on secondary highways the limit is 55 mph. Freeway on-ramps in the city are regulated by street lights during morning and evening rush hours. Drunk driving laws in Washington State are strict, and a 0.8% blood alcohol level is strictly enforced. Always strap children under age four or under 40 pounds into approved child-safety seats. Children over this age and weight traveling by road

in Washington State must still ride in an approved booster seat until they are age six or 60 pounds.

TRAFFIC

Traffic in Seattle is bad and getting worse. The I-5 corridor tends to be clogged with traffic heading into Downtown from both north and south from 6:30 to 9:30 each morning, and out again each evening from 2:30 to 6:30. It's not unusual for the heavy traffic pattern to continue throughout the day. Of the two bridges crossing Lake Washington (I-520 to the north and I-90 to the south), traffic is usually better on one or the other, so listen to local radio reports to decide which to use. On I-405, the north-south interstate highway on the east side of Lake Washington, the traffic is heavy during the traditional morning and evening rush hours.

CHILDREN IN SEATTLE

There's plenty for kids to enjoy in Seattle— green spaces, the waterfront, and urban adventure. Nearby are islands, beaches, inlets, and mountains to explore. If you're renting a car, don't forget to **arrange for a car seat** when you reserve. For general advice about traveling with children, consult *Fodor's FYI: Travel with Your Baby* (available in bookstores everywhere).

When you arrive look in local shops, newsstands, and bookstores for the free monthly publication *Seattle's Child,* which lists family-oriented events and activities. *Fodor's Around Seattle with Kids* (available in bookstores everywhere) can help you plan your days together.

🛈 **Local Information** *Seattle's Child* ⊠ 2107 Elliott Ave., Suite 303, Queen Anne ☎ 206/441-0191.

FLYING

Experts agree that it's a good idea to use safety seats aloft for children weighing less than 40 pounds. Airlines set their own policies: if you use a safety seat, U.S. carriers usually require that the child be ticketed, even if he or she is young enough to ride free, because the seats must be strapped into regular seats. And even if you pay the full adult fare for the seat, it may be worth it, especially on longer trips. Do **check your airline's policy about using safety seats during takeoff and landing.** Safety seats are not allowed everywhere in the plane, so get your seat assignments as early as possible.

When reserving, request children's meals or a freestanding bassinet (not available at all airlines) if you need them. But note that bulkhead seats, where you must sit to use the bassinet, may lack an overhead bin or storage space on the floor.

SIGHTS & ATTRACTIONS

Places that are especially appealing to children are indicated by a rubber-duckie icon (🦆) in the margin.

CONCIERGES

Concierges, found in many hotels, can help you with theater tickets and dinner reservations: a good one with connections may be able to get you seats for a hot show or prime-time dinner reservations at the restaurant of the moment. You can also turn to your hotel's concierge for help with travel arrangements, sightseeing plans, services ranging from aromatherapy to zipper repair, and emergencies. **Always tip** a concierge who has been of assistance (⇨ Tipping).

CONSUMER PROTECTION

Whether you're shopping for gifts or purchasing travel services, **pay with a major credit card** whenever possible, so you can cancel payment or get reimbursed if there's a problem (and you can provide documentation). If you're doing business with a particular company for the first time, contact your local Better Business Bureau and the attorney general's offices in your state and (for U.S. businesses) the company's home state as well. Have any complaints been filed? Finally, if you're buying a package or tour, always consider travel insurance that includes default coverage (⇨ Insurance).

🚹 **BBBs** Council of Better Business Bureaus ✉ 4200 Wilson Blvd., Suite 800, Arlington, VA 22203 ☎ 703/276-0100 🖷 703/525-8277 ⊕ www.bbb.org. 🚹 **Local BBBs** Washington Better Business Bureau 🖎 Box 68926, Sea-Tac, 98168-0926 ☎ 206/431-2222.

CRUISE TRAVEL

Seattle's expanding cruise industry now welcomes some of the world's largest ships to new docks on Elliott Bay. The city's strategic location along the West Coast means that it's just a day's journey by water to Canada or California, and you can reach Alaska or Mexico in less than a week. In addition to the major cruise lines, you can also sail around Elliott Bay, Lake Union, Lake Washington, or along a combination of local waterways.

Of the large ships, Norwegian Cruise Line offers seven-day summer cruises from Seattle to Alaska, as well as five-day cruises from Los Angeles to Vancouver, B. C. that stop in Seattle. The ships dock at Pier 66, the Bell Street Pier Cruise Terminal. Holland America Line, which has seven-day cruises to Alaska on the *MS Amsterdam,* and Princess Cruises, which offers seven-day Alaska cruises on the *Star Princess,* both dock at the Terminal 30 Cruise Facility south of Downtown.

To learn how to plan, choose, and book a cruise-ship voyage, consult *Fodor's FYI: Plan & Enjoy Your Cruise* (available in bookstores everywhere).

🚹 **Cruise Lines** Holland America Line 🖎 300 Elliott Ave. W ☎ 206/281-3535 or 877/932-4259 ⊕ www.hollandamerica.com. **Norwegian Cruise Line** 🖎 Bell Street Pier, 2203 Alaskan Way ☎ 206/615-3950 or 800/327-7030 ⊕ www.norwegiancruiselines.com. **Princess Cruise Lines** 🖎 2815 2nd Ave., Suite 400 Seattle 98121 ☎ 800/421-1700 ⊕ www.princess.com.

CUSTOMS & DUTIES

When shopping abroad, keep receipts for all purchases. Upon reentering the country, **be ready to show customs officials what you've bought.** Pack purchases together in an easily accessible place. If you think a duty is incorrect, appeal the assessment. If you object to the way your clearance was handled, note the inspector's badge number. In either case, first ask to see a supervisor. If the problem isn't resolved, write to the appropriate authorities, beginning with the port director at your point of entry.

IN SEATTLE

🚹 Sea-Tac U.S. Customs and Immigration office 🖎 South Satellite, near the International gates ☎ 206/553-7960 customs, 206/553-0467 immigration.

IN AUSTRALIA

Australian residents who are 18 or older may bring home A$400 worth of souvenirs and gifts (including jewelry), 250 cigarettes or 250 grams of cigars or other tobacco products, and 1,125 ml of alcohol (including wine, beer, and spirits). Residents under 18 may bring back A$200 worth of goods. Members of the same family traveling together may pool their allowances. Prohibited items include meat products. Seeds, plants, and fruits need to be declared upon arrival.

Australian Customs Service ⊡ Regional Director, Box 8, Sydney, NSW 2001 ☎ 02/9213-2000 or 1300/363263, 02/9364-7222 or 1800/803-006 quarantine-inquiry line ⊠ 02/9213-4043 ⊕ www.customs.gov.au.

IN CANADA

Canadian residents who have been out of Canada for at least seven days may bring in C$750 worth of goods duty-free. If you've been away fewer than seven days but more than 48 hours, the duty-free allowance drops to C$200. If your trip lasts 24 to 48 hours, the allowance is C$50. You may not pool allowances with family members. Goods claimed under the C$750 exemption may follow you by mail; those claimed under the lesser exemptions must accompany you. Alcohol and tobacco products may be included in the seven-day and 48-hour exemptions but not in the 24-hour exemption. If you meet the age requirements of the province or territory through which you reenter Canada, you may bring in, duty-free, 1.5 liters of wine or 1.14 liters (40 imperial ounces) of liquor or 24 12-ounce cans or bottles of beer or ale. Also, if you meet the local age requirement for tobacco products, you may bring in, duty-free, 200 cigarettes and 50 cigars. Check ahead of time with the Canada Customs and Revenue Agency or the Department of Agriculture for policies regarding meat products, seeds, plants, and fruits.

You may send an unlimited number of gifts (only one gift per recipient, however) worth up to C$60 each duty-free to Canada. Label the package UNSOLICITED GIFT—VALUE UNDER $60. Alcohol and tobacco are excluded.

Canada Customs and Revenue Agency ⊠ 2265 St. Laurent Blvd., Ottawa, Ontario K1G 4K3 ☎ 800/461-9999, 204/983-3500, 506/636-5064 ⊕ www.ccra.gc.ca.

IN NEW ZEALAND

All homeward-bound residents may bring back NZ$700 worth of souvenirs and gifts; passengers may not pool their allowances, and children can claim only the concession on goods intended for their own use. For those 17 or older, the duty-free allowance also includes 4.5 liters of wine or beer; one 1,125-ml bottle of spirits; and either 200 cigarettes, 250 grams of tobacco, 50 cigars, or a combination of the three up to 250 grams. Meat products, seeds, plants, and fruits must be declared upon arrival to the Agricultural Services Department.

New Zealand Customs ⊠ Head office: The Customhouse, 17–21 Whitmore St., Box 2218, Wellington ☎ 09/300-5399 or 0800/428-786 ⊕ www.customs.govt.nz.

IN THE U.K.

From countries outside the European Union, including the United States, you may bring home, duty-free, 200 cigarettes or 50 cigars; 1 liter of spirits or 2 liters of fortified or sparkling wine or liqueurs; 2 liters of still table wine; 60 ml of perfume; 250 ml of toilet water; plus £145 worth of other goods, including gifts and souvenirs. Prohibited items include meat products, seeds, plants, and fruits.

HM Customs and Excise ⊠ Portcullis House, 21 Cowbridge Rd. E, Cardiff CF11 9SS ☎ 0845/010-9000 or 0208/929-0152, 0208/929-6731 or 0208/910-3602 complaints ⊕ www.hmce.gov.uk.

DISABILITIES & ACCESSIBILITY

Most public buildings in Seattle offer access for people with disabilities, and all the rest rooms at Sea-Tac are wheelchair accessible. Metro buses are equipped with lifts and seat belts for wheelchairs, though none of the area car rental agencies have vehicles with hand controls. (Try contacting Access Mobility Systems, which has information about van rentals nationwide.) The Seattle/King County Convention and Visitors Bureau notes the wheelchair-accessibility of attractions and lodgings in its Seattle visitor and lodging brochures. The Huntleigh Skycap and Wheelchair Service offers wheelchair escort services at the airport.

Local Resources Access Mobility Systems ☎ 888/282-8267 ⊕ www.accessams.com. **Huntleigh Skycap and Wheelchair Service** ☎ 206/433-5281. **Seattle/King County Convention and Visitors Bureau** ⊠ 520 Pike St., Suite 1300, Downtown 98101 ☎ 206/461-5800 ⊕ www.seattleinsider.com.

LODGING

Despite the Americans with Disabilities Act, the definition of accessibility seems to differ from hotel to hotel. Some properties may be accessible by ADA standards for people with mobility problems but not for people with hearing or vision impairments, for example.

If you have mobility problems, ask for the lowest floor on which accessible services are offered. If you have a hearing impairment, check whether the hotel has devices to alert you visually to the ring of the telephone, a knock at the door, and a fire/emergency alarm. Some hotels provide these devices without charge. Discuss your needs with hotel personnel if this equipment isn't available, so that a staff member can personally alert you in the event of an emergency.

If you're bringing a guide dog, get authorization ahead of time and write down the name of the person with whom you spoke.

RESERVATIONS

When discussing accessibility with an operator or reservations agent, ask hard questions. Are there any stairs, inside *or* out? Are there grab bars next to the toilet *and* in the shower/tub? How wide is the doorway to the room? To the bathroom? For the most extensive facilities meeting the latest legal specifications, opt for newer accommodations. If you reserve through a toll-free number, consider also calling the hotel's local number to confirm the information from the central reservations office. Get confirmation in writing when you can.

SIGHTS & ATTRACTIONS

The street running through the Pike Place Market is paved in brick, and some of the pavement is rough, but the market is wheelchair accessible. The crowds get thick here during the peak tourist season, so expect slow-going. Aside from that, Seattle is a newer city so the majority of the other attractions are easily accessed by people using wheelchairs. The Seattle Art Museum has ramps and elevators as do the Space Needle and the other attractions at the Seattle Center. Pioneer Square has cobbled streets and sidewalks, but the street corners have been adapted with ramps.

TRANSPORTATION

Seattle ACCESS provides van transportation in King County for people with disabilities. You must register and make a reservation at least one day in advance of your trip. The trip is 50¢ each way.

7 ACCESS ☎ 206/689-3113 to register, 206/971-5522 or 800/201-8888 for reservations ⊕ transit.metrokc.gov/accessible/access.html.

7 Complaints Aviation Consumer Protection Division (⇨ Air Travel) for airline-related problems. **Departmental Office of Civil Rights** ✉ for general inquiries, U.S. Department of Transportation, S-30, 400 7th St. SW, Room 10215, Washington, DC 20590 ☎ 202/366-4648 ≋ 202/366-9371 ⊕ www.dot.gov/ost/docr/index.htm. **Disability Rights Section** ✉ NYAV, U.S. Department of Justice, Civil Rights Division, 950 Pennsylvania Ave. NW, Washington, DC 20530 ☎ ADA information line 202/514-0301, 800/514-0301, 202/514-0383 TTY, 800/514-0383 TTY ⊕ www.ada.gov. **U.S. Department of Transportation Hotline** ☎ for disability-related air-travel problems, 800/778-4838 or 800/455-9880 TTY.

TRAVEL AGENCIES

In the United States, the Americans with Disabilities Act requires that travel firms serve the needs of all travelers. Some agencies specialize in working with people with disabilities.

7 Travelers with Mobility Problems Access Adventures/B. Roberts Travel ✉ 206 Chestnut Ridge Rd., Scottsville, NY 14624 ☎ 585/889-9096 ⊕ www.brobertstravel.com, run by a former physical-rehabilitation counselor. **Accessible Vans of America** ✉ 9 Spielman Rd., Fairfield, NJ 07004 ☎ 877/282-8267, 888/282-8267, 973/808-9709 reservations ≋ 973/808-9713 ⊕ www.accessiblevans.com. **CareVacations** ✉ No. 5, 5110-50 Ave., Leduc, Alberta, Canada, T9E 6V4 ☎ 780/986-6404 or 877/478-7827 ≋ 780/986-8332 ⊕ www.carevacations.com, for group tours and cruise vacations. **Flying Wheels Travel** ✉ 143 W. Bridge St., Box 382, Owatonna, MN 55060 ☎ 507/451-5005 ≋ 507/451-1685 ⊕ www.flyingwheelstravel.com.

DISCOUNTS & DEALS

Be a smart shopper and compare all your options before making decisions. A plane ticket bought with a promotional coupon from travel clubs, coupon books, and direct-mail offers or purchased on the Internet may not be cheaper than the least expensive fare from a discount ticket agency. And always keep in mind that what you get is just as important as what you save.

CITYPASS

If you're planning to visit all or most of Seattle's top tourist destinations, buy a CityPass ticket book for $37 and you'll get 50% off admission to the Space Needle, the Seattle Art Museum, the Seattle Aquarium, the Pacific Science Center, the Woodland Park Zoo, and the Museum of Flight. The CityPass booklet, available at any of these attractions, is valid for nine consecutive days.

CityPass ☎ 888/299-6633 ⊕ www.citypass.com.

DISCOUNT RESERVATIONS

To save money, look into discount reservations services with Web sites and toll-free numbers, which use their buying power to get a better price on hotels, airline tickets (⇨ Air Travel), even car rentals. When booking a room, always **call the hotel's local toll-free number** (if one is available) rather than the central reservations number—you'll often get a better price. Always ask about special packages or corporate rates.

Airline Tickets Air 4 Less ☎ 800/AIR4LESS; low-fare specialist.

Hotel Rooms Accommodations Express ☎ 800/444-7666 or 800/277-1064 ⊕ www.accommodationsexpress.com. **Hotels.com** ☎ 800/246-8357 ⊕ www.hotels.com. **Quikbook** ☎ 800/789-9887 ⊕ www.quikbook.com. **RMC Travel** ☎ 800/245-5738 ⊕ www.rmcwebtravel.com. **Turbotrip.com** ☎ 800/473-7829 ⊕ www.turbotrip.com.

PACKAGE DEALS

Don't confuse packages and guided tours. When you buy a package, you travel on your own, just as though you had planned the trip yourself. Fly/drive packages, which combine airfare and car rental, are often a good deal. In cities, ask the local visitor's bureau about hotel packages that include tickets to major museum exhibits or other special events.

EMERGENCIES

The Doctor's Referral gives referrals of physicians and dentists in the Seattle area. You can also try Dental Referral, a national service, and the University of Washington Physicians Referral Service. Bartell

Drugs in Queen Anne and Rite Aid pharmacies in Factoria and Federal Way are open 24 hours. You'll also find pharmacies in most Safeway, QFC, and Fred Meyer supermarkets. Most Walgreens stores have drive-through windows.

Doctors & Dentists Dental Referral ☎ 800/511-8663. **Doctor's Referral** ☎ 206/622-9933. **University of Washington Physicians Referral Service** ☎ 800/826-1121.

Emergency Services Ambulance, Fire, and Police ☎ 911.

Hospitals Children's Hospital ⌂ 4800 Sand Point Way NE, Shoreline ☎ 206/526-2000 ⊕ www.seattlechildrens.org. **Harborview Medical Center** ⌂ 325 9th Ave., First Hill ☎ 206/731-3000 ⊕ www.washington.edu/medicine/. **Swedish Medical Center** ⌂ 747 Broadway, Capitol Hill ☎ 206/386-6000 ⊕ www.swedish.org.

Hot Lines AIDS Hotline ☎ 206/205-7837. **King County Sexual Assault Resource Center** ☎ 800/825-7273.

Late-Night Pharmacies Bartell Drugs ⌂ 600 1st Ave. N, Queen Anne ☎ 206/284-1354 ⊕ www.bartelldrugs.com. **Rite Aid** ⌂ 3905 Factoria Sq. Mall SE, off 128th Ave. SE, Bellevue ☎ 425/644-2925, 800/748-3243 for other locations ⌂ 2131 SW 336th St., Federal Way ☎ 253/952-2803. **Walgreens** ⌂ 859 NE Northgate Way, Northgate ☎ 206/417-0520 ⊕ www.walgreens.com ⌂ 5409 15th Ave. NW, Ballard ☎ 206/781-0056.

GAY & LESBIAN TRAVEL

Seattle is a progressive city with a vibrant gay scene. The greatest concentration of bars, restaurants, and shops serving the interests of gays and lesbians can be found on Capitol Hill. Each June the Gay Pride Parade is held on Broadway, the main thoroughfare of this popular Seattle neighborhood. For more information, pick up a copy of the *Seattle Gay News* or *The Stranger,* both of which are free weeklies.

For details about the gay and lesbian scene, consult *Fodor's Gay Guide to the USA* (available in bookstores everywhere).

Gay- & Lesbian-Friendly Travel Agencies Different Roads Travel ⌂ 8383 Wilshire Blvd., Suite 520, Beverly Hills, CA 90211 ☎ 323/651-5557 or 800/429-8747 (Ext. 14 for both) 🖷 323/651-3678 ✉ lgernert@tzell.com. **Kennedy Travel** ⌂ 130 W. 42nd St., Suite 401, New York, NY 10036 ☎ 212/840-8659, 800/237-7433 🖷 212/730-2269 ⊕ www.kennedytravel.com. **Now, Voyager** ⌂ 4406 18th St., San Francisco, CA 94114 ☎ 415/626-1169 or 800/255-6951 🖷 415/626-8626 ⊕ www.nowvoyager.com. **Skylink Travel and Tour** ⌂ 1455 N. Dutton

Ave., Suite A, Santa Rosa, CA 95401 ☎ 707/546–9888 or 800/225–5759 🖷 707/636–0951 serving lesbian travelers.

GUIDEBOOKS

Plan well and you won't be sorry. Guidebooks are excellent tools—and you can take them with you. You may want to check out the color-photo-illustrated Compass American Guides to the Pacific Northwest, Oregon, and Washington, all thorough on culture and history, or *Fodor's Road Guide USA: Oregon, Washington,* for comprehensive restaurant, hotel, and attractions listings for driving vacations. For more city coverage try *Fodor's Seattle.* All are available at online retailers and bookstores everywhere.

HOLIDAYS

Major national holidays are New Year's Day (Jan. 1); Martin Luther King Day (3rd Mon. in Jan.); Presidents' Day (3rd Mon. in Feb.); Memorial Day (last Mon. in May); Independence Day (July 4); Labor Day (1st Mon. in Sept.); Columbus Day (2nd Mon. in Oct.); Thanksgiving Day (4th Thurs. in Nov.); Christmas Eve and Christmas Day (Dec. 24 and 25); and New Year's Eve (Dec. 31).

INSURANCE

The most useful travel-insurance plan is a comprehensive policy that includes coverage for trip cancellation and interruption, default, trip delay, and medical expenses (with a waiver for preexisting conditions).

Without insurance you'll lose all or most of your money if you cancel your trip, regardless of the reason. Default insurance covers you if your tour operator, airline, or cruise line goes out of business. Trip-delay covers expenses that arise because of bad weather or mechanical delays. Study the fine print when comparing policies.

U.K. residents can buy a travel-insurance policy valid for most vacations taken during the year in which it's purchased (but check preexisting-condition coverage).

Always **buy travel policies directly from the insurance company**; if you buy them from a cruise line, airline, or tour operator that goes out of business you probably won't be covered for the agency or operator's default, a major risk. Before making

any purchase, review your existing health and home-owner's policies to find what they cover away from home.

🛈 Travel Insurers In the U.S.: **Access America** ✉ 6600 W. Broad St., Richmond, VA 23230 ☎ 800/284–8300 🖷 804/673–1491 or 800/346–9265 🌐 www.accessamerica.com. **Travel Guard International** ✉ 1145 Clark St., Stevens Point, WI 54481 ☎ 715/345–0505 or 800/826–1300 🖷 800/955–8785 🌐 www.travelguard.com.

FOR INTERNATIONAL TRAVELERS

For information on customs restrictions, *see* Customs and Duties.

CAR RENTAL

When picking up a rental car, non-U.S. residents need a voucher for any prepaid reservations that were made in the traveler's home country, a passport, a driver's license, and a travel policy that covers each driver.

CAR TRAVEL

Gas prices at this writing are about $1.79 a gallon (regular unleaded), $1.89 (unleaded plus), $1.99 (premium). Stations are plentiful, and stay open 24 hours along the highways. In rural areas, Sunday hours are limited, but you really can't get more than 30 mi without a refueling opportunity unless you're driving east of the Cascade Mountains.

All but the most rural or wooded roads are paved. Multilane, interstate highways I–5 (north–south) and I–90 (east–west) are the fastest routes to and from Seattle. Highways with three-digit numbers (like the 405 and 520 routes through Bellevue) encircle urban areas, which may have other limited-access expressways, freeways, and parkways. At this writing there were no toll roads in western Washington, but a toll bridge set to open in 2007 is under construction across the Tacoma Narrows channel. This is 48 mi south of Seattle, between Tacoma and Gig Harbor, the latter the gateway to the Kitsap and Olympic peninsulas.

Along larger highways, roadside stops with rest rooms, fast-food restaurants, and sundries stores are well spaced. State police and tow trucks patrol major highways and lend assistance to travelers in distress. If your car breaks down on an interstate, pull onto the shoulder and wait for help, or have your passengers wait while you walk to an emergency phone. If you carry a cell phone, dial *55, noting your location on the small green roadside mileage markers.

Driving in the United States is on the right. Do obey speed limits posted along roads and highways. Watch for lower limits in small towns and on back roads. On weekdays between 6 and 10 AM and again between 4 and 7 PM expect heavy traffic. To encourage carpooling, some freeways have special lanes for so-called high-occupancy vehicles (HOV)—cars carrying more than one passenger.

Bookstores, gas stations, convenience stores, and rest stops sell maps (about $3) and multiregion road atlases (about $10).

CONSULATES & EMBASSIES

Canada Canadian Consulate ⊠ Plaza 600 Bldg., 6th Ave. and Stewart St., 4th fl., ☎ 206/443-1777 ⊕ www.canada-seattle.org.

New Zealand New Zealand Consulate ⊠ 10649 North Beach Road, Bow, WA 98232 ☎ 360/766-8002 ⊕ www.nzemb.org/embassy/consulates.htm.

United Kingdom U.K. Consulate ⊠ 900 4th Ave., Suite 3001 ☎ 206/622-9255 ⊕ www.britainusa.com/consular/seattle.

CURRENCY

The dollar is the basic unit of U.S. currency. It has 100 cents. Coins are the copper penny (1¢); the silvery nickel (5¢), dime (10¢), quarter (25¢), and half-dollar (50¢); and the golden $1 coin, replacing a now-rare silver dollar. Bills are denominated $1, $5, $10, $20, $50, and $100, all green and identical in size; designs vary. In addition, you may come across a $2 bill, but the chances are slim. The exchange rate at this writing is $1.50 per British pound, 67¢ per Canadian dollar, 59¢ per Australian dollar, and 46¢ per New Zealand dollar.

ELECTRICITY

The U.S. standard is AC, 110 volts/60 cycles. Plugs have two flat pins set parallel to each other.

EMERGENCIES

For police, fire, or ambulance, **dial 911.**

INSURANCE

Britons and Australians need extra medical coverage when traveling overseas.

Insurance Information In Australia: **Insurance Council of Australia** ⊠ Insurance Enquiries and

Complaints, Level 3, 56 Pitt St., Sydney, NSW 2000 ☎ 1300/363683 or 02/9251-4456 ⊠ 02/9251-4453 ⊕ www.iecltd.com.au. In Canada: **RBC Insurance** ⊠ 6880 Financial Dr., Mississauga, Ontario L5N 7Y5 ☎ 800/565-3129 ⊠ 905/813-4704 ⊕ www. rbcinsurance.com. In New Zealand: **Insurance Council of New Zealand** ⊠ Level 7, 111-115 Customhouse Quay, Box 474, Wellington ☎ 04/472-5230 ⊠ 04/473-3011 ⊕ www.icnz.org.nz. In the U.K.: **Association of British Insurers** ⊠ 51 Gresham St., London EC2V 7HQ ☎ 020/7600-3333 ⊠ 020/7696-8999 ⊕ www.abi.org.uk.

MAIL & SHIPPING

You can buy stamps and aerograms and send letters and parcels in post offices. Stamp-dispensing machines can occasionally be found in airports, bus and train stations, office buildings, drugstores, and the like. You can also deposit mail in the stout, dark blue, steel bins at strategic locations everywhere and in the mail chutes of large buildings; pickup schedules are posted. You can deposit packages at public collection boxes as long as the parcels are affixed with proper postage and weigh less than one pound. Packages weighing one pound or more must be taken to a post office or handed to a postal carrier.

For mail sent within the United States, you need a 37¢ stamp for first-class letters weighing up to 1 ounce (23¢ for each additional ounce) and 23¢ for postcards. You pay 80¢ for 1-ounce airmail letters and 70¢ for airmail postcards to most other countries; to Canada and Mexico, you need a 60¢ stamp for a 1-ounce letter and 50¢ for a postcard. An aerogram—a single sheet of lightweight blue paper that folds into its own envelope, stamped for overseas airmail—costs 70¢.

To receive mail on the road, have it sent c/o General Delivery at your destination's main post office (use the correct five-digit ZIP code). You must pick up mail in person within 30 days and show a driver's license or passport.

PASSPORTS & VISAS

When traveling internationally, carry your passport even if you don't need one (it's always the best form of ID) and **make two photocopies of the data page** (one for someone at home and another for you, carried separately from your passport). If you lose your passport, promptly call the nearest embassy or consulate and the local police.

Visitor visas aren't necessary for Canadian or European Union citizens, or for citizens of Australia who are staying fewer than 90 days.

🛂 **Australian Citizens** **Passports Australia** ☎ 131–232 ⊕ www.passports.gov.au. **United States Consulate General** ✉ MLC Centre, Level 59, 19–29 Martin Pl., Sydney, NSW 2000 ☎ 02/9373–9200, 1902/941–641 fee-based visa-inquiry line ⊕ usembassy-australia.state.gov/sydney.

🛂 **Canadian Citizens** **Passport Office** ✉ to mail in applications: 200 Promenade du Portage, Hull, Québec J8X 4B7 ☎ 819/994–3500, 800/567–6868, 866/255–7655 TTY ⊕ www.ppt.gc.ca.

🛂 **New Zealand Citizens** **New Zealand Passports Office** ✉ For applications and information, Level 3, Boulcott House, 47 Boulcott St., Wellington ☎ 0800/22–5050 or 04/474–8100 ⊕ www. passports.govt.nz. **Embassy of the United States** ✉ 29 Fitzherbert Terr., Thorndon, Wellington ☎ 04/462–6000 ⊕ usembassy.org.nz. **U.S. Consulate General** ✉ Citibank Bldg., 3rd fl., 23 Customs St. E, Auckland ☎ 09/303–2724 ⊕ usembassy. org.nz.

🛂 **U.K. Citizens** **U.K. Passport Service** ☎ 0870/ 521–0410 ⊕ www.passport.gov.uk. **American Consulate General** ✉ Queen's House, 14 Queen St., Belfast, Northern Ireland BT1 6EQ ☎ 028/ 9032–8239 🖶 028/9024–8482 ⊕ www.usembassy. org.uk. **American Embassy** ✉ for visa and immigration information (enclose a SASE), Consular Information Unit, 24 Grosvenor Sq., London W1A 1AE ✉ to submit an application via mail, Visa Branch, 5 Upper Grosvenor St., London W1A 2JB ☎ 09068/ 200–290 recorded visa information or 09055/444– 546 operator service, both with per-minute charges, 0207/499–9000 main switchboard ⊕ www. usembassy.org.uk.

TELEPHONES

All U.S. telephone numbers consist of a three-digit area code and a seven-digit local number. Within many local calling areas, you dial only the seven-digit number. To call between area-code regions, dial "1" then all 10 digits; the same goes for calls to numbers prefixed by "800," "888," "866," and "877"—all toll free. For calls to numbers preceded by "900" you must pay—usually dearly.

For international calls, dial "011" followed by the country code and the local number. For help, dial "0" and ask for an overseas operator. The country code is 61 for Australia, 64 for New Zealand, 44 for

the United Kingdom. Calling Canada is the same as calling within the United States. Most local phone books list country codes and U.S. area codes. The country code for the United States is 1.

For operator assistance, dial "0." To obtain someone's phone number, call directory assistance at 555–1212 or occasionally 411 (free at public phones). To have the person you're calling foot the bill, phone collect; dial "0" instead of "1" before the 10-digit number.

At pay phones, instructions often are posted. Usually you insert coins in a slot (usually 25¢–50¢ for local calls) and wait for a steady tone before dialing. When you call long-distance, the operator tells you how much to insert; prepaid phone cards, widely available in various denominations, are easier. Call the number on the back, punch in the card's personal identification number when prompted, then dial your number.

MAIL & SHIPPING

There are post offices throughout Downtown Seattle and surrounding neighborhoods. They're generally well-staffed, and the lines move quickly.

🛂 **Post Offices** **Main Station** ✉ 301 Union St., Downtown ☎ 206/748–5417 or 800/275–8777. **Pioneer Square Station** ✉ 91 S. Jackson St., Pioneer Square ☎ 206/625–2293. **International District Station** ✉ 414 6th Ave. S, International District ☎ 206/625–2293. **Broadway Station** ✉ 101 E. Broadway, Capitol Hill ☎ 206/324–5474.

🛂 **Overnight Services** **Federal Express** ☎ 800/ 463–3339. **United Parcel Service** ☎ 800/742–5877. **United States Postal Service** ☎ 800/222–1811.

MEDIA

NEWSPAPERS & MAGAZINES

Seattle has two daily newspapers. The *Seattle Post-Intelligencer* is a Hearst paper, and the *Seattle Times* is locally owned. Both publish morning papers, and they publish the Saturday and Sunday papers jointly.

RADIO & TELEVISION

KUOW (94.9 FM) and KPLU (88.5 FM) are the local National Public Radio affiliates. KPLU also plays jazz 9 AM to 3 PM and 7:30 PM to 4 AM in between the news. Other stations include: KUBE (93.3 FM), pop music; KMPS (94.1 FM), country;

KBSG (97.3 FM), oldies; KING (98.1 FM), classical; KEZX (98.9 FM), smooth jazz; KISW (99.9 FM), hard rock; KZOK (102.5 FM), classic rock; KCMS (105.3 FM), pop Christian music; and KNDD (107.7 FM)—literally, "The End"—modern alternative rock. For news and traffic, the city turns on to KIRO (710 AM) and KNWX (770 AM). Christian programs are on KGNW (820 AM); for sports switch to KJR (950 AM). The main talk-show station is KOMO (1000 AM).

Channel 4, KOMO is the ABC affiliate. Channel 5, KING, is the NBC affiliate. Channel 7, KIRO, is the CBS affiliate. Channel 9, KCTS, is the public television station. Channel 13, KCPQ, is the Fox affiliate.

MONEY MATTERS

Prices throughout this guide are given for adults. Substantially reduced fees are almost always available for children, students, and senior citizens. For information on taxes, *see* Taxes.

ATMS

ATMs are *everywhere*. You can find them at banks, in grocery stores, convenience stores, many gas stations, restaurants, and bars. Most charge a 35¢ to $3 fee per transaction.

BANKS

You generally need an account to cash a personal check at a specific bank. There are also check-cashing services (which charge a fee) throughout Seattle. However, it's best to use credit cards, cash machines, and traveler's checks while you're traveling.

Bank of America, Seattle's largest American banking institution, has more than 50 area locations. Most are open weekdays 10–6 and some on Saturday 10–1. Key Bank has 40-plus branches. Hours are generally Monday–Thursday 9–5 and Friday 9–6. US Bank branches are open weekdays 9–5. Some are open Saturday 9–1. Washington Mutual's 40-plus branches have hours weekdays 9–6; some have hours Saturday 9–1. There are more than 30 branches of Wells Fargo; hours are weekdays 9–6. Some are open Saturday 9–2.
f Bank of America ☎ 206/461-0800 ⊕ www.bankofamerica.com. **Key Bank** ☎ 206/447-5767 ⊕ www.keybank.com. **US Bank** ☎ 800/872-2657 ⊕ www.usbank.com. **Washington Mutual** ☎ 800/

756-8000 ⊕ www.wamu.com. **Wells Fargo** ☎ 800/869-3557 ⊕ www.wellsfargo.com.

CREDIT CARDS

Throughout this guide, the following abbreviations are used: **AE**, American Express; **D**, Discover; **DC**, Diners Club; **MC**, MasterCard; and **V**, Visa.
f Reporting Lost Cards American Express ☎ 800/441-0519. **Diners Club** ☎ 800/234-6377. **Discover** ☎ 800/347-2683. **MasterCard** ☎ 800/622-7747. **Visa** ☎ 800/847-2911.

MONORAIL TRAVEL

Built for the 1962 World's Fair, the Seattle Monorail is a quick, convenient link between the Seattle Center and Downtown's Westlake Mall, located at Fourth Avenue and Pike Street. Making the 1-mi journey in just two minutes, the monorail departs both points every 10 minutes from 7:30 AM to 11 PM on weekdays and 9 AM to 11 PM weekends. The round-trip fare is $3; children 4 and under ride free. During weekends, Seattle Sonics basketball games, and the Folklife, Bite of Seattle, and Bumbershoot festivals—which all take place at the Seattle Center—you can park in the Bon-Macy's garage at Third Avenue and Stewart Street, take the monorail, and present your monorail ticket stub when you return for discounted parking rates of $5 on Friday and Saturday and $4 on Sunday and Monday.

A monorail for West Seattle, which would circle the California Avenue business core, is currently under construction.
f Seattle Center Monorail ☎ 206/905-2600 ⊕ www.seattlemonorail.com.

PACKING

Summer days in the Pacific Northwest are warm but evenings can cool off substantially. Your best bet is to **dress in layers**—sweatshirts, sweaters, and jackets are removed or put on as the day progresses. Chances are you'll need rain gear, too, especially if you're visiting in the winter. If you plan to explore the region's cities on foot, or if you choose to hike along mountain trails or beaches, bring comfortable walking shoes. Dining out is usually an informal affair, although some restaurants prefer men to wear a jacket and tie. If you plan on hiking or camping during the summer, insect repellent is a must.

In your carry-on luggage, pack an extra pair of eyeglasses or contact lenses and enough of any medication you take to last a few days longer than the entire trip. You may also ask your doctor to write a spare prescription using the drug's generic name, as brand names may vary from country to country. In luggage to be checked, **never pack prescription drugs, valuables, or undeveloped film.** And don't forget to carry with you the addresses of offices that handle refunds of lost traveler's checks. Check *Fodor's How to Pack* (available at online retailers and bookstores everywhere) for more tips.

To avoid customs and security delays, carry medications in their original packaging. Don't pack any sharp objects in your carry-on luggage, including knives of any size or material, scissors, and corkscrews, or anything else that might arouse suspicion.

To avoid having your checked luggage chosen for hand inspection, don't cram bags full. The U.S. Transportation Security Administration suggests packing shoes on top and placing personal items you don't want touched in clear plastic bags.

CHECKING LUGGAGE

You're allowed to carry aboard one bag and one personal article, such as a purse or a laptop computer. Make sure what you carry on fits under your seat or in the overhead bin. Get to the gate early, so you can board as soon as possible, before the overhead bins fill up.

Baggage allowances vary by carrier, destination, and ticket class. On international flights, you're usually allowed to check two bags weighing up to 70 pounds (32 kilograms) each, although a few airlines allow checked bags of up to 88 pounds (40 kilograms) in first class. Some international carriers don't allow more than 66 pounds (30 kilograms) per bag in business class and 44 pounds (20 kilograms) in economy. On domestic flights, the limit is usually 50 to 70 pounds (23 to 32 kilograms) per bag. In general, carry-on bags shouldn't exceed 40 pounds (18 kilograms). Most airlines won't accept bags that weigh more than 100 pounds (45 kilograms) on domestic or international flights. Check baggage restrictions with your carrier before you pack.

Airline liability for baggage is limited to $2,500 per person on flights within the United States. On international flights it amounts to $9.07 per pound or $20 per kilogram for checked baggage (roughly $640 per 70-pound bag), with a maximum of $634.90 per piece, and $400 per passenger for unchecked baggage. You can buy additional coverage at check-in for about $10 per $1,000 of coverage, but it often excludes a rather extensive list of items, shown on your airline ticket.

Before departure, itemize your bags' contents and their worth, and label the bags with your name, address, and phone number. (If you use your home address, cover it so potential thieves can't see it readily.) Include a label inside each bag and **pack a copy of your itinerary.** At check-in, make sure each bag is correctly tagged with the destination airport's three-letter code. Because some checked bags will be opened for hand inspection, the U.S. Transportation Security Administration (TSA) recommends that you leave luggage unlocked or use the plastic locks offered at check-in. TSA screeners place an inspection notice inside searched bags, which are re-sealed with a special lock.

If your bag has been searched and contents are missing or damaged, file a claim with the TSA Consumer Response Center as soon as possible. If your bags arrive damaged or fail to arrive at all, file a written report with the airline before leaving the airport.

7 Complaints **U.S. Transportation Security Administration Consumer Response Center** ☎ 866/289-9673 ⊕ www.tsa.gov.

REST ROOMS

All hotels and restaurants, and most grocery stores, parks, public beaches, ferries, and tourist attractions have clean, modern rest rooms.

SAFETY

Although the 1999 demonstrations against the World Trade Organization portrayed the city as chaotic, Seattle is generally calm. It's also relatively safe thanks to the numerous visible security personnel and the helpful, watchful residents who work together to keep crime rates down. The airport, ground transit links, ferries, and popular sights are well monitored by guards and cameras, and the city's knowledgeable travel personnel are on hand to help set visitors in the right direction. Festivals, parades, and sporting events are heavily patrolled by police. Tight rules apply as to what you can bring into stadiums, arenas, and performance venues; expect bag searches, X-ray machines, and/or metal detectors.

Use common sense and you'll avoid trouble: Always lock your car, and park in lighted areas after dark; don't walk alone during late hours; don't flash cash, jewelry, or valuables, particularly in crowded areas; and keep all valuables in a hidden pouch on your body or in your hotel safe. Keep an eye on your laptop computer at the airport, and lock it in the hotel safe when it's not in use. Keep your money well-guarded at markets and other crowded places or events, where distractions make it easy for pickpockets to prowl. Seattle's homeless panhandlers tend to frequent Pioneer Square, Belltown, Fremont, the U-District, and some area parks, but they're usually harmless.

SENIOR-CITIZEN TRAVEL

To qualify for age-related discounts, mention your senior-citizen status up front when booking hotel reservations (not when checking out) and before you're seated in restaurants (not when paying the bill). Be sure to have identification on hand. When renting a car, ask about promotional car-rental discounts, which can be cheaper than senior-citizen rates.

🚩 **Educational Programs** Elderhostel ✉ 11 Ave. de Lafayette, Boston, MA 02111-1746 ☎ 877/426-8056, 978/323-4141 international callers, 877/426-2167 TTY 🖷 877/426-2166 ⊕ www.elderhostel.org.

SIGHTSEEING TOURS

BALLOON

Over the Rainbow offers balloon tours in Woodinville in the spring and summer, weather permitting. They cost between $135 and $165 and include a morning champagne toast or a light supper at night.

BICYCLING

Blazing Saddles rents bikes and runs tours of the Burke Gilman Trail, the Ballard Locks, and Bainbridge Island. Terrene Tours organizes private day trips for groups of up to five for $580, which includes bike rental, guide, support van, lunch, and drinks. They can also set up overnight tours of the surrounding countryside and islands.

BOAT

Argosy Cruises sails around Elliott Bay (one hour, from Pier 55, $16), the Ballard Locks (2½ hours, from Pier 56, $30), and other area waterways. Let's Go Sailing permits passengers to take the helm, trim the sails, or simply enjoy the ride aboard the *Obsession* or the SC70 *Neptune's Car,* both 70-foot ocean racers. Three 1½-hour excursions ($23) depart daily from Pier 54. A 2½-hour sunset cruise ($38) is also available. Passengers can bring their own food on board.

BUS TOURS

Gray Line of Seattle operates bus and boat tours, including a six-hour Grand City Tour ($39) that includes many sights, lunch in Pike Place Market, and admission to the Space Needle observation deck.

CARRIAGE

Sealth Horse Carriages narrated tours ($50 per half hour, $100 per hour) trot away from the waterfront and Westlake Center.

ORIENTATION

For $36, Show Me Seattle takes up to 14 people in customized vans on day tours of the major sights, including the *Sleepless in Seattle* floating home, the Fremont Troll, and other offbeat stops. For the same price, Seattle Tours also has day tours of the city and its environs, with stops for picture taking. The Seattle Skyscrapers Tour visits all the major buildings of Downtown in about two hours for $12.

PLANE

Seattle Seaplanes' 20-minute scenic flight for $67.50 per person takes in views of Woodland Park Zoo, Downtown Seattle, and Microsoft. The company also schedules flying lessons, charter trips, and dinner flights to the San Juans and area islands. Take a 20-minute air tour with Seattle Flight for just $27 per person (up to 3), or an hour tour for $65 per person—with discounts for night flights. Kenmore Air makes scenic flights over the city, as well as to the San Juan Islands and Victoria, British Columbia.

TRAIN

The *Spirit of Washington* Dinner Train departs from Renton for a luxurious 3½-hour trip along the eastern shores of Lake Washington to the Columbia Winery in Woodinville. Sights include the Boeing Renton Plant, the Wilburton Trestle, and the Sammamish River Valley. Parlor seating is $60, or you can upgrade to the glass-encased dome for $75. For the same price you'll see Fourth of July fireworks or New Year's Eve festivities. The popular murder mystery tours are $80. Watch for winter specials, when children ride free.

WALKING

Chinatown Discovery Tours include four culinary excursions—from a light sampler to an eight-course banquet. The rates are $15 to $46, based on a minimum of four participants. Seattle Walking Tours creates customized, 2½-hour itineraries that cover specific areas of the city. These cost $15 per person for a minimum of three guests. Underground Seattle leads tours ($9) of the now-buried original storefronts and sidewalks of Pioneer Square are extremely popular. They offer an effective primer on early Seattle history, and it may be a good place to take cover if your aboveground tour starts to get soggy.

Tour Companies Argosy Cruises ☎ 206/623-4252 ⊕ www.argosycruises.com. **Blazing Saddles** ☎ 206/341-9994. **Chinatown Discovery Tours** ☎ 425/885-3085. **Gray Line of Seattle** ☎ 206/626-5208 or 800/426-7505 ⊕ www.graylineofseattle.com. **Kenmore Air** ☎ 425/486-1257 or 866/435-9524. **Let's Go Sailing** ☎ 206/624-3931. **Over the Rainbow** ☎ 206/364-0995 ⊕ www.letsgoballooning.com/Seattle. **Sealth Horse Carriages** ☎ 425/277-8282 ⊕ www8.bcity.com/heavyhorse. **Seattle Flight** ☎ 206/767-5234 ⊕ www.seattleflight.com. **Seattle Seaplanes** ☎ 800/637-5553 ⊕ www.seattleseaplanes.com. **Seattle Tours** ☎ 206/768-1234 ⊕ www.seattlecitytours.com. **Seattle Skyscrapers Tour** ☎ 206/667-9184. **Seattle Walking Tours** ☎ 425/885-3173 ⊕ www.seattlewalkingtours.com. **Show Me Seattle** ☎ 206/633-2489 ⊕ www.showmeseattle.com. *Spirit of Washington* **Dinner Train** ☎ 800/876-7245 ⊕ www.spiritofwashingtondinnertrain.com. **Terrene Tours** ☎ 206/325-5569. **Underground Seattle** ☎ 206/682-4646 ⊕ www.ohwy.com/wa/u/undertou.htm.

STREETCAR TRAVEL

The Waterfront Streetcar line of vintage 1920s-era trolleys from Melbourne, Australia, runs 1.6 mi south along Alaska Way from Pier 70, past the Washington State Ferries terminal at Piers 50 and 52, turning inland on Main Street, and passing through Pioneer Square before ending on South Jackson Street in the International District. It runs at about 20-minute intervals daily from 7 AM to 9 or 10 PM (less often and for fewer hours in winter). The fare is $1.25 from 9 to 3 and after 6, $1.50 during peak commuting hours. The stations and streetcars are wheelchair accessible.

Metropolitan Transit ☎ 206/553-3000 or 206/287-8463 for automated schedule line ⊕ transit.metrokc.gov.

STUDENTS IN SEATTLE

Most museums, attractions, and transportation options offer special rates to persons with valid student IDs. Ask if the special rate is not posted.

IDs & Services STA Travel ⊠ 10 Downing St., New York, NY 10014 ☎ 212/627-3111, 800/777-0112 24-hr service center ☐ 212/627-3387 ⊕ www.sta.com. **Travel Cuts** ⊠ 187 College St., Toronto, Ontario M5T 1P7, Canada ☎ 800/592-2887 in the U.S., 416/979-2406 or 866/246-9762 in Canada ☐ 416/979-8167 ⊕ www.travelcuts.com.

TAXES

There is a 15.6% hotel tax in Seattle for hotels with more than 20 rooms, 8.6% for properties with less than 20 rooms. Hotel tax is approximately 7.9% in areas outside of the city limits. There is an added 10% tax for renting cars at the airport.

SALES TAX

The sales tax in Washington is 8.6% and is applied to all purchases except groceries and prescription drugs. At restaurants you'll pay a 9.1% meal tax.

TAXIS

Rides generally run about $1.80 per mile, and it's usually easier to call for a taxi (no fee) than to flag down a ride on the street. There are no surcharges for late-night pickups. Taxis are readily available at most Downtown hotels. You can take an Atlas Towncar from the airport to your hotel for $45—or as far as Portland, Oregon, or Vancouver, British Columbia, for about $300. You can also hire a car and driver for the day; note that rates don't include the required 20% gratuity.

Taxi Companies Atlas Towncar ☎ 206/860-7777 or 888/646-0606 ⊕ www.atlastowncar.com. **Graytop Cab** ☎ 206/282-8222. **Orange Cab** ☎ 206/522-8800. **Yellow Cab** ☎ 206/622-6500.

TIME

Washington State is in the Pacific Time Zone, which is 2 hours later than Chicago, 3 hours later than New York, 8 hours later than London, and 18 hours later than Sydney.

TIPPING

Tips and service charges are usually not automatically added to a bill in the United States. If service is satisfactory, customers generally give waiters, waitresses, taxi drivers, barbers, hairdressers, and so forth, a tip of from 10% to 20% of the total bill. Bellhops, doormen, and porters at airports and railway stations are generally tipped $1 for each item of luggage. In Seattle there is no recognized system for tipping concierges. A gratuity of $2–$5 is suggested if you have the concierge arrange for a service such as restaurant reservations, theater tickets, or a town car, and $10–$20 if the service is more extensive or unusual, such as having a large bouquet of roses delivered on a Sunday.

TOURS & PACKAGES

Because everything is prearranged on a prepackaged tour or independent vacation, you spend less time planning—and often get it all at a good price.

BOOKING WITH AN AGENT

Travel agents are excellent resources. But it's a good idea to collect brochures from several agencies, as some agents' suggestions may be influenced by relationships with tour and package firms that reward them for volume sales. If you have a special interest, find an agent with expertise in that area; the American Society of Travel Agents (ASTA; ⇨ Travel Agencies) has a database of specialists worldwide. You can log on to the group's Web site to find an ASTA travel agent in your neighborhood.

Make sure your travel agent knows the accommodations and other services of the place being recommended. Ask about the

hotel's location, room size, beds, and whether it has a pool, room service, or programs for children, if you care about these. Has your agent been there in person or sent others whom you can contact?

Do some homework on your own, too: local tourism boards can provide information about lesser-known and small-niche operators, some of which may sell only direct.

BUYER BEWARE

Each year consumers are stranded or lose their money when tour operators—even large ones with excellent reputations—go out of business. So check out the operator. Ask several travel agents about its reputation, and try to **book with a company that has a consumer-protection program.** (Look for information in the company's brochure.) In the United States, members of the National Tour Association and the United States Tour Operators Association are required to set aside funds to cover payments and travel arrangements in the event that the company defaults. It's also a good idea to choose a company that participates in the American Society of Travel Agents' Tour Operator Program; ASTA will act as mediator in any disputes between you and your tour operator.

Remember that the more your package or tour includes, the better you can predict the ultimate cost of your vacation. Make sure you know exactly what is covered, and beware of hidden costs. Are taxes, tips, and transfers included? Entertainment and excursions? These can add up.

Tour-Operator Recommendations American Society of Travel Agents (⇨ Travel Agencies). **National Tour Association (NTA)** ✉ 546 E. Main St., Lexington, KY 40508 ☎ 859/226-4444 or 800/682-8886 🖷 859/226-4404 ⊕ www.ntaonline.com. **United States Tour Operators Association (USTOA)** ✉ 275 Madison Ave., Suite 2014, New York, NY 10016 ☎ 212/599-6599 🖷 212/599-6744 ⊕ www.ustoa.com.

TRAIN TRAVEL

Amtrak, the U.S. passenger rail system, has daily service to Seattle from the Midwest and California. The *Empire Builder* takes a northern route from Chicago to Seattle. The *Coast Starlight* begins in Southern California, makes stops throughout western Oregon and Washington, and terminates its route in Seattle. The once-daily *Mt. Baker International* takes a highly scenic coastal route from Seattle to Vancouver. There is not adequate train service in western Washington. The best regional train service is offered to Oregon and Vancouver, B.C.

Trains to and from Seattle have regular and business-class compartments. Cars with private bedrooms are available for multi-day trips (such as to Chicago), while "Custom Class" cars provide more legroom and complimentary refreshments on shorter routes (to Portland, for example). Reservations are necessary, and major credit cards are accepted.

Sounder Trains (commuter rails) are still a new phenomenon in Seattle—and as such, you can only travel north to the city in the mornings and south from Downtown during weekday evenings. Plans are in the works to create more round-trips and to extend service to communities north to Everett and from Lakewood to Tacoma. For now, trains leave Tacoma at 6:15 AM and 6:45 AM, with stops in Puyallup, Sumner, Auburn, Kent, and Tukwila prior to Seattle. Southbound trains leave Seattle at 5:10 and 5:35 PM.

It's $2 for one zone, $3 for two zones, and $4 from endpoint to endpoint; kids under six ride free. Tickets can be purchased at machines inside the stations or by mail. One-week, two-week, and monthly passes are also available. Transfers from Sounder Trains are accepted on buses throughout the region. For more information, contact Metropolitan Transit or Pierce Transit.

7 **Train Information Amtrak** ✉ King Street Station, 303 S. Jackson St., International District ☎ 206/382-4125 or 800/872-7245 ⊕ www.amtrak.com. **Metropolitan Transit** ☎ 206/553-3000 or 206/287-8463 for automated schedule line ⊕ transit.metrokc.gov. **Pierce Transit** ☎ 253/581-8000 ⊕ www.ptbus.pierce.wa.us. **Sounder Trains** ☎ 888/889-6368 ⊕ www.soundtransit.org.

TRAVEL AGENCIES

A good travel agent puts your needs first. Look for an agency that has been in business at least five years, emphasizes customer service, and has someone on staff who specializes in your destination. In addition, **make sure the agency belongs to a professional trade organization.** The American Society of Travel Agents (ASTA)—the largest and most influential

in the field with more than 20,000 members in some 140 countries—maintains and enforces a strict code of ethics and will step in to help mediate any agent-client disputes involving ASTA members if necessary. ASTA (whose motto is "Without a travel agent, you're on your own") also maintains a Web site that includes a directory of agents. (If a travel agency is also acting as your tour operator, *see* Buyer Beware *in* Tours and Packages.)

7 **Local Agent Referrals American Society of Travel Agents (ASTA)** ✉ 1101 King St., Suite 200, Alexandria, VA 22314 ☎ 703/739-2782 or 800/965-2782 24-hr hot line ⊞ 703/739-3268 ⊕ www.astanet.com. **Association of British Travel Agents** ✉ 68-71 Newman St., London W1T 3AH ☎ 020/7637-2444 ⊞ 020/7637-0713 ⊕ www.abta.com. **Association of Canadian Travel Agencies** ✉ 130 Albert St., Suite 1705, Ottawa, Ontario K1P 5G4 ☎ 613/237-3657 ⊞ 613/237-7052 ⊕ www.acta.ca. **Australian Federation of Travel Agents** ✉ Level 3, 309 Pitt St., Sydney, NSW 2000 ☎ 02/9264-3299 ⊞ 02/9264-1085 ⊕ www.afta.com.au. **Travel Agents' Association of New Zealand** ✉ Level 5, Tourism and Travel House, 79 Boulcott St., Box 1888, Wellington 6001 ☎ 04/499-0104 ⊞ 04/499-0786 ⊕ www.taanz.org.nz.

VISITOR INFORMATION

Learn more about foreign destinations by checking government-issued travel advisories and country information. For a broader picture, consider information from more than one country.

7 **Tourist Information Seattle/King County Convention and Visitors Bureau** ✉ 520 Pike St., Suite 1300, Downtown 98101 ☎ 206/461-5800 ⊕ www.seeseattle.org. **Seattle Visitor Center** ✉ Washington State Convention Center, 800 Convention Pl., Downtown 98104 ☎ 206/461-5840. **Washington State Convention & Trade Center** ✉ 800 Convention Pl., Downtown 98104 ☎ 206/447-5000 ⊕ www.wsctc.com. **Washington Tourism Development Division** ✐ Box 42500, Olympia, WA 98504 ☎ 360/725-5050 ⊕ www.tourism.wa.gov.

7 **Government Advisories Consular Affairs Bureau of Canada** ☎ 800/267-6788 or 613/944-6788 ⊕ www.voyage.gc.ca. **U.K. Foreign and Commonwealth Office** ✉ Travel Advice Unit, Consular Division, Old Admiralty Building, London SW1A 2PA ☎ 020/7008-0232 or 020/7008-0233 ⊕ www.fco.gov.uk/travel. **Australian Department of Foreign Affairs and Trade** ☎ 02/6261-1299 Consular Travel Advice Faxback Service ⊕ www.dfat.gov.au. **New Zealand Ministry of Foreign Affairs and Trade** ☎ 04/439-8000 ⊕ www.mft.govt.nz.

WEB SITES

Do check out the World Wide Web when planning your trip. You'll find everything from weather forecasts to virtual tours of famous cities. Be sure to visit Fodors.com (⊕ www.fodors.com), a complete travel-planning site. You can research prices and book plane tickets, hotel rooms, rental cars, vacation packages, and more. In addition, you can post your pressing questions in the Travel Talk section. Other planning tools include a currency converter and weather reports, and there are loads of links to travel resources.

The tourist boards sites will no doubt be your first stops. The home page for the Seattle Convention and Visitors Bureau is ⊕ www.seeseattle.org. For insight on the entire state, head to Washington State Tourism's ⊕ www.tourism.wa.gov. Information straight from the city's leaders is at ⊕ www.cityofseattle.net. Forget driving. Take public transportation—including the bus, streetcar, and water taxi. This site tells you how: ⊕ transit.metrokc.gov. OK. So you have to drive. The site ⊕ www.wsdot. wa.gov/traveler.html will help you deal with Seattle's horrific traffic problems.

Information on the International District and its shops, events, restaurants, and nightlife is at ⊕ www.internationaldistrict. org. West Seattle news and sight details are found at ⊕ www.westseattle.com, ⊕ www.wschamber.com, and ⊕ www. wsjunction.com. For all things Ballard, try ⊕ www.inballard.com. Find out what's going on around the University of Washington by logging on to ⊕ www. udistrictchamber.org. Reach the "Center of the Universe" at ⊕ www.fremont.com. Details about Wallingford are at ⊕ www. wallinford.org. To learn more about Bellevue, look to ⊕ www.ci.bellevue.wa.us and ⊕ www.bellevuechamber.org.

The *Seattle Post-Intelligencer* Web site (⊕ www.seattlepi.com) is full of breaking local and national news. The *Seattle Times* daily newspaper is one of the country's largest independently owned. Its Web site (⊕ www.seattletimes.com) has frequently updated local news and entertainment information. The site run by the irreverent weekly newspaper, *The Stranger* (⊕ www. thestranger.com), is a good place to find fun things to do—especially at night. The *Seattle Weekly* ⊕ www.seattleweekly. com focuses on local political coverage and entertainment.

EXPLORING SEATTLE

FODOR'S CHOICE

Ballard Locks, *Ballard*

Pike Place Market, *Downtown*

Pioneer Square District, *Downtown*

Seattle Asian Art Museum, *Capitol Hill*

Space Needle, *Queen Anne*

Washington Park Arboretum, *Capitol Hill*

Wing Luke Museum, *International District*

HIGHLY RECOMMENDED

Gasworks Park, *Fremont*

Kelsey Creek Farm and Park, *Bellevue*

Marymoor Park, *Redmond*

Nordic Heritage Museum, *Ballard*

Seattle Aquarium, *Downtown*

Seattle Art Museum, *Downtown*

Woodland Park Zoo, *Phinney Ridge*

Updated by
Holly S. Smith

SEATTLE IS A CITY OF MANY WATERS. It's defined by saltwater inlets and bays, freshwater lakes, and shipping canals that bisect its steep green hills, creating distinctive micro-landscapes along the water's edge. In the fishing harbors, high-tech trawlers are moored next to wooden fishing boats. On the lakes, funky floating homes crowd docks near swank yacht clubs. Diners have a choice between freshwater- and saltwater-front restaurants.

Seattle, like Rome, was built on seven hills—but a couple of hills have since been leveled. As the region's cultural center, the city is more the Athens of the Pacific Northwest than its Rome, with the sprawling campus of the University of Washington as its acropolis. As a visitor, you're likely to spend much of your time on only two of the surviving hills: Capitol Hill and Queen Anne Hill. The most definitive element of the natural and spiritual landscape, the hills are lofty, privileged perches from which residents are constantly reminded of the beauty of the forests, mountains, and waters just beyond the city.

The people of Seattle—a half-million within the city proper, another 2.5 million in the surrounding Puget Sound region—are a diversified bunch. The city has long had a vibrant Asian and Asian-American population, and well-established communities of Scandinavians, African-Americans, and Jews. Native Americans and Latinos live here, too. It's impossible to generalize about such a varied population, but the prototypical Seattleite was once summed up by a *New Yorker* cartoon in which one East Coast matron says to another, "They're backpacky, but nice."

That's quite true. In fact, so many Seattleites walk around with backpacks—even those dressed up for office or opera—that you begin to wonder if backpacks are de rigueur for well-dressed residents.

Although the skies here are cloudy part of the year, they aren't any more so than, say, Grand Rapids, Buffalo, or Chicago. Seattle actually gets less rain—and a lot less snow—than New York City. But Seattleites encourage the old joke that they don't tan, they rust. In the past, such comments discouraged outsiders from moving in. But during the last few decades, the population has boomed, thanks to such corporate giants as Microsoft, Nintendo, Alaska Airlines, Boeing, and Weyerhauser, as well as a plenitude of start-up sporting companies, travel-based businesses, and dot-com operations.

Seattle's climate and landscape encourage outdoor activities—hiking, sailing, mountain climbing, and softball in summer; skiing, snowshoeing, and snowboarding in winter. Long dark nights have made the city a haven for moviegoers and book readers—the number of art-house theaters has made this the Northwest's best city for catching independent and experimental films, and residents' per-capita book purchases are among North America's highest. There are two daily newspapers; a state-of-the-art convention center; two retractable-roof stadiums and an arena for hometown professional sports teams; a diverse music, dance club, and gallery scene; and top-notch ballet, opera, symphony, and theater companies. A major seaport, the city is a vital link in Pacific Rim trade and a growing port for major cruise lines.

Seattle's expansion has led to the usual big-city problems: increases in crime, homelessness, and traffic congestion. Many residents have fled north to the ever-growing suburbs of Bellevue, Kirkland, Redmond, Issaquah, Shoreline, and Bothell, and south to Renton, Kent, and Federal Way—all of which have swollen from quiet communities into sizable cities. Despite all the growing pains, though, Seattleites have a great love for their community and its natural surroundings; hence their firm com-

CAN YOU SAY "GEODUCK"?

SO YOU PACKED *Gore-Tex, khakis, and sensible shoes, and you've mastered the art of ordering complicated espresso drinks with urbane insouciance. Now if only you could pronounce Puyallup without raising local eyebrows. Here's a guide to a few of the Northwest's tongue-twisters.*

Alki *(AL-ki). Rhymes with high; the point where settlers first landed in this area.*

Geoduck *(GOOEY-duck). Gigantic clam grown in Puget (PEW-jet) Sound, sometimes weighing in at over 20 pounds. Often surrounded by gaping tourists at Pike Place Market.*

Kalaloch *(KLAY-lock). Popular scenic stretch on the wild Pacific side of the Olympic Peninsula.*

Poulsbo *(PAULS-bo). Charming Scandinavian town on Bainbridge Island treasured for its Norwegian bakeries.*

Puyallup *(pew-AL-up). Home of the Western Washington Fair, a month-long shindig held each September. Key phrase: "Do the Puyallup."*

Sequim *(skwim). Rhymes with swim. Between the Olympic Mountains and the Strait of Juan de Fuca (FEW-kah). Famous for Dungeness (dun-jen-NESS) crabs.*

Tacoma *(Tah-CO-mah). Growing city 30 mi south of Seattle, near Mt. Tahoma (Tah-ho-mah), a.k.a. Mt. Rainier (ray-NEAR).*

Yakima Valley *(YAK-him-uh). South central Washington's picturesque wine country.*

For the record, Washington's neighbor to the south is Oregon (OR-eh-gun), Spokane (spo-KAN) is eastern Washington's largest city, Lake Chelan (sha-LAN) is a spectacular body of water southwest of the Methow (MET-how) Valley, and that snow-capped volcano to the south is Mt. Rainier.

mitment to maintaining the area's reputation as one of the country's most livable places.

Getting Your Bearings

Two things are key to getting around and getting your bearings. First, because of the hills, comfortable walking shoes are a must. Second, to know Seattle is to know its neighborhoods, so read up on them and study the maps before heading out.

DOWNTOWN & ENVIRONS   Elliott Bay's brilliant waters push up against a striking skyline to form the heart of Downtown. The famous Pike Place Market is on the waterfront here. Belltown, to the north of Downtown, is compact but popular with the food-lovin', club-hoppin' crowd. Still farther north are the Seattle Center, the Space Needle, and a couple of museums—all in the lower portion of the Queen Anne district, which is lapped by the waters of Lake Union to the east.

Just south of Downtown is Pioneer Square, Seattle's oldest neighborhood. It's filled not only with massive redbrick and sandstone buildings but also with bistros, boutiques, and art galleries. Just to the southeast, the International District (I.D.) is a testament to Asia's influence on this port city. Chinese immigrants first came here in the mid-1800s to work in the lumber mills and on the railroads. Today the area is home not only to Chinese but also to Filipinos, Japanese, Koreans, and other Asian peoples.

Squeezed between Downtown's eastern edge and Capitol Hill, just north of the I.D., is First Hill, a little neighborhood of medical facilities, small businesses, and condos and apartments. Adjacent to and south of First Hill is the Central Area (also call the Central District or C.D.), the hub of Seattle's African-American community.

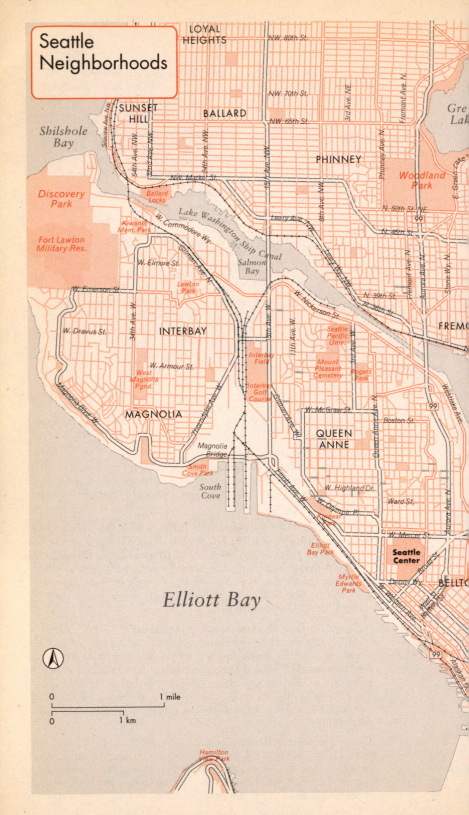

Seattle Neighborhoods

LOYAL HEIGHTS

NW. 80th St.

NW. 70th St.

SUNSET HILL

BALLARD

NW. 65th St.

3rd Ave. NE

PHINNEY

Fremont Ave. N.

Gre Lak

Shilshole Bay

NW. Market St.

Woodland Park

E. Green Lake Way

Discovery Park

Ballard Locks

Lake Washington Ship Canal

Leary Ave. NW

N. 50th St. NE

99

8th Ave. NW.

Fort Lawton Military Res.

Kiwanis Mem. Park

W. Commodore Wy.

Salmon Bay

N. 46th St.

Fremont Ave. N.

Stone Wy. N.

Aurora Ave. N.

W. Elmore St.

Gilman Ave. W.

W. Emerson St.

Lawton Park

W. Nickerson St.

N. 39th St.

N. 38th St.

FREMO

34th Ave. W.

W. Dravus St.

INTERBAY

5th Ave. W.

11th Ave. W.

Seattle Pacific Univ.

3rd Ave. N.

Westlake Ave. N.

W. Armour St.

West Magnolia Pgnd.

Interbay Field

Mount Pleasant Cemetery

Rogers Park

99

Magnolia Blvd. W.

Interbay Golf Course

W. McGraw St.

Boston St.

MAGNOLIA

Magnolia Bridge

Gilman Ave. W.

QUEEN ANNE

Queen Anne Ave. N.

1st Ave. N.

Aurora Ave. N.

Smith Cove Park

5th Ave. W.

W. Highland Dr.

Ward St.

South Cove

W. Olympic Pl.

Kinnear Park

W. Mercer St.

Elliott Bay

Elliott Bay Park

Seattle Center

BELLT

Myrtle Edwards Park

Denny Wy.

W. Western Ave.

Alaskan Fy.

99

0 ——— 1 mile

0 ——— 1 km

Hamilton View Park

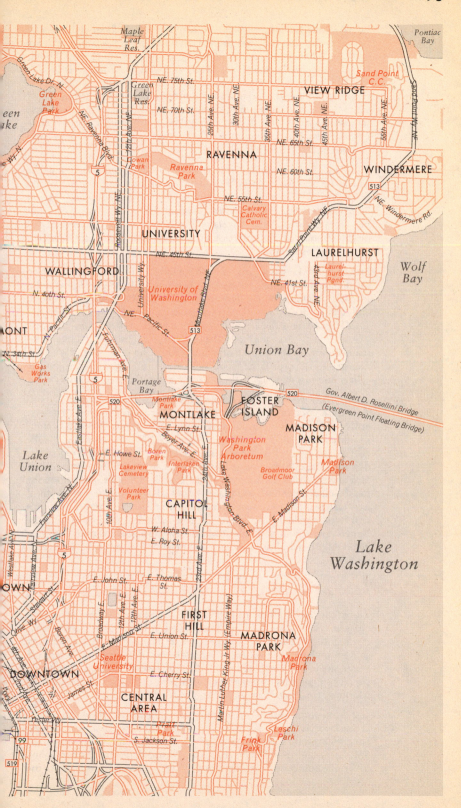

Edged by the Eastlake district—known for its houseboat colony—and Lake Union's southeastern shore, Capitol Hill has mind-blowing city and mountain views as well as dynamic people-watching. Stroll Broadway Avenue East between East Denny Way and East Roy Street or Pike and Pine between Boren Avenue and you'll find an eclectic collection of restaurants, bars, knickknack shops, and vintage clothing stores. You'll share the sidewalk with drag queens, club kids, college students, and senior citizens. North of East Denny Way is Madison Park, a quietly upscale, beachside community, complete with a village square of cafés and boutiques, on the shores of Lake Washington.

The University District (U-District), north of Capitol Hill, surrounds the University of Washington (UW) and buzzes with a youthful vibe. A stroll through the UW campus can include stops at its museums and Central Plaza, the nerve center for student activism. The Ave is a funky off-campus shopping area along University Way Northeast. To the north of this neighborhood is the Ravenna district of middle-class homes, homey shops, and family restaurants.

From Capitol Hill, you can take I–5 south to I–90, which heads east to the floating bridge that crosses Lake Washington to Mercer Island, with its palatial homes, parks, and protected wetlands. Bellevue, Kirkland, and Redmond are three affluent bedroom communities to the north and east. They, along with Mercer Island, form what has been called the city's "Gold Coast." Issaquah, on the southeastern shores of Lake Sammamish, is a growing residential area, while the core of Seattle's wine industry is just north in the Woodinville vineyards, where numerous wine cellars and tasting tours make the town a popular weekend retreat.

Immediately west of the U-District are Wallingford, a mix of small, boutiques, ethnic cafés, and modest homes; and Fremont, an artists' enclave. Still farther west is Ballard, a neighborhood with tidy streets, a Scandinavian heritage, and a thriving town square. Northwest of the U-District, Green Lake is a friendly, relaxing lakeside neighborhood of joggers, dog-walkers, cyclists, young professionals, and families. South of Ballard and the Lake Washington Ship Canal is Magnolia, a traditionally middle-class neighborhood that overlooks Puget Sound. Well south of here on a peninsula across Elliott Bay is West Seattle, where the region's first settlers staked their claim. Today it's a mix of the upscale and the beaten down, all along miles of beautiful shoreline, including the gorgeous Alki Beach. You can reach this neighborhood via the West Seattle Bridge.

DOWNTOWN, BELLTOWN, QUEEN ANNE

The Elliott Bay waterfront is the heart and soul of Seattle. Stretching along its waters is historic Pike Place Market, where vendors purvey handmade crafts, homemade goodies, and fresh food—from fresh-caught salmon and shellfish to fruits, veggies, and flowers—and waterside restaurants serve meals reflecting the Northwest's bounty. The Seattle Aquarium, with its awe-inspiring displays of underwater life, and the Maritime Discovery Center, are on the docks here.

Just north and slightly west of Downtown is Belltown. This former cool-cat enclave has gone decidedly upscale with a spattering of scenester shops, bars, and restaurants, but you can still find remnants of its edgy past. Still farther north is Queen Anne, whose upper reaches contain many luxurious houses and upscale shops. Lower Queen Anne is home to the

Seattle Center complex, the Space Needle, the Experience Music Project, the Science Fiction Experience, the Children's Museum, and the Pacific Science Center.

Numbers in the text correspond to numbers in the margin and on the Downtown Seattle & Environs map.

a good tour

Start your day with a walk to **Pike Place Market** ❶ ▶. Get there early as the vendors set up (9 AM weekdays and Saturday, or 10:30 AM Sunday), and before the crowds have arrived. Say hello to Rachel, the big brass pig that's the market's unofficial mascot. Have breakfast at an old-fashioned market eatery, or grab a latte and a sticky treat from the Three Girls Bakery before heading out to Steinbrueck Park to enjoy views over the bay. Ignore the panhandlers; they don't bite. And kick in a buck or so to the roaming street musicians.

If you enjoy innovative paintings and crafts both modern and old, stop next at the **Seattle Art Museum** ❷. Otherwise, after your market tour, take the Hillclimb steps down to the waterfront and spend a couple of hours at the **Seattle Aquarium** ❸. Next door is the **Seattle IMAX Dome Theater** ❹, which shows compelling nature-oriented films on an enormous screen. You can walk out on Piers 62 and 63 for a good view of Elliott Bay, then head north to the refurbished Bell Street Pier (66), a conference center and cruise ship docking area that contains several restaurants and **Odyssey Maritime Discovery Center** ❺. From here, head back toward the aquarium and then south along the waterfront to Yesler Way and Pioneer Square, with its many historic buildings, art galleries, boutiques, bookshops, and bars. Walk north along Fourth and Fifth avenues to the Downtown shopping district. Most of the exciting stores are within a few blocks of Westlake Center, at Fourth and Pine.

From Pioneer Square, you could take a quick jaunt six blocks south on Fourth Avenue to the dazzling new **Seattle Central Library** ❻, or head four blocks north on Fourth into Belltown, cutting down Bell Street toward Second Avenue. Return to Westlake Center and take the two-minute monorail ride to the Seattle Center, whose many sights include the **Space Needle** ❼.

If you have kids in tow, head to the fascinating interactive exhibits at the **Pacific Science Center** ❽ or at the **The Children's Museum** ❾. The **Experience Music Project** ❿, which celebrates American popular music, is known worldwide for architect Frank Gehry's daring design. Don't miss the Science Fiction Experience museum, also housed within. For a break afterward, consider walking west to the Olympic Sculpture Park at Alaskan Way and Broad Street.

Take the monorail back to **Westlake Center** ⓫, then walk east to Eighth Avenue and the **Washington State Convention and Trade Center** ⓬. Seattle's main visitor information center is inside the street-level mall at Convention Place.

TIMING   To see all the sights on this tour you really need two days. If you're pressed for time, choose just a couple—say, Pike Place Market or the Seattle Center, which can easily fill an entire morning, plus one museum or neighborhood for the afternoon.

What to See

❾ **The Children's Museum.** Enter this colorful spacious museum off the Seattle Center food court through a Northwest wilderness setting, with winding trails, hollow logs, and a waterfall. From here, you can explore a global village where rooms with kid-friendly props show everyday life in Ghana, the Philippines, and Japan. Another neighborhood contains an American post office, a fire station, and a grocery store. Cog City is a giant game of pipes, pulleys, and balls; and kids can test their talent in the mock recording studio. There's a small play area for infants and toddlers, and lots of crafts to help kids learn more about the exhibits. ⊠ *Seattle Center House, 305 Harrison St., Queen Anne* ☎ *206/441–1768* ⊕ *www.thechildrensmuseum.org* ⊠ *$6* ⊙ *Weekdays 10–5, weekends 10–6.*

⊘ ❿ **Experience Music Project.** Seattle's most controversial architectural statement is the 140,000-square-foot interactive museum celebrating American popular music. Architect Frank Gehry drew inspiration from electric guitars to achieve the building's curvy design. Funded by Microsoft co-founder Paul Allen, it's a fitting backdrop for the world's largest collection of Jimi Hendrix memorabilia, which is flanked by a gallery of guitars once owned by Bob Dylan, Hank Williams, Kurt Cobain, and the bands Pearl Jam, Soundgarden, and the Kingsmen. Experiment with instruments and recording equipment in the interactive Sound Lab, or attend music performances, workshops, and private events in the Sky Church concert hall, JBL Theater, Liquid Lounge bar, or Turntable Restaurant.

The **Science Fiction Experience** is another Paul Allen brainchild. For those who love sci-fi, the advisory board—Arthur C. Clarke, Ray Bradbury, Octavia Butler, Orson Scott Card, Syne Mitchell, Kim Stanley Robinson, and Greg Bear, among many others—says it all. This interactive multimedia museum truly takes you "out there" with spaceship rooms and a science-fiction heroes hall of fame. Fantastic Voyages focuses on time travel, Them! illustrates the fear of aliens, and Brave New Worlds explores the future. In Make Contact you can create your own journeys. ⊠ *5th Ave., between Broad St. and Thomas St., Queen Anne* ☎ *206/770–2700* ⊕ *www.emplive.com* ⊠ *$19.95* ⊙ *May 23–Sept. 1 Sun.–Thurs. 9–6, Fri. and Sat. 9–9; otherwise daily 9–5.*

⊘ ❺ **Odyssey Maritime Discovery Center.** Cultural and educational maritime exhibits on Puget Sound and ocean trade are the focus of this waterfront attraction. Learn all about the Northwest's fishing traditions with hands-on exhibits that include kayaking over computer-generated waters, loading a container ship, and listening in on boats radioing one another on Elliott Bay just outside. The adjacent Bell Street Conference Center hosts major local events and press conferences; see what's on tap. You can also shop the on-site fish market, dine on the catch of the day at the seafood restaurant, or spy on boaters docking at the marina or cruise ships putting into port. ⊠ *2205 Alaskan Way, Pier 66, Belltown* ☎ *206/374–4000* ⊕ *www.ody.org* ⊠ *$7* ⊙ *Mid-Sept.–mid-May, Tues.–Sat. 10–5, Sun. noon–5; otherwise Mon.–Sat. 10–5, Sun. noon–5.*

> **off the beaten path**

TILLICUM VILLAGE – Blake Island, about 30 minutes southwest of Seattle's Downtown docks, has a Native American village with a longhouse, an arts and crafts area, and a dining hall with a performance stage. Four-hour tours of the village include a boat ride from Pier 55, a salmon-bake, and the Native American musical production *Dance on the Wind.* Trails run through the surrounding Blake Island State Park's forests and along its beaches. There are also campgrounds. ☎ *206/933–8600 or 800/426–1205* ⊕ *www. tillicumvillage.com* ⊠ *Island and park free; tours $59.74* ⊙ *Island and park open year-round; Tillicum Village open Mar.–Dec.*

⊘ ❽ **Pacific Science Center.** With about 200 indoor and outdoor hands-on exhibits and a state-of-the-art planetarium, this is a great place for both

KIDS IN TOW?

ALTHOUGH SUMMER BRINGS beautiful, blue-sky days perfect for zoos, beaches, and parks, Seattle has plenty of grey, drizzly hours to fill in other months. Here are a few rainy-day destinations your wee one will enjoy.

Center for Wooden Boats: your kids can be skippers on an antique boat or Native American canoe.

Experience Music Project: unleash the musical prodigy within on the Sound Lab's state-of-the-art instruments.

Museum of History & Industry: find out what life was like for Seattle's earliest pioneers.

Pacific Science Center: moving dinosaurs, live small creatures, a butterfly room, lots of robots—and plenty of special exhibits.

Science Fiction Experience: kids can explore worlds in outer space—and their own imaginations.

The Children's Museum: plenty of colorful, educational interactivity to romp around in.

Tillicum Village: walk wooded trails, beach hike, view Native American arts and crafts, and enjoy a traditional salmon bake and costumed Native American performance on remote Blake Island.

Wing Luke Museum: marvel at kites, dragon puppets, and beautiful artwork, backdrops to educational segments on Asian historical contributions.

kids and grown-ups. The startling dinosaur exhibit is complete with moving robotic creatures, while Tech Zones has robots and virtual-reality games. Machines analyze human physiology in Body Works. The tropical butterfly house is stocked with farm-raised chrysalises weekly. Next door, IMAX movies and rock music, laser light shows run daily. ✉ *200 2nd Ave. N, Queen Anne* ☎ *206/443–2001* ⊕ *www.pacsci.org* ✉ *Center $9; IMAX $7.50–$8.50; light shows $5–$7.50* ☉ *Labor Day–Memorial Day, weekdays 10–5, weekends 10–6; otherwise daily 10–6.*

need a break?

Enter the **Olympic Sculpture Park** (✉ Broad St. and Alaskan Way, Belltown) at a transparent art pavilion connected by a gentle zigzag path to three very different gardens: Northwest foliage, urban plots, and shoreline environments shaped by water and wind. The park meanders from the water east across the highway and rail lines to the edge of the city, creating an uninterrupted earthen sculpture in itself— where does the land end and the art begin? Towering metal and stone figures and shapes are amid the grass and along walking paths, while informative signage promotes conservation of both local plants and shorelines. Festivals, performances, and exhibits by local and visiting artists are held in the pavilion throughout the year. Sandwiched between the Burlington Northern Railroad to the east and Elliott Bay to the west, the adjacent sliver of Myrtle Edwards Park is popular for walking, picnicking, and taking in sunsets. At this writing, the park is being developed; work is slated to be done in 2006.

👣 ⚑ ❶ **Pike Place Market.** Perhaps like many historical sites whose importance

Fodor'sChoice
★

is taken for granted, this institution started small. It dates from 1907, when the city issued permits allowing farmers to sell produce from wagons parked at Pike Place. Later the city built permanent stalls. At

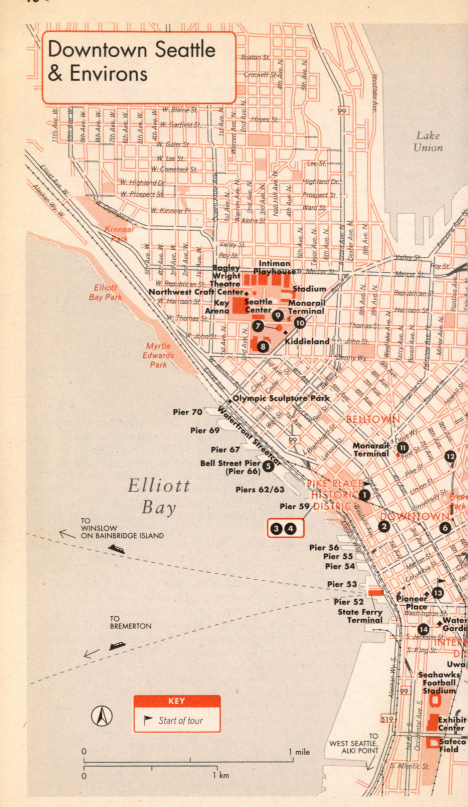

Downtown Seattle & Environs

Boston St.
Crockett St.
W. Blaine St.
W. Garfield St.
Hayes St.
11th Ave. W.
9th Ave. W.
8th Ave. W.
7th Ave. W.
6th Ave. W.
5th Ave. W.
4th Ave. W.
W. Galer St.
1st Ave. N.
Warren Ave. N.
99
W. Lee St.
W. Comstock St.
Lee St.
Elliott Ave. W.
Alaskan Wy. W.
W. Highland Dr.
W. Prospect St.
Highland Dr.
Queen Anne Ave. N.
1st Ave. N.
Warren Ave. N.
2nd Ave. N.
3rd Ave. N.
Nob Hill Ave. N.
5th Ave. N.
6th Ave. N.
Dexter Ave. N.
8th Ave. N.
Prospect St.
Ward St.
W. Kinnear Pl.
Aloha St.
Westlake Ave.

Lake Union

Kinnear Park

Valley St.
Roy St.

Olympic Dr.

Elliott Bay Park

5th Ave. W.
4th Ave. W.
3rd Ave. W.
2nd Ave. W.
1st Ave. W.
W. Republican St.
W. Harrison St.
W. Thomas St.
W. John St.

Bagley Wright Theatre
Intiman Playhouse
Northwest Craft Center
Stadium
Key Arena
Seattle Center
Monorail Terminal

Mercer St.
Valley St.
Roy St.
Republican St.
Harrison St.
Thomas St.
John St.

Taylor Ave. N.
5th Ave. N.
6th Ave. N.
7th Ave. N.
8th Ave. N.
Westlake Ave. N.
Terry Ave. N.
Boren Ave. N.
Fairview Ave. N.
Minor Ave. N.
Pontius Ave. N.

⑦ ⑨ ⑩
⑧ **Kiddieland**

Denny Wy.

Myrtle Edwards Park

Olympic Sculpture Park

Pier 70

Waterfront Streetcar

BELLTOWN

Pier 69

Pier 67

Monorail Terminal ⑪ ⑫
Olive Wy.
Pine St.

Bell Street Pier (Pier 66) ⑤

Piers 62/63

PIKE PLACE HISTORIC DISTRICT

Pike St.

Freeway Park

Pier 59

①

Western Ave.

DOWNTOWN

University St.

② ⑥

Elliott Bay

③ ④

Alaskan Wy.

TO WINSLOW ON BAINBRIDGE ISLAND

Pier 56
Pier 55
Pier 54

Marion St.
Columbia St.

Pier 53

⑬

Pier 52
State Ferry Terminal

Pioneer Place
Washington St.

TO BREMERTON

⑭ **Water Garden**

S. Jackson St.
S. King St.

INTER. DI...

Uwa...

99

Seahawks Football Stadium

KEY
▶ *Start of tour*

519

Exhibit Center

Safeco Field

0   1 mile
0   1 km

TO WEST SEATTLE, ALKI POINT

Occidental Ave. S.

S. Atlantic St.

one time the market was a madhouse of vendors hawking their produce and haggling with customers over prices. Some fishmongers still carry on this kind of frenzied banter, but chances are you won't get them to waver on their prices.

Urban renewal almost killed the market, but a group of residents, led by the late architect Victor Steinbrueck, rallied and voted it a historical asset in 1973. Many buildings have been restored, and the complex is connected to the waterfront by stairs and elevators. Booths sell seafood— which can be packed in dry ice for your flight home—produce, cheese, wine, spices, tea, coffee, and crafts. There are also several restaurants.

Although wandering at will is fun, free maps of the venue are available at several locations throughout the market. The map distinguishes among the various types of shops and stalls. Farmers who come to the market from as far away as the Yakima Valley, east of the Cascade Mountains, have first dibs on the tables, known as "farmers' tables," where they display and sell their own vegetables, fruits, or flowers. Vendors in the so-called high stalls often have fruits and vegetables or crafts that they've purchased locally to sell here. The superb quality of the high-stall produce helps to set Seattle's dining standards.

The shopkeepers who rent stores in the market sell such things as packaged food items, art, curios, pets, and more. Because the market is along a bluff, the main arcade stretches down the cliff face for several stories; many shops are below street level. Other shops and restaurants, some with courtyards, are in buildings east of Pike Place, and west of Western Avenue. ⊠ *Pike Pl. at Pike St., west of 1st Ave., Downtown* ☎ *206/682-7453* ⊕ *www.pikeplacemarket.org* ☉ *Mon.–Sat. 9–6, Sun. 11–5.*

need a break? **Three Girls Bakery** (⊠ **Pike Pl. Market, 1514 Pike Pl., Downtown** ☎ **206/622–1045), a 13-seat glassed-in lunch counter that's tucked behind a bakery outlet, serves sandwiches, soups, and pastries. Go for the chili and a hunk of Sicilian sourdough, or buy a loaf at the take-out counter, pick up some smoked salmon at the fish place next door, and head for a picnic table in Steinbrueck Park.**

★ ☾ ❸ **Seattle Aquarium.** From its cylindrical tank, an octopus welcomes you to the aquarium, whose darkened rooms and large, lighted tanks brilliantly display Pacific Northwest marine life. Look for crabs, eels, and anemones lingering in the background. The Tide Pool exhibit re-creates Washington's rocky coast and sandy beaches, complete with a 6,000-gallon wave that sweeps in over the ecosystem. Huge glass windows provide underwater views of seals and sea otters; you can go up top to watch them play in their pools. Kids love the Discovery Lab, where they can touch starfish, sea urchins, and sponges, then peek through microscopes at baby barnacles and jellyfish. They can also don scuba gear and animal costumes, scramble through a play area with fake hollow trees, or wrap up in the rubbery arms of a life-size replica of the Puget Sound octopus, which, at 100 pounds, is the world's largest, with an armspan of more than 10 feet. ⊠ *Pier 59 off Alaskan Way, Downtown* ☎ *206/386–4320* ⊕ *www.seattleaquarium.org* ⊠ *$8.50; $14 with IMAX admission* ☉ *Memorial Day–Labor Day, daily 10–7; Labor Day–Memorial Day, daily 10–5.*

off the beaten path **RUSSIAN COBRA SUBMARINE –** Just south of the ferry terminals, you can tour the torpedo rooms, sonar and radar areas, and crew quarters of a Russian-built Foxtrot Class attack submarine. From 1974 through 1994, this 284-foot sub patrolled the Arctic, Indian, and Pacific oceans on secret Cold War missions. Around 80 crew members spent up to three months at sea in this vessel, which had only three showers and two toilets. ⊠ *Pier 48, 101 Alaskan Way Downtown* ☎ *206/223–1767* ⊕ *www.russiansubseattle.com* ✉ *$10* ⊙ *Daily Sept.–May 9–5:30, June–Aug. 9–8.*

★ ❷ **Seattle Art Museum.** Postmodern architect Robert Venturi designed this five-story museum to be a work of art in itself: large-scale vertical fluting adorns the building's limestone exterior, accented by terra-cotta, cut granite, and marble. Sculptor Jonathan Borofsky's several-stories-high *Hammering Man* pounds away outside the front door. Inside, a large, airy, brightly lit hall is enlivened by two ancient Chinese stone camels. The pair once marked the entrance to the Asian Art Museum in Volunteer Park but had to be brought indoors because they weathered too rapidly in Seattle's moist clime.

The museum's extensive collection surveys Asian, Native American, African, Oceanic, and pre-Columbian art. Among the highlights are the anonymous 14th-century Buddhist masterwork *Monk at the Moment of Enlightenment* and Jackson Pollock's *Sea Change.* The café behind the lobby is a terrific lunch spot, and the shop carries souvenirs as well as international arts and crafts publications. The entrance ticket includes a free visit to the Seattle Asian Art Museum if used within a week. A ticket to the latter is good for $3 off admission here if used within one week. ⊠ *100 University St., Downtown* ☎ *206/654–3255* ⊕ *www. seattleartmuseum.org* ✉ *$7; free 1st Thurs. of month* ⊙ *Tues.–Sun. 10–5 (Thurs. until 9).*

⟳ **Seattle Center.** The 74-acre Seattle Center complex was built for the 1962 World's Fair. A rolling green campus organized around the massive International Fountain, the center includes an amusement park, theaters, exhibition halls, museums, shops, restaurants, a skateboard park, Key Arena, the Pacific Science Center, the Children's Museum, Marion Oliver McCaw Hall performance center, and the Space Needle. Among the arts groups based here are the Seattle Repertory Theatre, Intiman Theatre, the Seattle Opera, and the Pacific Northwest Ballet. The center hosts several professional sports teams: the Seattle Supersonics (NBA basketball), Sounders (soccer), Seadogs (indoor soccer), and Thunderbirds (amateur hockey). It's a bit cramped, and parking can be a nightmare, but the Seattle Center is the undisputed hub of the city's leisure life. It's also the site of three of the area's largest summer festivals: the Northwest Folklife Festival, Bite of Seattle, and Bumbershoot. In addition, the city's monorail travels between here and Westlake Center, a mall that's about a mile away.

At the southeast corner stands a statue of Chief Seattle, of the Duwamish tribe, with his right arm raised in welcome. Seattle was among the first Native Americans to have contact with the white explorers who came to the region. He was viewed as a great leader and peacemaker by his fellow tribesmen and as a friendly contact by the white settlers. The sculpture was created by local artist James Wehn in 1912 and dedicated by the chief's great-great granddaughter, Myrtle Loughery, on Founder's Day, November 13, 1912. After withstanding decades of rain and handling the statue was restored in 1975. ⊠ *Between 1st and 5th Aves. N and Denny Way and Mercer St., Queen Anne* ☎ *206/684–8582* ⊕ *www. seattlecenter.com.*

❻ **Seattle Central Library.** The structure that resembles a spaceship covered in delicate spiderweb threads is the hub of Seattle's 25-branch library system. Designed by Dutch architect Rem Koolhaas, the 11-story building houses 1.4 million books—the nonfiction titles on a four-level "book spiral" with continuous access—plus 400 computers, an auditorium, a "mixing chamber" floor of information desks, an area with materials in languages other than English, and a café. Floors zigzagging upward are visible from outside the metal facade. Intersecting beams, pipes, and trusses ensure that the costly building ($159 million plus) can withstand the region's regular earthquakes. ⊠ *1000 4th Ave., Downtown* ☎ *206/ 386–4636* ⊕ *www.spl.org* ⊗ *Mon.–Thurs. 9–9, Fri. 10:30–6, Sat. 9–6, Sun. 1–5.*

④ Seattle IMAX Dome Theater. The theater next to the aquarium shows 30- to 45-minute films on an enormous 180-degree curved screen several times a day, starting at 10 AM in summer. A big-deal Hexophonic sound system adds realism. Recent big-screen films have included *Extreme* sports action, *Bears,* and the *Living Sea. The Eruption of Mount St. Helens* is an awesome mainstay. A nice perk for weary-footed parents and their wee ones: kids under 5 are free. ⊠ *Pier 59 off Alaskan Way, Downtown* ☎ *206/622–1869* ⊕ *www.seattleimaxdome.com* ✉ *$7; second show same day $2; combination tickets including aquarium admission $14* ⊗ *Daily 10–5.*

Fodor's Choice
★

⑦ Space Needle. The distinctive exterior of the 520-foot-high Space Needle is visible throughout Downtown—but the view from the inside out is even better. A 42-second elevator ride up to the circular observation deck yields 360-degree vistas of Elliott Bay, Queen Anne Hill, the UW, and the Cascade Range. The Needle was built just in time for the World's Fair in 1962, but has since been refurbished with educational signs, interactive trivia game stations for kids, and the glass-enclosed SpaceBase store and Pavilion spiraling around the base of the tower. If you dine at the elite, top-floor SkyCity revolving restaurant, admission to the observation deck is free. Or, just enjoy views from the yummy coffee bar. ⊠ *5th Ave. and Broad St., Queen Anne* ☎ *206/443–2111 or 800/937–9582* ⊕ *www.spaceneedle.com* ✉ *$11* ⊗ *Sun.–Thurs. 9 AM–11 PM, Fri. and Sat. 9 AM–midnight.*

⑫ Washington State Convention and Trade Center. Seattle's vine-covered exhibition hall straddles I–5. The design of verdant Freeway Park south of here is intended to convey the spirit and flavor of the Pacific Northwest, which it does fairly well, considering the urban location. The street-level Visitor Information Center has maps, brochures, and event listings. ⊠ *Visitor Center: 800 Convention Pl., at 8th Ave. and Pike St., Downtown* ☎ *206/461–5840* ⊕ *www.wsctc.com* ⊗ *Memorial Day–Labor Day, daily 10–4; Labor Day–Memorial Day, weekdays 8:30–5, weekends 10–4.*

⑪ Westlake Center. This three-story mall is also a major terminus for buses and the Seattle Center Monorail, which was built for the 1962 World's Fair and connects Downtown to Seattle Center. The ground-level Made in Washington store showcases the state's products. Seattle's Downtown bus terminal is beneath the plaza. Underground walkways connect several business buildings between Fourth and Fifth avenues; on wet days, shoppers can walk from one store to the next without getting wet. ⊠ *400 Pine St., Downtown* ☎ *206/467–1600* ⊗ *Mon.–Fri. 9:30–9, Sat. 9:30–8, Sun. 11–6.*

SOUTH & EAST OF DOWNTOWN

A walk through Seattle's Pioneer Square and the International District (I.D.) provides a glimpse of the city as it appeared when rebuilt after the Great Fire of 1889. The rebuilding helped spur Seattle's transformation from a logging town to a Pacific Rim shipping center and a haven for immigrants from Asia and the Pacific islands. Most of this area's massive brick and sandstone buildings were constructed shortly after the fire on the ashes of the old, wooden downtown. These old buildings suffered some of the worst damage during an earthquake that rocked the city in February 2001. Many have undergone serious repairs. Still, the area remains lively.

Stretching north of the I.D., east of I–5 from around Madison Street to East Pine, lies First Hill, the home of many Downtown professional workers and a hub of Seattle's medical community. The adjoining Central Area is the cultural and residential heart of the African-American community, where mom-and-pop restaurants serve up soul food and historic neighborhood churches serve up food for the soul. South of Pioneer Square, stretching a mile or so past the sports stadiums down First Avenue South, is the quickly expanding Sodo industrial district, named for its location south of the former Kingdome indoor stadium.

Numbers in the text correspond to numbers in the margin and on the Downtown Seattle & Environs map.

a good tour

Begin at Pioneer Place, at First Avenue and Yesler Way, in the **Pioneer Square District 13** ▶. Explore the shops and historic buildings along First Avenue before heading to the **Klondike Gold Rush National Historical Park 14**, on Main Street two blocks south and one block east of Pioneer Place. As you continue east along Main Street to the **International District 15**, a restful stop is Waterfall Garden park, designed by Masao Kinoshita on the site where the messenger service that became United Parcel Service began operations.

Head south (right) on Second Avenue South and east (left) at South Jackson Street. You'll see Amtrak's King Street Station on your right as you head up South Jackson to Seventh Avenue, where the **Wing Luke Museum 16** surveys the past and present of immigrants from Asia and the Pacific islands and their descendants. The museum has walking-tour maps of historic buildings and businesses. One intriguing stop is the Uwajimaya store at Sixth Avenue South and South Dearborn Street (head south four blocks on Seventh Avenue South and turn right on South Dearborn Street). You can return to the harbor on one of the vintage Waterfront Streetcar trolleys—the southern terminus is at Fifth Avenue South and Jackson Street. You can catch a bus to Downtown at the same corner.

A drive through the neighborhoods directly east of Downtown takes in several sights amid the compact condominiums and modest free-standing dwellings. Head east on Cherry Street to the corner of Terry Avenue, where a cylindrical tiled dome marks the **Frye Art Museum 17**. Drive a block further to Boren, hang a left onto Madison Street, and continue east into the Central Area. At the intersection of 14th Avenue, you'll spot the tall white tower that fronts the sprawling **First African Methodist Episcopal Church 18**. Keep going east on Madison to 19th Avenue, then drive south to Cherry Street and the seemingly Aztec-inspired **Mount Zion Baptist Church 19**. Head back north on 19th Avenue to East Mercer Street to view the dreamlike colors of the **City in the Sky** Mural **20**. Drive east on Mercer to Martin Luther King Jr. Way, then south to East Cherry Street again, where you'll see the **Crespinel Martin Luther King Jr.** Mural **21** on the brick side of the Catfish Corner restaurant. Continue south on Martin Luther King Jr. Way to Yesler Way and the beige brick **Douglass Truth Neighborhood Library 22**.

TIMING You could breeze through Pioneer Square and the I.D. in a couple of hours—but why? These are rich, historically and culturally intriguing

CloseUp

ART TO GO

BUS SHELTERS AROUND THE CITY *are adorned with paintings to ease the boredom of waiting, but no work is more colorful than the Metro Transportation Tunnel, the mile-long bus tunnel that runs underground between the Convention Center (at Terry Avenue and Pine Street) and the International District. Among the artworks near the route's six stations are three 35-foot-long city-sanctioned murals—designed and installed by local artists Fay Jones, Gene Gentry McMahon, and Roger Shimomura—that provide abstract cartoonish interpretations of Downtown landmarks and street scenes in glorious palettes.*

It's also hard to miss the sculptures at the stops along the way. A favorite is the awe-inspiring Temple of Music, *created by Erin Shie Palmer, which tantalizes concertgoers bound for Benaroya Hall from the University Street Station. Best of all, you*

don't have to pay to see these works, since the tunnel falls within the city's "ride free zone." There are entrances to the tunnel at Ninth Avenue and Pine Street, at the Westlake Center Mall, at Third Avenue between Union and Seneca streets, at Third Avenue between Jefferson Street and Yesler Way, and at Fifth Avenue South and South Jackson Street.

areas with fascinating little shops, museums, and eateries, plus hidden green spaces and charming shaded spots to sit and take in the neighborhood. To wander through Pioneer Square's antiques stores, used bookshops, art galleries, and crafts boutiques—or to see all the wonders of the I.D., such as the herbal apothecaries, kitschy knickknack and housewares shops, Vietnamese noodle houses, Chinese dim sum restaurants, and Asian produce stalls—plan at least two hours for each. Add another two hours for an Underground Tour of Pioneer Square, which delves into Seattle's seedier history. Note that many Pioneer Square galleries, the Frye Art Museum, and the Wing Luke Museum are closed Monday.

What to See

(20) *City in the Sky* **Mural.** If you visit the popular Kingfish Café, you can still see the 3-D mural designed by Don Barrie, which has succumbed to the elements since its creation in 1974. Based on a Hopi Indian legend about evolution, the 70- × 30-foot painting is a sweeping dreamlike landscape of waves, green shores, and blue sky. You can sit and contemplate the mural on antique daybeds left outside by restaurant owners to handle the dining room's overflow. A foundation is seeking to restore the mural. ✉ *606 19th Ave. E Central Area.*

(21) *Crespinel Martin Luther King Jr.* **Mural.** Heading west on Cherry Street in the Central District, you'll see a 17-foot-tall mural of Dr. Martin Luther King Jr. gazing off in the distance thoughtfully. Pacific Northwest artist James Crespinel painted the mural in the summer of 1995 on the eastern face of the building that houses Catfish Corner, a soul food takeout place. ✉ *Corner of Martin Luther King Jr. Way and Cherry St. Central Area.*

㉒ Douglass Truth Neighborhood Library. Originally named the Yesler Library after Seattle businessman Henry Yesler, this simple brick, schoolhouse-style building is a hub of activity. Architects W. Marbury Somervell and Harlan Thomas designed the library, which opened in 1914 and today contains more than 9,000 books—many focusing on local and international experiences of African-Americans. At the request of local residents, who preferred that the name reflect the neighborhood's diversity, the library was renamed after Frederick Douglass and Sojourner Truth in 1975. ✉ *2300 E. Yesler Way, Central Area* ☎ *206/684–4704* ⊕ *www.spl.org* ⊙ *Mon.–Thurs. 10–9, Fri. 11:30–6, Sat. 10–6, Sun. 1–5.*

⑱ First African Methodist Episcopal Church. Founded in 1886, the state's oldest African-American church and the community's nexus has operated out of this historic building since 1912. The gospel choir is one of the city's best, and discussions with and among intellectuals, authors, artists, and the community are regularly scheduled. Rapidly growing church attendance—with 600 more members just since 2000—has led to an extra service out of a satellite site in Kent. ✉ *1522 14th Ave., Central Area* ☎ *206/324–3664 or 206/324–3665* ⊕ *www.fameseattle.org* ⊙ *Sun. 7:30 and 11, Kent service 9:30.*

⑰ Frye Art Museum. The tiled cylinder and adjacent museum were built in 1952 with funding from meat-packing millionaires. The permanent collection focuses on 19th- and 20th-century German, French, and American paintings and sculptures, including many European oils taken in trade for lard sold to bankrupt Germany after the Second World War. Temporary exhibits span Art Wolfe wildlife photos to exquisite Russian palace paintings. The museum also has drawing and ceramics studios; art, music, and craft classes; family activities; an auditorium; and a courtyard with a reflecting pool and waterfall. Nosh on light meals or sip coffee at the Gallery Café. Free tours run Sundays at 12:30 and 3. ✉ *704 Terry Ave., First Hill* ☎ *206/622–9250* ⊕ *www.fryeart.org* ▭ *Free* ⊙ *Tues.–Sat. 10–5 (Thurs. until 9), Sun. noon–5.*

⑮ International District. Bright welcome banners and 12-foot fiberglass dragons spinning in the wind capture the Asian spirit of the expanding International District (formerly called Chinatown). The I.D., as it's locally known, began as a haven for Chinese workers who came to the United States to work on the transcontinental railroad. The community has remained largely intact despite anti-Chinese riots and the forced eviction of Chinese residents during the 1880s and the internment of Japanese-Americans during World War II. About one-third of the residents are Chinese, one-third are Filipino, and another third come from elsewhere in Asia or the Pacific islands. Although today the main business anchor is the Uwajimaya Japanese superstore, there are also many small Asian restaurants, herbalists, acupuncturists, antiques shops, and private clubs for gambling and socializing. Look for the diamond-shape dragon signs in store windows—these establishments will give you a free-parking token.

You'll also find lots of green spaces. Kobe Terrace Park, at the top of Sixth Avenue next to the Nippon Kan Theater, surrounds an enormous concrete lantern, a gift symbolizing the bond between Seattle and its sister city, Kobe, Japan. Pea Patch garden plots spill down the south hillside; follow the trail to see the neighborhood's elderly residents tenderly planting flowers and vegetable seeds in the spring or harvesting their efforts in autumn. Leafy Hing Hay Park, at the corner of King and Maynard streets, includes an ornate pagoda that was designed and built in Taiwan. The district also stretches beneath the I-5 bridge, which is painted with festive red and yellow carp, and past the Pacific Rim Center to 12th Avenue. ⊠ *Between Yesler Way and S. Dearborn St. and 4th and 12th Aves.* ☎ *206/382–1197* ⊕ *www.internationaldistrict.org.*

need a break?

The **Seattle Deli** (⊠ 225 12th Ave., International District ☎ 206/328–1016) sounds like a typical sandwich shop, but it's actually a humble Vietnamese take-out joint with amazing, authentic food. Neighborhood workers line up as early as 7 AM for fresh-cooked, prewrapped rice and meat entrées, spring rolls, steamed buns, and—this being a deli—*banh mi* (sandwiches). Grab a bite and wander over to Hing Hay Park to watch the community in action, or to Kobe Terrace Park to take in the city views.

⑭ Klondike Gold Rush National Historical Park. A redbrick building with wooden floors and soaring ceilings contains a small museum illustrating Seattle's role in the 1897–98 gold rush in northwestern Canada's Klondike region. Displays show antique mining equipment, and the walls are lined with photos of gold diggers, explorers, and the hopeful families who followed them. Film presentations, gold-panning demonstrations, and rotating exhibits are scheduled throughout the year. Other sectors of this park are in southeast Alaska. ⊠ *117 S. Main St., Pioneer Square* ☎ *206/553–7220* ⊕ *www.nps.gov/klse/index.htm* ⌑ *Free* ⊙ *Daily 9–5.*

⑲ Mount Zion Baptist Church. Gospel-music fans are drawn to the church of the state's largest African-American congregation to catch the spirit through moving sermons and rousing song. The church's first gatherings began in 1890; back then its prayer meetings were held in people's houses and in a store. The church was incorporated in 1903, and after a number of moves, settled in its current simple but sturdy brick building. Eighteen stained-glass windows, each with an original design that honors a key African-American figure, glow within the sanctuary. Beneath the bell tower, James Washington's sculpture *The Oracle of Truth*, a gray boulder carved with the image of a lamb, is dedicated to children struggling to find truth. ⊠ *1634 19th Ave., Central Area* ☎ *206/322–6500* ⊕ *www.mountzion.net* ⊙ *Services Sun. 7:45 and 10:45.*

▶ ⑬ Pioneer Square District. Seattle's oldest neighborhood is a round-the-

Fodor'sChoice
★

clock hub of activity. Cafés, antiques shops, clothing boutiques, and art galleries fill elegantly renovated, turn-of-the-20th-century redbrick buildings lining the narrow streets that surround the historic central square. The district's most unique structure, the 42-story Smith Tower on Second Avenue and Yesler Way, was the tallest building west of the Mississippi when it was completed in 1914. By day, you'll see a mix of downtown workers and tourists strolling between the dining and arts spots, while darkness brings a frenzy of club-hoppers, plus late-night partyers spilling over from nearby festivals and stadium sports events. The ornate iron-and-glass pergola on First Avenue and Yesler Way marks the site where the pier and sawmill owned by Henry Yesler, one of Seattle's first businessmen, once operated. Actually, today's Yesler Way was the original "Skid Row," where in the 1880s timber was sent to the sawmill on a skid of small logs laid crossways and greased so that the cut trees would slide down to the mill. The area later grew into Seattle's first center of commerce. Many of the buildings you see today are replicas of the wood-frame structures destroyed by fire in 1889.

need a break?

Elliott Bay Books (⊠ 101 S. Main St., Pioneer Square ☎ 206/624–6600 or 800/962–5311 ⊕ www.elliottbaybook.com) is a local haunt for reading, relaxing, and respite. In addition to the light-filled, street-level bookstore with its creaky wood floors, there's a comfortable,

TUNNEL BACK IN TIME

When Seattle was rebuilt after the Great Fire of 1889, the city fathers wisely decided to raise the level of the old downtown, since it was so close to tidewater that sewers flowed backward during spring tides. But the old storefronts weren't torn down; new ones were simply added at the new street level. This left a ghostly underground city intact. Today, you can see these storefronts on a 1½-hour official walking tour of the musty passageways beneath Pioneer Square.

The **Seattle Underground Tour** starts in a public house that dates from 1890 and winds its way through five blocks of caverns. The guides are witty and knowledgeable, and the tour gives you a lively look at the city's Wild West past. ⊠ 608 1st Ave., Pioneer Square ☎ 206/682–4646 ⊕ www.undergroundtour.com ☎ $9 ☉ Ticket office daily 9:30–6; tour times vary but typically run 11–5.

brick-walled café downstairs. Order homemade sandwiches, salads, and soups at the deli counter, then settle down at one of the chunky wood tables. Desserts, like the hearty carrot cake, are first-rate—and enormous. Don't miss the hilarious (and often insightful) commentaries that cover the bathroom walls. The store is open weekdays 9:30 AM–10 PM, Saturdays 10–10, Sunday 11–7, and holidays 12–5.

👆 **16** **Wing Luke Museum.** Named for the Northwest's first Asian-American
Fodor's Choice elected official, this small, well-organized museum surveys the history
★ and cultures of people from Asia and the Pacific islands who settled in the Pacific Northwest. The emphasis is on how immigrants and their descendants have transformed and been transformed by American culture. The permanent collection includes costumes, fabrics, crafts, basketry, photographs, and Chinese traditional medicines. ⊠ 407 7th Ave. S, International District ☎ 206/623–5124 ⊕ www.wingluke.org ☎ $4 ☉ Tues.–Fri. 11–4:30, weekends noon–4.

off the beaten path

SAFECO FIELD – This 47,000-seat, grass turf, open-air baseball stadium with the retractable roof replaced the famous but dilapidated cement Kingdome in 1999. Wear comfortable shoes: the one-hour tour ($3) takes you down to the field, into the dugouts, back to the press and locker rooms, and up to the posh box seats. Buy tickets in the sports shop and check out the baseball memorabilia upstairs while you wait. Afterward, head across the street to the Pyramid Alehouse for a brew. ⊠ 1st Ave. S, Sodo ☎ 206/622–4487 ⊕ www.mariners.mlb.com ☎ $3 ☉ Apr.–Oct. non-game day tours at 10:30, 12:30, and 2:30, game-day tours at 10:30 and 12:30; Nov.–Mar. tours Tues.–Sun. at 10:30 and 12:30.

CAPITOL HILL

With its mix of theaters and churches, coffeehouses and nightclubs, stately homes and student apartments, Capitol Hill demonstrates Seattle's diversity. It's a great place for strolling, admiring the mansions and gardens from more ostentatious eras, wandering through colorful boutiques and used bookshops, and refueling in tasty ethnic eateries. Drives through the neighborhood's narrow streets are leisurely on clear weekends, as everyone on the road slows down to take in the 360-degree views of Puget Sound, Lake Washington, and the snowy, serrated peaks of the Olympic and Cascade ranges.

Numbers in the text correspond to numbers in the margin and on the Capitol Hill & the U–District map.

From Downtown, walk up Pine Street to Melrose Avenue and fortify yourself with a jolt of java (and perhaps an artsy new hardcover) at the Bauhaus. Continue east along the **Pike–Pine corridor** 23 ⌐ on Pine Street to Broadway and turn left (but don't miss the art deco Egyptian Theater to the right). Passing Seattle Central Community College you'll cross Denny Way, the unofficial threshold of the **Broadway shopping district** 24. After six blocks, the road bears to the right, becoming 10th Avenue East.

You'll notice many beautiful homes on the side streets off 10th Avenue East in either direction as you continue north to Prospect Street. Turn right at Prospect Street and gird yourself for another hill. Continue on to 14th Avenue East and turn left (north) to enter **Volunteer Park** 25. After walking around a picturesque water tower (with a good view from the top), you'll see the Volunteer Park Conservatory straight ahead, the reservoir to your left, and the **Seattle Asian Art Museum** 26 to your right. Leave the park to the east via Galer Street. Walk north along 15th Avenue East to visit **Lakeview Cemetery** 27 (where Bruce Lee lies in repose), or turn right (south) and walk four blocks to shops and cafés. To return Downtown, continue walking south on 15th Avenue East and west on Pine Street (if you've had enough walking, catch Metro Bus 10 at this intersection; it heads toward Pike Place Market). At Broadway, cut one block south to Pike Street for the rest of the walk. The above tour is a good survey of Capitol Hill, but it's by no means complete. The **Washington Park Arboretum** 28, for example, is too far to walk; catch Metro Bus 11 heading northeast along East Madison Street, or drive.

TIMING

Simply walking this tour requires about four hours—two if you start and end in the Broadway shopping district. Allow at least two hours for shopping the Pike–Pine corridor and Broadway, an hour for the Asian Art Museum, and a half hour for the conservatory. The amount of time you spend at Bruce Lee's grave is between you and Mr. Lee. Allow two hours for the arboretum, where losing track of time, and yourself, is pretty much the point.

What to See

24 **Broadway Shopping District.** Seattle's youth-oriented culture, old money, and gay scene all converge on this lively, laid-back stretch of Broadway East between East Denny Way and East Roy Street. Complete with plenty of cafés, record shops, vintage clothing stores, and the obligatory art-house movie theater, Harvard Exit, it's great place to stroll, sip coffee, or have a brew. The three-story **Broadway Market** (✉ 401 Broadway E, Capitol Hill) has the Gap and Urban Outfitters along with some smaller and funkier boutiques, a Myer grocery store, a branch of the discount Ticket/Ticket source, and a cinema. The glaring sign for **Dick's Drive-In** (✉ 115 Broadway E, Capitol Hill) beckons to all who see it—a Deluxe Burger and a shake at 1 AM is a quintessential Seattle experience. The avenue's appeal is that it's generally safe at all hours and has fascinating people-watching and a lot of cool stuff—specialty coffee, handmade chocolates, sushi, salsa, boutique accessories, kitschy knickknacks.

Between Pine and Roy streets artist Jack Mackie inlaid seven sets of bronze dancing footprints demonstrating the steps for the tango, the waltz, the foxtrot, and others. Don't feel embarrassed about prancing out these ballroom dances. Even the most conservative Seattleites occasionally dance on this sidewalk. Look closely at the steps near Roy Street to see coffee beans in the concrete, a nod to the region's love affair with java.

Near Pine Street is a dedication to the city's most worshiped rock-and-roll icon—Jimi Hendrix. His bronze effigy holds a guitar, and from the looks of things he hasn't just kissed the sky, he's made out with it. Buckled at the knees with his hand up, head thrown back, and eyes squeezed shut, Seattle's legendary son is frozen in the midst of what seems a particularly ear-splitting riff. Frequently someone will leave an offering—a flower, a cigarette, or even a joint—in his outstretched fingers.

27 **Lakeview Cemetery.** One of the region's most beautiful cemeteries looks east toward Lake Washington from its elevated hillside directly north of Volunteer Park. Bruce Lee's grave and that of his son Brandon are the most visited sites. Several of Seattle's founding families are also interred here (their bodies were moved from a pioneer cemetery when Denny Hill was leveled to make room for the motels, car dealerships, and parking lots of the Denny Regrade south of Lake Union). Ask for a map at the cemetery office.

Capitol Hill natives are loathe to tell people about the **Louisa Boren Lookout** (✉ 1555 15th Ave. E [at Garfield St.], Capitol Hill) in a little park across from Lakeview Cemetery. Here you can sit on the bench under the tree at the park's center and gaze upon a carpet of treetops in Interlake Park below. Unobstructed views of Lake Washington and the U-District are available rain or shine, but on the clearest days the Cascade Mountains complete the picture. ✉ *1554 15th Ave. E, Capitol Hill* ☎ *206/322–1582* ✉ *Free* ⊙ *Mon.–Sat. 9–4:30.*

23 **Pike–Pine Corridor.** An increasingly popular center of activity, this funky strip between Downtown and the south end of the Broadway shopping district contains galleries, thrift shops, designer retro furniture stores, and restaurants. Stop in for a drink at the famous **Cha Cha Lounge** (✉ 506 E. Pine St., Capitol Hill), a dark hipster hangout decked out in south-of-the-border flair. On weekends the strip is hopping as club kids and drag performers flock to the alley entrance of **Neighbors** (✉ 1509 Broadway [at E. Pike St.], Capitol Hill), Seattle's oldest gay bar, for disco dancing that lasts until 4 AM.

26 **Seattle Asian Art Museum.** This 1933 Art Moderne edifice fits surprisingly
Fodor'sChoice   well with the stark plaza stretching from the front door to the edge of a
★   bluff, and with the lush plants of Volunteer Park. The museum's collections include thousands of paintings, sculptures, pottery, and textiles from China, Japan, India, Korea, and several southeast Asian countries, many collected by the late Eugene Fuller, Seattle's most famous art collector. Children's crafts tables provide activities related to current exhibits, and free gallery tours are available by appointment. A ticket to the museum is good for $3 off admission to the Seattle Art Museum if used within one week. Likewise, a ticket from the Seattle Art Museum gets you free admission here within the same time frame. ✉ *Volunteer Park, 1400 E. Prospect St., Capitol Hill* ☎ *206/654–3100, 206/654–3123 for gallery tours* ⊕ *www.seattleartmuseum.org* ✉ *$3; free 1st Thurs. and Sat. of month* ⊙ *Tues.–Sun. 10–5 (Thurs. until 9); call for tour schedule.*

25 **Volunteer Park.** High above the mansions of North Capitol Hill sits 45-acre Volunteer Park, a grassy expanse perfect for picnicking, sunbathing, reading, and strolling. You can tell this is one of the city's older parks by the size of the trees and the rhododendrons, many of which were planted more than a hundred years ago. The Olmsted Brothers, the premier landscape architects of the day, helped with the final design in 1904,

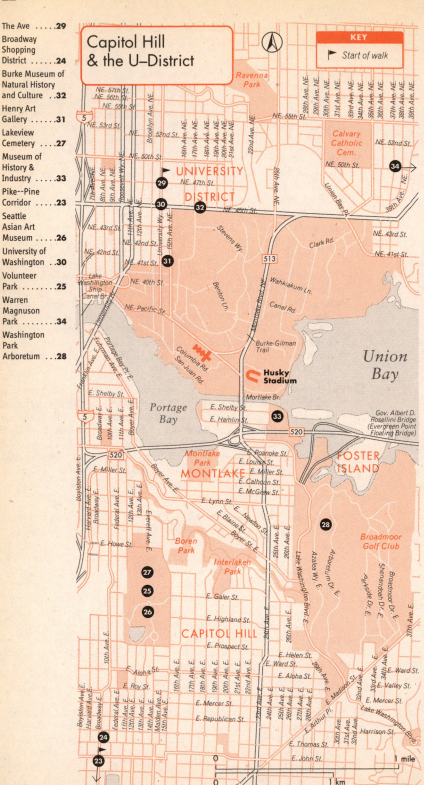

Capitol Hill & the U–District

KEY

▶ Start of walk

and the park has changed surprisingly little since then. From a traffic circle at the park's south entrance, it's a mere 108 steps to some great views at the top of the 75-foot-high water tower, built circa 1906.

Beside the lake in the center of the park is the Seattle Asian Art Museum. Across from the museum is the romantic **Volunteer Park Conservatory** (☎ 206/684–4743). This Victorian-style greenhouse, completed in 1912, is one of only three conservatories remaining in the U.S. from the lavish golden age predating World War I (the other two are the W. W. Seymour Conservatory in Tacoma's Wright Park, and the Conservatory of Flowers in San Francisco's Golden Gate Park). The magnificent collection of tropical plants was accumulated largely by donation (like the artwork in the nearby museum). The extensive Anna Clise Orchid Collection, begun in 1919, is at its most spectacular in late fall and early winter, when most of the flowers are in full bloom. The conservatory also has some splendid palm trees, a well-stocked koi pond, and, almost incongruously, a magnificent collection of cacti and other succulents. A focal point of the park, at the western edge of the 445-foot-high hill and in front of the Asian Art Museum, is Isamu Noguchi's sculpture *Black Sun,* carved from a 30-ton block of black granite. Many seem to enjoy taking photos of the Space Needle framed in the 9-foot, 9-inch hole of the "sun." ✉ *Park entrance: 14th Ave. E at Prospect St., Capitol Hill* ⊕ *www.ci.seattle.wa.us/seattle/parks/parkspaces/volpark. htm* ✉ *Free* ☾ *Park: daily dawn–dusk; Conservatory: May–mid-September, daily 10–7, otherwise 10–4.*

☾ ㉘ **Washington Park Arboretum.** The 230-acre arboretum has more than
Fodor'sChoice 130 endangered plants, plus more than 40,000 native and exotic trees,
★ shrubs, and vines from some 4,800 different species and cultivars. In warm winters, flowering cherries and plums bloom in its protected valleys as early as late February, while the flowering shrubs in Rhododendron Glen and Azalea Way are in full bloom March through June. In autumn, trees and shrubs glow in hues of crimson, pumpkin, and lemon; in winter, plantings chosen specially for their stark and colorful branches dominate the landscape. From March through October, visit the peaceful **Japanese Garden** (☎ 206/684–4725 ✉ $3), a compressed world of mountains, forests, rivers, lakes, and tablelands, open from 10 AM until sunset. The pond, lined with blooming water irises in spring, has turtles and brightly colored koi. An authentic Japanese tea house is reserved for tea ceremonies and instruction on the art of tea. The Graham Visitors Center at the park's north end has descriptions of the arboretum's flora and fauna, as well as brochures, a garden gift shop, and self-guided walking tour maps. ✉ *2300 Arboretum Dr. E, Capitol Hill* ☎ *206/543–8800* ⊕ *depts.washington.edu/wpa* ✉ *Free* ☾ *Park daily 7 AM–sunset; visitors center daily 10–4.*

UNIVERSITY DISTRICT

The U-District, as this area is called locally, is bounded by Ravenna Boulevard to the north, the Montlake Cut waterway (connecting Lake Union and Lake Washington) to the south, 25th Avenue Northeast to the east, and I–5 to the west. A stroll through the University of Washington campus can include stops at its museums and other cultural attractions. To get a whiff of the slightly anarchic energy that fuels this part of town, head off campus to "The Ave," the student-oriented shopping area along University Way Northeast.

Numbers in the text correspond to numbers in the margin and on the Capitol Hill & the U–District map.

Start at Northeast 45th Street and University Way Northeast. Proceed south on **The Ave** (University Way) **29** ► through the heart of the district's many shopping and dining options. Turn left at Northeast Campus Parkway, stopping by the visitor center at the **University of Washington 30**. Straight ahead at the end of the block is the **Henry Art Gallery 31**. Continue east to Central Plaza, better known as Red Square. On clear days you'll be rewarded with views of Mt. Rainier to the southeast. Walk down Rainier Vista (past the Frosh Pond and fountain) to Stevens Way, turning left into Sylvan Grove, a gorgeous outdoor theater. Return via Rainier Vista to Red Square and strike out due north. A walk along shady Memorial Way past the commuter lot deposits you at the **Burke Museum of Natural History and Culture 32**. From the Burke step out onto Northeast 45th Street, walking two longish blocks to the left to return to University Way Northeast. If you want to continue farther afield, drive south over the Montlake Bridge to the **Museum of History & Industry 33**, where you can explore Seattle's growth and development through hands-on exhibits that trace its seafaring, golddigging, timber-felling, neighborhood-melding traditions. Afterward, walk the marshy trail and watch the Canadian geese in adjacent McCurdy Park. Finish your tour with an afternoon visit to **Warren Magnuson Park 34**, also known as Sand Point Magnuson Park, a relaxing place to toss a football, fly a kite, or catch some rays.

TIMING   This walk takes about two hours, plus two hours to tour the Museum of History & Industry and another half-hour to explore McCurdy Park. You can easily spend an hour each in the Henry Art Gallery and Burke Museum and an additional hour (or two) on The Ave.

What to See

► **29** **The Ave.** University Way Northeast, the hub of University of Washington social life, has all the activities you would expect to find in a student-oriented district—great coffeehouses, cinemas, clothing stores, bars, and cheap ethnic restaurants, along with panhandlers and pockets of grime. The major action along The Ave is between 42nd and 50th streets, though there are more shops and restaurants as University Way continues north to 58th Street and the entrance to Ravenna Park.

need a break?   Stop in the **Big Time Brewery** (✉ 4133 University Way NE, University District ☎ 206/545–4509 ⊕ www.bigtimebrewery.com), with its soaring ceilings and yellow brick exterior, to take a free weekday tour and sample one of at least 10 original beers on tap daily. Sidle up to the antique bar to kick a couple back, then put a quarter in the jukebox and stroll around to scan the vast bottle and can collection, historic brewery photos, and antique beer memorabilia. After you've loosened up, dare your friends to a shuffleboard game.

☾ **32** **Burke Museum of Natural History and Culture.** Totem poles mark the entrance to this museum of regional history, where exhibits survey the land and cultures of the Pacific Northwest. Highlights include memorabilia from Washington's 35 Native American tribes: costumes and masks, tools, baskets, blankets, and cookware, among many other items. You can also explore the surrounding terrain through dioramas and displays of local archeological finds. For $1 more on the admission price, you get same-day admission to the Henry Art Gallery. ✉ *University of Washington campus, 17th Ave. NE and NE 45th St., University District* ☎ 206/543–

TIME TO RELAX

A DAY EXPLORING SEATTLE *will involve lots of cardio: walking through markets and museums, perhaps some hiking or boating—and climbing those hills. Take a break to relax at one of these famed spas, and you'll understand why those who live here seem so at ease: They know how to manage stress.*

Gene Juarez Salon and Spa. *Change into the signature kimono-style robe and sip a cinnamon tea while you wait for your trendy "stand-up haircut": you stand while the stylist snips away. Patrons also get a foot soak and have use of the eucalyptus steam chamber. Luxury treatments include wraps, massages, facials, waxing, manicures, and pedicures.* ✉ *607 Pine St., Downtown* ☎ *206/326–6000* ✉ *Bellevue Galleria, 550 106th Ave. NE, Bellevue* ☎ *425/455–5511* ⊕ *www. genejuarez.com* ✉ *Redmond Town Center, 16495 NE 74th St., Redmond* ☎ *425/882–9000.*

Habitude Salon, Day Spa & Gallery. *Beamed ceilings, polished wood floors, plush furnishings, and tropical scents relax you the moment you enter. Indulge in a single treatment or in such packages as Beneath the Spring Thaw Falls (hydrating glow, massage, scalp treatment, sauna, and smoothie). Other offerings include the Hot Rocks detox sauna, Rainforest Steam Shower, delectable spa lunches, and door-to-door town car service. It's the state's only Aveda Lifestyle spa.* ✉ *2801 NW Market St., Ballard* ☎ *206/782–2898* ⊕ *www.habitude.com.*

Spa Bellisima. *Envelop yourself in a polar fleece robe, sink into a soft lounge chair, sip an herbal tea, and await simple luxury. Scented candles and soothing music surround you during your facial or massage, which use only certified organic botanicals, oils, and herbal essences. Custom-blended creams from ingredients such as honey, sesame seeds, and citrus are applied beneath diaphanous gauze "clouds." Bellisima (outrageously beautiful) is how you'll feel when you leave.* ✉ *2620 2nd Ave., Belltown* ☎ *206/ 956–4156.*

Spa del Lago. *Golden light, shining wood floors, and butter-cream-color walls wrap you in warmth, inviting you to relax for a hot stone massage, salt glow, mud wrap, or a sports shave or body bronzing. Acupuncture, teen facials, and expectant-mother massages are also available.* ✉ *1929 43rd Ave. E, Suite 100, Madison Park* ☎ *206/322–5246.*

Spa at the Woodmark. *Your hosts are a soothing team of licensed aestheticians, masseuses, and nail technicians who'll help you "practice doing nothing." Sound inviting? How about heated beds, facials accompanied by upper-body massages, monthly price-slashing specials, and a bag of samples to take home? The "Just for Him" package includes a facial, manicure, pedicure, massage, and snack. Top off your visit with a meal by the hotel's executive chef.* ✉ *Woodmark Hotel, 1200 Carillon Point, Kirkland* ☎ *425/ 822–3700 or 800/323–7500.*

Spa at Willows Lodge. *Often included among the world's top romantic getaways by international travel magazines, this spa surrounds a tranquil outdoor hot tub. Opt for a soothing massage, expert skin treatments, or hand and foot pampering. Weekday clients can try the "Northwest Express" package, which includes a massage, body polish, and facial.* ✉ *Willows Lodge, 14580 NE 145th St., Woodinville* ☎ *425/424–2900.*

Ummelina International Day Spa. *Hand-carved Javanese doors open into this tranquil, luxurious, Asian-inspired spa. Relax beneath a warm waterfall, take a steamy, scented sauna, or submit to a mud wrap or smoothing body scrub. The three-hour Equator package for couples includes all this and more. Linger over the experience with a cup of delicately flavored tea.* ✉ *1525 4th Ave., Downtown* ☎ *206/624–1370.*

5590 ⊕ *www.washington.edu/burkemuseum* ⌨ *$5.50* ⊙ *Daily 10–5 (Thurs. until 8).*

㉛ Henry Art Gallery. The works by Northwest artists at this contemporary art gallery are culled from several genres and include photography, 19th- and 20th-century paintings, and textiles from the permanent collection. The Henry also hosts important touring multimedia exhibitions. One installation, *Volume: Bed of Sound,* encouraged visitors to listen rather than look—and lie upon a huge bed fitted with headphones while doing so. Other exhibits have included the work of Wolfgang Laib and Alexis Rockman. ⊠ *University of Washington campus, 15th Ave. NE and NE 41st St., University District* ☎ *206/543–2280* ⊕ *www.henryart. org* ⌨ *$5* ⊙ *Tues.–Sun. 11–5 (Thurs. until 8).*

㉝ Museum of History & Industry. Few places are better equipped to help you get a handle on the history of the Pacific Northwest. Since 1952 this museum has collected objects (some dating to 1780) that chronicle the region's economic, social, and cultural history. Factory and mining equipment, gramophones, clothing, newspapers, and everyday items from yesteryear are all on display, many along the re-created Seattle street from the 1880s. The interactive exhibits encourage kids to have fun and learn. On weekends look for educational presentations, family workshops, and historical walks. Students, teachers, and history buffs are always roaming the vast museum library. ⊠ *2700 24th Ave. E (across the Montlake Bridge from the University, on the south side of Union Bay), University District* ☎ *206/324–1126* ⊕ *www.seattlehistory.org* ⌨ *$7; free first Thurs. of the month* ⊙ *Daily 10–5; first Thurs. 10–8.*

off the beaten path

NORTHWEST PUPPET MUSEUM – In a renovated church in the Maple Leaf neighborhood, the only puppet center in the Northwest highlights the renowned marionettes of the Carter family. The museum's mission is to present a top-quality, international puppet theater where children and adults alike can be entertained, learn puppetry skills, and appreciate puppetry traditions from around the world. The Carters are professional puppeteers trained by masters from Italy, Romania, and China. They have performed in festivals from Scotland to Uzbekistan. For their talents they have received a Fulbright Award and a UNIMA/USA Citation of Excellence, the highest award in American puppet theater. Recent shows include *The Nutcracker, The Travels of Babar,* and *The Adventures of Sinbad.* Also on-site are a museum, theater, research library, picnic area, playground, and shop where puppet-making workshops and marionette classes are held. ⊠ *9123 15th Ave. NE, University District, Take I–5 north, Exit 171 to Lake City Way, turn left on 15th Ave. NE and continue to 92nd St.* ☎ *206/523–2579* ⊕ *www. nwpuppet.org* ⌨ *Varies by performance* ⊙ *Call for performance and workshop schedules.*

㉚ University of Washington. The "U-Dub" is popular slang for this 35,000-student university founded in downtown Seattle in 1861. The campus moved to Denny Hall in 1895, and the Alaska-Yukon-Pacific Exposition hosted here in 1909 brought national attention to the Northwest. The UW is respected for its research and graduate programs in medicine, nursing, oceanography, Asian studies, drama, physiology, and social work, among many others. Its athletic teams—particularly football and women's basketball—have strong regional followings, and Red Square is the nerve center for student activity and politics. By the way, "red" refers to the square's brick paving, not to the students' political inclinations, though it's here that you'll see animal-rights, environmental, and other advocates attempting to rouse the masses. On sunny days the steps are filled with students sunbathing, studying, or hanging out.

One of North America's premier research sources, **Suzzallo Library** (✉ Center of UW campus [near Red Sq.], University District ☎ 206/543–0242) is a spectacular example of Gothic architecture. Some 35 mi of book-filled shelves are housed in this heart of the university's massive library system, with more than 6 million catalogued volumes and microform materials combined here and in 22 campus branches. Hours are Monday–Thursday 7:30 AM–midnight, Friday 7:30–6, Saturday 9–5, and Sunday noon–midnight.

One of UW's first buildings contains the **Campus Observatory** (✉ Corner of NE 45th St. and 17th Ave. NE, University District ☎ 206/543–0126), one of the oldest working refractive telescopes in the West. This antique isn't terribly large (a mere 6″ diameter), but it gives you a good look at the moon, various planets, and other astral objects. No scientific research is performed here. The observatory is on the north end of the campus, near the Burke Museum. ✉ *University Visitor Information Center, 4014 University Way NE, near NE 45th St., University District* ☎ *206/543–9198* ⊕ *www.washington.edu* ⌛ *Free* ☉ *Daily 8–5.*

need a break?
Nouveau Dorm (✉ **Stevens Way and Whitman Ct., University District** ☎ **206/616–8026), in McMahon Hall on the UW campus, has an eight-station cafeteria where the food is cheap, filling, and—surprise!—actually pretty good. Mix your own meats, sauces, and veggies at the Mongolian grill; order a well-rounded, dinner-size plate at Abundo; or just grab a tasty slice of pizza, a sandwich, or a burger. The furnishings are elegant, and the large windows frame pretty campus views.**

34 **Warren Magnuson Park.** Jutting into Lake Washington northeast of the University District is this beachside area, also called Sand Point Magnuson Park. Innovative art is threaded through the grounds, including *Soundgarden,* a series of aluminum tubes mounted to catch the wind and create flutelike music. (Yes, Seattle's famous band named itself after this sculpture.) Morning walkers and joggers often rest on the whale-shape benches to watch the sun rise over Lake Washington—a spectacle that's especially lovely when accompanied by this gentle soundtrack. The sculpture is in the northern part of the park, through the turnstile and across *Moby Dick* Bridge (embedded with quotes from Melville's novel). ✉ *Park entrance: Sand Point Way NE at 65th St., University District.*

NORTH & WEST OF DOWNTOWN

Fremont has been called "Seattle's Greenwich Village," and the neighborhood's residents—many of them artists—do little to challenge the image. "The Artists' Republic of Fremont," as many prefer to call it, brims with sass and self-confidence—with many galleries, restaurants, coffeehouses, antiques shops, and pubs where it's easy to lose track of time. East of Fremont is Wallingford, an inviting neighborhood of bungalow homes, boutiques, small restaurants, stores selling handmade crafts, and used clothes and bookshops. Phinney Ridge, a small residential area, and the Woodland Park Zoo are north of Fremont. Ballard, with its strong Scandinavian heritage and fishing traditions, lies to the west. Magnolia sits south across the ship canal from Ballard, filling out the peninsula west of Queen Anne to Discovery Park—one of Seattle's favorite outdoor spots. The hilly gathering of modest middle-class homes and stunning ocean-view mansions is encircled by the popular sunset drives of Magnolia Boulevard and Gilman Avenue West.

a good
tour

Numbers in the text correspond to numbers in the margin and on the North & West of Downtown map.

Coming from downtown, you'll probably enter Fremont via the Fremont Bridge, one of the world's busiest drawbridges. **Fremont Center** 35 ▸ is tiny and can easily be explored by intuition. Here's one strategy: proceed north on Fremont Avenue North. Stop at the corner of North 34th Street to check out one of Fremont's "hysterical sites"—the *Waiting for the Interurban* sculpture. The life-size human statues may be draped with all manner of funky garb. Don't worry, it's not vandalism. It's a tradition.

Continue up to North 35th Street and turn right. Walk two blocks to the Aurora Bridge (you'll be standing underneath it). Turn left and walk one block, but approach with care. The "Fremont Troll"—a whimsical concrete monster that lurks beneath the bridge—jealously guards his Volkswagen Beetle. Head back along North 36th Street, making a hard left at the statue of Lenin (seriously) at Fremont Place, the first street after you cross Fremont Avenue North. Walk a half block southeast, go right at the crosswalk, and then make a right on North 35th Street. At the end of the block is the 53-foot Fremont Rocket, "officially" designating the center of the universe.

Walk straight ahead one long block to Phinney Avenue, then turn left and continue one block to the Ship Canal. On the right is Canal Park. Linger here, or turn left on North 34th Street and return to the Fremont Bridge.

Other area attractions are best reached by car, bus, or bike. The **Woodland Park Zoo** 36 is due north of Fremont via Fremont Avenue North (catch Bus 5 from the northeast corner of Fremont Avenue North and North 39th Street). **Green Lake** 37, with its park full of grassy hills, walkways, and sports courts, is northeast of the Woodland Park Zoo on Highway 99 (Aurora Avenue North). **Gasworks Park** 38, on North Northlake Way, on Lake Union's north shore, is less than a 2-mi drive southeast of Fremont. The **Ballard Locks** 39 are west of Fremont (take Bus 28 from the corner of Fremont Avenue North and North 35th Street to Northwest Market Street and Eighth Avenue North and transfer to Bus 44 or, on weekdays only, Bus 46, heading west). A long block north of the Ballard Locks, on 32nd Avenue Northwest, is the **Nordic Heritage Museum** 40, which traces the immigration of Scandinavians to America and the Northwest, as well as their general history and culture. **Discovery Park** 41 is a walk of less than 1 mi from the south entrance to the Ballard Locks. Head west (right) on Commodore Way and south (left) on 40th Street.

TIMING   The walk around Fremont takes an hour at most, but the neighborhood is meant for strolling, browsing, sipping, and shopping. Plan to spend a full morning or a good part of an afternoon. You could easily spend two hours at the Ballard Locks or the Nordic Heritage Museum, and several hours at the Woodland Park Zoo, Green Lake, or Discovery Park.

What to See

39   **Ballard Locks.** This passage in the 8-mi Lake Washington Ship Canal connects Puget Sound's saltwater Shilshole Bay to freshwater Lake Washington and Lake Union. Officially titled the Hiram M. Chittenden Locks and completed in 1917, the structure now services 100,000 boats yearly by raising and lowering water levels 6 feet to 26 feet. An estimated half million salmon and trout make the same journey from

FodorsChoice
★

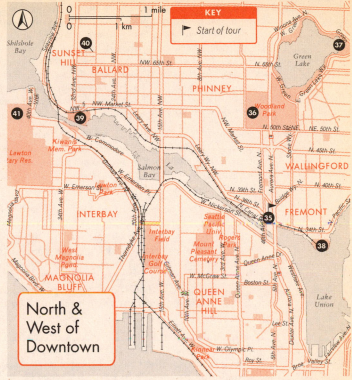

North & West of Downtown

saltwater to fresh each year on the fish ladder, with waterline windows showing the 21 rising platforms where they migrate to their spawning grounds June through October. Along the south side of the locks is a 1,200-foot promenade with a footbridge, a fishing pier, and an observation deck. West are the lovely, 7-acre Carl English Jr. Botanic Gardens, with ornamental patches of native and exotic plants. Guided tours start at the nearby visitor center, where you'll find displays on the locks' history and operation, as well as several fanciful sculptures by local artists. From downtown, take Bus 15 or 18 to the stop at Northwest Market Street and 15th Avenue Northwest, then transfer to Bus 44 or (weekdays) 46 heading west on Market Street. ✉ *3015 NW 54th St.; from Fremont, head north on Leary Way NW, west on NW Market St., and south on 54th St., Ballard* ☎ *206/783–7059* ⊕ *www.nws.usace.army. mil/opdiv/lwsc* ✉ *Free* ⏱ *Locks daily 7 AM–9 PM; visitor center mid-May to mid-Sept., daily 10–6; mid-Sept. to mid-May, Thurs.–Mon. 11–4; call for tour information.*

off the beaten path **CENTER FOR WOODEN BOATS –** Though slightly off the main drag at the south end of Lake Union, the center is a great place to launch your expedition if you're interested in exploring the water (or just the waterfront). Check out the 1897 schooner *Wawona* and the other historic vessels on display, watch the staff at work on a restoration, rent a boat at the Oarhouse for a sail around the lake, or have a picnic. ✉ *1010 Valley St., Queen Anne* ☎ *206/382–2628* ⊕ *www. cwb.org* ✉ *Free* ⏱ *May–Labor Day, museum daily 11–7 (boat livery noon until 7); Labor Day–late Sept., museum and boat livery Wed.–Mon. 11–6; late Sept.–May, museum and boat livery Wed.–Mon 11–5.*

(41) Discovery Park. At 534 acres, this former military base is a wildlife sanctuary and Seattle's largest park. You can hike through cool forests, explore saltwater beaches, or take in views of Puget Sound and Mt. Rainier. A 2.8-mi trail traverses this urban wilderness. ⊕ *From downtown Seattle take Elliott Avenue north until it becomes 15th Ave. NW, turn left on W. Emerson, right on Gilman Ave. W, left on W. Fort St., and right on E. Government Way* ✉ *3801 E. Government Way, Magnolia* ☎ *206/386–4236* ⊕ *www.ci.seattle.wa.us/parks/parkspaces/discovparkindex. htm* ✉ *Free* ☺ *Park daily 6 AM–11 PM, visitor center daily 8:30–5.*

▶ **(35) Fremont Center.** The self-styled "Republic of Fremont" is one of Seattle's most distinctive neighborhoods. The center is an eclectic strip of Fremont Avenue stretching from the ship canal at the south end to North 36th Street, with shops and cafés two blocks on either side. The area also contains many lighthearted attractions.

Beneath the Aurora Bridge lurks the gigantic, bearded *Fremont Troll* with a gleaming eye and a pouty lip. Eighteen feet tall and not so handsome, he clutches a real Volkswagen Beetle in his massive left hand. The gray giant watches over the neighborhood, and even allows people to crawl up on his shoulders for the obligatory photo. The troll appeared in 1991, commissioned by the Fremont Arts Council. The statue only looks frightening around Halloween, when, presiding over a wild parade, he has a bicycle-wheel rim as a nose ring and a giant spider crawling on his shoulder.

When Russian counterrevolutionaries knocked over a 7-ton **statue of Lenin** in 1989, they couldn't have known it would end up in Fremont. A Seattle-area man named Lewis Carpenter toted the striding bronze Red from Slovakia to Seattle in 1989, and when he died in 1994, the statue made its way to the neighborhood's Sunday flea market. Soon he was ousted from this den of capitalism, and today he sits in front of a burrito joint on North 36th Street, between Fremont and Evanston avenues.

Fremont's signature statue, *Waiting for the Interurban,* frequently fools those who drive by and wonder why this crowd looks so still and happy. In reality it's a cast aluminum sculpture of five figures, one holding a small child. Residents enjoy dressing and ornamenting the figures for holidays, birthdays, homecomings—just about any joyful occasion. Look closely at the dog circling the legs of one figure and you'll see it wears the face of a bearded, ornery-looking man. As the story goes, the one-time honorary mayor of Fremont, Armen Stepanian, was upset with Richard Beyer for choosing himself as the artist to create the statue when no one else applied to the Fremont Arts Council for the job. Beyer had the final word in the brouhaha by putting Stepanian's face on the canine. The sculpture is on North 34th Street, just over the Fremont Bridge at Fremont Avenue. Walk another block to the corner of North 35th Street and Evanston Avenue, then look up to spot the 53-foot, Russian-built **Fremont Rocket.**

need a break? **The Essential Baking Co.** (✉ 1604 N. 34th St., Fremont ☎ 206/545–3804) is the quick-stop place to grab a warm loaf of bread, or coffee and a sinfully flaky baked treat. If you're hungry, you can also linger for a simple lunch with a twist—roasted tomatoes and watercress added to the grilled goat cheese and cheddar sandwich, for example. Top off the meal by sampling the handmade organic chocolates.

★ ☺ **(38) Gasworks Park.** Despite the hulking remains of an old gas plant here, the open, hilly, 20-acre park is actually easy on the eyes. Colorful kites soar in the air and bright-hued spinnakers bob offshore in Lake Union on summer days. Get a glimpse of downtown Seattle from the zodiac sculpture at the top of the hill, or feed the ducks on the lake. The sand-bottom playground has monkey bars, wooden platforms, and a spinning metal merry-go-round. Crowds throng to picnic and jam at the outdoor summer concerts, movies, and city-stopping Fourth of July fireworks display. ⊠ *North end of Lake Union, N. Northlake Way and Meridian Ave. N, Fremont* ⊘ *Daily 4 AM–11:30 PM.*

need a break?

Julia's in Wallingford (⊠ 4401 Wallingford Ave. N, Wallingford ☎ 206/633–1175), across from the Wallingford Center, is a busy café that fills quickly with diners craving hearty American, Mexican, and Mediterranean dishes. Meals are served all day—egg scrambles, gazpacho, burritos, pasta—with lots of soups, salads, and snacks, plus vegetarian options. Beer and wine are available.

07 Green Lake. Cross beneath Highway 99 (Aurora Avenue North) from the Woodland Park Zoo to a beautiful 342-acre park wrapped around a lovely lake. Take a boat out on the water; play basketball, tennis, baseball, or soccer on the nearby courts; or jog, blade, or bike the 3-mi lakeside trail. A first-rate play area includes a giant sandbox, swings, slides, and all the climbing equipment a child could ever dream of—plus lots of grassy areas and benches where adults can take a break. The park is generally packed (about 1 million people visit each year), especially on weekday evenings, when many Seattleites come to see and be seen. And you'd better love dogs; the canine to human ratio here is just about even. Surrounding the park are peaceful middle- and upper-class homes, plus a compact commercial district where you can grab a whole-wheat burrito and fresh carrot juice—or a full-fat latte and a chunk of chocolate cake. ⊠ *E. Green Lake Dr. N and W. Green Lake Dr. N, Green Lake.*

★ ☺ **40 Nordic Heritage Museum.** The only educational institute in the country to focus solely on Nordic cultures, this museum in a renovated early 1900s schoolhouse traces Scandinavian art, artifacts, and heritage all the way from Viking times. Behind the redbrick walls, nine permanent galleries on three floors give an in-depth look at how immigrants from Denmark, Finland, Iceland, Norway, and Sweden came to America and settled in the Pacific Northwest. Among the finds are textiles, china, books, tools, and photographs brought from the old countries. Delve into Nordic history at the extensive library; learn a few phrases at the on-site Scandinavian Language Institute; or join in a class or children's program on Nordic arts and crafts. The temporary galleries display paintings, sculpture, and photography by contemporary artists. ⊠ *3014 NW 67th St., Ballard* ☎ *206/789–5707* ⊕ *www.nordicmuseum.com* ⊠ *$4* ⊘ *Tues.–Sat. 10–4, Sun. noon–4.*

★ ☺ **36 Woodland Park Zoo.** Many of the 300 species of animals in this 92-acre botanical garden roam freely in habitat areas that have won several design awards. A jaguar exhibit is the center of the Tropical Rain Forest area where rare cats, frogs, and birds evoke South American jungles. The Butterflies & Blooms exhibit ($1) shows off the amazing beauty and variety of the winged creatures and describes their relationship with local flora. With authentic thatch-roof buildings, the African Village has a replica school room overlooking animals roaming the savanna; the Asian Elephant Forest trail takes you through a Thai village; and the Northern Trail winds past rocky habitats where brown bears, wolves, mountain goats, and otters scramble and play. The terrain is mostly flat, making it easy for wheelchairs and strollers (which can be rented) to negotiate. Kids love the barnyard, bug house, and the adjacent wooded play yard with its rope spider web, giant gopher burrow, and otter slides. ⊠ *5500 Phinney Ave. N, Phinney Ridge* ☎ *206/684–4800* ⊕ *www.zoo.org* ✉ *$9* ⊘ *Mid-Mar.–Apr. and mid-Sept.–mid-Oct., daily 9:30–5; May–mid-Sept., daily 9:30–6; mid-Oct.–mid-Mar., daily 9:30–4.*

THE EASTSIDE

On the far side of Lake Washington is East King County, the center of which is Bellevue. First across the floating bridge, though, is Mercer Island, a wooded, residential island community. Continue over the bridge, hang a left, and you're in Bellevue, a fast-growing city that now rivals Seattle for shoppers, conventions, and coveted living space. Top-name hotels, top-rated dining spots, renowned museums, a chic music and performance center, a professional theater, and numerous parks, gardens, and beaches have helped give Bellevue its own bustling, elite, yet internationally spiced character. Its charming core is still evident, however, in the many early-20th-century buildings of the original town square and outlying residential areas.

North of Bellevue, Kirkland is a pleasant town on the eastern shores of Lake Washington. It's very pedestrian-friendly, with shops, galleries, and restaurants all along the water. North of Bellevue, rustic Woodinville is best known for the Chateau Ste. Michelle and Columbia wineries; the Redhook Brewery, founded in Seattle; and Molbak's Nursery. Redmond, just east of Kirkland, has grown by leaps and bounds since Microsoft chose the small town for its corporate headquarters. In sports circles, Redmond is also known as the "Bicycle Capital of the Northwest" because of its first-rate Velodrome at Marymoor Park.

Southeast of Bellevue, in the foothills at the south end of Lake Sammamish, Issaquah is a scenic bedroom community coming into its own with gatherings of upscale shops and gated neighborhoods of modern mansions. Yet salmon still run seasonally in local streams—an event celebrated with the Annual Salmon Days Festival. East of Issaquah lies the rural community of North Bend. A truck stop that was the setting for the TV serial *Twin Peaks*, the town gets its name from a bend in the Snoqualmie River, which here turns north. The surrounding scenery is beautiful, dominated by 4,167-foot Mt. Si (with many popular hiking trails), 4,420-foot Mt. Washington, and 4,788-foot Mt. Tenerife.

What to See

Bellevue Botanical Gardens. This beautiful, 36-acre public area in the middle of Wilburton Hill Park is encircled by spectacular perennial borders, brilliant rhododendron displays, and patches of alpine and rock gardens. A log cabin exhibits implements of pioneer life. The visitor center is open daily during park hours. ⊠ *12001 Main St., Bellevue* ☎ *425/451–3755* ⊕ *www.bellevuebotanical.org* ✉ *Free* ⊘ *May–Sept., daily 10–6, Oct.–Apr., daily 10–4.*

Boehm's Chocolate Factory. Follow the delicious aromas through the mountains to the Edelweiss Chalet, where you'll find sweets as delicious as those produced in Switzerland. Tours (by reservation only) run July through September, but the factory is open year-round. You can't sample, but you can purchase what you see at the front shop. If you overindulge, work off the calories with a stroll through the adjacent garden. ⊠ *255 NE Gilman Blvd., Issaquah* ☎ *425/392–6652* ⊕ *www. boehms.com* ✉ *Free* ⊘ *Weekdays 9–6, Sun. 11–6.*

Burke-Gilman/Sammamish River Trail. The 27-mi-long, paved Burke-Gilman Trail runs from Seattle's Gasworks Park, on Lake Union, east

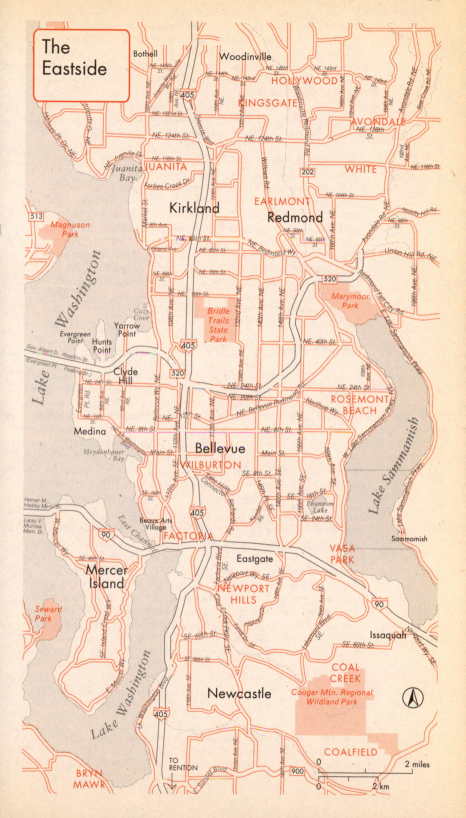

The
Eastside

along an old railroad right-of-way along the ship canal and then north along Lake Washington's western shore. At Blyth Park in Bothell, the trail becomes the Sammamish River Trail and continues for 10 mi to Marymoor Park, in Redmond. Energetic Seattleites take the trail to Marymoor for the annual Heritage Festival and Fourth of July Fireworks. Except for a stretch of the Sammamish River Trail between Woodinville and Marymoor Park where horses are permitted on a parallel trail, the path is limited to walkers, runners, and bicyclists. ✛ *Take I–90 east to north I–405, then Exit 23 east (S.R. 522) to Woodinville.*

off the beaten path

JIMI HENDRIX GRAVE SITE – Since his death in 1970, the famed guitarist has rested in Greenwood Cemetery. Refurbishments will add a memorial with a domed roof, granite columns, a waterfall, and a life-size bronze sculpture depicting Hendrix striking a stance from his 1969 performance at Woodstock. ✛ *Take I–5 south to I–405 north and the WA–169 south (SE Maple Valley Hwy.) exit, keeping left at fork in the ramp. Merge onto SE Maple Valley Hwy./WA–169 north. Take a right on Sunset Blvd. N, then a right at NE 3rd St. Continue 1 mi, as NE 3rd St. becomes NE 4th St. Turn right at the third light.* ⊠ *3rd and Monroe Sts., Renton* ☎ *425/255–1511* ⊕ *www.jimihendrixmemorial.com* ☼ *Daily sunrise–sunset* ☞ *Inquire at the office; a counselor will direct you to the site.*

Chateau Ste. Michelle Winery. One of the state's oldest wineries is 15 mi northeast of Seattle on 87 wooded acres. Once part of the estate of lumber baron Fred Stimson, it includes the original trout ponds, a carriage house, a caretaker's cottage, formal gardens, and the 1912 family manor house (which is on the National Register of Historic Places). Complimentary wine tastings and cellar tours run throughout the day. You're also invited to picnic and explore the grounds on your own; the wine shop sells delicatessen items. During the summer Chateau Ste. Michelle hosts nationally known performers and arts events in its amphitheater. ✛ *From downtown Seattle take I–90 east to north I–405; take Exit 23 east (S.R. 522) to Woodinville exit.* ⊠ *14111 NE 145th St., Woodinville* ☎ *425/415–3300* ⊕ *www.ste-michelle.com* ⊞ *Free* ☼ *Daily 10:30–4:30.*

Columbia Winery. A group of University of Washington professors founded this winery in 1962, making it the state's oldest. Using only European vinifera-style grapes grown in eastern Washington, the founders' aim was to take advantage of the fact that the vineyards share the same latitude as the best wine-producing areas of France. Complimentary wine tastings are held daily; cellar tours are on weekends. The gift shop is open year-round and sells wines and wine-related merchandise. Columbia hosts special food-and-wine events throughout the year. It's also the final destination of the **Spirit of Washington Dinner Train** (☎ 800/876–7245 ⊞ $47–$69 ⊕ www.spiritofwashingtondinnertrain.com), which originates in Renton and makes the three-hour trip along the eastern shores of Lake Washington. ⊠ *14030 NE 145th St., Woodinville., From downtown Seattle take I–90 east to north I–405; take Exit 23 east (S.R. 522) to Woodinville exit, go right. Go right again on 175th St., and left on Hwy. 202.* ☎ *425/488–2776 or 800/488–2347* ⊕ *www.columbiawinery. com* ⊞ *Free* ☼ *Daily 10–7.*

Cougar Mountain Regional Wildland Park. This spectacular park in the "Issaquah Alps" has more than 36 mi of hiking trails and 12 mi of bridle trails within its 3,000-plus acres. The Indian Trail, believed to date back 8,000 years, was part of a trade route that the Native Americans used to reach North Bend and the Cascades. Thick pine forests rise to spectacular mountaintop views; there are waterfalls, deep caves, and the remnants of a former mining town. Look for deer, black bears, bobcats, bald eagles, and pileated woodpeckers, among many other woodland creatures. ✉ *18201 SE Cougar Mountain Dr. From downtown Seattle take I–90 east; follow signs to park beyond Issaquah, Issaquah* ⊙ *Daily 8 AM–dusk.*

Cougar Mountain Zoo. It's not just named for the mountain; this really is the place to see cougars up close. You'll also find reindeer and other Northwest creatures as well as parrots, macaws, and such endangered international species as lemurs and cheetahs. You can see everything in an hour, making this a good sight for young ones. ✉ *19525 SE 54th St., Issaquah* ☎ *425/391–5508* ⊕ *www.cougarmountainzoo.org* 💲 *$8* ⊙ *Mar.–Oct., Fri.–Sun. 10–5.*

Issaquah Salmon Hatchery. Depending on what time of the year you visit the hatchery, you can see adult salmon, their eggs, or juveniles waiting to be released into the ocean. ✉ *125 W. Sunset Way, Issaquah* ☎ *425/391–9094* 💲 *Free* ⊙ *Daily 8–4:30.*

★ **Kelsey Creek Farm and Park.** With wide lawns, wood bridges curving over bubbling streams, and easy, paved walking paths through groomed gardens, this Bellevue park is a local favorite of families. Farm animals—which you can pet—roam the fields surrounding two enormous, white, Cape Dutch–style barns where smaller animals like rabbits and ducks are caged. The playground is most fun for children four and under, but big kids will get a kick out of spotting wildlife in the brooks and marshes. ✉ *SE 4th Pl., Bellevue* ☎ *425/455–7688* 💲 *Free* ⊙ *Daily 7–6.*

Lake Sammamish State Park. Eastsiders flock to this day-use park in the summer to soak up the sunshine on the sandy beach, then to cool off in the frigid lake waters. Speedboats and kayaks zip through the waves out past the swimming float; landlubbers stick to the trails behind the shore. Picnic tables are crowded on weekends—and it's best to bring your own basket rather than test the greasy concessions. ✉ *Off I–90W, Issaquah* ☎ *425/455–7010 or 800/233–0321* ⊕ *www.parks.wa.gov* 💲 *Free* ⊙ *Daily dawn–dusk.*

Lake Washington Floating Bridge. Officially titled the Lacey V. Murrow Floating Bridge, the span took 18 months to build and was the largest bridge of its kind when it opened in 1940. Stretching 3,387 feet (1¼ mi), it has 25 floating concrete pontoons—each one 14 feet high, 59 feet wide, and 350 feet long—kept in place with 65-ton anchors. Its four lanes, part of I–90, take east- and west-bound traffic from east Seattle to the north end of Mercer Island and on to Lake Washington just south of Bellevue, contributing to Mercer Island's growth. In 1989, the Evergreen Point Floating Bridge opened next to it, adding three general-purpose lanes and two carpool lanes. The following year a week of high winds and rain sunk the original bridge, which wasn't rebuilt until three years later. ✉ *I–90 from east Seattle to Mercer Island.*

★ **Marymoor Park.** This 640-acre park has the famous Marymoor Velodrome—the Pacific Northwest's sole cycling arena—a 45-foot-high climbing rock, game fields, tennis courts, a model airplane launching area, off-leash dog space, and the Pea Patch community garden. You can row on Lake Sammamish, fish off a pier, or head straight to the picnic grounds or to the Willowmoor Farm, an estate in the park. It has a Dutch-style windmill and the historic Clise Mansion, which contains the Marymoor Museum of Eastside History.

Marymoor has some of the best bird-watching in this largely urban area. It's possible to spot some 24 resident species, including great blue herons, belted kingfishers, buffleheads, short-eared and barn owls, and red-tailed hawks. Occasionally, bald eagles soar past the lakefront. The Sammamish River, which flows through the western section of the park, is an important salmon spawning stream. King County Parks naturalists periodically give guided wildlife tours. With all these attractions, it's no wonder the park has more than 1 million visitors annually—about ¼ of the state's population.

If hiking is your thing, you can get here via two regional trails. (There are several internal hiking trails as well.) The Sammamish River Trail, which connects to the Burke-Gilman Trail in Bothell, completes a 27-mi path to Seattle's Fremont neighborhood. The Bridle Crest Trail winds west for 2 mi to Bridle Trails State Park in Bellevue. The King County Park System also purchased 11 mi of former railroad right-of-way on the east shore of Lake Sammamish for the East Lake Sammamish Trail, which links Marymoor Park with Lake Sammamish State Park in Issaquah and the Mountains to Sound Greenway.

The annual Heritage Festival held here is the Eastside's premier Fourth of July event, with live music, dancing, historical exhibits, arts, crafts, and fireworks. Festivities for the Evergreen Horse Classic and WOMAD (World of Music, Arts, and Dance) are also held at the park. ⊠ 6046 *W. Lake Sammamish Pkwy. NE, Redmond* ☎ 425/296–4232 ☉ *Daily 8 AM–dusk.*

Molbak's Nursery. This gardening store is more than just a nursery, it's an institution where locals gather for coffee in a central conservatory surrounded by lush tropical plants (all of which are for sale). Unlike many other modern nurseries, Molbak's still grows its own plants instead of having them shipped in from bulk outlets, and, thus, has had an incredible impact on the local garden scene. ✛ *From downtown Seattle take I–90 east to north I–405. Take Exit 23 east (S.R. 522) to Woodinville exit* ⊠ *13625 NE 175th St., Woodinville* ☎ 425/483–5000 ⊕ *www.molbaks.com.*

☞ **Rosalie Whyel Museum of Doll Art.** Thousands of dolls span the ages and the world in this three-story museum. Displays include everything from antique porcelain models to state-of-the-art baby dolls that seem almost real. Related items such as detailed miniature houses, toys, clothing, strollers, and cribs show every aspect of a little girl's dream world—and yes, the ubiquitous Barbie is here. The gift shop stocks many unique items, but shop early or you'll compete with senior bus tour crowds picking up goodies for the grandkids. ⊠ *1116 108th Ave. NE, Bellevue* ☎ 425/455–1116 or 800/440–3655 ⊕ *www.dollart.com* ☒ *$6* ☉ *Mon.–Sat. 10–5, Sun. 1–5.*

need a break?

If you're crossing the I–90 bridge to or from Bellevue, take a beach break at Mercer Island's 77-acre **Luther Burbank Park** (⊠ 2040 84th Ave. [at SE 24th St.], Mercer Island ☎ 206/296–8687). There are beautiful views of Lake Washington from the tennis courts, picnic tables, and grassy volleyball area—and from the network of fishing and sunning piers right over the choppy waves. A slim ½-mi dirt trail leads through the lakeside forest to a sandy swimming area. The shady playground's sloping brick pyramids and tunnel mazes are perfect for little climbers; your dog can make friends in the off-leash area.

WEST SEATTLE

Cross the bridge to West Seattle and it's another world altogether. Jutting out into Elliott Bay and Puget Sound, separated from the city by the Duwamish waterway, this suburb covers most of the city's western peninsula—and, indeed, it has an identity of its own. The first white settlers parked their boat at Alki Point in 1851, planning to build a major city here until they discovered a deeper logging port at today's Pioneer Square. Alki Point Lighthouse sits on the peninsula's northwest tip, a place for classic sunset views. In summer, throngs hang out at Alki Beach—Seattle's taste of California—while others head for the trails and playgrounds of Lincoln Park to the west. The main shopping and dining areas line Alki Avenue, next to the beach, and California and Fauntleroy avenues on the way to the ferry docks.

What to See

Alki Point. Part beach and part park, threaded by biking and running paths, this is the place where David Denny, John Low, and Lee Terry arrived in September 1851, ready to found a city. They stayed here for six months before moving to what is now Pioneer Square; a marker shows where they landed. Also in the park is one of 195 Lady Liberty replicas found around the country. This one, near the 2700 block of Alki Avenue SW, was erected by Boy Scouts in 1952 as part of their national "Strengthening the Arm of Liberty" campaign. The so-called Miss Liberty (or Little Liberty) is a popular meeting point for beachfront picnics and dates. Marvel at the lustrous 50 acres of rugged old-growth forest at **Schmitz Park** (⊠ 5551 SW Admiral Way, West Seattle), steps from Alki Beach. Along the neighborhood's southwest edge, near the Fauntleroy ferry terminal, **Lincoln Park** (⊠ 5551 SW Admiral Way, West Seattle) sets acres of old forests, rocky beaches, and such recreational facilities as a playground, a pool, and tennis courts, against views of Puget Sound.

West Seattle Junction. Walk through West Seattle's business district, amid the line of small restaurants, shops, and businesses, and you'll come across works of art depicting scenes from local history. A few play tricks with perspective, reminiscent of the paintings Wile E. Coyote used in his attempts to trick the Roadrunner. *The Junction* is a perfect example: If not for the row of neatly trimmed laurel bushes just beneath the wall upon which it's painted, you might be tempted to walk right into the picture's 1918 street scene, painted from the perspective of a streetcar. Another mural is taken from a postcard of 1920s Alki. The most colorful, however, is the *The Hi-Yu Parade,* with its rendition of a *Wizard of Oz*–theme float reminding locals of a 1973 summer celebration. ⊠ *Along California Ave. SW and Fauntleroy Way SW (between 44th and 47th Aves.), West Seattle* ⊕ *www.westseattle.com/site/murals.*

off the beaten path

MUSEUM OF FLIGHT – Boeing, the world's largest builder of aircraft, was founded in Seattle in 1916. So it's not surprising that this facility at Boeing Field, south of the International District, is one of the city's best museums. It's especially fun for kids, who can climb in many of the aircraft and pretend to fly, make flight-related crafts, or attend special programs. The Red Barn, Boeing's original airplane factory, houses an exhibit on the history of flight. The Great Gallery, a dramatic structure designed by Ibsen Nelson, contains more than 20 vintage airplanes. ⊠ 9404 E. Marginal Way S (take I–5 south to Exit 158; turn right on Marginal Way S), Renton ☎ 206/764–5720 ⊕ www.museumofflight. org ⊠ $9.50 ⊙ Fri.–Wed. 10–5, Thurs. 10–9.

WHERE TO EAT

2

FODOR'S CHOICE

Cafe Juanita, *Kirkland*

Dahlia Lounge, *Downtown*

Hing Loon, *International District*

Lampreia, *Belltown*

Le Gourmand, *Phinney*

Le Pichet, *Downtown*

Marco's Supper Club, *Belltown*

Oceanaire, *Downtown*

Ray's Boathouse, *Ballard*

Restaurant Zoë, *Belltown*

Rover's, *Madison Valley*

Salumi, *Pioneer Square*

HIGHLY RECOMMENDED

Bis on Main, *Bellevue*

Brad's Swingside Cafe, *Fremont*

Brasa, *Belltown*

Earth & Ocean, *Downtown*

El Camino, *Fremont*

El Puerco Lloron, *Downtown*

Etta's Seafood, *Belltown*

Fandango, *Belltown*

Jones Barbecue, *Rainier Valley*

Monsoon, *Capitol Hill*

1200 Bistro, *Capitol Hill*

Waterfront Seafood Grill, *Belltown*

Yarrow Bay Grill, *Kirkland*

Updated by
Julie Fay

WHAT WAS ONCE A MEAT-AND-POTATOES TOWN is now a culinary capital in its own right. It started with Chinese, Japanese, and French chefs who were inspired by the quality of local produce and seafood and able to cater to an upwardly mobile clientele spawned by the region's software industry. Young American chefs soon moved in and, applying lessons learned from their foreign-born mentors, raised the quality of local cookery even higher. Seattle's culinary revolution seems never-ending. Even long-established restaurants that once depended largely on exquisite views and expense-account clients have adjusted their menus to serve the increasingly sophisticated tastes of Seattle diners.

The best restaurants in Seattle, unlike other cities, are spread throughout its neighborhoods—from Downtown and the urban renewal zone of Belltown north to Green Lake and Phinney Ridge and east Madison Valley and beyond. Several nationally famous restaurants share waterfront locations on downtown piers, the shores of Lake Union, the Ship Canal, and Shilshole Bay—along with splendid views—with fast-food eateries. Small but excellent noodle shops, and *taquerias,* which sell tacos and other light Mexican fare, are sprouting up in the Rainier Valley's ethnic neighborhoods as well as in West Seattle and areas in the south of the city.

In general, Downtown, Pike Place Market, and Pioneer Square are *the* places to do lunch. Restaurants here also serve dinner, but much of Downtown's evening action centers around hotel restaurants and a handful of places popular with the "in" crowd. Pioneer Square, on the other hand, comes alive at night with music, comedy acts, and other entertainment. Several restaurants and sports bars cater to fans attending games at Safeco Field. Restaurants and cafés (as well as shops) on Capitol Hill and in Belltown also come to life in the evening. On warm nights, the sidewalk tables of Belltown and the decks of waterfront restaurants are packed with diners.

WHAT IT COSTS				
$$$$	$$$	$$	$	¢
AT DINNER over $32	$24–$32	$16–$24	$8–$16	under $8

Prices are per person for a main course, excluding tax and tip.

IN & AROUND DOWNTOWN

Downtown

American

$$–$$$$ ✕ **13 Coins.** In Seattle's forward-looking food scene, this is the land that time forgot, circa 1967. Open 24 hours a day, 13 Coins is a longtime favorite of Seattle's nighthawk population. Menu benchmarks include liver and onions, jumbo shrimp on ice, and platters of steak and pasta big enough to stuff a logger. The rich breakfasts include such dinosaurs as Italian-sausage frittatas and eggs Benedict. Seafood dishes aren't quite up to Seattle's high standards, but the steamed clams and the baked king salmon fillet are decent. For dessert, the New York–style cheesecake comes with an "endless" cup of coffee. ⊠ *1125 Boren Ave. N, Downtown* ☎ *206/682–2513* ⌁ *Reservations not accepted* ▭ *AE, D, MC, V.*

¢–$$ ✕ **Athenian Inn.** The Athenian is a quintessential old-time Pike Place Market restaurant, with a wall-to-wall window view of Puget Sound and rather standard (but well-prepared) food ranging from seafood appetizers to grilled steaks. Breakfast is served all day. This place has survived just about every culinary fad in the past and will probably do so well into the 22nd century. The bar is stocked with more than 300 imported wines, as well as spirits. ⊠ *1517 Pike Pl., Downtown* ☎ *206/624–7166* ⊟ *AE, D, MC, V* ⏱ *Closed Sun.*

Contemporary

$$–$$$
Fodor'sChoice
★

✕ **Dahlia Lounge.** Romantic Dahlia—with dimly lit valentine-red walls—worked its magic on Tom Hanks and Meg Ryan in *Sleepless in Seattle*. It's cozy and then some, but the food plays its part, too. Crab cakes, served as an entrée or an appetizer, lead an ever-changing regionally oriented menu. Other standouts are seared ahi tuna, near-perfect gnocchi, and such desserts as coconut-cream pie and fresh fruit cobblers. Seattle's most energetic restaurateur, chef-owner Tom Douglas also owns Etta's Seafood in Pike Place Market, and the excellent Palace Kitchen on Fifth Avenue. But Dahlia is the one that makes your heart go pitter-pat. ⊠ *2001 4th Ave., Downtown* ☎ *206/682–4142* ⚲ *Reservations essential* ⊟ *AE, D, DC, MC, V* ⏱ *No lunch weekends.*

$$–$$$

✕ **Place Pigalle.** Large windows look out on Elliott Bay in this cozy spot tucked behind a meat vendor in Pike Place Market's main arcade. In nice weather, open windows let in the fresh salt breeze. Flowers brighten each table, and the staff is warm and welcoming. Despite its name, this is a very American restaurant. Go for the rich oyster stew, the Dungeness crab (in season), or the fish of the day. Local microbrews are usually on tap, and the wine list is thoughtfully compact. ⊠ *81 Pike Place Market, Downtown* ☎ *206/624–1756* ⊟ *AE, MC, V* ⏱ *Closed Sun.*

★ $$

✕ **Earth & Ocean.** Rarely are both the chef and the pastry chef as noteworthy as they are here. Chef Johnathan Sundstrom hits a homerun with his shepherd's pie, a scrumptious oxtail and foraged mushroom stew with a mashed potato crust. Also routinely offered are two tasting menus, the meatless "Grower's Menu" and the "Menu Sauvage." Pastry chef Sue McCown's desserts are a wonder of whimsy and yum. In Sue's world, a pair of shortbread ladies' legs kick out of a banana dessert served in a martini stem, and warm chocolate oozes out of cake served with a hot fudge dipping sauce in her beloved creation, www.chocolate.com. ⊠ *W Hotel, 1112 4th Ave., Downtown* ☎ *206/264–6060* ⚲ *Reservations essential* ⊟ *AE, DC, MC, V* ⏱ *Closed Sun. No lunch.*

$–$$

✕ **Library Bistro.** The Alexis Hotel's dining room is a warm and beckoning place to settle in for cocktails or a meal. As the name suggests, the place is filled with books. The high-backed booths and comfy couches invite diners to meet and linger. Veteran chef Matt Costello (Dahlia Lounge, Etta's) has created a casual bistro menu with down-to-earth pricing. Look for the pumpkin ravioli in brown butter, crispy fried chicken wings with cilantro dipping sauce, and braised short ribs with sweet potato hash. The congenial wine director, David LeClaire, is an excellent resource for navigating the impressive collection of Northwest wines. ⊠ *Alexis Hotel, 1007 1st Ave., Downtown* ☎ *206/624–3646* ⚲ *Reservations essential* ⊟ *AE, D, DC, MC, V* ⏱ *No lunch weekends or dinner on Sunday.*

$–$$

✕ **Sazerac.** The spunky restaurant at the Hotel Monaco gleefully thumbs its nose at the traveler's fallback: the hotel dining room. "Big dawg" Jan Birnbaum presides over a whimsical (if not downright goofy) patchwork of Northwest and American favorites with quirky southern accents. The cedar-plank smoked salmon sits comfortably alongside collard greens; the braised pork shoulder gets "apple-cider luv sauce" and "soft sexy grits." A lively bar (with late-night service) and an indulgent dessert list—proffering such delights as peach grunt (similar to cobbler, but loaded

2

Mealtimes
Many of Seattle's better restaurants serve only dinner and are closed on Sunday; many that serve lunch during the week do not do so on weekends. Unless otherwise noted, the restaurants listed are open daily for lunch and dinner. Downtown Seattle restaurants generally serve food until 10 PM on weekdays and later on Friday and Saturday. Outside the city, restaurants stop serving around 9 PM.

Reservations
Seattleites dine out often, so reservations are always a good idea. Reviews note only where they are essential or not accepted. Reservations can often be made a day in advance, but you might have to make them several weeks ahead at the most popular restaurants. If you've just arrived in town and heard about a popular restaurant, it doesn't hurt to call. Seattle's maître d's are very accommodating to out-of-towners and might be willing to you fit in on short notice. Book as far ahead as you can, and reconfirm as soon as you arrive.

Smoking
Smoking in restaurants and bars is legal in Washington State. Whether or not it's allowed in particular establishments is at the discretion of the owner.

Tipping
Most Seattleites tip 15%–20%. You should leave 25% if the service was outstanding, or the server or kitchen fulfilled special requests.

What to Wear
In the last decade, Seattle dining has become very informal. It used to be that restaurants requiring jackets and ties always kept some in reserve for customers who arrived without them—but that's no longer the case. There's some indication that tastes might be changing once again, and that service, if not dress, is becoming more formal. To be on the safe side, in nicer restaurants women should wear dressy slacks or a casual dress to dinner; although it's rarely required, men can't go wrong with a sports coat or blazer. We mention dress only when men are required to wear a jacket or a jacket and tie.

Wine, Beer & Spirits
The liquor laws in the State of Washington are stringent. Spirits are sold only in state-run liquor stores, and liquor stores are closed on Sunday. Cocktails are only sold in restaurants that serve a full menu. The laws are less strict regarding wine and beer, which can be readily found in grocery and convenience stores. Taverns that don't serve food are permitted to serve beer and wine.

---

with peaches) and chocolate cake—round out the fun. ✉ *1101 4th Ave., Downtown* ☎ *206/624–7755* ▭ *AE, D, DC, MC, V.*

Delicatessen

¢–$ ✕ **Roxy's Diner.** This kosher deli/diner does a great job with such traditional fare as chicken noodle and chicken matzo-ball soup, blintzes, knishes, latkes, and sandwiches. The latter include kosher hot dogs, pastrami, corned beef, chopped chicken liver, and kippered salmon. For dessert, try the *rugalach* (cookies filled with fruit, nuts, and jam). The place has been known to make New Yorkers homesick. Breakfast is served

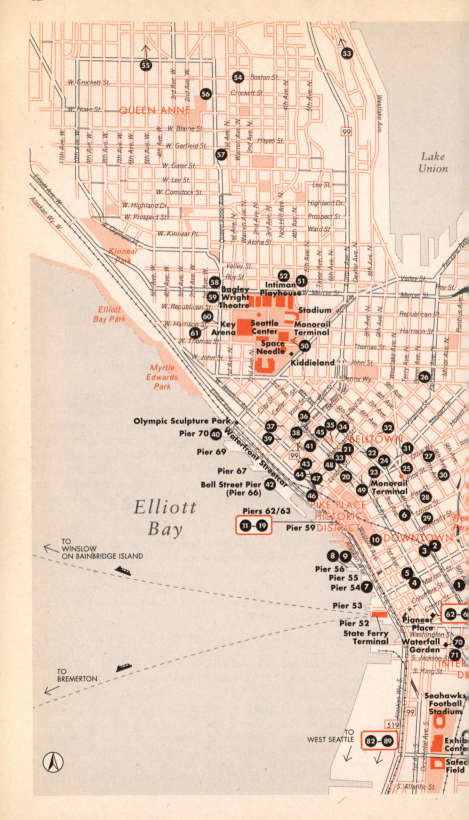

Where to Eat In & Around Downtown

on the weekends. ⊠ *1329 1st Ave., Downtown* ☎ *206/381–8800* 🍴 *Reservations not accepted* ▭ *AE, D, MC, V* ☉ *No dinner.*

Eclectic

$$–$$$ ✕ **Andaluca.** This secluded spot downstairs at the Mayflower Park Hotel offers a synthesis of fresh local ingredients and Mediterranean flavors. Small plates can act as starters or be combined for a satisfying meal. A Dungeness crab tower with avocado, hearts of palm, and gazpacho salsa is cool and light, while the beef tenderloin with pears and blue cheese is a glorious trip to the opposite end of the sensory spectrum. ⊠ *407 Olive Way, Downtown* ☎ *206/382–6999* ▭ *AE, D, DC, MC, V.*

¢–$$ ✕ **Fare Start.** The homeless men and women who operate this café, a project of the FareStart job-training program, prepare an American-style lunch of sandwiches, burgers, and fries during the week. Reservations are essential for the $17 Thursday dinner, prepared by a guest chef from a restaurant such as Ray's Boathouse or the Metropolitan Grill. The cuisine changes with the chef. Whenever you go, you're assured a great meal for a great cause and a real taste of Seattle's community spirit. ⊠ *1902 2nd Ave., Downtown* ☎ *206/443–1233* ▭ *D, MC, V* ☉ *No lunch weekends. No dinner Fri.–Wed.*

French

$$–$$$$ ✕ **Campagne.** The white walls, picture windows, snowy linens, fresh flowers, and candles at this urbane restaurant overlooking Pike Place Market and Elliott Bay evoke Provence. So does the robust French country fare, with starters such as seafood sausage, and calamari fillets with ground almonds. Main plates include panfried scallops with a green-peppercorn and tarragon sauce, cinnamon-roasted quail served with carrot and orange essence, and Oregon rabbit with an apricot-cider and green-peppercorn sauce. Campagne is open only for dinner, but the adjacent Café Campagne serves breakfast, lunch, and dinner daily. ⊠ *Inn at the Market, 86 Pine St., Downtown* ☎ *206/728–2800* 🍴 *Reservations essential* ▭ *AE, DC, MC, V* ☉ *No lunch.*

$$–$$$ ✕ **Brasserie Margaux.** The Warwick Hotel, on Downtown's northern fringe, is a longtime favorite of visiting stars, but until now it had no restaurant to match the quality of its rooms. That changed when Brasserie Margaux replaced the long-struggling Liaison restaurant. Stephen Desgaches, a bright young French chef, works magic with such tasty fare as salmon carpaccio with pink peppercorns, avocado, and shrimp; marinated tuna; and mussels steamed in a tomato broth laced with anise liqueur. ⊠ *401 Lenora St., Downtown* ☎ *206/777–1990* 🍴 *Reservations essential* ▭ *AE, DC, MC, V* ☉ *No lunch weekends.*

$$–$$$ ✕ **Le Pichet.** Slate tabletops, tile floor, and rolled-zinc bar transport you out of Downtown Seattle and into Paris, 1934. Blackboards spell out the specials. Wines are served from the earthenware *pichets* that inspired the brasserie's name. The menu is heartbreakingly French: at lunch there are rustic pâtés and *jambon et fromage* (ham and cheese) sandwiches on crusty baguettes; dinner sees homemade sausages, daily fish specials, and steak tartare. The roast chicken (for two) takes an hour to prepare and is worth every second you'll wait. It's enough to make you think the French invented soul food. Dinner reservations are essential. ⊠ *1933 1st Ave., Downtown* ☎ *206/256–1499* ▭ *MC, V.*

Fodor's Choice
★

$$–$$$ ✕ **Maximilien.** Despite its great views of the Sound and the Olympics, Maximilien remains a well-kept secret. That's because it's tucked away in Pike Place Market behind Market Spice and a butcher shop, and it's not easy to find unless you know the way. Persevere; you'll be delighted. Under previous owner François Kissel, Maximilien was one of Julia Child's favorite Seattle restaurants. Nothing much has changed under the current owner (and former employee) Axel Macé: the bistro-style food is

still very good, and the mood is still very French. ⊠ *1333 5th Ave., Downtown* ☎ *206/682–7270* ⊟ *AE, D, DC, MC, V* ☯ *Closed Sun.*

$ ✕ **Crepe de Paris.** Seattle's oldest French restaurant is still going strong, perhaps because it has bucked the trends, and serves up good, old-fashioned French fare. It has all the accoutrements to keep the Downtown crowd and visiting businesspeople happy: a full bar, happy hour, and, in warm weather, seating on the open-air terrace. In the evening, there's cabaret entertainment as well. ⊠ *1333 5th Ave., Downtown* ☎ *206/623–4111* ⊟ *AE, D, DC, MC, V* ☯ *Closed Sun.*

Irish

$–$$ ✕ **Kells.** Tucked into a quiet spot along Pike Place Market's Post Alley, this bustling restaurant-pub has been Seattle's favorite Irish hangout for more than a decade. The beer selection leans heavily on Irish brews, but the dinner menu offers both Irish and Northwest favorites, from Irish stew to seafood pastas. It's open every day of the week from 11:30 AM to 2 AM. ⊠ *1919 Post Alley, Downtown* ☎ *206/728–1916* ⊟ *AE, MC, V.*

Italian

$–$$ ✕ **Pink Door.** With its Post Alley entrance and meager signage, many enjoy the Pink Door's speak-easiness almost as much as the savory Italian food. In warm months patrons partake on the deck shaded by a grape arbor while enjoying the stunning view of Elliott Bay. The roasted garlic and tapenade are eminently sharable appetizers; spaghetti *alla puttanesca* (with anchovies, capers, and tomatoes), and cioppino are standout entrées. The whimsical bar is often crowded, the staff is saucy and irreverent, and cabaret acts regularly perform on a small corner stage. There's no place quite like it. ⊠ *1919 Post Alley, Downtown* ☎ *206/443–3241* ⊟ *AE, MC, V* ☯ *Closed Sun. and Mon.*

¢–$$ ✕ **Il Fornaio.** This Italian restaurant dominates the Pacific Place Mall that houses it. When shopping, there seems to be an opportunity to give them your custom at every turn. There's a casual café on the street level, then an even more casual espresso counter on the mall's first level, and finally the elegant full-service dining room. Though the fresh breads and wood-fired pizzas are widely acclaimed, the entire menu has much to offer. Noteworthy are the seasonal antipasti, vegetarian minestrone, handmade ravioli stuffed with Swiss chard, and the rosemary-scented rotisserie chicken. ⊠ *600 Pine St. Downtown* ☎ *206/264–0994* ⊟ *AE, DC, MC, V.*

Latin

$ ✕ **Copacabana.** Much of the strategy that preserved Pike Place Market in the 1960s was hatched at this small Bolivian café. The food served here includes such tasty fare as spicy shrimp soup, *saltenas* (savory meat-and-vegetable pies), paella, and *pescado á la Español* (halibut in a saffron-tomato-onion sauce). Tasty food, cold beer, and great views are good reasons to linger. ⊠ *1520 1st Ave., Downtown* ☎ *206/622–6359* ⊟ *AE, D, MC, V* 🍴 *Reservations not accepted* ☯ *No dinner Sun. in summer.*

Mexican

★ ¢–$ ✕ **El Puerco Lloron.** This funky, cafeteria-style diner has some open-air terrace seating on the Pike Place Market Hillclimb, offering views of Elliott Bay on sunny days. It's also got some of Seattle's best and most authentic Mexican cooking—simple, tasty, and inexpensive. Even Mexican natives swear by it. More ambitious highlights include perfect *chiles rellenos* (mild green peppers that are breaded, stuffed with cheese, and fried) and a particularly flavorful guacamole. ⊠ *501 Western Ave., Downtown* ☎ *206/624–0541* ⊟ *AE, MC, V.*

Pan-Asian

$$–$$$$ ✗ **Dragonfish.** From the pachinko machines around the bar to the colorful origami and rattan fans on the ceiling, kid-friendly Dragonfish is a festive, freewheeling place that takes advantage of Seattleites' yen for Pan-Asian cuisine. The seafood and noodle specialties are worth investigating, but the small plates from the grill are the real stars on the flashy menu. Try the Korean *bulgogi,* skirt steak marinated in tangy soy, ginger, and *mirin* (a sweet rice wine), or the chicken wings in a caramel-ginger sauce. Accompany your meal with a lime-leaf and lemongrass "limontini." ⊠ *722 Pine St., Downtown* ☎ *206/467–7777* ▭ *AE, D, DC, MC, V.*

$–$$$ ✗ **Wild Ginger.** The seafood and Southeast Asian fare at this restaurant ranges from mild Cantonese to spicier Vietnamese, Thai, and Korean dishes. Specialties include *satay* (skewered and grilled chunks of beef, chicken, or vegetables with a spicy peanut sauce). In fact, the satay bar, where you can sip local brews and eat skewered tidbits until 2 AM, is a neighborhood hangout. The clubby dining room has high ceilings and lots of mahogany and Asian art. You might want to try the live crab cooked to order, sweetly flavored duck, wonderful soups, or one of the fine vegetarian options. ⊠ *1401 3rd Ave., Downtown* ☎ *206/623–4450* ▭ *AE, D, DC, MC, V* ☽ *No lunch Sun.*

Seafood

$$–$$$$ ✗ **Elliott's Oyster House.** No place in Seattle serves better Dungeness crab or oysters than Elliott's, which has gotten the presentation of fresh seafood down to a fine art. You can't go wrong with the local rockfish or salmon. The dining room is bright, and there's a great view of Elliott Bay and of the harbor tour boats next door. On sunny days the place is packed with diners from all over the country who have come to learn what Seattle is all about. They've probably picked the right place. ⊠ *Pier 56, off Alaskan Way, Downtown* ☎ *206/623–4340* ▭ *AE, DC, MC, V.*

$$–$$$$ ✗ **Steamers.** This friendly restaurant serves fish-and-chips, freshly steamed clams, and other local seafood favorites in a casual setting a cut above fast-food take-out. The flame-broiled burgers are tasty, too. On sunny days you can sit outside on the dock and have your steamers and beer alfresco. ⊠ *Pier 56, off Alaskan Way, Downtown* ☎ *206/623–2066* ⚞ *Reservations not accepted* ▭ *D, MC, V.*

$–$$$ ✗ **Ivar's Acres of Clams.** A big restaurant on an old waterfront shipping pier, with windows overlooking Elliott Bay, this old Seattle favorite has held its own against the influx of bright new restaurants throughout the years. Look for seasonal dinners as well as local standbys such as fish-and-chips and Atlantic salmon. ⊠ *Pier 54, Downtown* ☎ *206/624–6852* ▭ *AE, MC, V.*

$–$$$ ✗ **Oceanaire.** For years Seattle restaurateurs have been trying to create
Fodor'sChoice the quintessential seafood restaurant, and wouldn't you know, a pair
★ of midwestern businessmen have managed to pull it off. The stylish room is reminiscent of a 1930s supperclub, with plush booths and a circular oyster bar. Chef Kevin Davis has created a superbly fun retro menu complete with clams casino, oysters Rockefeller, up to 25 varieties of the freshest seafood, and a circa 1920s green goddess salad dressing. When is the last time you saw baked Alaska on a menu? Portions are huge, so plan to share. ⊠ *1700 7th Ave., Downtown* ☎ *206/267–2277* ▭ *AE, D, DC, MC, V* ☽ *No lunch weekends.*

$–$$ ✗ **McCormick's Fish House.** Happy hours at this clubby restaurant are popular with the after-work crowd; prices are good, and the bar menu has a good selection of dishes—burgers, spring rolls, taquitas, oysters, and more. The dining room specializes in typical steak and seafood fare. The raw bar here has largest selection of oysters in town. There's open-air dining in front. ✉ *722 4th Ave., Downtown* ☎ *206/682–3900* ⏱ *No lunch weekends* 🖃 *AE, D, DC, MC, V.*

¢ ✕ **Emmett Watson's Oyster Bar.** This unpretentious spot can be hard to find—it's in the back of Pike Place Market's Soames-Dunn Building, facing a small flower-bedecked courtyard. But for those who know their oysters, finding this place is worth the effort. Not only are the oysters very fresh and the beer icy cold, but both are inexpensive and available in any number of varieties. If you don't like oysters, try the salmon soup or the fish-and-chips—flaky pieces of fish with very little grease. ✉ *1916 Pike Pl., Downtown* ☎ *206/448–7721* ⌦ *Reservations not accepted* 🖃 *No credit cards* ⏱ *No dinner Sun.*

Steak

$$$$ ✕ **Morton's of Chicago.** This outlet of the famous Chicago steak emporium has taken Seattle by storm. The menu's high points are lamb and veal chops and prime midwestern steaks, but the seafood dishes are also very popular. Hardly anyone seems to mind that the prices are a bit steep, or that the dining room is two flights of steps below street level. The place always seems packed to capacity. Which means that you really should have a confirmed reservation before stepping out. ✉ *1511 6th Ave., Downtown* ☎ *206/223–0550* 🖃 *AE, MC, V* ⏱ *No lunch weekends.*

$$–$$$$ ✕ **Metropolitan Grill.** This favorite lunch spot of the white-collar crowd is not for timid eaters: custom-aged mesquite-broiled steaks—arguably the best in Seattle—are huge and come with baked potatoes or pasta. Even the veal chop is extra thick. Lamb, chicken, and seafood entrées are also on the menu. Onion rings and sautéed mushrooms are popular accompaniments. Among its many virtues, the Met Grill does one dish better than anyone else in Seattle: the exceptionally flavorful hamburger is about as delicious as grilled meat can get. ✉ *818 2nd Ave., Downtown* ☎ *206/624–3287* 🖃 *AE, D, DC, MC, V* ⏱ *No lunch weekends.*

Belltown

American

$–$$ ✕ **Frontier Room.** A bold 2002 makeover transformed this longtime Seattle resident from skid-row seedy to cowboy kitsch. The cowhide booths in the bar and original tongue-and-groove paneling discovered during the remodel set the proper carnivorous mood. Oysters Frontier (from the appetizer menu) brings together broiled oysters, arugula, and a punchy, bisque-like sauce with all the subtlety of a monster truck show. Barbecue offerings get an A for effort by focusing on the meat and the smoke, not the sauce. The St. Louis Ribs are flavorful, if a bit dry; the moist, tender pulled pork is better. It's very crowded on weekend nights. ✉ *2203 1st Ave., Belltown* ☎ *206/956–7427* 🖃 *AE, D, MC, V* ⏱ *Closed Sun. and Mon.*

Contemporary

$$$$ ✕ **Lampreia.** The beige-and-gold interior of this Belltown restaurant is the perfect backdrop for chef-owner Scott Carsberg's sophisticated cuisine. After an appetizer of cream of polenta soup with shiitake mushrooms, try one of the seasonal menu's second courses—perhaps squid-and-salmon-filled cannelloni—before moving on to a main course of pheasant with apple-champagne sauerkraut or lamb with pesto and whipped potatoes. The clear flavors of such desserts as lemon mousse with strawberry sauce are a soothing conclusion to an exciting experience. ✉ *2400 1st Ave., Belltown* ☎ *206/443–3301* ⌦ *Reservations essential* 🖃 *AE, MC, V* ⏱ *Closed Sun.–Mon. No lunch.*

FodorsChoice ★

$$$–$$$$ ✕ **El Gaucho.** Dress to impress here—you don't want to be outclassed by the waistcoated waitstaff that coolly navigates the packed floor of

this retro steak house. El Gaucho serves some of the city's most basic, most satisfying fare in a swanky, expansive room. For the complete show, order the items prepared table-side. From the flaming lamb shish kebab to the cool Caesar salad (possibly the city's best), the virtuoso presentation seems to make everything taste better. Ritzy yet comfortable, El Gaucho makes you relax no matter how stressful your day. ⊠ *2505 1st Ave., Belltown* ☎ *206/728–1337* ⌖ *Reservations essential* ▭ *AE, MC, V* ⊗ *No lunch.*

\$\$–\$\$\$ ✕ **Cascadia.** Water flows over the "rain window," a 9-foot-long panel of glass, etched with a design of the Cascade mountain range, that separates the kitchen and the cherry-wood-paneled dining room at this elegant restaurant. Chef Kerry Sears uses fresh regional produce, seafood, meat, and game to create memorable meals, which might include smoked Oregon Muscovy duck with pears and creamed collard greens, marinated sea bass with roasted potatoes and caviar dressing, or crab steak with chanterelles. Seven-course tasting menus (\$55–\$90) showcase the Northwest's culinary best. ⊠ *2328 1st Ave., Belltown* ☎ *206/ 448–8884* ⌖ *Reservations essential* ▭ *AE, DC, MC, V* ⊗ *Closed Sun. No lunch.*

\$\$
FodorśChoice
★
✕ **Restaurant Zoë.** Reservations are sought after at this chic eatery on a high-trafficked Belltown corner. Its tall windows, lively bar scene, and charming waitstaff add to the popularity, which comes mainly from its inspired kitchen. The considerable talents of chef-owner Scott Staples can be seen in his house-smoked hanger steak served with mashed potatoes, parsnips, and veal jus and his pan-seared sea scallops served over asparagus herb risotto with smoked bacon and blood-orange vinaigrette. Ease into your meal with an adventurous and expertly executed appetizer, remaining mindful of the house-made desserts that await you. ⊠ *2137 2nd Ave., Belltown* ☎ *206/256–2060* ▭ *AE, D, MC, V* ⊗ *No lunch.*

\$–\$\$ ✕ **Flying Fish.** This joint is jumping, some might even think it noisy, but rest assured, there's nothing noisy about the food. It is sublime. Chef Christine Keff is a genius in the kitchen, and consistently produces innovative, high-quality dishes. Keff was among the first to introduce Seattleites to the joys of shared plates, and it's a pleasure—and sometimes torture—to see servers walk by with large platters heaped high with steaming clams or mussels, spicy crab cakes, or whole Dungeness crab, fried oysters, crisp-fried calamari, or whole steamed rockfish. Her fish tacos are delicious, as is her no-nonsense fried chicken. ⊠ *2234 1st Ave., Belltown* ☎ *206/728–8595* ▭ *AE, D, MC, V* ⊗ *No lunch.*

Eclectic

\$–\$\$\$ ✕ **Palace Kitchen.** The star of this chic yet convivial Tom Douglas eatery (he's also responsible for Dahlia Lounge and Etta's) may be the 45-foot bar, but the real show takes place in the giant open kitchen at the back. Sausages, sweet-pea ravioli, salmon carpaccio, and a nightly selection of exotic cheeses vie for your attention on the ever-changing menu of small plates. There are also always a few entrées, 10 fantastic desserts, and a rotisserie special from the apple-wood grill. ⊠ *2030 5th Ave., Belltown* ☎ *206/448–2001* ▭ *AE, D, DC, MC, V* ⊗ *No lunch.*

\$–\$\$
FodorśChoice
★
✕ **Marco's Supper Club.** Multiregional cuisine is the specialty of this casual, family-owned restaurant with shrimp-color walls and mismatched flatware. Marco's loyal, steady following is a testament to how good the cooking here is. Start with the fried sage-leaf appetizer with chipotle-garlic aioli and tomatillo salsa, then move on to sesame-crusted ahi tuna, Jamaican jerk chicken, or a pork porterhouse in an almond mole sauce. ⊠ *2510 1st Ave., Belltown* ☎ *206/441–7801* ▭ *AE, MC, V* ⊗ *No lunch weekends.*

Italian

$–$$ ✕ **Belltown Billiards.** Good food is the draw at this popular lunch spot, after-work rendezvous, and upscale night-owl perch. Lunch is mostly soups, salads, simple pasta dishes, and hearty specials like the herb-coated New York steak with linguine marinara. Lighter appetites will enjoy the fish of the day or the bruschetta with soup and salad. For dinner, pastas range from a simple linguine *aglio olio* (with garlic, oregano, and crushed red peppers) to a more adventurous penne *carrittira* (with shiitake mushrooms and red pepper flakes in a vodka-tomato cream sauce). Panini and other sandwiches are served into the early-morning hours. ⊠ *190 Blanchard St. (underneath the Queen City Grill), Belltown* ☎ *206/448–6779* 🖷 *206/441–9513* ▭ *AE, MC, V* ☉ *Closed Sun.–Mon.*

Japanese

$$–$$$$ ✕ **Nikko.** The ultrachic sushi bar is the architectural centerpiece at sophisticated Nikko in the Westin Hotel, where chefs prepare some of the best sushi and sashimi in Seattle. On the regular menu, the Kasu sake–marinated cod and the teriyaki salmon are consistent winners. Try to get here early to grab a private tatami room or a booth, and be prepared to splurge. ⊠ *Westin Hotel, 1900 5th Ave., Belltown* ☎ *206/322–4641* ▭ *AE, D, DC, MC, V* ☉ *Closed Sun. No lunch Sat.*

$$–$$$ ✕ **Saito's Japanese Café and Bar.** Fusion won't fly at this Belltown restaurant, sushi bar, and lounge. Traditional appetizers include *kaarage* (marinated, breaded, and deep-fried chicken), *gyoza* (steamed pork dumplings), and *kakifry* (panfried oysters). Chef Yutaka Saito drapes elegant, enormous slices of the freshest fish over pillows of rice in his exquisite nigiri sushi. Aside from the gorgeous sushi and sashimi, consider the *unajyu* (broiled freshwater eel with a tangy sweet sauce), *salmon misozuke* (brushed with red miso, baked slowly, and served with caramelized turnips), and *tonkatsu* (breaded and fried pork cutlet). The full bar stocks more than 30 different sakes. ⊠ *2122 2nd Ave., Belltown* ☎ *206/728–1333* ▭ *AE, D, DC, MC, V* ☉ *Closed Sun. No lunch Sat.*

$$–$$$ ✕ **Shiro's.** Willfully unconcerned with atmosphere, this simple spot is a real curiosity amid Belltown's chic establishments. The focus is entirely on the exceptional menu of authentic Japanese fare. Indulge your curiosity with the more exotic offerings. Seaweed becomes a haute cuisine dish at this formal but friendly café, and a sure hand guides the sushi bar. ⊠ *2401 2nd Ave., Belltown* ☎ *206/443–9844* ▭ *AE, MC, V* ☉ *Closed Sun.*

Latin

★ **$–$$** ✕ **Fandango.** Fandango is so much fun it should be called "*fun*dango," and so Latin it seems sunny even on a drizzly Seattle day. Aside from the quality of food made by owner-chef Christine Keff, Fandango might owe some of its popularity to its silent partners—Edgar Martinez, one of the Seattle Mariners' hottest players, and Dave Valle, a TV baseball commentator and former Mariners catcher. Specialties include Tarascan bean-and-tomato soup; creamy walnut-and-chipotle soup; crisply fried squid; Brazilian seafood stew; and suckling pig with zucchini, poblano chiles, and onions. The bar, a favorite late-night hangout, has an enticing menu, plus 50 different tequilas. ⊠ *2313 1st Ave., Belltown* ☎ *206/441–1188* ▭ *DC, MC, V* ☉ *No lunch.*

Mediterranean

★ **$$–$$$** ✕ **Brasa.** When famous Seattle chefs set out to open their own restaurants, the results are often even more spectacular than they were in the places they left behind. That's certainly true for Brasa, which has become a Seattle favorite since Tamara Murphy, formerly of Campagne, opened its Belltown doors. Locals go for such delectable dishes as Spanish fried squid, squid-ink risotto, braised short ribs with a red-wine glaze, and polenta cake. More traditional but equally toothsome and carefully prepared are the beef tenderloin and monkfish. ✉ *2107 3rd Ave., Belltown* ☎ *206/728–4220* ⚚ *Reservations essential* ▭ *AE, DC, MC, V* ✆ *No lunch.*

Pan-Asian

$ ✗ **Noodle Ranch.** Tongue planted firmly in cheek, Noodle Ranch bills itself as Belltown's purveyor of "Pan-Asian vittles." Standouts on chef Nga Bui's inexpensive menu include sugar-cane shrimp, Japanese eggplant in ginger, and a spicy basil stir-fry. The gentle sense of humor evident in the restaurant's name carries over to the dressed-down design scheme. ✉ *2228 2nd Ave., Belltown* ☎ *206/728–0463* ▭ *AE, MC, V* ✆ *Closed Sun.*

Seafood

$$–$$$$ ✗ **Anthony's Pier 66.** The straightforward preparations allow the seafood to speak for itself. The menu includes many items found elsewhere: raw oysters, steamed clams, mussels, and Dungeness crab, as well as the usual Northwest fish: halibut, rockfish, lingcod, and petrale sole. Everything is very good and very tasty and, in the true Northwest tradition, not at all pretentious. Best of all, the views are truly outstanding. ✉ *2201 Alaskan Way (Bell St./Pier 66), Belltown* ☎ *206/448–6688* ▭ *AE, D, MC, V.*

★ $$–$$$$ ✗ **Waterfront Seafood Grill.** With its spectacular view, impeccable service, and inventively prepared seafood, Waterfront has all of the fine-dining bases covered. You can catch the sunset from the spacious bar, where cocktails and appetizers such as the salt-and-pepper prawns with lime vinaigrette and tuna tempura are served. The menu's largely Asian-influenced entrées might include sesame-seared sea bass with baby bok choy and coconut jasmine rice, or lobster risotto with butternut squash and snow peas. Although seafood is the focal point, the menu always includes a vegetarian dish as well as many meat dishes, such as rack of lamb with honey lavender demi-glace. ✉ *Pier 70, 2801 Alaskan Way, Belltown* ☎ *206/956–9171* ▭ *AE, DC, MC, V* ✆ *No lunch.*

$–$$$ ✗ **Queen City Grill.** North of Pike Place Market, the Queen City Grill made this area fashionable long before the ritzy condos and swell boutiques moved into adjacent Belltown. Best of all, its seafood menu is now better than ever. The kitchen has the perfect touch for fresh shellfish and fish, from Dungeness crab to ahi tuna; the vast wine list is locally famous. Queen City's philosophy is simple and very Northwest: to serve the freshest possible seafood, simply grilled, and prepared to enhance natural flavors. ✉ *2201 1st Ave., Belltown* ☎ *206/443–0975* ▭ *AE, D, DC MC, V* ✆ *No lunch weekends.*

$$ ✗ **Fish Club.** Zoning laws prohibit the kind of signage that a "seafood-centric" restaurant this good deserves. In the Marriott Waterfront Hotel looking across Alaskan Way at Elliott Bay, the Fish Club is the creation of celebrity chef Todd English. The food is sublime and the presentation is distinctive. Boulliabaise comes served in an earthenware crock, the shrimp cocktail (with a powerful Bloody Mary/horseradish sauce), on a bed of crushed ice, and the bacon-wrapped tenderloin sits in a moat of demi-glace in a deep soup plate. Valet parking is complimentary. ✉ *2100 Alaskan Way, Belltown* ☎ *206/256–1040* ▭ *AE, DC, MC, V.*

★ $–$$ ✗ **Etta's Seafood.** Tom Douglas's restaurant near Pike Place Market has a sleek and slightly whimsical design and views of Victor Steinbrueck Park. Try the Dungeness crab cakes in season or the various Washington oysters on the half shell. Brunch, served on weekends, always includes zesty seafood omelets, but the chef also does justice to French toast, eggs and bacon, and Mexican-influenced breakfast dishes. ✉ *2020 Western Ave., Belltown* ☎ *206/443–6000* ▭ *AE, D, DC, MC, V.*

ON THE MENU

SEATTLE IS A FOOD CITY, with easy access to an incredible bounty of foods from land and sea, both wild and farm-raised. Many Seattleites tend kitchen gardens, hunt and fish, trap crabs, dig clams, harvest berries in season, and cross the mountains to pick fruit in the Wenatchee and Yakima valleys. Gathering fresh foods at the source has honed local palates: Seattleites know—by taste, smell, and touch—when foods are fresh and at their peak.

Wild salmon has played an important role in local cookery, but its importance has diminished due to a decades-long decline in stocks. Still plentiful are halibut, rockfish, Dungeness crab, spot prawns, and geoduck clams as well as blackberries, huckleberries, mushrooms, and wild greens.

Seattle's chefs purchase ingredients whenever possible from regional farms, orchards, and dairies. Asparagus, tomatoes, and hot peppers arrive from the Yakima Valley; mild onions from Walla Walla; apricots and pears from Wenatchee; apples from Lake Chelan. Lamb and beef come from dryland pastures, while clams and oysters are harvested from tidal flats in Samish Bay, the Hood Canal, and Willapa Bay. Even salmon is now farmed, and thus available year-round. Pike Place Market, a local institution since 1907, is another source of high-quality ingredients.

Because Seattle is a multiethnic city, local cooks and chefs have evolved several cooking styles. Preparations can be very plain, such as razor clams dipped in milk, egg, and cracker crumbs and panfried, or complex, like meat and seafood dishes enhanced by fruit sauces in the Sephardic tradition. Local chefs' obsessions with the freshest seasonal ingredients may make it difficult to get the same dish twice— especially at top-notch restaurants, where menus change seasonally, if not daily.

Perhaps the most important tenet of Northwest cuisine is that foods be enhanced without masking their natural flavors. That has spawned all manner of innovation. At Rover's (considered by many to be the city's finest restaurant), Dungeness crab cakes might be accompanied by beets marinated in a rare old balsamic vinegar, whereas a neighborhood café might proffer diner-style Dungeness crab and cheddar-cheese melts served with french fries or potato salad. You can always count on finding plain, cooked Dungeness crab accompanied by melted butter and lots of oven-fresh bread.

Preparations of other local seafood favorites—including mussels, shrimp, scallops, and calamari—show similar creativity from restaurant to restaurant. And the same holds true for fowl, including Washington state chicken, Muscovy duck, squab, and such meats as rabbit, lamb, and New York steak.

Comfort food has its niche here, too, with yummy clam chowder, buttermilk-batter fried chicken with mashed potatoes, pasta and smoked salmon, and pan-roasted breast of duck with aromatic spices. No Northwest meal is complete, of course, without a bottle of wine from a regional winery or ale from a local microbrewery.

Queen Anne

American

$$–$$$$ ✗ **Canlis.** Little has changed at this Seattle institution since the '50s, when steak served by kimono-clad waitresses represented the pinnacle of high living. The waitresses still wear kimonos, the view across Lake Union is as good as ever, and Canlis remains the only dining establishment in town with a dress code (no tennis shoes or blue jeans, and men must wear a jacket)—quite unusual for this casual town. Besides the famous steaks, there are equally famous Quilcene Bay oysters and fresh fish in season. Every year since 1997 Canlis has been the recipient of *Wine Spectator* magazine's Grand Award for its wine list and service. ⊠ *2576 Aurora Ave. N, Queen Anne* ☎ *206/283–3313* ⌂ *Reservations essential* ⌂ *Jacket required* ▭ *AE, DC, MC, V* ☉ *Closed Sun. No lunch.*

$–$$ ✗ **Five Spot.** Up the hill from Seattle Center, the unpretentious Five Spot has a regional American menu that makes a new stop every four months or so—Key West, Little Italy, New Orleans, Santa Fe, and the fictitious "Springfield" are a few of the most recent ones. At the restaurant's cousins, Jitterbug in Wallingford, the Coastal Kitchen in Capitol Hill, and Endolyne Joe's in West Seattle, the same rotating menu strategy applies, with more international flavor but equally satisfying results. This is a popular spot for Sunday brunch. ⊠ *1502 Queen Anne Ave. N, Queen Anne* ☎ *206/285–7768* ▭ *MC, V.*

$–$$ ✗ **Paragon.** A comfortable neighborhood bistro, Paragon has a classy bar out front and a dining room in back that serves rustic Northwest cuisine. Look for skirt steak, lemon chicken, and pork chops as well as fresh fish. ⊠ *2125 Queen Anne Ave. N, Queen Anne* ☎ *206/283–4548* ▭ *AE, MC, V.*

$–$$ ✗ **Turntable Restaurant.** On the street level of the Experience Music Project, this raucous restaurant serves up fine vittles at *almost* bargain prices. The menu runs the gamut from home-style classics like buttermilk-batter fried chicken and turkey potpie, to portobello mushroom and tofu napoleons. Adventurous pizzas, hamburgers done right, and house specials using local ingredients—including Dungeness crab chowder and Hood Canal clams steamed in microbrew beer—are also good bets. From its perch over the dining room, the Liquid Lounge sends down big, delicious cocktails: try their double lemon drop. ⊠ *Experience Music Project, 325 5th Ave. N, Queen Anne* ☎ *206/770–2777* ▭ *AE, D, DC, MC, V.*

Chinese

$–$$ ✗ **Bamboo Garden.** You can't tell that from the menu, but the Bamboo Garden serves some of the city's best vegetarian (and kosher) food in Seattle. The Chinese dishes are listed by their traditional names even though all of the "meat"—including fish, chicken, pork, and beef—is made from gluten or other vegetarian substitutes. The dining room is simple, with the usual Oriental accoutrements. ⊠ *364 N. Roy St., Queen Anne* ☎ *206/282–6616* ▭ *AE, D, MC, V* ☉ *No lunch weekends.*

Contemporary

$–$$$ ✗ **Kaspar's.** A decidedly unglamorous interior and a location amid Lower Queen Anne Hill's low-rise office buildings and light-industry warehouses focus diners' attention where it belongs—on chef-owner Kaspar Donier's finely wrought contemporary cuisine. Seafood, steak, and poultry options abound. The Muscovy duck with bosc pears, and the Hanoi-style sea bass with fennel and green onions are especially appealing. The five-course Northwest seafood dinner is a lifeline for the indecisive. Kaspar's proximity to Seattle Center makes it a natural destination before or after your evening's entertainment, but the food insists that you take your time. ✉ *19 W. Harrison St., west of Queen Anne Ave. N, Queen Anne* ☎ *206/298–0123* ▭ *AE, MC, V* ⊘ *Closed Sun.–Mon. No lunch.*

Mexican

$–$$ ✕ **Peso's Kitchen & Lounge.** "Have a Margarita . . . at NOON!" proclaims the $3 happy hour menu at this "meet market" near the Seattle Center. There is no denying that the bar drives the show at this lively establishment that can best be described as Goth-Mex (think Madonna's "Like a Prayer" video). Nevertheless, the predictable Mexican menu delivers with above-average execution. The grilled prawns, carne asada, fish tacos, and Gulf-style crab cakes are winners. And, as you might imagine, the bartenders do have a special way with everyone's favorite tequila-and-lime cocktail. ✉ *605 Queen Anne Ave. N, Queen Anne* ☎ *206/283–9353* ▭ *AE, MC, V.*

Pan-Asian

$ ✕ **Chinoise Café.** This small, very popular neighborhood café with tightly packed in tables serves a number of simple Asian dishes, from sushi and *bento* boxes to seafood stir-fried with black-bean sauce, and Vietnamese spring rolls. Their successful formula is duplicated at the Madison Valley and I.D. locations. ✉ *12 Boston St., Queen Anne* ☎ *206/284–6671* ✉ *610 5th Ave. S, International District* ☎ *206/254–0413* ✉ *2801 E. Madison, Madison Valley* ☎ *206/323–0171* ▭ *AE, D, DC, MC, V.*

Seafood

$–$$$ ✕ **Chinook's.** Large windows in this big, rather sterile family seafood house overlook fishing boats moored in Salmon Bay, one of the home ports of the Alaska salmon fleet. Not surprisingly, the restaurant is known for its king salmon and for the particularly pretty views from its patio. The wait for a table can be grueling on busy nights. Breakfast is available on weekends. ✉ *1900 W. Nickerson, Queen Anne* ☎ *206/283–4665* ⌨ *Reservations not accepted* ▭ *AE, MC, V.*

Thai

¢–$ ✕ **Bahn Thai.** Because of the variety and high quality of its dishes, Bahn Thai, a pioneer in local Thai food, is still one of the city's best and most popular places, so it's a good idea to make a reservation. Start your meal with a skewer of tangy chicken or pork satay, or with the *tod mun goong* (spicy fish cake), and continue with hot and sour soup, and one of the many prawn or fish dishes. The deep-fried fish with garlic sauce is particularly good—and you can order it extra spicy. Evenings here are relaxed and romantic. ✉ *409 Roy St., Queen Anne* ☎ *206/283–0444* ▭ *AE, DC, MC, V* ⊘ *No lunch weekends.*

International District & Pioneer Square

Café

¢–$ ✕ **Cafe Paloma.** You might swoon over the interior of this tiny café close to several art galleries, with its decorative bronze trays and big baskets full of glossy eggplants and tomatoes. Along with coffee service, there's light lunch and dinner fare with a Mediterranean/Turkish accent: handmade dolmas, hummus, and *baba ghanoush* (an eggplant puree made with yogurt—not tahini—in this case). The daily lunch specials can veer toward down-home American, though: a juicy pork tenderloin is frequently the centerpiece of the midday meal. ✉ *93 Yesler Way, Pioneer Square* ☎ *206/405–1920* ▭ *MC, V.*

Cajun

¢–$ ✕ **New Orleans.** Aspirations to authenticity demand more than a name, and better versions of Creole and Cajun cuisine can be had elsewhere in Seattle. But at least they put filé powder (a woodsy-flavored spice) and okra in the gumbo, and crayfish shows up on the menu. And the setting—unpretentious tables in a high-ceiling, 19th-century brick building—comes as close to the French Quarter as you can get on the West Coast. After dinner, it transmogrifies into one of the Pioneer Square bars, with blues the predominant genre. ⊠ *114 1st Ave. S, Pioneer Square* ☎ *206/622–2563* ▭ *AE, MC, V.*

Chinese

$–$$$ ✕ **Top Gun.** This modest storefront restaurant brims with regulars devoted to the dim sum served daily from 10 until 3. House specialties include succulent *siu mai* (steamed pork dumplings), fried cubes of tofu with prawns, pork-filled *hum bao,* salt-and-pepper squid, and crisp *gai-lan* (Chinese broccoli) drizzled with a soy sauce–based dressing. Save room for the dessert cart: the buttery, bite-size egg tarts melt in your mouth, and the mango pudding turns many first-timers into repeat customers. ⊠ *668 S. King St., International District* ☎ *206/623–6606* ▭ *MC, V.*

$ ✕ **Hing Loon.** Food magic happens in this eatery with bright fluorescent
Fodor'sChoice lighting, shiny linoleum floors, and large round laminate tables. Although
★ many Chinese chefs may head to Linyen after hours, this is where they purportedly come for noodles. The walls are covered with menu specials handwritten (in Cantonese and English) on paper place mats. Employ the friendly waitstaff to help make your selections. Dishes of particular note are the stuffed eggplant, crispy fried chicken, *Funn* noodles, and any of the seafood offerings. ⊠ *628 S. Weller St., International District* ☎ *206/682–2828* ▭ *MC, V.*

$ ✕ **Linyen.** If it weren't in the International District, you'd consider this elegant restaurant an upscale American café. But don't let the interior decoration fool you: the first-rate food is authentically Asian. This is the place where Chinese chefs come to eat late at night after they've closed their own kitchens. Favorite dishes include the honey walnut prawns and the Peking duck. ⊠ *424 7th Ave. S, International District* ☎ *206/ 622–8181* ▭ *AE, MC, V.*

Delicatessen

¢ ✕ **Bakeman's Restaurant.** Low on frills but high on personality, this well-lighted lunchery attracts a steady stream of business suits with its signature turkey and meat-loaf sandwiches, both served on fluffy white bread. Your window of opportunity is small: it's open weekdays from 10 to 3. Bakeman's is within easy striking distance of Pioneer Square, but the feel is far from touristy. ⊠ *122 Cherry St., Pioneer Square* ☎ *206/622–3375* ⌂ *Reservations not accepted* ▭ *No credit cards* ◷ *Closed weekends. No dinner.*

Italian

$–$$$$ ✕ **Il Terrazzo Carmine.** Ceiling-to-floor draperies lend the dining room understated dignity, and intoxicating aromas waft from the kitchen. The chef blends Tuscan-style and regional southern Italian cooking to create soul satisfying dishes such as veal osso buco, homemade ravioli, pasta with seafood, and roast duck with wild cherry sauce. ⊠ *411 1st Ave. S, Pioneer Square* ☎ *206/467–7797* ◷ *Closed Sun. No lunch Sat.* ▭ *AE, D, DC, MC, V.*

$–$$$ ✕ **Luigi's Grotto.** This underground (literally) restaurant feels like an Italian countryside trattoria. Try the raisin-sweetened calamari or the spinach salad. ⊠ *102 Cherry St., Pioneer Square* ☎ *206/343–9517* ◷ *No lunch weekends* ▭ *AE, D, DC, MC, V.*

$ ✕ **Trattoria Mitchelli.** Although the food is good, Trattoria Mitchelli is important for another reason: It's open until 4 AM most nights, and opens at 7 AM. Its Pioneer Square location may account for this, as many pub crawlers find "the Trat" a hospitable establishment for winding up an evening (and for getting some much-needed late-night/early-morning sustenance). The food is traditional—thin crust, applewood-fired pizzas; sizable pasta dishes; Caesar salads with anchovies (if you want them). ⊠ *84 Yesler Way, Pioneer Square* ☎ *206/623–3883* ⌨ *Reservations not accepted* ⊟ *AE, MC, V.*

¢–$ ✕ **Salumi.** The kind chef-owner Armandino Batali (father of famed New York chef Mario Batali) doles out samples of his fabulous house-cured meats while you wait for a table (which you must be willing to share) at this postage-stamp of a place. Order a meatball, oxtail, sausage, or lamb sandwich—and get samples of your runners-up. Mainly this is a lunch spot, though every Friday Batali serves dinner to a lucky few (reservations are made as much as 12 months ahead). The house wine served at lunch is strong, inexpensive, and good. ⊠ *309 3rd Ave. S, Pioneer Square* ☎ *206/621–8772* ⊟ *AE, D, DC, MC, V.*

Fodor'sChoice ★

Japanese

¢–$ ✕ **Takohachi.** Comfort food at a comfortable price is the name of the game at this popular little restaurant. The emphasis is on fried foods such as *tonkatsu* (breaded pork cutlet) and *kaarage* (breaded boneless chicken), but the *nabe* (cabbage soup) is also quite delicious. There are only two types of sushi on the menu—California roll and a *battera* (mackerel and sweet rice stuffed in a fried tofu pouch)—and neither is available at lunch. ⊠ *610 S. Jackson St., International District* ☎ *206/682–1828* ⊟ *MC, V* ☉ *Closed Sun. No lunch Sat.*

Malaysian

¢–$ ✕ **Malay Satay Hut.** Grilled flat breads, called *roti canai* (unstuffed) and *roti relur* (stuffed with egg, green onion, and red pepper), are a specialty here. The roti are served with a curry dipping sauce studded with chunks of chicken and potato. Other menu favorites include Buddhist Yam Pot (scallops and prawns served in a ring of cooked shredded yam), Belachan string beans (string beans and prawns tossed in a spicy sauce), mango chicken, any of the curries, and the banana pancakes. ⊠ *212 12th Ave. S, International District* ☎ *206/324–4091* ⊟ *MC, V.*

Pan-Asian

¢–$ ✕ **Uwajimaya Village Food Court.** Not only an outstanding grocery and gift shop, Uwajimaya also has a hoppin' food court offering a quick tour of Asian cuisines at lunch-counter prices. For Japanese or Chinese, the deli offers sushi, teriyaki, and barbecued duck. For Vietnamese food, try the fresh spring rolls, served with hot chili sauce, at Saigon Bistro. Shilla has Korean grilled beef and kim chee stew, and there are Filipino lumpia to be found at Inay's Kitchen. The Honeymoon Tea Shop sells *pearl tea,* a cold drink served with a fat straw for sucking up the tapioca balls at the bottom of the cup. ⊠ *600 5th Ave. S, International District* ☎ *206/624–6248* ⊟ *MC, V.*

Vietnamese

¢–$ ✕ **Cafe Hue.** Cafe Hue seems a bit like its namesake old colonial capital—its glories past now, quiet and reflective. Once this café helped introduce Seattle to Vietnamese food; now its dishes seem a bit wan compared with the explosion of Thai and Pan-Asian menus, all tangier and saucier. The building, a late-19th-century stone-and-brick beauty, is still grand as ever. But the food—chicken and fish, lightly sauced, with rice and Asian vegetables—leaves you wondering if something hasn't been left out. ⊠ *312 2nd Ave. S, Pioneer Square* ☎ *206/625–9833* ⊟ *MC, V* ☉ *No dinner Sun.*

CloseUp

WHERE TO REFUEL AROUND TOWN

HERE ARE SOME PLACES *to consider when you are short on time or cash. A few are chains; most are locally owned. Some have* seating, some don't; but all are popular, quick, affordable, and central.

Alki Bakery. *This West Seattle coffee shop–bakery–lunch counter has views of Alki Beach and beyond.*

Dick's Drive-In. *Seattle's classic burger chain has several locations. Only the Queen Anne branch has seating.*

El Puerco Lloron. *Authentic Mexican food served cafeteria-style on the Pike Place Market Hill Climb.*

Ezell's Fried Chicken. *There's no seating at this Central Area spot, but a take-out box of fried chicken, rolls, and a couple of sides makes a fine picnic.*

Il Fornaio. *Both the café and the espresso bar on the first floor of Pacific Place*

mall have coffee, salads, sandwiches, and seating.

Ivar's Acres of Clams. *Clam chowder and fish-and-chips are the specialties at this waterfront landmark next to the Coleman Dock ferry terminal. There's seating indoors and out.*

Pagliacci. *Counter service only at this pizzeria near the UW. There are some salads on the menu, and plenty of seats.*

Salumi. *Italian meatball sandwiches, hearty wines, Armandino Batali, and a big shared table—Enough said?*

Uwajimaya Village Food Court. *Several stands sell Asian fast foods in the heart of Seattle's International District. Uwajimaya's deli carries Japanese and Chinese dishes, Inay's Kitchen specializes in Filipino cuisine. Aloha Plates serves— you guessed it—Hawaiian. The long shared tables are often crowded.*

¢–$ ✗ **Saigon Bistro.** Great values and weekend crowds are found at this bistro, the entrance of which is somewhat elusively located through the back parking lot of the Asian Plaza at 12th and Jackson. Noteworthy dishes include a turmeric-scented mung bean crepe filled with shrimp and scallops served on a cafeteria tray (we're not kidding) mounded with lettuce leaves and pungent herbs, fresh summer rolls stuffed with a filling of your choice (including green mango), traditional *pho* (noodle soups), and such savory dishes as lemongrass-marinated grilled skirt steak and deep-fried pork spring rolls. Parking is free. ✉ *1032 S. Jackson St., International District* ☎ *206/329–4939* ▭ *MC, V.*

¢ ✗ **Saigon Gourmet.** This small café is about as plain as they get, but the food is superb and incredibly inexpensive. Aficionados make special trips for the Cambodian soup and the shrimp rolls, but don't overlook the unusual papaya with beef jerky. Parking can be a problem, but the food rewards your patience. ✉ *502 S. King St., International District* ☎ *206/624–2611* ⌨ *Reservations not accepted* ▭ *MC, V* ☼ *Closed Mon.*

Central Area & Environs

American

¢–$ ✗ **Ezell's Fried Chicken.** Hands-down, this is *the* place in Seattle for fried chicken. From the counter you can watch cooks bread the chicken pieces before tossing them into deep fryers. Both original and spicy flavors are terrific, but be warned that the spicy is exactly that. The rolls are big, fluffy, and baked in generously greased muffin tins. Here you'll also find Faygo sodas. Ezell's is across from Garfield High School (alma mater of Quincy Jones and Jimi Hendrix), so you'll want to steer clear during the lunch hour to avoid the stampede of students. ✉ *501 23rd Ave., Central Area* ☎ *206/324–4141* ▭ *No credit cards.*

Barbecue

★ ¢–$ ✗ **Jones Bar-B-Que.** Good barbecue in Seattle is about as commonplace as a sunny Thanksgiving Day. So be thankful there's Jones. About 4 mi south of Downtown, in Rainier Valley, Jones hits all the barbecue notes: ribs, brisket, chicken, hot links, all arrive falling-off-the-bone tender, smoky, and full of flavor. The sauce is homemade from a family recipe and comes in three levels of heat. Sides include sweet and savory baked beans, cornbread, and collard greens. The combinations offer the best value. Homemade desserts include peach cobbler and three kinds of pie: sweet potato, pecan, and apple. ✉ *3216 S. Hudson St., Rainier Valley* ☎ *206/725–0447* ▭ *No credit cards* ⊘ *Closed Mon.*

Ethiopian

¢–$ ✗ **Assimba Ethiopian Cuisine.** Eat with your hands here using *dabo*, bread made with semolina, spiced with cumin, and basted with butter and oil. Chef Messelu Feide Messeret has attracted quite a following by offering both traditional fare and twists on tradition: The Assimba combo is a house favorite—Messert takes a typically vegetarian dish and covers it with an Ethiopian beef sauce. ✉ *2722 E. Cherry St., Central Area* ☎ *206/322–1019* ▭ *AE, D, DC, MC, V* ⊘ *Closed Sun.*

West Seattle

American

$–$$ ✗ **Endolyne Joe's.** The creators of the Coastal Kitchen and Jitterbug have found their latest home at what was once the last stop on the trolley car line from Alki to Fauntleroy. Here you'll find pan-roasted mussels, breaded flounder, and chicken dredged in crunchy corn flakes and fried. The brick and old growth timbers of the structure, which was built in the '20s, have been used to their full advantage to give the room an authentic saloon flavor. As always with this group of restaurants, the sundaes are dreamy, with special honors going to the coconut ice cream hot fudge sundae served with homemade coconut brittle. ✉ *9261 45th St. SW, West Seattle* ☎ *206/937–5637* ▭ *MC, V.*

$ ✗ **Luna Park Cafe.** This place is about as retro as it gets, complete with tabletop jukeboxes. Actually, it's not really retro, since the café has never changed. It's still more or less what it was in the '60s—an upscale sit-down hamburger and sandwich joint that has updated by adding vegetarian "burgers" and espresso to its menu. But the milk shakes are as rich as ever, the breakfasts are as huge as always, and the burgers can be a tad unctuous. The Luna Park is one of the best places in the city to take children, who get a kick out of putting quarters into the jukeboxes. ✉ *2918 SW Avalon Way, West Seattle* ☎ *206/935–7250* ▭ *AE, D, MC, V.*

Barbecue

¢–$$ ✗ **Backporch BBQ.** Outdoors and at the rear of a neighborhood tavern, this place is barely more than a little porch kitchen with three picnic tables, but the sweet, tender brisket and boneless pork practically fall apart at the touch of a fork. Fruitwood-smoked meats slow-cook here for 10 to 12 hours, says the owner. You have four choices of sauce intensity: mild, spicy, turbo, and nitro. Sides are done well, too; look for home-baked corn bread and corn on the cob. Get ribs elsewhere, but come here for the other meats, which you can also buy by the pound. ✉ *6459 California Ave. SW, West Seattle* ☎ *206/932–RIBS* ▭ *MC, V.*

Café

¢ ✗ **Alki Bakery.** You can't help but notice the pies bursting with fruit and the pillowy cakes filling the café's attractive display case. But before you indulge, order a colorful salad or fettuccine with roasted vegetables, and take in the wide, calming view of the Olympics and Bainbridge Island. This bakery does a brisk business and also owns a retail outlet in Georgetown, south Seattle. ⊠ *2738 Alki Ave. SW, West Seattle* ☎ *206/ 935–1352* ▭ *AE, D, MC, V.*

Greek

$–$$ ✕ **Ephesus Restaurant.** Neighborhood joints like this one are well worth the trip west. With a garden that provides a good amount of the restaurant's produce—Ephesus is in an old house—you can expect the emphasis to be on fresh, seasonal fare. If it's summer, order a salad; in winter try one of the *topraks* (oven-baked stews made with chunks of meat, potatoes, onions, and other veggies). They're rich and comforting on a cold and rainy day. ⊠ *5245 California Ave. SW, West Seattle* ☎ *206/ 937–3302* ⌲ *Reservations essential* ▭ *MC, V* ☉ *No lunch.*

Pizza

¢–$$ ✕ **Pegasus Pizza.** Seattle's favorite pizzeria is known for its tasty, exquisitely sauced and flavorful pizzas (with uncommonly crisp crusts), and its delicious pastas. The pizza here is so good that it conjures thoughts of the ancient Greeks, who invented the first pizza, and of the ancient Romans who appropriated it when they conquered the Greek colony at Neapolis. A notable Greek salad is so large it easily feeds four. In summer there's outside dining (with views of the beach). ⊠ *2758 Alki Ave. SW, West Seattle* ☎ *206/932–4849* ▭ *AE, D, MC, V* ☞ *No smoking.*

Seafood

$$–$$$ ✕ **Salty's on Alki.** Famed for its Sunday and holiday brunches and its view of Seattle's skyline across the harbor, Salty's offers more in the way of quantity than quality—and a bit too much of its namesake ingredient. But it's a couple steps up from the mainstream seafood chains. And, oh, that view. ⊠ *1936 Harbor Ave. W (just past port complex), West Seattle* ☎ *206/937–1600* ▭ *AE, MC, V.*

¢–$ ✕ **Sunfish Cafe.** Alki's neighbors love Sunfish, and it does a thriving business despite its lack of variety. Unfancy grilled "fishkebabs," stews, and chowders are the fare, and it's cheap, quick, and good. Take a beach stroll before or after dinner—the sun setting over the Olympics washes the entire landscape in gold. ⊠ *2800 Alki Ave. SW (at SW 62nd St.) West Seattle* ☎ *206/938–4112* ▭ *No credit cards* ☉ *Closed Mon.*

NORTH & EAST OF DOWNTOWN

Capitol Hill & Madison Park

American

¢ ✕ **Dick's Drive-In.** This chain of orange hamburger stands has changed little since the 1950s. The fries are handcut, the shakes are hand dipped (i.e., made with hard ice cream), and the burgers are just handy. The top-of-the-line burger, Dick's Deluxe ($2.08), has two beef patties, American cheese, lettuce, onions and is slathered in their special tartar sauce. Many folks swear by the frill-free plain cheeseburger ($1.20). Open until 2 AM daily, these drive-ins are as popular with families and students as they are with folks girding themselves against hangovers after a night out on the town. ⊠ *1115 Broadway E, Capitol Hill* ☎ *206/323–1300* ▭ *No credit cards* ⊠ *111 NE 45th St., Wallingford* ☎ *206/632–5125* ⊠ *500 Queen Anne Ave. N, Queen Anne* ☎ *206/285–5155* ▭ *No credit cards.*

¢ ✕ **Kidd Valley.** It's not quite the bargain wonderland that Dick's Drive-In is, but Kidd Valley has more. More types of sandwiches, more varieties of shakes, and more places to sit. If you are looking to consume an entire day's allotment of calories in one meal, this is the place for you. People come here primarily for the burgers and shakes, but Kidd Valley has onion rings, veggie burgers, and chicken club sandwiches, too. ✉ *135 15th Ave. E, Capitol Hill* ☎ *206/328–8133* ▭ *MC, V* ✉ *5502 25th Ave. NE, University District* ☎ *206/522–0890* ▭ *MC, V* ✉ *531 Queen Anne Ave. N, Queen Anne* ☎ *206/284–0184* ▭ *MC, V.*

Café

¢ ✗ **B&O Espresso.** Capitol Hill hipsters and solitary types frequent this local favorite that serves its own European-inspired pastries like chocolate raspberry torte and espresso mousse torte. Appetizers are available each evening, and weekends see brunch. ✉ *204 Belmont Ave. E, Capitol Hill* ☎ *206/322–5028* ⊘ *No lunch* ▭ *MC, V.*

Contemporary

$$$–$$$$ ✗ **Hunt Club.** Dark wood and plush seating provide a traditional backdrop for chef Brian Scheehser's preparations of Pacific Northwest meat and seafood. The house-made squash ravioli or saffron mussel bisque are excellent starters. Entrées on the seasonal menu include succulent jumbo prawns, pan-roasted sea scallops served with truffle risotto, and steak with garlic mashed potatoes and paper-thin onion rings. ✉ *Sorrento Hotel, 900 E. Madison St., First Hill* ☎ *206/622–6400* ▭ *AE, DC, MC, V.*

$–$$ ✗ **Coastal Kitchen.** Here's a chic yet casual place with a three-tiered menu. Local restaurant gurus Jeremy Hardy and Peter Levy (of Queen Anne's Five Spot and Wallingford's Jitterbug fame) hit on a surefire formula with their hearty diner-style dishes served alongside Southern-accented meals. The cooks also concoct a rotating menu with cuisines of such far-flung coastal places as Oaxaca, Vietnam, and Barcelona, to name a few. The experiments don't always work, but you can't knock their adventurous spirit. Besides, you can always fall back on the roast chicken with creamy mashed potatoes or the marinated pork chop. ✉ *429 15th Ave. E, Capitol Hill* ☎ *206/322–1145* ▭ *MC, V.*

$–$$ ✗ **Rosebud.** A home away from home, Rosebud is there when you need it. From the brunch served daily from 9 to 2 to the cozy happy hour, this is a place where you can go to relax. The walls are red, the booths and couches are covered in striped slipcovers. There are a few nods to *Citizen Kane* (a sled, a movie poster), but they're subtle nods. On the varied menu you'll find eggs blackstone (a Benedict-style breakfast dish with bacon and black-peppercorn sauce); pasta with duck confit, Italian kale, and pecorino cheese; and braised lamb shanks served with pea vines. ✉ *719 E. Pike St., Capitol Hill* ☎ *206/323–6636* ▭ *AE, D, MC, V.*

★ $–$$ ✗ **1200 Bistro and Lounge.** The interior glows at this comfortable bistro, which is half lounge, half restaurant. Both sides stay plenty busy due to the expertly prepared food and cocktails. Friendly servers make you feel like you're dining in the home of a dear friend—who also happens to be an excellent cook. Portions are generous, and the plates are artfully arranged. Menu favorites include the Muscovy duck served with roasted fingerling potatoes and green-peppercorn demi-glace; filet mignon with scalloped blue cheese potatoes; and a vegetable gratin with wilted spinach, caramelized onions, and feta cheese. ✉ *1200 E. Pike St., Capitol Hill* ☎ *206/320–1200* ▭ *AE, MC, V* ⊘ *No lunch.*

French

$$$$ ✗ **Rover's.** The restaurant of Thierry Rautureau, one of the Northwest's **Fodor'sChoice** most imaginative chefs, is an essential destination on any Seattle culinary tour. Sea scallops, venison, squab, lobster, and rabbit are frequent ★ offerings (vegetarian items are also available) on the restaurant's prix-fixe menu. Traditional accoutrements such as foie gras and truffles pay homage to Rautereau's French roots, but bold combinations of local in-

gredients are evidence of his wanderlust. The service at Rover's is excellent—friendly but unobtrusive—the setting romantic, and the presentation stunning. ⊠ *2808 E. Madison St., Madison Valley* ☎ *206/325–7442* ⚐ *Reservations essential* ▤ *AE, MC, V* ☉ *Closed Sun. and Mon. No lunch.*

$$–$$$ ✕ **Cassis.** Everything served at candlelit Cassis is made on the premises by chef Charlie Durham or pastry chef Brandy Bassett, right down to the bread. In season a Yakima Valley farmer delivers a weekly truckload of freshly harvested produce grown exclusively for the Cassis kitchen. Specialties include panfried calves' liver, mussels *marinière* (with herbs and white wine), and fish soup topped with a rouille. A rotating selection of 10 wines are available by the glass, and three house wines are offered by the *pichet* (small pitcher). The menu changes monthly, and a prix-fixe menu is offered Sunday through Thursday before 7 PM. ⊠ *2359 10th Ave., Capitol Hill* ☎ *206/329–0580* ⚐ *Reservations essential* ▤ *AE, MC, V.*

$$ ✕ **Madison Park Cafe.** Karen Binder's small, vaguely French neighborhood café is a local institution. Although this spot has been in the past widely known for its breakfast and lunch, recent years have brought a greater emphasis on the dinner service. Popular dishes on the ever-changing evening menu have included cassoulet, oysters in a Pernod cream sauce, pepper steak, and traditional rack of lamb. For warm-weather dining, there's a secluded cobblestone courtyard shaded by trees and scented by more than 12 species of lilies. In summer, foods cooked on an outdoor brick grill add to the delicious aromas wafting from the kitchen. ⊠ *1807 42nd Ave. E, Madison Park* ☎ *206/324–2626* ▤ *AE, MC, V* ☉ *No dinner Sun.–Mon.*

Italian

$–$$$ ✕ **Cafe Lago.** Hugely popular with locals, Cafe Lago specializes in wood-fired pizzas and light handmade pastas. The lasagna—ricotta, béchamel, and cherry-tomato sauce amid paper-thin pasta sheets—perfectly represents the menu's inclination toward the simply satisfying yet exquisitely prepared. Spare table settings, high ceilings, and a friendly atmosphere make the restaurant suitable for a night out with friends or a romantic interlude. ⊠ *2305 24th Ave. E, Capitol Hill* ☎ *206/329–8005* ▤ *D, DC, MC, V* ☉ *Closed Mon. No lunch.*

Southern

¢–$$ ✕ **Kingfish Cafe.** Good Southern cooking is such a novelty in Seattle that the three sisters who own and operate Kingfish are local celebrities. Here you can get a good po'boy (served on a proper po'boy roll) with green tomatoes, fried chicken, pulled pork, scrumptious crab cakes, and, of course, sweet potato pie. The place is spare but elegant, with monochrome photographs culled from family albums. ⊠ *602 19th Ave. E, Capitol Hill* ☎ *206/320–8757* ⚐ *Reservations not accepted* ▤ *MC, V* ☉ *Closed Tues. No lunch weekends.*

Southwestern

$ ✕ **Cactus.** It's worth the drive to Madison Park to experience the rich flavors and colorful decor. The food, which displays Native American, Spanish, and Mexican influences, will satisfy many palates, from the vegetarian to the carnivorous. From the tapas bar, sample the marinated eggplant, garlic shrimp, or tuna *escabeche* (in a spicy, vinegar-based marinade). Larger plates include vegetarian chilis rellenos, grilled pork with chipotle peppers, and a flavorful ancho-chili and cinnamon-roasted chicken. ⊠ *4220 E. Madison St., Madison Park* ☎ *206/324–4140* ▤ *D, DC, MC, V.*

Thai

$ ✕ **Siam.** Thai cooking is so ubiquitous in Seattle that it's almost mainstream. With this amount of competition, it's a testament to Siam that it remains so popular. Start your meal with satay or the city's best *tom kah gai*—a soup of coconut, lemongrass, chicken, and mushrooms. Entrées include curries, noodle dishes, and many prawn, chicken, and fish dishes. Specify one to five stars according to your tolerance for heat. ⊠ *616 Broadway, Capitol Hill* ☎ *206/324–0892* ▭ *AE, MC, V* ☉ *No lunch weekends.*

Vegetarian

$ ✕ **Cafe Flora.** This sophisticated Madison Park café attracts vegetarians and meat eaters for full-flavored, artistically presented meals. An adventurous menu includes portobello mushroom Wellington, fajitas, and polenta topped with onion, rosemary, and mushrooms. Sunday brunch draws a crowd. ⊠ *2901 E. Madison St., Madison Valley* ☎ *206/325–9100* ▭ *MC, V* ☉ *Closed Mon.*

¢ ✕ **Gravity Bar.** Sprout-filled sandwiches and other healthful foods are dished up at this congenial juice bar with a sci-fi-industrial interior. The juices—from any number of fruits and vegetables, solo or in combo—are often zippier than the solid food. ⊠ *415 Broadway E, Capitol Hill* ☎ *206/325–7186* ▭ *No credit cards.*

Vietnamese

★ ¢–$$ ✕ **Monsoon.** This elegant restaurant and wine bar sits unobtrusively on a Capitol Hill avenue, letting its classic Saigon cuisine make the splashy statements. Staff favorites include the caramelized gulf shrimp served with jasmine rice, the catfish claypot with chili-lime sauce, and the lemongrass tofu. Exotic homemade ice creams include jackfruit or lychee and muscat, but the restaurant's most famous dessert is the crème caramel. The wine cellar has more than 500 bottles of wine guaranteed to complement the sublime work of the chef. ⊠ *615 19th Ave. E., Capitol Hill* ☎ *206/325–2111* ▭ *MC, V* ☉ *Closed Mon.*

University District

American

$ ✕ **Portage Bay Cafe.** This casual, contemporary café is a favorite hangout with the university crowd. Try the pot roast, pork chops, duck, and crab cakes. Breakfast is served, as is weekend brunch, and on nice days there is open-air dining. ⊠ *4130 Roosevelt Ave. NE, University District* ☎ *206/547–8230* ▭ *AE, D, MC, V.*

Brazilian

$–$$ ✕ **Tempero Do Brasil.** Folks come from far afield to this festive place for a taste of Brazil. The popular cod, prawn, and halibut dishes simmered in golden coconut-based sauces are complex and satisfying; entrées arrive with moist, chewy long-grain rice and delectable black beans. For a larger meal, try the charbroiled Argentine steak, *bife grelhado*. Finish with cold passionfruit mousse or tangy guava paste served with farmer's cheese, and strong dark coffee. The outstanding food, attention to detail, and earnest staff make dining here a pleasure. The airy patio is perfect for icy Brazilian cocktails in the summer. ⊠ *5628 University Way NE, University District* ☎ *206/523–6229* ▭ *AE, MC, DC, V* ☉ *Closed Mon.*

Café

¢ ✕ **Ugly Mug.** Pleasantly worn couches, lamps on the tables, and jazz standards on the stereo recall the funky Seattle that once was. A sign at the cash register admonishes, "Friends don't let friends go to Starbucks!" Indeed, the Ugly Mug doesn't aspire to be anything more than itself,

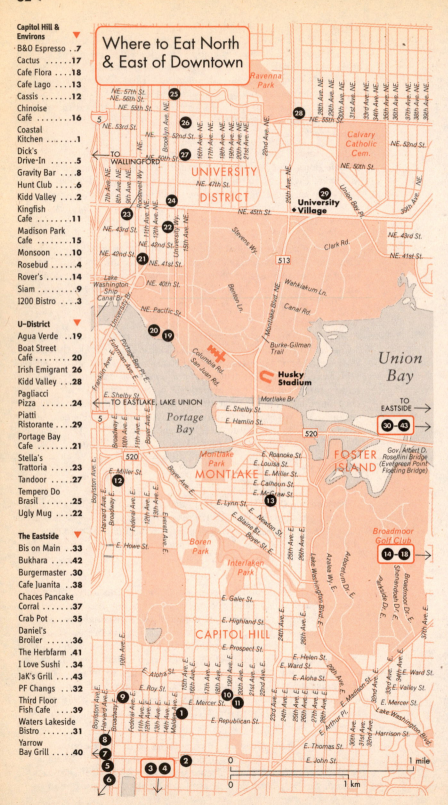

Where to Eat North & East of Downtown

with warming, inventive soups like garbanzo-cabbage or black bean cooked with wine and orange zest. The meat-loaf sandwich, with its wonderfully smoky flavor, makes you want seconds. For breakfast, try the Belgian waffles with yogurt and fruit, or the exceptional raspberry scone. ⊠ *1309 NE 43rd St., University District* ☎ *206/547–3219* ▭ *No credit cards.*

French

$–$$ ✕ **Boat Street Café.** A sunny day at the Boat Street Café is a treat for the senses. Open windows bring the scent of flowers and the clink of boats bobbing nearby as the kitchen sends enticing aromas to your table. The crab cakes evoke the Pacific Northwest; the chicken in tarragon cream sauce savors of France; and the fresh scallop ravioli might remind you of Italy. American touches are present in oven-roasted prawns, pork in blackberry sauce, and a sweet corn flan. The simple and spare interior has a rustic grace that belies the sophistication of the food. ⊠ *909 NE Boat St., University District* ☎ *206/632–4602* ▭ *No credit cards* ⊙ *Closed Mon. No dinner Sun.–Tues.*

Indian

$ ✕ **Tandoor.** In a neighborhood largely populated by starving students, U-District restaurants are usually cheap, and Tandoor is no exception. The northern Indian menu focuses on tandoori (meat cooked in a clay oven, over charcoal) dishes, though it's the special naan (round leavened flat bread, in this case stuffed with chicken and nuts), lamb vindaloo (a spicy curry stew served over basmati rice), and curried meat and vegetable mulligatawny soup that really sing. An additional bonus: the beer and wine, like the food, are bargain priced. ⊠ *5024 University Way NE, University District* ☎ *206/523–7477* ▭ *AE, D, DC, MC, V.*

Irish

¢–$ ✕ **Irish Emigrant.** If authenticity means something to you, this is a true Irish bar, owned by Irish folks (they may be the ones playing that fiddle you hear) with lots of Irish regulars. That said, lots of the patrons are UW students who do get loud and rowdy on occasion. In addition to the ubiquitous (and properly poured) pint of Guinness, provisions include bangers and mash (Angus sausages and mashed potatoes), fish-and-chips, and chicken potpie. Shoot some pool, or just shoot the breeze with your friends. For those with minds like a lint trap, Monday is trivia night. ⊠ *5260 University Way NE, University District* ☎ *206/525–2955* ▭ *AE, MC, V* ⊙ *No lunch weekdays.*

Italian

$–$$ ✕ **Piatti Ristorante.** The staff is friendly, and everything about this place is casual. There's a fireside dining room; if it's warm you can sit on one of two patios. What more could you ask for? The rotisserie chicken is a favorite, as well as the chicken marsala. Or try the ravioli stuffed with arugula and ricotta. ⊠ *2800 NE University Village, University District* ☎ *206/524–9088* ▭ *AE, DC, MC, V.*

$ ✕ **Stella's Trattoria.** Paintings by local artists brighten the three dark, cavernlike dining rooms at this all-night trattoria. The food is standard Italian; try the melanzane parmigiana, which is eggplant browned in the pan and topped with marinara, mozzarella, and Parmesan, served with garlic pasta. There's open-air dining on the sidewalk out front. ⊠ *4500 9th Ave., University District* ☎ *206/633–1100* ▭ *AE, D, MC, V.*

Mexican

¢–$ ✕ **Agua Verde.** You can rent kayaks at Agua Verde, which is on a street bordering Portage Bay and surrounded by boat repair shops. The food here has been described as Baja California Mexican, which may refer as much to the bright, beachy colors as it does to the cuisine. Tacos aren't dripping with grease, cheese, or sour cream, and choices include fish and chile-chicken. With a nod to the U-District diet, there are lots of vegetarian items. Regulars swear by the black-bean cakes and *mangodillas*, quesadillas with mango and poblano chiles. Warning: The fresh-lime margaritas may hike your otherwise small bill. ⊠ *1303 NE Boat St., University District* ☎ *206/545–8570* ▭ *MC, V* ⟟ *Sun. lunch take-out only.*

Pizza

$–$$ ✕ **Pagliacci Pizza.** These days, down-and-dirty pizza is hard to find. Pagliacci ascetically adheres to a thin-crust, no-nonsense ethic which includes, yes, amazing, a cheese-and-tomato-sauce pie. That's all. Just pizza. It's almost zen. ⊠ *4529 University Way NE, University District* ☎ *206/ 632–0421* ▭ *AE, MC, V.*

The Eastside

American

¢–$ ✕ **Burgermaster.** Since 1952, carhops at this drive-in have been serving people at their car windows. The specialty, of course, is hamburgers, but the drive-in also serves fresh and savory fish sandwiches. ⊠ *10606 Northup Way, Bellevue* ☎ *425/827–9566* ▭ *AE, D, DC, MC, V.*

¢   ✕ **Chaces Pancake Corral.** Chaces has been in the breakfast business since 1958. Here is where you are going to find "old Bellevue" enjoying an endless cup of coffee, a chitty chat with the neighbors, and a waitstaff that knows them by name. The menu offers no surprises, but plenty of pancakes, cured meats, egg dishes, and more than one flavor of syrup. Expect to wait for a table on the weekends. ⊠ *1606 Bellevue Way SE, Bellevue* ☎ *425/454–8888* ▭ *MC, V.*

Chinese

¢–$ ✕ **PF Changs.** This upscale chain in The Lodge at Bellevue Square serves beautiful Chinese food in a lively dining room. The chicken in lettuce wraps are popular, the salt-and-pepper calamari pack a flavorful punch, and the Cantonese roasted duck served with steamed buns and hoisin sauce is a hearty choice. Upon request the kitchen will prepare Szechwan long beans and asparagus tossed together so you won't have to choose between the two. White and brown rice are available, and all dishes are served family style. ⊠ *525 Bellevue Square, Bellevue* ☎ *425/637–3582* ▭ *AE, MC, V.*

Contemporary

$$$$ ✕ **The Herbfarm.** The sumptuous, nine-course, prix-fixe meals served at this restaurant 10 mi northeast of Kirkland are the paradigm for Pacific Northwest cuisine. The delectables you will encounter include goat cheese biscuits, green pickled walnuts, and salmon with a sauce of fresh herbs. ⊠ *14590 NE 145th St., Woodinville* ☎ *206/784–2222* ⌔ *Reservations essential* ☉ *No lunch* ▭ *AE, MC, V.*

$$–$$$ ✕ **Waters Lakeside Bistro.** Panoramic views dominate this dining room inside the Woodmark Hotel. The restaurant's "bistro cuisine" includes Dungeness crab cakes, tenderloin steaks, and pan-seared salmon. Outdoor seating under canvas umbrellas is available during the warmer months. Breakfast is also available. ⊠ *1200 Carillon Point, Kirkland* ☎ *425/803–5595* ☉ *No dinner Sun.* ▭ *AE, DC, MC, V.*

Continental

★ $–$$ ✕ **Bis on Main.** The intimate, romantic dining room is given special flair from the rotating exhibits of modern art that adorn the walls. The most popular of the many scrumptious entrées are the crab cakes and the crispy

POPULAR WITH PARENTS

WHEN DINING WITH children, most parents are looking for three things: french fries, crayons, and an understanding waitstaff (high chairs and booster seats don't hurt either). Here are few good bets for families.

Anthony's Pier 66. Children are welcome at the fish bar (where they mix a mean Shirley Temple) and in the more formal dining room. Kids love to watch the tugboats and ferries in the busy harbor.

Coastal Kitchen/Jitterbug/5 Spot/ Endolyne Joes. These neighborhood restaurants are endlessly family-friendly. The sundaes alone are worth a trip.

Etta's. Tom Douglas named this restaurant, one of three he owns, after his daughter. The jovial staff will make you feel right at home with your own daughters and sons.

Ivar's Salmon House. At water level on the Ship Canal, and filled with Native American artifacts, Ivar's has been a family favorite for generations.

Kidd Valley. Burgers, fries, shakes, and more in an indestructible fast-food restaurant.

Oceanaire. Three words: flaming baked Alaska.

Palisades/Maggie Bluff's. Palisades has a big weekend brunch buffet, where kids can fill their own plates, and food for feeding the fish in the pond. Maggie Bluff's has a kid's menu and places from which to watch for sailboats.

Portage Bay Café. An easy place to take the family for breakfast.

Red Mill. Some say the burgers here are the best in town, and the Greenwood location is only blocks from the Woodland Park Zoo.

---

garlic chicken, a free-range chicken deboned and marinated and then pan-seared, roasted, and served with horseradish mashed potatoes. ✉ *10213 Main St., Bellevue* ☎ *425/455–2033* ▭ *AE, D, DC, MC, V* ✺ *No lunch on weekends.*

Indian

$ ✗ **Bukhara of India.** This pleasant suburban restaurant has a standard repertory of aromatic and spicy Indian dishes such as tandoori chicken, samosas, and curries. It's a welcome addition to the culinary desert of the far Eastside. ✉ *317 NW Gilman Blvd., Issaquah* ☎ *425/392–8743* ▭ *AE, D, DC, MC, V.*

Italian

$$–$$$ ✗ **Cafe Juanita.** Under the direction of chef-owner Holly Smith, this ro-
Fodor'sChoice mantic Eastside favorite focuses on traditional northern Italian recipes
★ while allowing for exploration of other Italian cuisines. The menu changes daily as Smith uses the freshest ingredients available, many of which come from the restaurant's own garden. Favorites plates include a smoked trout served with pickled wild ramps; braised rabbit served over a chickpea-flour crepe; and a rich grilled rib-eye steak drizzled with red-wine syrup. ✉ *9702 NE 120th Pl., Kirkland* ☎ *425/823–1505* ▭ *MC, V* ✺ *Closed Mon. No lunch.*

Japanese

$–$$ ✗ **I Love Sushi.** This is the Bellevue original of one of Seattle's most popular sushi bars. It's bigger and more bustling than its Lake Union offspring, and the food is every bit as good. The chefs occasionally bring in rare treats from around the world, but local specialties such as geoduck or salmon are available year-round. Start with some salty *edamame*— fresh green soybeans in the shell that you draw out with your teeth.

✉ *11818 NE 8th St., Bellevue* ☎*425/454–5706* ⚠ *Reservations essential* ▭ *MC, V* ◷ *No lunch Sun.* ✉ *1001 Fairview Ave. N, Eastlake* ☎ *206/625–9604* ⚠ *Reservations essential* ▭ *MC, V* ◷ *No lunch Sun.*

Seafood

$$–$$$$ ✕ **Third Floor Fish Cafe.** This elegant restaurant with a great view (and an ugly name) is a popular Eastside dining spot. Chef Scott Staples, who put the café on the map, has left to open a place of his own (Restaurant Zoë), and his sous chef, Greg Campbell, has taken the helm. Campbell has a sure touch with Mediterranean-style fish, and he handles meats equally well. The menu focuses on fresh, preferably local, seafood (such as wild Pacific salmon or pan-seared scallops), but also includes chicken, lamb (as in cabernet-braised lamb shanks), and beef tenderloin. ✉ *205 Lake St. S, Kirkland* ☎ *425/822–3553* ⚠ *Reservations essential* ▭ *AE, D, MC, V* ◷ *No lunch.*

★ $$–$$$$ ✕ **Yarrow Bay Grill.** This pleasant waterfront-view restaurant on Lake Union, south of Kirkland, always serves good food and has excellent service, making it one of the best restaurants east of Lake Washington. The Beach Cafe at Yarrow Bay, the Grill's informal downstairs offshoot, has tables closer to the water, the menu is less formal, and the prices are lower. ✉ *1270 Carillon Point, off Lake Washington Blvd., Kirkland* ☎ *425/889–9052* ▭ *AE, DC, MC, V.*

$–$$$ ✕ **Crab Pot Restaurant.** Sitting on Lake Washington, with spectacular views of Seattle, the restaurant is famous for its *seafeasts*: seafood poured over butcher paper. A mallet is all that stands between you and your meal. The menu also includes steak and chicken entrées. ✉ *2 Lake Bellevue Dr., Bellevue* ☎ *425/455–2244* ▭ *AE, D, DC, MC, V.*

Steak

$$–$$$ ✕ **Daniel's Broiler.** Occupying the entire 21st floor of the Bank of America building, this restaurant has unbeatable views of Mt. Rainier, Seattle, the Cascades, and Lake Washington. Known primarily for its high-quality steaks, the restaurant also serves an assortment of seafood, including cold water lobster tail. ✉ *10500 NE 8th St., 21st fl., Bellevue* ☎ *425/462–4662* ▭ *AE, D, DC, MC, V* ◷ *No lunch weekends.*

$–$$$ ✕ **JaK's Grill.** The specialty of this popular local restaurant is steak; people come from all around for it. The menu also includes seafood dishes and pastas. The large, open dining room is often loud and boisterous. ✉ *14 Front St., Issaquah* ☎ *425/837–8834* ▭ *DC, MC, V* ◷ *No lunch.*

NORTH & WEST OF DOWNTOWN

Eastlake

American

$–$$ ✕ **Bluwater Bistro.** This upscale (and upstairs) dining room has one of the better views of Lake Union, its boats, people, wildlife, and floatplanes. The menu is simple, but the dishes are tasty: fresh seafood, roasted chicken, stuffed pork chops, New York steak topped with blue cheese, and other comfort foods. In warm weather, there's an outside, water-level dining area. The bistro offers complimentary valet parking and free boat moorage. ✉ *1001 Fairview Ave. N, Eastlake* ☎ *206/447–0769* ▭ *MC, V.*

¢–$ ✕ **14 Carrot Cafe.** This popular breakfast and lunch place has changed owners several times in the last two decades, yet somehow the restaurant stays the same. Only the cinnamon rolls are not as good as they used to be. But specials such as biscuits in gravy and the pancakes du jour still sell like hotcakes. The egg dishes are consistently good, and the Tahitian French toast, made with tahini, is as popular as ever. Don't get upset about the crowd packing the place on weekends: most live within walking distance, and this is their neighborhood café. ✉ *2305 Eastlake Ave. E, Eastlake* ☎ *206/324–1442* ▭ *MC, V* ⊘ *No dinner.*

Eclectic

$$ ✕ **Bandoleone.** From the simple austerity of the dining room to the festive deck decorated with colorful Mexican paper cutouts, the mood here is romantic and fun. The unpretentiousness suits the sophisticated menu that roams across Spain, the Caribbean, and Central and South America. A grilled ahi tuna entrée comes with papaya black-bean salsa; the eggplant relleno is stuffed with squash, summer corn, sweet onions, and goat cheese. Tequila-cured salmon gravlax and a banana-macadamia empanada with tamarind dipping sauce highlight the outstanding tapas selections. The gravlax also appears on the imaginative and inexpensive weekend brunch menu, served between 9 and 2. ✉ *2241 Eastlake Ave. E, Eastlake* ☎ *206/329–7559* ▭ *MC, V* ⊘ *No lunch.*

Italian

$–$$ ✕ **Cucina! Cucina! Italian Cafe.** This boisterous, noisy Italian pasta and pizza house has one of the best decks from which to enjoy Lake Union on a sunny day. The pastas are decent; the pizzas come from a wood-fired oven; and there's a good selection of local microbrews. Prices are reasonable. The bar is one of the city's most popular places for singles. ✉ *901 Fairview Ave. N, Eastlake* ☎ *206/447–2782* ▭ *AE, D, MC, V.*

$–$$ ✕ **Serafina.** To many loyal patrons, Serafina is *the* perfect neighborhood café. Some claim the restaurant also has the best Italian food in Seattle. And then there's the romance: burnt-sienna walls topped by a forest-green ceiling convey the feeling of a lush (and perhaps decadent) garden villa—a sense heightened by the small sheltered courtyard out back. Menu highlights include grilled eggplant layered and baked with prosciutto, goat cheese, and tomatoes, and the fresh mussels steamed with smoked tomatoes, *harissa* (spicy hot sauce made with chilies, garlic, cumin, coriander, and olive oil), leeks, and sweet vermouth. As an added attraction, there is live jazz every night except Monday. ✉ *2043 Eastlake Ave. E, Eastlake* ☎ *206/323–0807* ▭ *MC, V* ⊘ *No lunch weekends.*

Wallingford

Contemporary

$–$$ ✕ **Jitterbug.** With its cozy booths and white tablecloths, this tiny diner-cum-bistro has a rotating menu of international ethnic cuisine—just like its companion café, the Coastal Kitchen. On the basic menu you'll find pork chops and juicy rib-eye steak, with specials like halibut with pasta in white wine sauce or pan-seared marlin. For breakfast, try the cheery gingerbread waffles. As at the Coastal, the voices heard in the bathrooms are hilarious, wooden-sounding foreign-language lessons on tape. ✉ *2114 N. 45th St., Wallingford* ☎ *206/547–6313* ▭ *MC, V* ⊘ *No dinner Sun.*

Hawaiian

$–$$ ✕ **Luau Polynesian Lounge.** Anything that claims to be a Polynesian lounge had better deliver some authentic South Pacific ambience. Teeny tiny Luau does it up right, and for better or worse without the grass-skirted servers. In the thatched-roof bar you can order a cocktail served in a ceramic coconut mug and the *pupu* platter (an assortment of spicy appetizers, like the fabulous hot-and-sour, five-spice beef short ribs). Or grab a table to order entrées that include Kahlua pork sandwiches and coconut-crusted Hawaiian game fish in a curry broth. ✉ *2253 N. 56th St., Wallingford* ☎ *206/633–5828* ▭ *AE, MC, V* ⊘ *No lunch.*

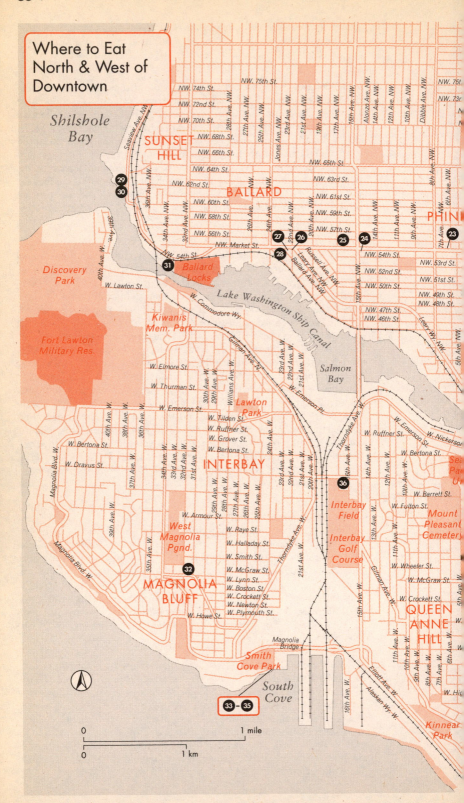

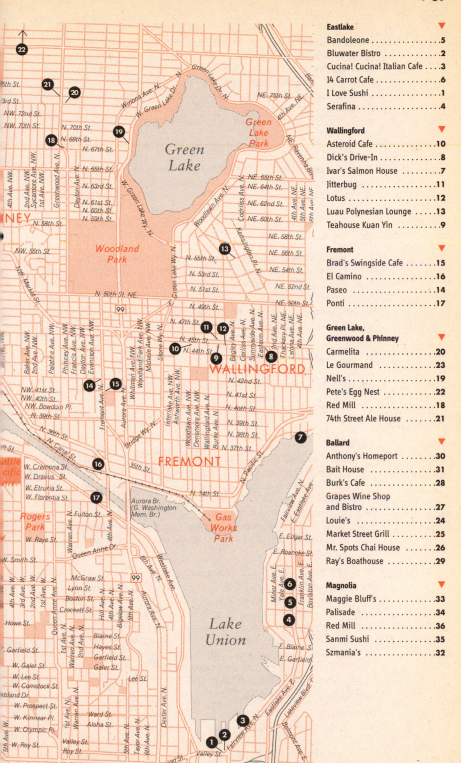

Italian

$–$$ ✕ **Asteroid Cafe.** Three rock 'n' rollers who didn't like the sound of "starving musician" created this tiny Wallingford eatery where pasta rules. Nearly three dozen kinds are offered: from savory portobello ravioli in a sage-and-butter sauce to ultra-spicy chicken diablo. Servings are huge, so be smart and share your entrée. And, especially if you ordered the diablo, cool off with the homemade sorbet, served in frozen lemon or orange rinds. ✉ *1605 N. 45th St., Wallingford* ☎ *206/547–2514* ▭ *AE, D, DC, MC, V* ⊗ *No lunch.*

Seafood

$–$$$ ✕ **Ivar's Salmon House.** This long dining room facing Lake Union has original Northwest Indian artwork collected by the former owner. You can dine inside or out on the deck; the fish-and-chips and alder-smoked salmon are good bets. There's brunch on Sunday. ✉ *401 NE Northlake Way, Wallingford* ☎ *206/632–0767* ▭ *AE, MC, V.*

Tea

¢ ✕ **Teahouse Kuan Yin.** There's almost as much ginger, ginseng, and philosophy in evidence here as classic black or green tea; the New Age healthful ethic is in full swing. Rich scones, berry pies, and green-tea ice cream leaven the mix. The adjoining bookstore focuses on travel and world understanding. Kuan Yin, the shop's namesake, is the goddess of mercy. ✉ *1911 N. 45th St., Wallingford* ☎ *206/632–2055* ▭ *MC, V.*

Thai

¢–$ ✕ **Lotus.** This Thai eatery has quick service and simple, tasty curries and noodles. Try the spicy eggplant stir-fry for a welcome change from the usual chicken-shrimp Thai hegemony. ✉ *2101 N. 45th St., Wallingford* ☎ *206/632–2300* ▭ *MC, V.*

Fremont

Cuban

$ ✕ **Paseo.** The centerpiece of Lorenzo Lorenzo's slim Cuban-influenced menu is a highly secret sauce that was years in the making; word has it that Lorenzo even hides the recipe from his employees. The marinated pork sandwich, topped with sautéed onions, is doused with this sauce and keeps folks coming back for more. The entrées are also a bargain, from scallops with cilantro to prawns in red sauce. ✉ *4225 Fremont Ave. N, Fremont* ☎ *206/545–7440* ▭ *No credit cards* ⊗ *No lunch Sun.*

Italian

★ **$–$$** ✕ **Brad's Swingside Cafe.** You've probably dreamed of finding a place like this—funky, cramped, and dear to the heart of the owner. Lots of people share this dream, so you can expect to wait a while on weekends. Chef-owner Brad Inserra, who likes to come out and chat—so long as you don't dis the Pittsburgh Pirates—bills Swingside as Seattle's "best little Italian restaurant," but don't come expecting spaghetti and meatballs. You will find an imaginative lamb-and-venison stew with coconut milk, orange, and mango. Be sure to ask the server what wine Inserra recommends. He's always right. ✉ *4212 Fremont Ave. N, Fremont* ☎ *206/633–4057* ▭ *MC, V* ⊗ *Closed Sun. No lunch.*

Mexican

★ **¢–$** ✕ **El Camino.** Loose, loud, and funky, this Fremont storefront restaurant gives its own irreverent Northwest interpretation of Mexican cuisine. Rock-shrimp quesadillas, chipotle-pepper and garlic sea bass, and duck with a spicy green sauce are typical of the kitchen's gentle spin. Even a green salad becomes transformed with toasted pumpkin seeds on crispy romaine with a cool garlic, lime juice, and cilantro dressing. You can eat until midnight, although there's no better place to chill on a summer afternoon than El Camino's deck. A tart margarita, served in a pint glass, makes the perfect accessory. ⊠ *607 N. 35th St., Fremont* ☎ *206/632–7303* 🍽 *AE, DC, MC, V* ⊘ *No lunch weekdays.*

Seafood

$$–$$$ ✗ **Ponti.** Working in a placid canal-side location, in a villalike setting a stone's throw from the Fremont and Aurora bridges, chef Alvin Binuya builds culinary bridges between Northwest ingredients and Mediterranean and Asian techniques. Alaskan king crab legs with a chardonnay butter and herb mayonnaise manifest the kitchen's classic restraint; the grilled mahimahi with satsuma potato gratin and shallot jus walks on the wilder side. ⊠ *3014 3rd Ave. N, Fremont* ☎ *206/284–3000* 🍽 *AE, DC, MC, V.*

Green Lake, Greenwood & Phinney

American

¢–$ ✗ **Pete's Egg Nest.** You'll notice right away that almost everybody knows everybody else here. This is truly a neighborhood restaurant where locals meet over breakfast and lunch to exchange news or just shoot the breeze. No one ever seems in a hurry. The service is friendly and efficient, but never rushed. Nor are you. Plus, even with coffee and juice, your meal will set you back less than $10. But the food here is not just inexpensive. It's truly tasty and well-prepared, which seems to be the formula that brings back the locals over and over again. ⊠ *7717 Greenwood Ave. N, Greenwood* ☎ *206/784–5348* 🍽 *MC, V* ⊘ *No dinner.*

¢–$ ✗ **74th Street Ale House.** This neighborhood restaurant-pub is busy at lunch, but gets really crowded at night. For locals, it's a great place to walk to after you get home from work and want to unwind—and you wisely refuse to drive after a pitcher of microbrew. You can experience the locally famous chicken on rye, and steamed mussels, as well as soups and pasta specials—all dishes you can enjoy without having to critically appraise. The bar has a great beer selection. ⊠ *7401 Greenwood Ave. N, Greenwood* ☎ *206/784–2955* 🍽 *MC, V.*

Contemporary

$$$–$$$$
Fodor'sChoice
★

✗ **Le Gourmand.** Not every chef cares enough to grow the poppies that provide the seeds for his homemade crackers. Chef-owner Bruce Naftaly does. This man has routinely worked the line since taking the helm at this neighborhood restaurant in the early 1980s. Bruce uses classic French techniques and locally grown ingredients to create stunning dishes such as his roast duckling with black currant sauce (using homemade cassis); or king salmon poached in champagne and gooseberry sauce. Pastry chef Sara Naftaly's dessert menu might include a flourless chocolate cake with raspberries and almond crème anglaise. ⊠ *425 NW Market St., Phinney* ☎ *206/784–3463* 🚭 *Reservations essential* 🍽 *AE, MC, V.*

$$–$$$ ✗ **Nell's.** Nell's is a bright spot on the Seattle dining scene. Chef-owner Philip Mihalski's ever-changing menu focuses on coaxing maximum performance from the freshest of seasonal regional ingredients. Employing broadly European techniques, Mihalski creates such dishes as seared sea scallops with a curry cream sauce and shavings of black truffle over a puree of cauliflower, and poached halibut in kaffir lime broth with roasted spring onions. Suggested appetizers include a fantastic onion tart with hazelnut butter and Jerusalem artichoke chips, and seared foie gras in duck broth over a puree of turnips. ⊠ *6804 E. Greenlake Way N, Green Lake* ☎ *206/524–4044* 🍽 *AE, MC, V* ⊘ *No lunch.*

Vegetarian

$$ ✕ **Carmelita.** You don't have to leave your taste buds at home when you want to indulge in healthy vegetarian dishes: Everything on the menu is fresh and well prepared: from the grilled bread salad with chèvre and fava beans to the baby artichoke, chickpea, and tomato "bouillabaisse." You will not notice the absence of fish, fowl, or meat stocks in the preparations. This is a popular place, so reservations are recommended. ✉ 7314 Greenwood Ave., Greenwood ☎ 206/706–7703 ▭ MC, V ⊗ Closed Mon.

Ballard

American

¢ ✕ **Bait House.** It's no joke: In the summer fishermen stop here at 4 AM to pick up their bait (but the kitchen's closed then). You can come during a more reasonable hour for a deli sandwich, crab cocktail, the famous open-faced crab-cheese melt, and definitely for the view. The patio and the small, crooked, rough-hewn dining room overlook boats gliding by on their way to the Ballard Locks. Take a peek behind the counter, too: All hot food is baked or warmed in little toaster ovens. Expect nautical charm. ✉ 5517 Seaview Ave. NW (between Ballard Locks and train bridge overpass), Ballard ☎ 206/297–9109 ▭ MC, V ⊗ Closed Mon. No dinner Sun. or Tues.

Café

¢–$ ✕ **Grapes Wine Shop and Bistro.** Amid a number of tables and a comfy sofa, the wine-and-cheese merchant's counter area is usually a jumble of paperwork and magazines. Piaf's voice might be resonating up to the rafters, though; a sea breeze from Shilshole Bay might be drifting in, and the grilled cheese sandwich of the day on rustic bread might be scrumptious raclette, a nutty, semifirm cheese similar to Gruyère. The large selection of wine by the glass and bottle is a veritable tour of Italy's wine regions. ✉ 5424 Ballard Ave. NW, Ballard ☎ 206/297–1460 ▭ D, MC, V.

Cajun/Creole

$–$$ ✕ **Burk's Cafe.** With homey wood floors, a tiny but comfortable bar, and plenty of light, immaculate Burk's is well versed in gumbos, jambalayas, and ribs, making it a godsend in a city with relatively few Creole restaurants. Big crocks of hot pickled okra sit on each table; servers are competent and even witty. The blackened rockfish is exceedingly tender inside, and the alder-wood-smoked sausages are made on the premises. Try the fetching sandwiches, which come on chewy rolls. Be warned: most dishes are extra spicy and can't be made milder. ✉ 52411 Ballard Ave. NW, Ballard ☎ 206/782–0091 ▭ MC, V ⊗ Closed Sun.–Mon.

Chinese

¢–$ ✕ **Louie's.** Louie's looks straight out of a 1960s James Bond flick. Cavernous booths, mirror-paneled walls, and a huge (reservable) banquet room can make for a fun excursion. Besides the Cantonese/Szechuan fare, the menu includes dim sum and American chow like burgers and roast beef au jus sandwiches. Like many Chinese restaurants in town, Louie's is open past midnight on weekends. ✉ 5100 15th Ave. NW (just north of Ballard Bridge), Ballard ☎ 206/782–8855 ▭ AE, D, MC, V ⊗ No lunch weekends.

Contemporary

$–$$ ✕ **Market Street Grill.** In a space that mixes restrained, cool design elements with the warmth of candlelit tables, chef John Paul Kunselman oversees the Northwest menu. You can pair a number of attractive starters to make whole meals: warm lobster and artichoke salad, shrimp cakes with watercress mayonnaise, and foie gras with sweetbreads. The entrées, seasonally focused and equally appetizing, range from sea scallop potpie to grilled pork tenderloin with shaved Reggiano Parmigiano and porcini risotto cake. ⊠ *1744 NW Market St., Ballard* ☎ *206/789–6766* ▤ *AE, D, MC, V* ⊙ *No lunch.*

Seafood

$$–$$$$ ✕ **Anthony's Homeport.** This is a comfortable waterfront restaurant where ample outside dining in protected nooks allows you a sea breeze and great views without getting blasted by gales. The seafood preparations are as good as those of the more upscale Ray's, next door. But this restaurant's true claim to fame rests on its annual Oyster Olympics, a madcap oyster-shucking, oyster-judging, oyster-slurping event held in late March. ⊠ *6135 Seaview Ave. NW (at the Shilshole Marina), Ballard* ☎ *206/783–0780* ▤ *AE, MC, V.*

$$–$$$$ ✕ **Ray's Boathouse.** The view of Puget Sound might be the big draw here,

Fodor's Choice but the seafood is also impeccably fresh and well prepared. Perennial
★ favorites include broiled salmon, Kasu sake-marinated cod, Dungeness crab, and regional oysters on the half shell. Ray's has a split personality: there's a fancy dining room downstairs and a casual café and bar upstairs. In warm weather you can sit on the deck outside the café and watch the parade of fishing boats, tugs, and pleasure craft floating past, almost right below your table. ⊠ *6049 Seaview Ave. NW, Ballard* ☎ *206/789–3770* ⌂ *Reservations essential (dining room); reservations not accepted (café)* ▤ *AE, DC, MC, V.*

Tea

¢ ✕ **Mr. Spots Chai House.** In-the-know locals won't put up with syrupy-sweet competitors once they've partaken of Mr. Spots' peppery, subtle drink dubbed Morning Glory Chai. In fact, what started as a chai-brewing operation in owner Jessica Vidican-Neisius's basement quickly became a successful wholesale business with a storefront café (and computers with Internet access). Tea is worshiped here, so you'll find high-quality leaf as well as unusual blends including rose congou, plum, and hair-point green, along with jars of more mysterious herbs. The thumbnail-size menu offers an especially gooey and satisfying grilled cheese. ⊠ *2213 NW Market St., Ballard* ☎ *206/297–CHAI* ▤ *MC, V.*

Magnolia

American

¢–$ ✕ **Maggie Bluff's.** Super casual and kid-friendly, this spot right on the marina is popular with boaters coming in from a day at sea. On nice days there is outdoor seating, for the rainy days you can watch the weather and the bobbing sailboats from indoors. The menu is filled with burgers, Caesar salads, Buffalo wings, and the like. The full bar maintains a selection of local brews on tap. ⊠ *2601 W. Marina Pl., Magnolia* ☎ *206/ 283–8322.*

¢ ✕ **Red Mill.** Seattleites have been seduced by the Red Mill. Burgers here are superbly crafted by a crack assembly-line staff. You can order one dressed simply, with lettuce and smoky "Mill Sauce" mayo, or more elaborately, with menu combinations of luscious roasted Anaheim peppers, blue cheese, red onion jam, or Tillamook cheddar. Vegetarians note: Order the meatless patties as substitutions on the regular burger menu, rather than from the veggie menu—the regular burger buns and dressings are much better. ⊠ *1613 W. Dravus, Magnolia* ☎ *206/284–6363* ⊠ *316 N. 67th St., Greenwood* ☎ *206/783–6362.*

Contemporary

$–$$ ✗ **Szmania's.** Ludger Szmania's comfortable, open-kitchen restaurant is a regional favorite with such dishes as herb-roasted Alaskan halibut with pinot noir–onion sauce, seared ahi tuna on a black rice cake with a red Thai curry sauce, roasted duckling with smoked raspberry barbecue sauce, and grilled New York steak with a balsamic onion cabernet sauvignon glacé. Dishes come in small and large sizes to give you the option of tasting more than one. The wine list has more than 165 vintages from around the world. Szmania's is always full, perhaps because its prices are so reasonable for Seattle. There's outside dining in nice weather. ⊠ *3321 McGraw St., Magnolia Village, Magnolia* ☎ *206/284–7305* ▭ *AE, MC, V* ☉ *Closed Sun. No lunch.*

Japanese

$–$$$ ✗ **Sanmi Sushi.** If you tell people that your favorite sushi restaurant is Magnolia's Sanmi Sushi, you'll either get a blank look or a suspicious one, like "How'd you know about Sanmi?" Devotees swear that there's no better such place in Seattle. The unpretentious restaurant's owner is also the head sushi chef, and his wife is the hostess. Not only will you be treated graciously and eat some fabulous fresh fish, but you've got a gorgeous view of the Magnolia marina. If you order nothing else, try the scallop roll. You won't find more buttery scallops anywhere. ⊠ *2601 W. Marina Pl. (off the Magnolia Bridge), Magnolia* ☎ *206/283–9978* ▭ *AE, MC, V* ☉ *Closed Mon. No lunch weekends.*

Seafood

$$$–$$$$ ✗ **Palisade.** The short ride to the Magnolia neighborhood yields a stunning view back across the bay to the lights of Downtown. And there's no better place to take in the vista than this restaurant at the Elliott Bay Marina. Palisade scores points for its playfully exotic ambience—complete with a gurgling indoor stream. As for the food, the simpler preparations, especially the signature plank-broiled salmon, are most satisfying. Maggie Bluffs, an informal café downstairs, is a great spot for lunch on a breezy summer afternoon. ✛ *From downtown, take Elliott Ave. northwest across Magnolia Bridge to Elliott Bay Marina exit* ⊠ *2601 W. Marina Pl., Magnolia* ☎ *206/285–1000* ▭ *AE, D, DC, MC, V.*

WHERE TO STAY

FODOR'S CHOICE

Alexis Hotel, *Downtown*

Fairmont Olympic Hotel, *Downtown*

Gaslight Inn, *Capitol Hill*

Inn at Harbor Steps, *Downtown*

Inn at the Market, *Downtown*

WSeattle, *Downtown*

HIGHLY RECOMMENDED

Ace Hotel, *Belltown*

Bellevue Club Hotel, *Bellevue*

Elliott Grand Hyatt, *Downtown*

Hotel Monaco, *Downtown*

Marriott, *Downtown*

Marriott Waterfront, *Belltown*

Panama Hotel, *International District*

Sorrento Hotel, *First Hill*

Watertown Hotel, *University District*

Willows Lodge, *Woodinville*

Woodmark Hotel, *Kirkland*

Updated by
Julie Fay

TO GET THE MOST OUT OF SEATTLE'S LODGING SCENE, identify your preferences. Most properties specialize in something or have one or two key features. For some it's state-of-the-art business services, for others it may be romance and pampering.

If you want a view of the Cascades, the Olympics, Elliott Bay, or Lake Union, then look to such high-rises as the Elliott Grand Hyatt, the Sheraton, and the Westin. The vistas from the floor-to-ceiling windows at the WSeattle are dizzying, and the panoramic views at the Inn at the Market and the Edgewater Hotel make you feel part of the scenery. Such moderately priced options as the Ace Hotel and Pensione Nichols have the same striking views as their more expensive cousins. If unforgettably comfortable beds are important, try the Fairmont Olympic or WSeattle. For pampering, choose the Alexis, with its on-site Aveda spa. For the best business services pick a hotel close to the convention center: the Elliott Grand Hyatt, the Madison, the Sheraton, the Westin, the W, or the Fairmont Olympic. If an early morning flight has you worried about rush-hour snarls on I–5, opt for a hotel near the Sea-Tac airport.

Most of Seattle's hotels are Downtown, but there are good deals to be had in the outlying neighborhoods, and some places will transport you to and from Downtown for free. Both of the Marriotts at Lake Union, for example, offer a shuttle to the Pike Place Market, Westlake Center, the Space Needle, and Pier 70. Bed-and-breakfasts on Capitol Hill are a manageable walk from Downtown and are near boutiques, restaurants, bars, and movie theaters.

Less expensive but still tasteful lodging options (rates often include parking) are available in the University District, which is well served by the city's buses and which has affordable restaurants, trendy shops, and lots of pubs. Both Belltown and Queen Anne attract a wealthier, more staid clientele. Queen Anne is perfect for those attending sights and cultural events at the Seattle Center. Bellevue is desirable to travelers with business on the Eastside, shoppers, and those looking for proximity to outdoor activities in the Cascades. Although the Fremont neighborhood has attracted commercial and residential newcomers, it has few lodgings. The closest bets are the Marriott Courtyard at Lake Union or the Chelsea Station near the Woodland Park Zoo.

Seattle's peak season is May through September, with August at the pinnacle. You aren't likely to have trouble booking a room the rest of the year as long as your visit doesn't coincide with major conventions, or arts or sporting events. But to make sure you won't go sleepless, the best advice remains to book as far in advance as possible.

WHAT IT COSTS				
	$$$$	$$$	$$	$	¢
FOR 2 PEOPLE	over $250	$200–$250	$150–$200	$100–$150	under $100

Price categories are assigned based on the range between the least and most expensive standard double rooms in high season. Tax (17%) is extra.

Assume that hotels operate on the European Plan (EP, with no meals) unless specified that they use the All-inclusive (all meals and some drinks and activities), Continental Plan (CP, with a Continental breakfast), Modified American Plan (MAP, with breakfast and dinner), or the Full American Plan (FAP, with all meals). All hotels listed have private bath, heat, air-conditioning, TV, and phone unless otherwise noted.

The lodgings listed are the cream of the crop in each price category. We always list the facilities that are available—but don't specify whether they cost extra: when pricing accommodations, always ask what's included and what entails an additional charge. Also, be sure to inquire about reduced rates. Many hotels offer special weekend rates, sometimes up to 50% off regular prices. Note, however, that such deals aren't usually available in peak summer months, when hotels are full.

In & Around Downtown

Downtown & Belltown

★ **$$$$** ✠ **Elliott Grand Hyatt.** The Elliott was built as part of an expansion of the Washington State Convention Center. Both projects appear to have been designed to appeal to Seattleites in the high-tech industry. The hotel offers state-of-the-art Internet access (100Mb/s), Virtual Private Network technology, video conference rooms, and a 151-seat theater with data ports at every seat. Rooms on the upper floors have views of Elliott Bay, Lake Union, and the Cascade and Olympic Mountain ranges. Carrara marble floors, Vesuvio granite counters, and oversize soaking tubs are standard in all of the guest bathrooms. ✉ *721 Pine St., Downtown 98101* ☎ *206/774–1234* 🖷 *206/774–6311* ⊕ *www.hyatt.com* 🛏 *317 rooms, 108 suites* ⌂ *Restaurant, café, room service, in-room data ports, minibars, gym, bar, theater, laundry service, concierge, meeting rooms, parking (fee), no-smoking rooms* ▤ *AE, D, DC, MC, V.*

$$$$ ✠ **Fairmont Olympic Hotel.** This is the place to stay in town for incom-
Fodor's Choice parable elegance and service. The 1920s Renaissance Revival–style
★ Olympic is the grande dame of Seattle hotels. Marble, wood paneling, thick rugs, and plush armchairs adorn the public spaces; graceful staircases lead to ballrooms. The Georgian (the hotel's premier dining room) and a gilded balcony overlook the lobby. Sizable guest rooms are done in soothing yellows, blues, and greens; each is furnished with a sofa, desk, and other period reproduction pieces. Amenities include chocolates on your pillow, complimentary shoe shines, and the morning newspaper. ✉ *411 University St., Downtown 98101* ☎ *206/621–1700 or 800/ 223–8772* 🖷 *206/682–9633* ⊕ *www.fairmont.com* 🛏 *450 rooms* ⌂ *3 restaurants, room service, in-room data ports, in-room safes, minibars, refrigerators, indoor pool, health club, lounge, children's programs (ages 0–17), laundry service, concierge, meeting rooms, parking (fee)* ▤ *AE, D, DC, MC, V.*

★ **$$$$** ✠ **Hotel Monaco.** Goldfish in your room are among the fun touches at this luxury hotel in a former office building in the heart of the Financial District. The light and whimsical lobby has high ceilings and hand-painted nautical murals inspired by the fresco at the Palace of Knossos in Crete. A pleasing blend of bold and bright colors and patterns graces the spacious guest rooms. In-room amenities include voice mail, irons, hair dryers, coffeemakers, and stereos with CD players. The hotel really lays out the red carpet for pets. ✉ *1101 4th Ave., Downtown 98101* ☎ *206/621–1770 or 800/945–2240* 🖷 *206/621–7779* ⊕ *www.monaco-seattle.com* 🛏 *144 rooms, 45 suites* ⌂ *Restaurant, room service, in-room data ports, in-room fax, gym, bar, dry cleaning, laundry service, concierge, business services, meeting rooms, airport shuttle, parking (fee), some pets allowed, no-smoking rooms* ▤ *AE, D, DC, MC, V.*

$$$$ ✠ **Hotel Vintage Park.** Each guest room in this medium-size hotel is named for a Washington winery or vineyard. The theme extends to complimentary wine served each evening in the lobby while patrons relax on richly upholstered sofas and chairs facing a marble fireplace. Rooms—decorated in dark green, plum, deep red, taupe, and gold—have custom-made cherry furniture and original artwork. If you're literary-minded, hotel staff will deliver your choice of titles from the Seattle Public Library. The athletically inclined can have exercise equipment brought to

CloseUp

LODGING ALTERNATIVES

BOOK AS FAR IN ADVANCE *as possible if you're coming from May through September. And know that big, high-rise hotels and chain motels aren't your only lodging options.*

Apartment Rentals & Home Exchanges

A furnished rental can save you money, especially if you're traveling with a group. You can also exchange your home for someone else's by joining a home-exchange organization, which will send you its updated listings of available exchanges for a year and will include your own listing in at least one of them.

Home-Exchange Clubs: HomeLink International ✇ Box 47747, Tampa, FL 33647 ☎ 813/975–9825 or 800/638–3841 ⊕ www.homelink.org ✉ $75 per year. **Intervac U.S.** ✇ Box 590504, San Francisco, CA 94159 ☎ 800/756–4663 ⊕ www.intervacus.com ✉ $125 yearly fee.

Local Rental Agents: Accommodations Plus ☎ 425/455–2773 ⊕ www.aplusnw. com. **Apartment Hunters** ☎ 206/770–0111 ⊕ www.apthunters.com. **Apartment Insider** ☎ 206/284–2441 ⊕ www. apartmentinsider.com. **Apartment Locators** ☎ 206/524–1111.

Rental Listings: ApartmentGuide–Greater Puget Sound ☎ 425/545–4431 ⊕ www. ApartmentGuide.com. **For Rent Magazine** ☎ 425/487–2869 ⊕ www.aptsforrent. com. **Seattle Rent Tech** ☎ 206/322–5544 ⊕ seattle.renttech.com/web.

B&Bs

Seattle's B&Bs are primarily in historic homes with the exception of the Wall Street Inn (in a former apartment building) and the Inn at Harbor Steps (in a modern residential high-rise). Make reservations as far in advance as possible; refunds are usually possible up to 10 days before arrival, but investigate whether you can lose your deposit. Sometimes a fine of $35 is levied for cancellations.

Reservation Services: Bed & Breakfast Association of Seattle ☎ 206/547–1020 ⊕ www.seattlebandbs.com. **Northwest**

Bed & Breakfast Reservation Service ✉ 610 SW Broadway, Portland, OR 97205 ☎ 503/243–7616. In the United Kingdom: **American Bed & Breakfast, Inter-Bed Network** ✉ 31 Ernest Rd., Colchester, Essex CO7 9LQ ☎ 0206/223162.

Hostels

In some 5,000 locations in more than 70 countries around the world, Hostelling International (HI), the umbrella group for a number of national youth-hostel associations, offers single-sex, dorm-style beds and, at many hostels, accommodations for couples and families. Membership in any HI national hostel association, open to travelers of all ages, allows you to stay in HI-affiliated hostels at member rates, about $10–$25 per night. Members have priority if the hostel is full and are eligible for discounts, even on rail and bus travel in some countries.

Local Information: Hostelling International Seattle ✉ 84 Union St. ☎ 206/622–5443 or 888/622–5443 ⊕ www. hiseattle.org.

Main Organizations: Australian Youth Hostel Association ✉ 10 Mallett St., Camperdown, NSW 2050, Australia ☎ 02/9565–1699 ⊕ www.yha.org.au. **Hostelling International—American Youth Hostels** ✉ 733 15th St. NW, Suite 840, Washington, DC 20005 ☎ 202/783–6161 ⊕ www.hiayh.org. **Hostelling International—Canada** ✉ 400–205 Catherine St., Ottawa, Ontario K2P 1C3, Canada ☎ 613/237–7884 ⊕ www. hostellingintl.ca. **Youth Hostel Association of England and Wales** ✉ Trevelyan House, 8 St. Stephen's Hill, St. Albans, Hertfordshire AL1 2DY, U.K. ☎ 0870/8708808 ⊕ www.yha.org.uk. **Youth Hostels Association of New Zealand** ✉ Box 436, Christchurch, New Zealand ☎ 03/379–9970 ⊕ www.yha.org.nz.

their rooms. Tulio, the hotel restaurant, is a popular spot for rustic Italian fare. ⊠ *1100 5th Ave., Downtown 98101* ☎ *206/624–8000 or 800/624–4433* 🖶 *206/623–0568* 🌐 *www.vintagepark.com* 🛏 *126 rooms* ♺ *Restaurant, room service, in-room data ports, minibars, refrigerators, spa, laundry service, concierge, meeting rooms, parking (fee), no-smoking floors* ▤ *AE, D, DC, MC, V.*

$$$$ 🏨 **Seattle Sheraton Hotel and Towers.** Business travelers are the primary patrons of this high-rise hotel close to shopping and the convention center. The busy lobby has a comfortable open lounge which is ideal for people watching and enjoying the notable collection of art glass produced by well-known Northwest artist Dale Chihuly. Guest rooms are plain, yet generously proportioned. Views here are mostly territorial, but you can get a glimpse Elliott Bay or Lake Union on or above the 20th floor. The rooms on the top five floors, larger and more elegant than those below, include concierge service and complimentary Continental breakfast. All rooms have two-line phones. ⊠ *1400 6th Ave., Downtown 98101* ☎ *206/621–9000 or 800/325–3535* 🖶 *206/621–8441* 🌐 *www.sheraton.com/seattle* 🛏 *800 rooms, 40 suites* ♺ *3 restaurants, room service, in-room data ports, in-room safes, minibars, indoor pool, health club, 2 bars, laundry service, concierge, meeting rooms, parking (fee), no-smoking rooms* ▤ *AE, D, DC, MC, V.*

$$$–$$$$ 🏨 **Alexis Hotel.** The European-style Alexis occupies two restored build-
Fodor'sChoice ings near the waterfront. Complimentary wine is served 5:30–6:30 in
★ the lobby bar, a prelude to the attentive service you'll receive throughout your stay. Rooms, in subdued colors, are decorated in imported Italian and French fabrics, with antique and reproduction furniture. Some suites have whirlpool tubs or wood-burning fireplaces, and some have marble fixtures. Unfortunately, views are limited, and rooms facing First Avenue can be noisy. Amenities include in-room cordless phones, shoe shines, the morning newspaper, and access to workout facilities. Pets are welcome. ⊠ *1007 1st Ave., Downtown 98104* ☎ *206/624–4844 or 800/426–7033* 🖶 *206/621–9009* 🌐 *www.alexishotel.com* 🛏 *65 rooms, 44 suites* ♺ *Restaurant, room service, in-room data ports, minibars, refrigerators, gym, massage, steam room, bar, lobby lounge, laundry service, concierge, meeting rooms, parking (fee), no-smoking floors* ▤ *AE, D, DC, MC, V.*

$$$–$$$$ 🏨 **Edgewater.** The only hotel that sits on a pier beside Elliott Bay, the Edgewater has spacious waterfront accommodations with balconies providing views of ferries, barges, and the Olympic Mountains. All rooms, including those facing Alaskan Way, have fireplaces and are decorated in rustic plaids and peeled-log furniture. From the lobby's comfortable sofas and chairs, you can sometimes watch sea lions frolicking in the bay. A courtesy van shuttles patrons to the Downtown area on a first-come, first-served basis. ⊠ *Pier 67, 2411 Alaskan Way, Belltown 98121* ☎ *206/728–7000 or 800/624–0670* 🖶 *206/441–4119* 🌐 *www.noblehousehotels. com* 🛏 *237 rooms* ♺ *Restaurant, room service, in-room data ports, minibars, gym, bicycles, bar, laundry service, concierge, meeting rooms, parking (fee), no-smoking rooms* ▤ *AE, D, DC, MC, V.*

$$$–$$$$ 🏨 **Westin Hotel.** The flagship of the Westin chain often hosts U.S. presidents and other visiting dignitaries. Northeast of Pike Place Market, Seattle's largest hotel is easily recognizable by its twin cylindrical towers. The innovative design gives all rooms terrific views of Puget Sound, Lake Union, the Space Needle, or the city. Airy guest rooms are furnished in a simple, high-quality style; some are equipped with speakerphones and modem hookups. ⊠ *1900 5th Ave., Downtown 98101* ☎ *206/728–1000 or 800/228–3000* 🖶 *206/727–5896* 🌐 *www.westin.com* 🛏 *822 rooms, 43 suites* ♺ *3 restaurants, room service, in-room data ports, some in-room fax, in-room safes, minibars, indoor pool, gym, hair salon, mas-*

sage, 2 bars, children's programs (ages 0–17), laundry service, concierge, business services, convention center, car rental, parking (fee), no-smoking floors ▤ *AE, D, DC, MC, V.*

$$$–$$$$

Fodor'sChoice

★

▥ **WSeattle.** Easily Seattle's coolest hotel, "the W" manages to maintain a welcoming and relaxed tone. Candlelight and custom-designed board games encourage lingering around the lobby fireplace on deep couches strewn with throw pillows. Nearby bookshelves hold art books, and rough-hewn wood bowls cradle shiny green apples. Decorated in black, brown, and French blue, guest rooms are almost austere, but beds are exceptionally comfortable with pillow-top mattresses and 100% goose-down pillows and comforters. Floor-to-ceiling windows maximize striking views of the Sound and the city. Cotton robes plus an iron, ironing board, coffeemaker, and hair dryer are standard amenities. ▢ *1112 4th Ave., Downtown 98101* ☎ *206/264–6000 or 877/946–8357* ▨ *206/264–6100* ⊕ *www.whotels.com* ⇌ *419 rooms, 16 suites* ⌂ *Restaurant, room service, in-room data ports, in-room safes, minibars, gym, bar, laundry service, concierge, business services, meeting rooms, parking (fee), no-smoking floors* ▤ *AE, D, DC, MC, V.*

$$–$$$$

Fodor'sChoice

★

▥ **Inn at the Market.** This sophisticated yet unpretentious property up the street from Pike Place Market oozes personality. The good-size rooms have comfortable modern furniture and small touches such as fresh flowers and ceramic sculptures. Ask for a room with views of the Market and Elliott Bay. Coffee and the morning newspaper are complimentary. Comfortably furnished with Adirondack chairs, the fifth-floor deck overlooks the water and the Market. Restaurants include Campagne and the less formal yet equally romantic café Bacco, which serves tasty variations on breakfast classics. For a fee you have access to a health club and spa down the street. ▢ *86 Pine St., Downtown 98101* ☎ *206/443–3600 or 800/446–4484* ▨ *206/448–0631* ⊕ *www.innatthemarket.com* ⇌ *60 rooms, 10 suites* ⌂ *3 restaurants, room service, in-room data ports, refrigerators, laundry service, concierge, meeting room, parking (fee), no-smoking rooms* ▤ *AE, D, DC, MC, V.*

★ $$$

▥ **Marriott Waterfront.** Finally, another hotel takes advantage of Seattle's prime waterfront real estate. All rooms face the water (half have balconies) in this long narrow building overlooking the shoreline. For the best views, book the north tower. The elegant lobby has cascading Italian chandeliers, walnut detailing, glass-tile mosaic floors, and back-lit walls of fused onyx and glass. High tea is served in the gallery, a breezeway that joins the lobby with Todd English's Fish Club Restaurant. Wireless Internet access is available in all of the hotel's public spaces. Irons, ironing boards, hair dryers, and a complimentary newspaper come with each room. ▢ *2100 Alaskan Way (between Piers 62/63 and Pier 66), Belltown 98121* ☎ *206/443–5000 or 800/228–9290* ▨ *206/256–1100* ⊕ *www.gowestmarriott.com/seattlewaterfront* ⇌ *345 rooms, 13 suites* ⌂ *Restaurant, bar, café, room service, in-room data ports, indoor-outdoor pool, gym, bar, dry cleaning, laundry service, concierge, concierge floor, business services, meeting rooms, airport shuttle, parking (fee), no-smoking rooms* ▤ *AE, D, DC, MC, V.*

$$$

▥ **Paramount Hotel.** The Paramount is a château-style hotel close to fine dining, shopping, and high-tech entertainment sites including Gameworks, Niketown, and a 16-screen multiplex theater. Inside, the comfortable lobby—with a fireplace, bookshelves, and period reproductions—looks like a country gentleman's smoking parlor. Decorated in hunter green and beige with gray accents, guest rooms are quiet but small. All have work areas, lounge chairs, and large bathrooms. ▢ *724 Pine St., Downtown 98101* ☎ *206/292–9500 or 800/663–1144* ▨ *206/292–8610* ⊕ *www.paramounthotelseattle.com* ⇌ *146 rooms, 2 suites* ⌂ *Restaurant, room service, in-room data ports, cable TV with movies and video* *games, gym, laundry service, concierge, meeting rooms, parking (fee), no-smoking rooms* ☐ *AE, D, DC, MC, V.*

$$$ 🏨 **Seattle Hilton.** Just west of I–5, the Seattle Hilton is a popular site for meetings and conventions. The rooms, tasteful but nondescript, have soothing color schemes. Providing excellent views of the city, the Top of the Hilton bar-restaurant serves well-prepared salmon dishes and other local specialties. An underground passage connects the Hilton with the Rainier Square shopping concourse, the 5th Avenue Theater, and the convention center. ✉ *1301 6th Ave., Downtown 98101* ☎ *206/624–0500, 800/542–7700, or 800/426–0535* 🖷 *206/682–9029* ⊕ *www.hilton. com* ⇥ *237 rooms, 3 suites* ⚑ *2 restaurants, room service, in-room data ports, minibars, gym, piano bar, laundry service, concierge, business services, meeting rooms, parking (fee), no-smoking floors* ☐ *AE, D, DC, MC, V.*

$$–$$$ 🏨 **Inn at Harbor Steps.** On the lower floors of a high-rise residential building, this hotel is a departure for Four Sisters Inns, whose collection of
Fodor's Choice small hotels focuses on quaint city and country properties. The en-
★ trance and corridors, in muted gray, tan, and sage, have something of a yuppie-dormitory feel, but guest rooms are large, with high ceilings, gas fireplaces, and tidy kitchenettes. Bathrooms accommodate large tubs (some of them whirlpools) and oversize glass-enclosed shower stalls. A tempting breakfast buffet is served in the dining room. Complimentary hors d'oeuvres, wine, and tea are served each afternoon in the library. ✉ *1221 1st Ave., Downtown 98101* ☎ *206/748–0973 or 888/728–8910* 🖷 *206/748–0533* ⊕ *www.foursisters.com* ⇥ *30 rooms* ⚑ *In-room data ports, refrigerators, indoor pool, gym, sauna, basketball, laundry facilities, laundry service, concierge, meeting room, parking (fee)* ☐ *AE, MC, V* ⦿ *BP.*

$$–$$$ 🏨 **Red Lion Hotel on 5th Avenue.** In the heart of Downtown, this former bank headquarters is a comfortable business-oriented hotel convenient to the shopping and financial districts. Service is warm and professional; the public spaces have high ceilings, tall windows, and dark-wood paneling. Lining the lobby are sitting areas with couches and overstuffed chairs upholstered in olive green and aubergine velvets and brocades. Guest rooms are mid-size and attractively appointed in a green and pink botanical theme. Rooms on the Executive floors, 17–20, have exquisite views of Puget Sound or the city skyline. All rooms are equipped with coffeemakers, hair dryers, irons, and ironing boards. ✉ *1415 5th Ave., Downtown 98101* ☎ *206/971–8000 or 800/325–4000* 🖷 *206/ 971–8100* ⊕ *www.redlion.com/5thave* ⇥ *287 rooms, 10 suites* ⚑ *Restaurant, room service, in-room data ports, gym, laundry service, concierge, business services, meeting rooms, parking (fee), no-smoking rooms* ☐ *AE, D, DC, MC, V.*

$$–$$$ 🏨 **Summerfield Suites by Wyndham.** Next to the convention center and overlooking I–5, Summerfield Suites is ideal for an extended business stay. Guest rooms are simply decorated in hues of burgundy and green. Most of the rooms are suites, which have full kitchens, living rooms with gas fireplaces, and separate bedrooms. Street-facing rooms have views of Lake Union, but the exhaust fumes and noise from traffic below are a deterrent to using the balconies from which the scenery is best admired. Rooms are remarkably quiet, however, when doors and windows are kept closed. ✉ *1011 Pike St., Downtown 98101* ☎ *206/682–8282 or 800/833–4353* 🖷 *206/682–5315* ⊕ *www.summerfieldseattle.com* ⇥ *10 rooms, 183 suites* ⚑ *In-room data ports, pool, gym, sauna, laundry facilities, laundry service, meeting rooms, parking (fee), no-smoking rooms* ☐ *AE, D, DC, MC, V* ⦿ *CP.*

$$–$$$ 🏨 **Warwick Hotel.** Service is friendly and leisurely (but not slow) at the Warwick, which is part of an international chain. The rooms are un-

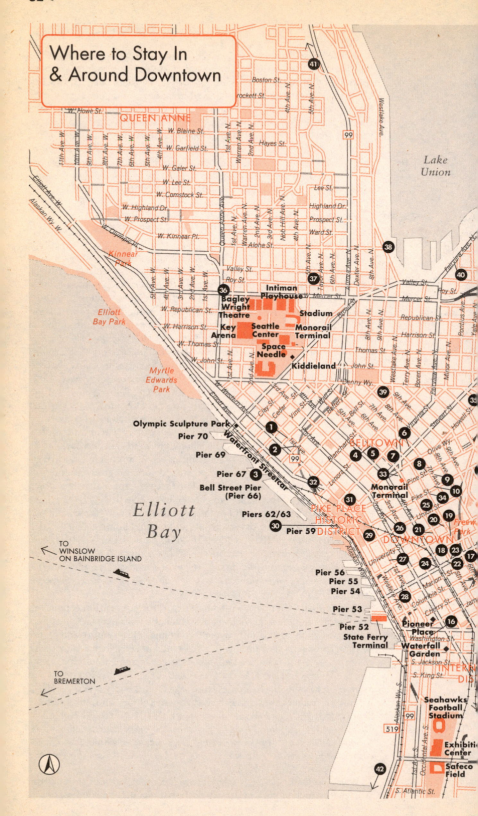

Where to Stay In & Around Downtown

QUEEN ANNE

Lake Union

Kinnear Park

Elliott Bay Park

Myrtle Edwards Park

Bagley Wright Theatre

Intiman Playhouse

Stadium

Key Arena

Seattle Center

Monorail Terminal

Space Needle

Kiddieland

Olympic Sculpture Park

Pier 70

Waterfront Streetcar

Pier 69

Pier 67

Bell Street Pier (Pier 66)

Elliott Bay

BELLTOWN

Monorail Terminal

Piers 62/63

PIKE PLACE HISTORIC DISTRICT

Pier 59

DOWNTOWN

Freeway Park

TO WINSLOW ON BAINBRIDGE ISLAND

University St

Pier 56

Pier 55

Pier 54

TO BREMERTON

Pier 53

Pier 52

State Ferry Terminal

Pioneer Place

Waterfall Garden

INTERN'L DIST

Seahawks Football Stadium

Exhibition Center

Safeco Field

Downtown & Belltown ▼

Ace Hotel 2
Alexis Hotel 28
Claremont Hotel 5
Crowne Plaza 19
Edgewater 3
Elliott Grand Hyatt 9
Fairmont
Olympic Hotel 21
Green Tortoise
Backpacker's Hotel . . .26
Hostel International
Seattle 29
Hotel Monaco 24
Hotel Vintage Park 18
Inn at Harbor Steps . . .27
Inn at the Market 30
Madison
Renaissance 17
Marriott Springhill
Suites 35
Marriott Waterfront . . .32
Mayflower Park
Hotel 33
Pacific Plaza 23
Paramount Hotel 8
Pensione Nichols 31
La Quinta 39
Red Lion Hotel on
5th Avenue 25
Roosevelt Hotel 10
Seattle Hilton 20
Seattle Sheraton
Hotel and Towers 34
Summerfield Suites
by Wyndham 11
Vance Hotel 6
Wall Street Inn 1
Warwick Hotel 4
WSeattle 22
Westin Hotel 7

**International District &
Pioneer Square** ▼
Amaranth Inn 14
Panama Hotel 15
Pioneer Square
Hotel 16

First Hill ▼
Inn at
Virginia Mason 12
Sorrento 13

Lake Union & Fremont ▼
Chelsea Station 41
Marriott Courtyard 38
Marriott
Residence Inn 40

Queen Anne ▼
Hampton Inn
and Suites 37
MarQueen Hotel 36

West Seattle ▼
Villa Heidelberg 42

**Seattle-Tacoma
International Airport** ▼
Coast Gateway Hotel . . .49
Doubletree Hotel
Seattle Airport 45
Doubletree Inn,
Doubletree Suites 44
Hilton Seattle
Airport and
Conference Center 46
Marriott Sea-Tac 43
Red Lion Hotel:
Seattle Airport 47
Wyndham Garden
Hotel 48

CloseUp

WITH CHILDREN?

MOST HOTELS IN SEATTLE ALLOW children under a certain age to stay in their parents' room at no extra charge, but others charge for them as extra adults; be sure to find out the cutoff age for children's discounts. Cribs are usually available upon request and hotel staff can assist you in finding a reputable baby-sitter.

The Fairmont Olympic Hotel has a swimming pool and offers outstanding children's amenities such as toys and games, room service menu with a Winnie-the-Pooh theme, and child-size furniture and bathrobes. Families are made welcome at the Marriott Residence Inn on Lake Union. All the guest accommodations have kitchens and bedrooms off living rooms. The large atrium-style lobby has a waterfall and several sitting areas stocked with books and games. The Sheraton's big rooms, rooftop pool, and proximity to

FAO Schwarz toy store (it's across the street) make it popular with families. It's a favorite during the holidays, when the lobby is filled with bigger-than-life gingerbread houses built by chef/architect teams. In the U-District, the laid-back University Inn has an outdoor pool, free parking, and the Portage Bay Cafe—a great place to dine with kids.

Best Choices: Fairmont Olympic Hotel ✉ 411 University St. ☎ 206/621–1700 or 800/223–8772 ⊕ www.fourseasons. com. **Marriott Residence Inn** ✉ 800 Fairview Ave. N ☎ 206/624–6000, 800/331–3131 for central reservations ⊕ www.marriott.com. **Seattle Sheraton Hotel and Towers** ✉ 1400 6th Ave. ☎ 206/621–9000 or 800/325–3535 ⊕ www.sheraton.com/seattle. **University Inn** ✉ 4140 Roosevelt Way NE ☎ 206/ 632–5055 or 800/733–3855 ⊕ www. universityinnseattle.com.

derstated without being bland; most have small balconies providing Downtown views. Furnishings tend toward the traditional rather than the modern. Brasserie Margeaux, the hotel restaurant-lounge, is a welcome retreat after a day in this bustling neighborhood. The Warwick offers 24-hour courtesy transportation within Downtown. ✉ 401 Lenora St., Belltown 98121 ☎ 206/443–4300 or 800/426–9280 🖷 206/448–1662 ⊕ www.warwickhotels.com ➲ 225 rooms, 4 suites ⚫ Restaurant, room service, in-room data ports, indoor pool, gym, hot tub, sauna, bar, concierge, parking (fee), no-smoking rooms ▭ AE, D, DC, MC, V.

$–$$$ 🏨 **Mayflower Park Hotel.** Brass fixtures, antiques, and lacquered screens give a muted Asian feel to the public and private spaces at this older property near the Westlake Center. Service is smooth and unobtrusive. Rooms are on the small side, but the Mayflower Park is so sturdily constructed that it's much quieter than many modern downtown hotels. You'll have privileges at a nearby health club. ✉ 405 Olive Way, Downtown 98101 ☎ 206/623–8700 or 800/426–5100 🖷 206/382–6997 ⊕ www. mayflowerpark.com ➲ 159 rooms, 13 suites ⚫ Restaurant, room service, gym, bar, laundry service, business services, meeting rooms, parking (fee), no-smoking rooms ▭ AE, D, DC, MC, V.

$$ 🏨 **Claremont Hotel.** The small lobby of this historic 1926 property has an understated beauty and lots of charm. The original marble wainscoting and fireplace have been affectionately preserved and are accented by a rich terra-cotta wall finish. Guest rooms run the gamut from cramped and viewless standards to spacious suites, some with kitchens. Many rooms have large walk-in closets; all of the bathrooms have been restored in keeping with their original style. The hotel's two-story ballroom is popular for weddings and other festivities. ✉ 2000 4th Ave., Downtown 98121 ☎ 206/448–8600 or 800/448–8601 🖷 206/441–7140 ⊕ www.claremonthotel.com ➲ 30 rooms, 80 suites ⚫ Restaurant, in-

room data ports, gym, laundry service, meeting rooms, parking (fee), no-smoking rooms ▭ *AE, D, DC, MC, V.*

$$ ▧ **Crowne Plaza.** A favorite of business travelers, the Crowne Plaza is directly off I–5, midway between First Hill and the financial district. The lobby is small and plainly appointed in teal and cream with brass accents and potted plants. Rooms are quiet and spacious, with lounge chairs and work areas. All have views of Harbor Island to the south and Elliott Bay, Seattle Center, and the Space Needle to the north. The relaxed and friendly staff is very attentive. ⊠ *1113 6th Ave., Downtown 98101* ☎ *206/464–1980 or 800/521–2762* 🖶 *206/340–1617* ⊕ *www.basshotels. com* 🛏 *415 rooms, 28 suites* ♨ *Restaurant, room service, in-room data ports, health club, sauna, bar, laundry service, concierge, business services, meeting rooms, parking (fee), some pets allowed, no-smoking rooms* ▭ *AE, D, DC, MC, V.*

$$ ▧ **Madison Renaissance.** Rooms at this high-rise between Downtown and I–5 are decorated in deep green, burgundy, and brown, with metal accents and dark-wood furniture. Good views of Downtown, Elliott Bay, and the Cascades can be had from rooms above the 10th floor—above the 20th, they're excellent. Guests on the club-level floors get complimentary Continental breakfast and their own concierge. Amenities on all floors include free coffee, the morning newspaper, and shoe shines. The rooftop health club has a 40-foot pool. ⊠ *515 Madison St., Downtown 98104* ☎ *206/583–0300 or 800/278–4159* 🖶 *206/622–8635* ⊕ *www.renaissance.com* 🛏 *466 rooms, 88 suites* ♨ *2 restaurants, room service, in-room data ports, minibars, pool, hot tub, bar, laundry service, concierge, meeting rooms, parking (fee)* ▭ *AE, D, DC, MC, V* ⦿ *CP.*

$–$$ ▧ **Pensione Nichols.** One block from Pike Place Market, this B&B's location can't be beat. Some rooms have shared bath, but both of the second-floor suites have their own, as well as an enclosed balcony, full kitchen, separate bedroom, and large living room. Evidence of the owner's former life as an antiques collector and shop owner are apparent in the furnishings throughout. Each of the third-floor rooms is unique; most have skylights rather than windows. Breakfast consists of warm breads and fruit fresh from the market served in the natural-light-filled common area overlooking Elliott Bay. ⊠ *1923 1st Ave., Downtown 98101* ☎ *206/441–7125 or 800/440–7125* 🛏 *10 rooms with shared bath; 2 suites with bath* ▭ *AE, D, DC, MC, V* ⦿ *CP.*

$–$$ ▧ **Roosevelt Hotel.** An older hotel near the convention center and the shopping district, the Roosevelt has an elegant lobby with a grand piano, a fireplace, a Chinese lacquered screen, and walls of windows— a great place to relax and watch the foot traffic outside. Smallish rooms are furnished with period reproductions upholstered in mellow pinks and greens. Thanks to the insulated windows you can enjoy city views without hearing street noise. Some bathrooms have their original tile work, but there isn't much counter space. ⊠ *1531 7th Ave., Downtown* ☎ *206/621–1200 or 800/582–0157* 🖶 *206/233–0335* ⊕ *www. coasthotels.com* 🛏 *138 rooms, 13 suites* ♨ *Restaurant, room service, in-room data ports, gym, bar, laundry service, meeting rooms, parking (fee), no-smoking rooms* ▭ *AE, D, DC, MC, V.*

$ ▧ **Marriott Springhill Suites.** On the eastern edge of downtown, Springhill Suites is removed from the city center's bustle. Decorated in cheery yellows, the lobby is open and airy, with large windows, deep couches, a TV tuned to MSNBC, and stacks of *Wall Street Journal*s. The all-suites accommodations—with large desks, high-speed Internet access, and separate sleeping areas—reinforce the impression that the hotel caters to business people as well as leisure travelers. The darkish rooms come equipped with dual-line speakerphones, irons, ironing boards, and coffeemakers.

A free shuttle takes you to one of three places Downtown. ✉ *1800 Yale Ave., Downtown 98101* ☎*206/254–0500 or 888/287–9400* 🖷*206/254–0990* ⊕ *www.springhillsuites.com* 🖙 *234 suites* ⚶ *Restaurant, in-room data ports, microwave, refrigerator, exercise equipment, indoor pool, hot tub, lobby lounge, laundry facilities, business services, parking (fee), no-smoking rooms* ▭ *AE, D, DC, MC, V* ⦿ CP.

$ 🏨 **Wall Street Inn.** Built in the 1950s as a land base for merchant marines, this prime piece of Belltown real estate is now a homey land base for visitors. Guest rooms are comfortably furnished in an appealing mix of styles; some still have Murphy beds. A handful of rooms have kitchenettes, and seven have peek-a-boo views of Elliott Bay and the Olympic Mountains. Partake of the extensive Continental breakfast in front of the fire, on the patio, or back in your room. All rooms have hair dryers, robes, and slippers. ✉ *2507 1st Ave., Belltown 98121* ☎ *206/448–0125* 🖷 *206/448–2406* ⊕ *www.wallstreetinn.com* 🖙 *20 rooms* ⚶ *In-room data ports, some kitchenettes, refrigerators, business services, parking (fee)* ▭ *AE, MC, V* ⦿ CP.

★ ¢–$$ 🏨 **Ace Hotel.** "You are beautiful" is etched into every vanity mirror at this ultrahip, super-friendly hostelry in Belltown, and the color scheme is white on white, evoking the movie set for *Sleeper*. Offering the squeaky clean functionality of a Norwegian budget hotel, The Ace serves the nightclubbing public in the most modern of styles. Half the rooms sleep "one or two humans" and share bathrooms. Suites are larger and have full private bathrooms hidden behind rotating walls. Thoughtful amenities in these somewhat austere deluxe accommodations include condoms, *Kama Sutra* books, energy bars, and bottled water. ✉ *2423 1st Ave., Belltown 98121* ☎*206/448–4721* 🖷*206/374–0745* ⊕*www.theacehotel. com* 🖙 *24 rooms* ⚶ *Restaurant, room service, in-room data ports, parking (fee), no-smoking rooms* ▭ *AE, D, DC, MC, V.*

¢–$ 🏨 **La Quinta.** The exterior of this otherwise plain building is visible for many blocks due to its five-story mural of frolicking orcas. The whale theme is continued in the lobby where bright paintings of the black and white cetaceans by the artist known simply as "Wyland" hang by the dozen. The suites, which have kitchenettes and separate bedrooms, show less wear than do the regular guest rooms. La Quinta surprises with its many amenities—from high-speed Internet access to warm cookies in the lobby—and its friendly service. All rooms have hair dryers, irons, ironing boards, and coffeemakers. ✉ *2224 8th Ave., Belltown 98121* ☎ *206/624–6820 or 800/437–4867* 🖷 *206/467–6926* ⊕ *www. lq.com* 🖙 *50 rooms, 12 suites* ⚶ *In-room data ports, microwaves, refrigerators, exercise equipment, hot tub, sauna, laundry facilities, business services, free parking, some pets allowed (fee), no-smoking rooms* ▭ *AE, D, DC, MC, V* ⦿ CP.

¢–$ 🏨 **Pacific Plaza.** Locally owned and independently operated, this 1929 property maintains a low profile in a neighborhood filled with fancy hotels. Its Fourth Avenue entrance is through a coffee shop, and its Spring Street entrance is marked only by a small awning. Location (it is across the street from the new Rem Koolhaas library building), skilled management, and the fair price make this one of the best lodging bargains downtown. Guest beds have tan leather headboards and sage green spreads. The small-ish rooms all have ceiling fans and city views. Irons, ironing boards, hair dryers, and coffeemakers are standard. ✉ *400 Spring St., Downtown 98104* ☎ *206/623–3900 or 800/426–1165* 🖷*206/623–2059* ⊕*www.pacificplazahotel.com* 🖙*159 rooms* ⚶ *Restaurant, coffee shop, pizzeria, concierge, parking (fee), no-smoking rooms* ▭ *AE, D, DC, MC, V.*

¢–$ 🏨 **Vance Hotel.** Close to shopping and the Convention Center, this historic hotel does a tidy little business keeping the budget traveler close to the major Downtown attractions. The small lobby is impressively elegant with its dark marble, original millwork, and deep blue walls. The guest rooms are clean and bright: pretty yellow fabrics were used to create a cheery effect. Rooms facing Stewart Street can get a little noisy during peak traffic times. ⊠ *620 Stewart St., Downtown 98101* ☎ *206/441–4200 or 877/956–8500* 🖷 *206/443–5754* 🌐 *www.vancehotel.com* 🖙 *169 rooms* ⚫ *Restaurant, concierge, laundry service, parking (fee), no-smoking floors* 🖃 *AE, D, DC, MC, V.*

¢   🖼 **Green Tortoise Backpacker's Hotel.** Kitchen privileges are included with the accommodations at this hostellike hotel one block from the Pike Place Market on a gritty stretch of Second Avenue. This facility is a bit grubby, and some of the front-desk staffers are terminally crabby, but the price is tough to beat. For $20 you can let a bed in a dorm room and spend your days fraternizing with the adventurous, young, international clientele that makes this place a vital travel hub. ⊠ *1525 2nd Ave., Downtown 98101* ☎ *206/340–1222* 🖷 *206/623–3207* 🌐 *www.greentortoise.net* 🖙 *7 private rooms, 30 dorm rooms all share bath* ⚫ *Laundry facilities* 🖃 *MC, V.*

¢   🖼 **Hostel International Seattle.** For about $20 a night you'll get a dorm-room bed at this hostel near Pike Place Market and the Seattle Art Museum. As is usual with youth hostels around the world, there's a dining room, and kitchen privileges are included in the price. June through August reservations with a credit card are essential. ⊠ *84 Union St., Downtown 98101* ☎ *206/622–5443 or 888/622–5443* 🌐 *www.hiseattle.org* 🖙 *10 private rooms, 20 dorm rooms, all share bath* ⚫ *Library, laundry facilities* 🖃 *AE, MC, V.*

International District & Pioneer Square

$$ 🖼 **Pioneer Square Hotel.** The street-level saloon helps set a decidedly Old West tone at this 1914 workmen's hotel that's now part of the Best Western chain. But the charm stops at the door. Rooms, though spacious, have standard-issue furnishings and a predominantly pink and green color scheme. Quarters at the back of the hotel face an air shaft, creating dark but peaceful refuges. For a fee, you can use the facilities at a nearby health club. ⊠ *77 Yesler Way, Pioneer Square 98104* ☎ *206/340–1234* 🖷 *206/467–0707* 🌐 *www.pioneersquare.com* 🖙 *75 rooms, 3 suites* ⚫ *Coffee shop, room service, in-room data ports, pub, laundry service, concierge, business services, meeting rooms, parking (fee), no-smoking rooms* 🖃 *AE, D, DC, MC, V* 🍽 *CP.*

¢–$ 🖼 **Amaranth Inn.** An old Craftsman home just blocks from Chinatown has been restored and converted into a spacious, sunny B&B. Common areas include a sunroom, a parlor, and a formal breakfast room. Guest rooms are done in creams and pale greens with touches of lace and brocades in bedspreads and window treatments; seven have private baths and gas fireplaces. The full breakfast served here ranges from straightforward egg dishes with sausage or bacon to French toast with seasonal fruit, and always includes juice, pastries, coffee, and a selection of teas. ⊠ *1451 S. Main St., International District 98144* ☎ *206/720–7161 or 800/720–7161* 🖷 *206/323–0772* 🌐 *www.amaranthinn.com* 🖙 *8 rooms (2 with shared bath)* ⚫ *Dining room, free parking; no smoking* 🖃 *AE, D, DC, MC, V* 🍽 *BP.*

★ ¢   🖼 **Panama Hotel.** From the unused traditional Japanese bathhouse in the basement to the lovingly restored teahouse and the unclaimed belongings of families interned during WWII, this 1910 three-story walk-up is almost a time capsule of Japanese culture in Seattle. Owner Pam Johnson sees to many distinctive touches throughout. Climb the steep creaky stairs to immaculate rooms featuring hand-embroidered cotton coverlets, kitschy Asian mementos, and armoires made from refrigerator crates during the 1940s. Rooms have sinks but share bathrooms. Rates include a teahouse breakfast of fresh doughnuts and hot beverages. A TV can usually be delivered to you upon request. ⊠ 605½ S. Main St., International District 98104 ☎ 206/223–9242 🖷 206/624–4947 ⊕ www.panamahotelseattle.com ➷ 100 rooms share bath ♨ Tea shop, laundry facilities, Internet; no room phones, no room TVs, no smoking ⊟ AE, D, MC, V ⦿ CP.

First Hill

★ $$$–$$$$ 🏨 **Sorrento.** Built in 1909, the Sorrento was designed to look like an Italian villa, with a dramatic circular driveway surrounding a palm-fringed fountain. Sitting high on First Hill, the hotel overlooks Downtown and Elliott Bay. Rooms are quiet and comfortable, although some are quite small. The largest are the corner suites, which have spacious baths and some antique furnishings. In the lobby, the dark-paneled Fireside Lounge is an inviting spot for coffee, tea, or cocktails; the Hunt Club serves Pacific Northwest dishes. Limousine service within the downtown area is complimentary, as are privileges at a nearby athletic club. ⊠ 900 Madison St., First Hill 98104 ☎ 206/622–6400 or 800/426–1265 🖷 206/343–6155 ⊕ www.hotelsorrento.com ➷ 76 rooms, 42 suites ♨ Restaurant, room service, in-room data ports, in-room fax, minibars, bar, dry cleaning, laundry service, concierge, business services, meeting rooms, parking (fee) ⊟ AE, D, DC, MC, V.

$–$$$ 🏨 **Inn at Virginia Mason.** As it's owned by the Virginia Mason Medical Center, this hotel draws quite a few "medical guests" whose treatment keeps them in the city for multiple days. Few folks know that it's open to the general public as well. The large rooms have an air of history; a few even have original wood-burning fireplaces surrounded by beautiful 1920s tile. In warmer months you can enjoy city views from the rooftop garden. The popular Rhododendron Restaurant serves simple healthful fare in the lobby and adjoining courtyard. ⊠ 1006 Spring St., First Hill 98104 ☎ 206/583–6453 or 800/283–6453 🖷 206/223–7545 ➷ 79 rooms ♨ Restaurant, in-room data ports, cable TV, business services, parking (fee); no smoking ⊟ AE, D, DC, MC, V.

Lake Union & Fremont

$$–$$$ 🏨 **Marriott Residence Inn.** An extended-stay hotel on scenic Lake Union, the Marriott is perfect for families. All accommodations are one- or two-bedroom suites, each with a living room and a fully equipped kitchen. Decorated in greens and blues, the comfortable rooms get plenty of natural light. The lobby, in a seven-story atrium with a waterfall, has many areas in which to relax, watch TV, play games, or peruse the cookbooks displayed on bookshelves. Room rates include complimentary shuttle service within a 2½-mi radius of the hotel. ⊠ 800 Fairview Ave. N, Lake Union 98109 ☎ 206/624–6000 or 800/331–3131 🖷 206/223–8160 ⊕ www.marriott.com ➷ 234 suites ♨ Kitchens, cable TV, indoor pool, gym, sauna, parking (fee), no-smoking rooms ⊟ AE, D, DC, MC, V ⦿ CP.

$–$$ 🏨 **Chelsea Station.** In a classic Seattle neighborhood across from the Woodland Park Zoo, this B&B offers warm hospitality in a quiet locale. The parlor and breakfast rooms are done in sage green and have Mission-style oak furniture, brocade upholstery, lace curtains, and works by local artists. Spacious guest rooms, each with a writing desk, have both antique and contemporary furnishings. The accommodations in front have views of the Cascades. One suite has a piano, another a kitchen. Several rooms have adjoining doors, useful for families or larger groups. Breakfast can be tailored to your dietary needs upon request. ⊠ 4915 Linden Ave. N, Fremont 98103 ☎ 206/547–6077 or 800/400–6077 🖷 206/632–5107 ⊕ www.bandbseattle.com ➷ 2 rooms, 7 suites ♨ In-room data ports ⊟ AE, D, DC, MC, V ⦿ BP.

$–$$ 🖼 **Marriott Courtyard.** Comfort and convenience more than make up for this hotel's lack of charm. The perks: Lake Union and Space Needle views, a courtesy shuttle (to and from the Space Needle, Convention Center, Westlake Center, Pike Place Market, and the Waterfront), inexpensive parking, a cozy lobby lounge, a pool, and a business center. Guest rooms are sunny, spacious, and done in shades of green and burgundy. Each has a coffeemaker, an iron, and an ironing board. Critically acclaimed restaurants are within walking distance, and the Wooden Boat Center is across the street. ⊠ *925 Westlake Ave. N (at Aloha St.), Lake Union 98109* ☎ *206/213–0100 or 800/321–2211* 🖷 *206/433–4443* ⊕ *www.courtyard.com* 🛏 *250 rooms, 2 suites* ♻ *Restaurant, room service, in-room data ports, indoor pool, hot tub, gym, bar, dry cleaning, laundry facilities, business services, meeting rooms, parking (fee), no-smoking rooms* ⊟ *AE, D, DC, MC, V.*

Queen Anne

$$–$$$ 🖼 **MarQueen Hotel.** At the foot of Queen Anne Hill, just blocks from the Seattle Center, the MarQueen is ideal for patrons of the opera, ballet, theater, or Key Arena sporting events. Formerly an apartment building, this 1918 brick hotel has a dark lobby with marble floors, overstuffed furniture, Asian-style lacquered screens, and a grand staircase overlooking a garden mural painted on a facing building. The spacious guest rooms, furnished with reproduction antiques, all have kitchens and sitting areas. A complimentary newspaper is left outside the door each morning. ⊠ *600 Queen Ave. N, Queen Anne 98109* ☎ *206/282–7407 or 888/445–3076* 🖷 *206/283–1499* ⊕ *www.marqueen.com* 🛏 *47 rooms, 4 suites* ♻ *Room service, in-room data ports, kitchenettes, minibars, microwaves, refrigerators, cable TV, dry cleaning, laundry service, concierge, meeting room, parking (fee), no-smoking rooms* ⊟ *AE, D, DC, MC, V.*

$–$$ 🖼 **Hampton Inn and Suites.** During the week, this utilitarian property caters primarily to business travelers; on weekends it's an attractive choice if you plan to attend events held at the nearby Seattle Center. About half the rooms are suites, each with a gas fireplace, kitchen, and balcony. Standard rooms are furnished with desks and overstuffed chairs. Some rooms also have sofas and kitchenettes; all rooms have hair dryers, irons, ironing boards, and coffeemakers. ⊠ *700 5th Ave. N (at Roy St.), Queen Anne 98109* ☎ *206/282–7700 or 800/426–7866* 🖷 *206/282–3325* ⊕ *www.hamptoninn.com* 🛏 *124 rooms, 74 suites* ♻ *In-room data ports, refrigerators, cable TV, gym, laundry service, business services, meeting rooms, free parking* ⊟ *AE, D, DC, MC, V* ⊚ *CP.*

West Seattle

¢–$ 🖼 **Villa Heidelberg.** Surrounded by manicured lawns and flower-filled gardens, this 1909 Craftsman has a wide porch from which you can see Puget Sound. The charms of the interior include hardwood floors, embossed wallpaper, and lace tablecloths. Rooms are appointed with comfortable Arts and Crafts furnishings and many have splendid views of the sound, garden, or mountains. Breakfast is served in the formal dining room on a table bedecked with what seem to be different sets of china, linen, and glassware each day. ⊠ *4845 45th Ave. SW, West Seattle 98116* ☎ *206/938–3658 or 800/671–2942* 🖷 *206/935–7077* ⊕ *www.villaheidelberg.com* 🛏 *4 rooms with shared bath, 2 suites* ♻ *Cable TV; no kids under 6, no smoking* ⊟ *AE, MC, V* ⊚ *BP.*

Seattle-Tacoma International Airport

$–$$$$ 🖼 **Doubletree Inn, Doubletree Suites.** These two hotels across the street from each other are adjacent to the Southcenter shopping mall and convenient to business-park offices. The Inn is a classic Pacific North-

CloseUp

MOUNTAINS MAJESTY

MANY HOTELS ARE POSITIONED to take maximum advantage of breathtaking views of the Cascades and Olympics, Elliott Bay, Lake Washington, and the pièce de résistance, Mt. Rainier. When the clouds break, soak in the sights, and save your memories for the rainy days.

The Edgewater: Get a water-level view of ferries and other harbor traffic on Elliott Bay from this Pier 67 location.

Elliott Grand Hyatt: A viewing lounge on the 27th floor is available to guests on the concierge levels.

Inn at the Market: Elliott Bay and the Pike Place Market are right outside your window.

Madison Renaissance: The rooftop health club, complete with pool and hot tub, has a breathtaking cityscape vista.

Pensione Nichols: The suites have enclosed balconies and sweeping views of Elliott Bay.

Seattle Sheraton Hotel and Towers: An Olympic-size pool and gym with a view are on the top floor of this 35-story hotel.

Westin Hotel: These twin circular towers offer panoramas of all the sights, natural and man-made.

WSeattle: The floor-to-ceiling windows offer dizzying views of the city and/or Elliott Bay from rooms from the 15th floor up.

The Woodmark: Lake Washington views complement the Woodmark's understated elegance.

University Tower: From this art deco U-District beacon you can see Mt. Rainier, the UW campus, any of the city's lakes, or Downtown's skyline, depending on which way your room faces.

---

west–style lodge; its rooms are smaller and less lavish than those in the suites across the street, but they're perfectly fine and cost at least $25 less. Suites have sofas, tables and chairs, and wet bars. ⊠ *Doubletree Inn, 205 Strander Blvd., Southcenter 98188* ☎ *206/575–8220 or 800/ 325–8733* 🖷 *206/575–4743* ↩ *193 rooms, 5 suites* ⚲ *Room service, coffee shop, dining room, 2 pools (1 indoor), bar, meeting rooms, airport shuttle, free parking, no-smoking rooms* ⊠ *Doubletree Suites, 16500 Southcenter Pkwy., Southcenter 98188* ☎ *206/575–8220 or 800/325–8733* 🖷 *206/575–4743* ⊕ *www.doubletreehotels.com* ↩ *221 suites* ⚲ *Restaurant, room service, refrigerators, indoor pool, health club, hot tub, sauna, racquetball, bar, meeting rooms, airport shuttle, free parking, no-smoking rooms* 🖃 *AE, D, DC, MC, V.*

★ **$$** 🆑 **Marriott Sea-Tac.** The luxurious Marriott has a five-story, 21,000-square-foot tropical atrium complete with a waterfall, a dining area, an indoor pool, and a lounge. In the guest rooms, greens and mauves compliment dark-wood and brass furnishings. If you must stay in the airport environs, this is your most comfortable option. ⊠ *3201 S. 176th St., Sea-Tac 98188* ☎ *206/241–2000 or 800/643–5479* 🖷 *206/248–0789* ⊕ *www.marriott.com* ↩ *459 rooms* ⚲ *Restaurant, room service, in-room data ports, indoor pool, health club, hot tubs, sauna, lobby lounge, laundry service, concierge, meeting rooms, airport shuttle, free parking, no-smoking rooms* 🖃 *AE, D, DC, MC, V.*

$ 🆑 **Doubletree Hotel Seattle Airport.** The lobby of this large convention hotel has wood parquet floors and a fireplace; it's furnished in colors of autumn leaves. Just five minutes from the airport and 10 minutes from Southcenter shopping mall, it serves its primarily corporate clientele well. The orange, yellow, and burgundy color scheme of the lobby is carried into the spacious guest rooms. Some of the suites here are equipped with whirlpool tubs, and the Lakeside Suite—on one corner of the building—

has a wraparound balcony overlooking Bow Lake. Irons, ironing boards, and hair dryers are standard equipment. ⊠ *18740 Pacific Hwy. S, Sea-Tac 98188* ☎ *206/246–8600* 🖷 *206/431–8687* ⊕ *www.doubletreehotels. com* ⇨ *837 rooms, 13 suites* ♧ *3 restaurants, room service, in-room data ports, pool, gym, hair salon, 2 bars, laundry service, meeting rooms, airport shuttle, parking (fee)* ▭ *AE, D, DC, MC, V.*

$ 🏨 **Hilton Seattle Airport and Conference Center.** Only a half-hour drive from Downtown, and directly across the street from Sea-Tac airport, this hotel and conference center were designed with the business traveler in mind. Rooms are spacious and cheery, decorated in pale yellows, greens, and burgundy. All come equipped with work desks, iron, ironing board, hair dryer, and robes. In addition to smaller meeting rooms, a full service conference center, which can accommodate up to 1,000 guests, is connected to the hotel by a breezeway. ⊠ *17620 Pacific Hwy. S, Sea-Tac 98188* ☎ *206/244–4800* 🖷 *206/248–4499* ⊕ *www.hilton.com* ⇨ *175 rooms, 3 suites* ♧ *Restaurant, room service, in-room data ports, mini-bars, refrigerators, cable TV, pool, gym, lounge, dry cleaning, laundry facilities, laundry service, concierge, business services, convention center, meeting rooms, airport shuttle, free parking, no-smoking rooms* ▭ *AE, D, DC, MC, V.*

$ 🏨 **Red Lion Hotel: Seattle Airport.** The enthusiastic and helpful staff at this conveniently located property make it attractive to business or leisure travelers. You are welcome to play the baby grand piano in the small but comfortable lobby. All rooms come equipped with Nintendo systems. Rooms in the rear have views of Bow Lake. ⊠ *18220 International Blvd., Sea-Tac 98188* ☎ *206/246–5535 or 800/733–5466* 🖷 *206/246–9733* ⊕ *www.redlion.com* ⇨ *146 rooms* ♧ *Restaurant, room service, pool, gym, hot tub, sauna, bar, business services, meeting rooms, airport shuttle, free parking* ▭ *AE, D, DC, MC, V.*

¢–$ 🏨 **Wyndham Garden Hotel.** Convenient airport access is a plus here. The elegant lobby has a fireplace, a marble floor, and comfortable furniture. Rooms have large desks, overstuffed chairs, irons and boards, coffeemakers, and hair dryers. ⊠ *18118 Pacific Hwy. S, Sea-Tac 98188* ☎ *206/244–6666* 🖷 *206/244–6679* ⊕ *www.wyndham.com* ⇨ *180 rooms, 24 suites* ♧ *Restaurant, room service, in-room data ports, indoor pool, gym, lobby lounge, laundry facilities, laundry service, meeting rooms, airport shuttle, free parking, no-smoking floors* ▭ *AE, D, DC, MC, V.*

¢   🏨 **Coast Gateway Hotel.** You're allowed to play the baby grand piano in the lobby of this no-frills hotel one block south of Sea-Tac airport. The subdued guest rooms are furnished in light wood and calming greens. Nintendo, WebTV, and HBO are all included in the price of the room. Irons, ironing boards, hair dryers, and coffeemakers are also standard. ⊠ *18415 Pacific Hwy. S, Sea-Tac 98188* ☎ *206/248–8200 or 800/663–1144* 🖷 *206/244–1198* ⊕ *www.coasthotels.com* ⇨ *145 rooms* ♧ *Room service, in-room data ports, gym, dry cleaning, meeting room, airport shuttle, free parking, no-smoking floors* ▭ *AE, D, DC, MC, V* ⏷⏺ *CP.*

North & East of Downtown

Capitol Hill

$–$$ 🏨 **Hill House.** Housed in a pair of expertly restored 1903 Victorian homes, this is a B&B where emphasis is placed on the latter "B." Former restaurateur and current inn owner Herman Foster turns out elaborate made-to-order breakfasts daily—everything from smoked-salmon eggs Benedict to walnut bread French toast. In the guest rooms antique beds sport crisp cotton coverlets over down comforters, and you'll always find fresh flowers, homemade soaps, ice water, and plush robes. ⊠ *1113 E. John St., Capitol Hill 98102* ☎ *206/720–7161 or 800/720–7161* 🖷 *206/323–0772* 🌐 *www.seattlebnb.com* 🖘 *7 rooms, 5 with private bath* ⚐ *Free parking* ▭ *AE, D, DC, MC, V* ⦿ *BP.*

¢–$$ 🏨 **Bacon Mansion.** On a tree-lined street near Volunteer Park, this 1909 Tudor is surrounded by gardens. The first-floor living room is filled with comfortable furniture and lots of natural light; it also has a grand piano. Each unique guest room is appointed with collectibles old and new. The Capitol Suite has a pine four-poster, a carved oak fireplace, and a view of the Space Needle; from the floral-themed Iris Room you can see Mt. Rainier. Several rooms have hideaway beds in addition to the queen-size beds that are the norm. The restored carriage house provides larger quarters; upstairs, the former chauffeur's quarters now serve as a cozy loft. ⊠ *959 Broadway Ave. E (at E. Prospect St.), Capitol Hill 98102* ☎ *206/329–1864 or 800/240–1864* 🖷 *206/860–9025* 🌐 *www.baconmansion.com* 🖘 *11 rooms, 2 share bath; 2 suites* ⚐ *In-room data ports, some refrigerators, library; no a/c, no smoking* ▭ *AE, D, DC, MC, V* ⦿ *CP.*

¢–$$ 🏨 **Gaslight Inn.** Rooms here range from a crow's nest with peeled-log
furniture and Navajo-print fabrics to suites with gas fireplaces and antique carved beds. There's also an apartment with a blown-glass chandelier and views of Downtown and Elliott Bay. The large common areas evoke a gentlemen's club, with oak wainscoting, animal statuary, high ceilings, and hunter-green carpet. One owner's past career as a professional painter is evident in the impeccable custom-mixed finishes throughout the inn. Those staying in studios and suites receive free off-street parking. ⊠ *1727 15th Ave., Capitol Hill 98122* ☎ *206/325–3654* 🖷 *206/328–4803* 🌐 *www.gaslight-inn.com* 🖘 *9 rooms, 7 suites* ⚐ *Pool, laundry facilities, no-smoking rooms* ▭ *AE, MC, V* ⦿ *CP.*

$ 🏨 **Bed and Breakfast on Broadway.** Proprietors Don Fabian and Russel Lyons go out of their way to make you feel comfortable in their home. A Steinway grand piano dominates the music room, and antiques and art, including paintings by co-host Lyons, fill the living room. Queen-size beds with goose-down comforters are standard in the guest rooms, two of which have enclosed balconies. The inn is near restaurants, movie theaters, shops, and a bus stop. ⊠ *722 Broadway Ave. E, Capitol Hill 98102* ☎ *206/329–8933 or 888/329–8933* 🖷 *206/726–0918* 🌐 *www.bbonbroadway.com* 🖘 *4 rooms* ⚐ *Free parking, no-smoking rooms* ▭ *AE, D, DC, MC, V* ⦿ *CP.*

¢–$ 🏨 **Salisbury House.** Built in 1904, this Craftsman house sits on a wide, tree-lined street. The spacious rooms contain an eclectic collection of furniture, including some antiques. The basement suite has a private entrance and phone line, a fireplace, and a whirlpool bath. The Rose Room is filled with rose chintz and has a canopy bed, the Lavender Room is furnished in white wicker, and the Blue Room has a private deck overlooking the garden. ⊠ *750 16th Ave. E, Capitol Hill 98112* ☎ *206/328–8682* 🖷 *206/720–1019* 🌐 *www.salisburyhouse.com* 🖘 *4 rooms, 1 suite* ⚐ *Dining room, in-room data ports, business services; no a/c, no cable TV in some rooms, no kids under 12, no smoking* ▭ *AE, DC, MC, V* ⦿ *BP.*

University District

$–$$ 🏨 **University Inn.** This impeccably maintained inn has earned its popularity by steadfastly offering clean friendly lodging in a city where the price for a room is liable to cause "sticker shock." It's mainly frequented by travelers with business at the UW or the surrounding medical facilities, although leisure travelers also find themselves at home here. The traditional guest rooms in the original wing, built in the 1960s, have smallish bathrooms, but on the plus side, many have balconies. A newer wing was built in the late 1980s; its junior suites have such amenities as microwaves and refrigerators. ✉ *4140 Roosevelt Way NE, University District 98105* ☎ *206/632–5055 or 800/733–3855* 🖷 *206/547–4937* ⊕ *www.universityinnseattle.com* 📧 *102 rooms* ♨ *Restaurant, in-room data ports, in-room safes, some microwaves, some refrigerators, outdoor pool, exercise equipment, hot tub, dry cleaning, laundry facilities, meeting rooms, free parking, no-smoking floors* 🖃 *AE, D, DC, MC, V* ⦿| *CP.*

$–$$ 🏨 **University Suites.** A companion to the Chambered Nautilus, this property is a four-plex that was converted to suites with kitchenettes in 1998. Three of the units have separate bedrooms. The Ravenna has hardwood floors throughout, an antique cast-iron bed, and herb print tiles in the kitchen. The remaining suites have carpeting. The Cascades Suite has two bedrooms and, from the porch, a breathtaking view of its namesake mountains. Expertly prepared breakfasts are served at the B&B next door. Whereas they always include granola, perhaps you'll be lucky enough to try the owner's famed stuffed French toast. ✉ *5005 22nd Ave. NE, University District 98105* ☎ *206/522–2536* 🖷 *206/528–0898* ⊕ *www.chamberednautilus.com* 📧 *4 rooms* ♨ *Kitchenettes, microwaves, refrigerators, cable TV with movies; no smoking* 🖃 *AE, MC, V* ⦿| *BP.*

★ $–$$ 🏨 **Watertown Hotel.** The developer of this property is a boater and an architect, and his predilection and profession are reflected in the exposed concrete and metal construction, porthole windows in bathroom doors, and the clean lines of the fountains and pools. Grasses and smooth river rock enhance the landscaping, while specially commissioned artworks add visual interest to the public areas. In the guest rooms, space-saving closets are accessible from two sides, big operable windows let in lots of light, and blackout curtains let you keep things dark. Rooms have full-length mirrors and come with irons, ironing boards, and coffeemakers. Free wine tastings nightly. ✉ *4242 Roosevelt Way NE, University District 98105* ☎ *206/826–4242 or 800/944–4242* 🖷 *206/315–4242* ⊕ *www.watertownseattle.com* 📧 *155 rooms* ♨ *Restaurant, in-room data ports, in-room safes, microwaves, refrigerators, exercise equipment, bicycles, laundry facilities, meeting rooms, free parking; no smoking* 🖃 *AE, D, DC, MC, V* ⦿| *CP.*

$ 🏨 **Chambered Nautilus.** You can't miss the bright red door of this Georgian Colonial Revival home near the University of Washington. Its big living room has Oriental rugs, a fireplace, and a sideboard stocked with cookies and coffee. Each guest room has a queen-size bed with down comforters, and many have private porches. Two have fireplaces. The Scallop Room has a wood-burning stove and is trimmed in khaki and green, while the larger Sunrise Room has yellow walls and crisp blue and white bedding. The noteworthy breakfasts might include roasted pears with caramel sauce or individual crustless quiches in ramekins. ✉ *5005 22nd Ave. NE, University District 98105* ☎ *206/522–2536* 🖷 *206/528–0898* ⊕ *www.chamberednautilus.com* 📧 *6 rooms, 4 suites* ♨ *Cable TV; no kids under 8, no smoking* 🖃 *AE, MC, V* ⦿| *BP.*

$ 🏨 **University Tower.** Within blocks of the University of Washington, this 1931 property (owned by the Best Western chain) has been restored to its original art deco elegance. Guest rooms are bathed in soothing shades of white with bright-red lounge chairs for bold contrast. The rooms, whose amenities include coffeemakers, hair dryers, and irons with ironing boards, have unparalleled views of the university, Mt. Rainier, Green Lake, or Lake Union. Rates include the morning newspaper and Continental breakfast. ✉ *4507 Brooklyn Ave. NE, University District 98105* ☎ *206/634–2000 or 800/899–0251* 🖷 *206/547–6029* ⊕ *www.*

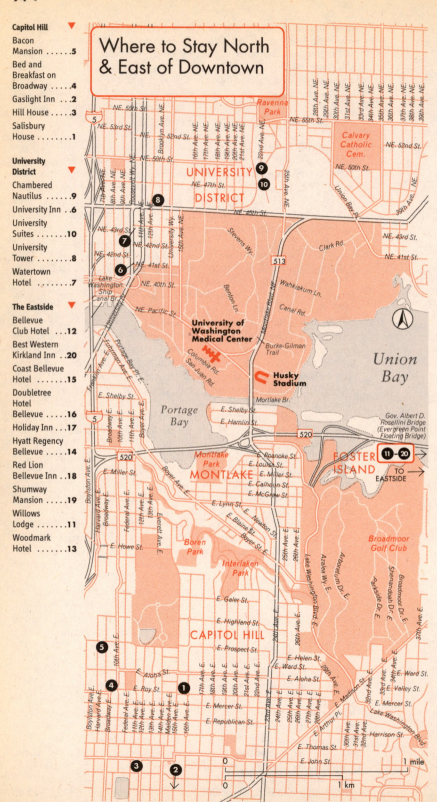

Where to Stay North & East of Downtown

meany.com ⌘ *155 rooms* ⌂ *Restaurant, in-room data ports, gym, bar, laundry service, concierge, meeting rooms, free parking, no-smoking rooms* ▱ *AE, D, DC, MC, V* ⛾ *CP.*

The Eastside

★ **$$$$** ▥ **Willows Lodge.** A dramatically lit old growth Douglas Fir snag greets you at the entrance to this luxury spa hotel. Timbers salvaged from a 19th-century warehouse lend a warm rustic counterpoint to the lodge's sleek modern design. A floor-to-ceiling stone fireplace dominates the lobby, and contemporary Native-American prints and sculptures by area artists adorn the walls and gardens. All guest rooms have fireplaces, oversize soaking tubs, and CD and DVD players. Bathrooms have a pair of free-standing stone sinks that resemble salad bowls and have industrial-looking spigots. The spa offers both beauty and rejuvenating treatments. ✉ *14580 NE 145th St., Woodinville 98072* ☎ *425/424–3900 or 877/424–3930* 🖶 *425/424–2585* ⊕ *www.willowslodge.com* ⌘ *83 rooms, 5 suites* ⌂ *Restaurant, room service, in-room data ports, in-room safes, minibars, refrigerators, pool, gym, spa, bar, laundry service, concierge, business services, meeting rooms, free parking* ⛾ *CP* ▱ *AE, D, DC, MC, V.*

★ **$$$–$$$$** ▥ **Bellevue Club Hotel.** This modern boutique hotel has won numerous design awards. Warm earthtones coupled with the clever use of lighting create the illusion of sunlight even when it's raining outside. Original oil paintings by Northwest artist Mark Rediske hang in each room. Pillows made from African Kuba textiles, Turkish area rugs, and *raku* pottery offset cherry furniture. All rooms have plush armchairs and large, spa-inspired, limestone-tile bathrooms with tubs and separate glass-enclosed showers. ✉ *11200 SE 6th St., Bellevue 98004* ☎ *425/454–4424 or 800/579–1110* 🖶 *425/688–3101* ⊕ *www.bellevueclub.com/hotel.htm* ⌘ *64 rooms, 3 suites* ⌂ *2 restaurants, room service, in-room data ports, in-room safes, minibars, refrigerators, tennis court, pool, health club, hot tub, spa, basketball, lounge, laundry service, concierge, business services, meeting rooms, parking (fee)* ▱ *AE, DC, MC, V.*

★ **$$$–$$$$** ▥ **Woodmark Hotel.** The Woodmark is the only hotel on Lake Washington's shores. Its contemporary-style rooms—which face the water, a courtyard, or the street—are done in shades of café au lait, taupe, and ecru. Numerous amenities include terry bathrobes, coffeemakers, irons, hair dryers, complimentary shoe shines, and the morning paper. A circular staircase, descending from the lobby to the Library Bar, passes a huge bay window with a panoramic view of Lake Washington. Waters Bistro serves Pacific Rim cuisine, with dishes such as lemongrass steamed clams, and grilled halibut with roasted onion-ginger relish. ✉ *1200 Carillon Pt., Kirkland 98033* ☎ *425/822–3700 or 800/822–3700* 🖶 *425/822–3699* ⊕ *www.thewoodmark.com* ⌘ *79 rooms, 21 suites* ⌂ *Restaurant, room service, in-room data ports, in-room safes, minibars, refrigerators, gym, spa, bar, laundry service, concierge, business services, meeting rooms, parking (fee)* ▱ *AE, DC, MC, V.*

$$$ ▥ **Hyatt Regency Bellevue.** Near Bellevue Square and other downtown Bellevue shopping centers, the Hyatt looks like any other sleek high-rise, but its interior is adorned with huge displays of fresh flowers and such Asian touches as antique Japanese chests. Rooms are understated, with dark wood and earth tones predominating. Deluxe suites include two bedrooms, bar facilities, and meeting rooms with desks and full-length tables. You'll have access to a health club and pool that share a courtyard with the hotel. The restaurant serves excellent and reasonably priced breakfast, lunch, and dinner; an English-style pub and sports bar serves lunch and dinner. ✉ *900 Bellevue Way NE, Bellevue 98004* ☎ *425/462–2626* 🖶 *425/646–7567* ⊕ *www.hyatt.com* ⌘ *353 rooms,*

29 suites △ Restaurant, room service, sports bar, laundry service, concierge, Internet, meeting rooms, parking (fee), no-smoking rooms ▤ *AE, D, DC, MC, V.*

$–$$ ▣ **Coast Bellevue Hotel.** A 20-minute walk from Bellevue Square, this hotel has a number of town-house suites, suitable for two to four people, with sleeping lofts and wood-burning fireplaces. Rooms facing the courtyard are larger and quieter than the others. A substantial, complimentary appetizer buffet, served in the lounge weekdays between 5 and 7, includes seafood and roast beef. ⊠ *625 116th Ave. NE, Bellevue 98004* ☎ *425/455–9444 or 800/663–1144* 🖷 *425/455–2154* ⊕ *www.coasthotels. com* 🛏 *160 rooms, 16 suites △ Restaurant, room service, pool, gym, lounge, dry cleaning, laundry facilities, business services, meeting rooms, free parking, no-smoking rooms* ▤ *AE, D, DC, MC, V.*

$–$$ ▣ **Doubletree Hotel Bellevue.** The 10-story Doubletree has an airy atrium filled with trees, shrubs, and flowering plants. The property also has a formal restaurant, a lounge with two dance floors, and oversize guest rooms decorated in hunter green, burgundy, and beige. Suites have wet bars and whirlpool tubs. ⊠ *300 112th Ave. SE, Bellevue 98004* ☎ *425/455–1300 or 800/733–5466* 🖷 *425/455–0466* ⊕ *www.doubletreehotels. com* 🛏 *348 rooms, 5 suites △ 2 restaurants, room service, in-room data ports, cable TV, pool, gym, hair salon, bar, shop, dry cleaning, laundry service, concierge, business services, meeting rooms, free parking, no-smoking rooms* ▤ *AE, D, DC, MC, V.*

$ ▣ **Holiday Inn.** Winners of the "Quality Excellence" award for service from 1997 to 2003, this two-story chain hotel off I–90 in Issaquah is nothing if not friendly. Comfortable guest rooms have triple-sheeted beds piled high with pillows. Black-and-white photos of flowers hang on the walls, and each room comes with a workstation, lounge chair, and ottoman. Also standard are irons, ironing boards, coffeemakers, and hair dryers. Although primarily frequented by corporate travelers, families are welcome—and kids eat free. A surprisingly whimsical touch here is the salmon-shape swimming pool. ⊠ *1801 12th Ave. NW, Issaquah 98027* ☎ *425/392–6421* 🖷 *425/391–4650* ⊕ *www.holiday-inn.com/sea-issaquah* 🛏 *100 rooms △ Restaurant, lobby lounge, room service, in-room data ports, cable TV, pool, wading pool, bar, laundry facilities, business services* ▤ *AE, D, DC, MC, V.*

$ ▣ **Red Lion Bellevue Inn.** Just west of I–405 in downtown Bellevue, this Red Lion's landscaped gardens are full of rhododendrons and azaleas. Guest rooms are spacious: Those on the first floor have patios, while second-floor accommodations have balconies overlooking the pool and gardens. Irons, ironing boards, hair dryers, and coffeemakers are standard equipment in all rooms. ⊠ *11211 Main St., Bellevue 98004* ☎ *425/455–5240* 🖷 *425/455–0654* ⊕ *www.redlion.com* 🛏 *181 rooms △ Restaurant, room service, in-room data ports, refrigerators, cable TV, pool, exercise equipment, bar (with entertainment), meeting rooms, business services, free parking* ▤ *AE, D, DC, MC, V.*

¢–$ ▣ **Shumway Mansion.** This B&B at Juanita Beach is close to downtown Kirkland. Oriental carpets and a gas fireplace lend warmth to its parlor. Guest rooms are named after local towns: The Kirkland Suite has a separate sitting area for reading, watching TV, or trying to catch a glimpse of Lake Washington through the trees: a task more easily accomplished in the winter months. The Redmond offers a four-poster bed and a sitting porch. A full breakfast is served each morning; there are homemade cookies in the evening. ⊠ *11410 99th Pl. NE, Kirkland 98033* ☎ *425/823–2303* 🖷 *425/822–0421* ⊕ *www.shumwaymansion.com* 🛏 *8 rooms △ In-room data ports, business services; no a/c, no kids under 12, no smoking* ▤ *AE, MC, V* ⋈*I BP.*

¢ 🏨 **Best Western Kirkland Inn.** This chain hotel's location at Exit 20A just off I–405 makes it popular with tour operators, corporate travelers, and shoppers. Just 1 mi from malls, dining, and Lake Washington, the no-nonsense rooms make a great base for exploring Kirkland. Standard rooms face the freeway and can be noisy, the deluxe rooms mirror the standard rooms in size, yet have microwaves and refrigerators and face the quiet side. Four of the deluxe rooms come with whirlpool tubs. All rooms have irons, ironing boards, and hair dryers. ✉ *12223 NE 116th St., Kirkland 98034* ☎ *425/822–2300 or 800/332–4200* 🖷 *425/889–9616* 🌐 *www.bestwestern.com* 🛏 *110 rooms* ♨ *Some in-room hot tubs, some microwaves, some refrigerators, cable TV with movies, outdoor pool, hot tub, laundry facilities, some pets allowed, no-smoking rooms* 💳 *AE, D, DC, MC, V* ⦿ *CP.*

NIGHTLIFE & THE ARTS

4

FODOR'S CHOICE

Bada Lounge, *Belltown*

Dimitriou's Jazz Alley, *Downtown*

5th Avenue Theater, *Downtown*

Marion Oliver McCaw Hall, *Queen Anne*

Seattle Symphony, *Downtown*

Vivace Roasteria, *Capitol Hill*

HIGHLY RECOMMENDED

NIGHTLIFE Alibi Room, *Downtown*

The Baltic Room, *Capitol Hill*

Century Ballroom, *Capitol Hill*

The Fenix, *Pioneer Square*

Garage, *Capitol Hill*

Redhook Brewery, *Woodinville*

ARTS Cinerama, *Belltown*

Elliot Bay Book Co, *Pioneer Square*

Greg Kucera Gallery, *Pioneer Square*

Northwest Actors Studio, *Capitol Hill*

Seattle Art Museum, *Downtown*

Updated by
Holly S. Smith

SEATTLE HAS BEEN CAREFULLY TENDING ITS CREATIVE COMMUNITIES for decades. Twenty-five years ago, a large, well-funded theater scene began to develop, the Seattle International Film Festival was founded, and rock musicians were often seen carting their equipment between the many lively clubs. When the high-tech boom of the 1990s drew the eyes of the nation to the Pacific Northwest, Seattle was ready for the spotlight.

Today, the city's dynamic theater scene is a highly regarded proving ground for Broadway, and the film festival draws the finest in world cinema here each spring. The ethereal McCaw Hall is a first-class venue for opera and ballet, and Benaroya Hall, with its outstanding acoustics, is a premier symphony hall. Families enjoy the Children's Theatre, the Northwest Puppet Center, and the many summertime folk art and music festivals. Intrepid club crawlers thrive amid the trendy bars and edgy dance clubs. Mix up your choices, add a pint of traditional ale or a stem of Washington wine to the evening, and your taste of Northwest nightlife will be complete.

NIGHTLIFE

The high-tech revolution turned Seattle from a quiet city, noted for its natural beauty and slow pace, to a buzzing, innovative metropolis whose sights and sounds continue to reflect the information sector's fast pace. The grunge rock legacy of Nirvana and Pearl Jam is still felt in the city's music venues, which also showcase up-and-coming pop, punk, heavy metal, and alternative bands. Dance clubs on Capitol Hill and the Pike–Pine corridor reverberate with the rhythms of disco and house music. The places known for country, jazz, or blues are authentic and friendly.

The Stranger and *Seattle Weekly* (distributed city-wide on Thursday) give detailed music, art, and nightlife listings, as well as hot tips and suggestions for the week's events. Friday editions of the *Seattle Times* and the *Seattle Post-Intelligencer* include weekend pullout sections detailing arts and entertainment events. Shows usually begin around 9 PM, and cover charges range from $5 for local acts and weeknight admissions to $20 for touring acts. The joint cover charge of $10 gets you into up to 10 Pioneer Square blues, jazz, and rock clubs. Bars and clubs stay open until 2 AM, with the rare exception of alcohol-free after-hours events.

Neighborhoods with high concentrations of clubs and bars include Ballard, Pioneer Square, Capitol Hill, the University District, and Belltown. On-street parking is usually plentiful, but crowded Capitol Hill and Downtown also have lots and garages. Cabs are abundant and buses run until around midnight, so you don't have to drive at all.

Ticketmaster (☎ 206/628–0888 ⊕ www.ticketmaster.com) sells tickets to most arts, entertainment, and sports events in the Seattle area. The two locations of **Ticket/Ticket** (✉ Broadway Market, 401 Broadway E, 2nd fl., Capitol Hill ☎ 206/324–2744 ✉ Pike Place Information Booth, 1st Ave. and Pike St., Downtown ☎ 206/682–7453 Ext. 226) sell half-price tickets to many events on the day of the show (or the previous day for a matinee). Sales are cash and in-person only. The independent online ticket company ⊕ www.ticketweb.com sells local-event tickets. For movie show times and theater locations of current releases, call the *Seattle Times* **InfoLine** (☎ 206/464–2000 Ext. 3456).

Arcades

GameWorks (✉ 7th Ave. and Pike St., Downtown ☎ 206/521–0952), a Steven Spielberg–Sega collaboration, has virtual-reality technology, arcade games, and high-tech road racing. It's free to go inside, but individual game costs run up quickly; look for such play-all-you-want specials as the Summer Fun Pass ($30 per day). On Thursday night girls pay just $10; after 9 PM guys can buy the Thrill Pass for $20.

LaserDome (⊠ Pacific Science Center, 200 2nd Ave. N, Queen Anne ☎ 206/443–2850). Rock and roll never looked or sounded better than in this laser light show, which pulsates to the sounds of artists ranging from Britney Spears and the Backstreet Boys to Green Day, Nirvana, and Pearl Jam.

Shorty's (⊠ 2222 2nd Ave., Belltown ☎ 206/441–5449). Tired of waiting for your table at a packed Belltown restaurant? Enjoy a few games of pinball here instead. With some old-school favorites and all the most popular video games, this is a haven for folks who still have a touch of the kid in their souls. There are cold beer and hot dogs to boot!

Bars

★ **Alibi Room** (⊠ 85 Post Alley, Downtown ☎ 206/623–3180), a wood-paneled bar in Pike Place Market, is where well-dressed Seattle film-industry talents sip double martinis and hash out ideas while taking in splendid views of Elliott Bay or studying the scripts, handbills, and movie posters that line the walls. It's a miraculously ever-cool yet low-key place. Stop by for a drink—potent vodka creations are the specialty—or a meal, or stay to catch a live band and dance.

Anthony's Home Port (⊠ 6135 Seaview Ave. NW, Ballard ☎ 206/783–0780) is part of a sophisticated Northwest seafood chain. The bar has glorious views of sailboats slicing through Shilshole Bay, and the bartenders make a delectable, spiced Bloody Mary.

Art Bar (⊠ 1516 2nd Ave., Belltown ☎ 206/622–4344) has high ceilings, exposed-brick walls, and artfully arranged paintings and sculptures. Escape the crush of the main "gallery" by heading to the more subdued lounge, which has a pool table, in back. Entertainment could be a jazz ensemble, a DJ, or an author reading—it really depends on the night.

Fodor'sChoice ★ **Bada Lounge** (⊠ 2230 1st Ave., Belltown ☎ 206/374–8717) is a sleek spot with a New York vibe, an Asian-inspired menu, and a Parisian-pretty crowd. Regulars on the club circuit slink up to the posh, crimson-lit alcove to sip pricey drinks and nibble on sushi. "Hypnotic," an open-mike showcase for actors, poets, singers, and storytellers happens the second and fourth Monday of each month.

Capitol Club (⊠ 414 E. Pine St., Capitol Hill ☎ 206/325–2149) is a sumptuous escape where you can sprawl upon tasseled floor cushions to dish with your friends and dine on Middle Eastern treats. Peek into the private Blue Room, where the powerful and famous dine in peace—but even they can't smoke until after 10 PM.

Cascadia (⊠ 2328 1st Ave., Belltown ☎ 206/448–8884) is opulent and classy, with jazz-piano background music and a cascading water feature. Floor-to-ceiling windows and a working fireplace make even the rainiest evenings cozy and picturesque. Sip a top-label Northwest wine at the cherrywood bar, where drinks are backlit by a golden glow.

Cha Cha Lounge (⊠ 504 E. Pine St., Capitol Hill ☎ 206/329–1101) is a dark bohemian place, where up-and-comers congregate under the thatched roof of the crimson-walled main bar or at tables in the smoky back room. The sign on the door says it all: IF YOU ARE RACIST, SEXIST, HOMOPHOBIC, OR AN A - - - - - -, DON'T COME IN.

Lead Gallery Wine Bar (⊠ 1022 1st Ave., Belltown ☎ 206/623–6240) lets you sip a savory Washington vintage while wandering through a gallery of contemporary art. After a couple of glasses you might just plunk down your credit card for a one-of-a-kind work.

Linda's Tavern (⊠ 707 E. Pine St., Capitol Hill ☎ 206/325–1220), with its buffalo head and its wagon-wheel lights, is as western as a Montana cowboy bar, albeit one that's smack in the middle of the urbane Pike–Pine corridor. A neighborhood crowd gossips over a jukebox that beats out everything from lounge to punk.

Mudshark Bar (✉ 2411 Alaskan Way, Pier 67, Downtown ☎ 206/728–7000), above the water at the Edgewater hotel, has superb views of Elliott Bay and the Olympic Mountains. Huge windows surround the elegant, light-filled space, which is often filled with delicate, jazzy piano music. Tuesday through Sunday you can ask the pianist to play your favorite tunes—and the audience might sing along.

Oliver's (✉ 405 Olive Way, Downtown ☎ 206/382–6995), in the Mayflower Park Hotel, is the perfect place for an early-evening drink. In fact, having a cocktail here is like having high tea in some parts of the world. Wingback chairs, low tables, and lots of natural light make it easy to relax after a hectic day.

Palomino (✉ 1420 5th Ave., Downtown ☎ 206/623–1300) is a classy place to stop for a drink after a shopping spree. Gleaming marble, wood, and glass accents surround the city's longest bar, and original paintings by the late Seattle artist Ambrose Patterson (who once shared gallery space in Paris with Matisse) grace the walls. An adjacent lounge serves tapas and drinks.

Red Door (✉ 3401 Evanston Ave. N, Fremont ☎ 206/547–7521), a one-time biker dive nicknamed "Loud Door" for its weekend cacophony, has moved twice and acquired considerable polish through the years. Fremont's diverse crowds mingle, sample multiple microbrews, and slurp back beer-steamed clams.

Sunset Tavern (✉ 5433 Ballard Ave. NW, Ballard ☎ 206/784–4880), a Chinese restaurant turned trendy bar, attracts everyone from college punks and sorority chicks to post-grad nomads and neighborhood old-timers. All come for the ever-changing music acts and Wednesday night karaoke backed by a live band.

The Terrace (✉ Fairmont Olympic Hotel, 411 University St., Downtown ☎ 206/621–1700), a stately piano lounge in one of Seattle's finest hotels, is the place to enjoy a cigar with your cocktail. Test the waitstaff's savoir faire by polling them about the city's best restaurants.

Tini Bigs (✉ 100 Denny Way, Queen Anne ☎ 206/284–0931) attracts successful-looking couples, who drink martinis (there are 27 variations served here) and chat about each other through a thin, cigar-smoke haze. Black walls and shiny tables dimly lit with pink lights ensure the stylish a proper stage.

Virginia Inn (✉ 1937 1st Ave., Downtown ☎ 206/728–1937) blends the gaiety of the Pike Place Market district with the artsy vibe from neighboring Belltown. It's an institution, really; the kind of place where crowds spill out onto the patio on warm summer evenings.

Brewpubs

Seattle brewpubs churn out many high-quality beers for local distribution. Those listed below also serve food and nonalcoholic beverages; some have a cover charge if there's live music. Most have unique house brands on tap, and those with on-site breweries also conduct tours.

Big Time Brewery (✉ 4133 University Way NE, University District ☎ 206/545–4509) belongs more in yuppieville than the U-District, with its neat brick walls, polished wood floors, and vintage memorabilia. At least 10 beers—including pale ale, amber, and porter—are always on tap; tours of the adjacent brewery tell the whole story.

Dad Watson's (✉ 3601 Fremont Ave., Fremont ☎ 206/632–6505), which offers the same 17 brews as its sister operations, Six Ales and McMenamin's, is a popular stop on the Fremont Pub Crawl.

Elysian Brewing Company (✉ 1221 E. Pike St., Capitol Hill ☎ 206/860–1920), a large, industrial-looking space with a brewery in back, lets you sample house concoctions at the copper-stamped upstairs bar or in the downstairs lounge.

Elysian Tangle Town (✉ 2601 N. 55th St., Fremont ☎ 206/547–5929), owned by the same people as Capitol Hill's Elysian Brewing Company, is a snug, one-room, neighborhood bar that carries the same brews as its sister operation along with a few specialties of its own.

Hales Ales Brewery and Pub (✉ 4301 Leary Way NW, Fremont ☎ 206/782–0737) produces unique English-style ales and the nitrogen-conditioned Cream Ale, Special Bitter, and Stout. The pub's signature brews are its Pale Ale and Amber Ale; order a taster's "flight" if you want to test the rest.

McMenamin's (✉ 200 Roy St., Queen Anne ☎ 206/285–4722) is part of the same Portland-based brewpub chain as Six Ales, with the same brands on tap. It's a no-smoking spot that's a madhouse when Seattle Center events let out.

Pike Pub and Brewery (✉ 1415 1st Ave., Downtown ☎ 206/622–6044) is a cavernous bar and restaurant operated by the brewers of the renowned Pike Place Pale Ale. It also houses the Seattle Microbrewery Museum and an excellent shop with home-brewing supplies.

Pyramid Alehouse (✉ 91 S. Royal Brougham Way, at 1st Ave. S, Downtown ☎ 206/682–3377), a loud festive spot south of Pioneer Square and across from Safeco Field, brews the varied Pyramid line—including a top-notch Hefeweizen and an Apricot Ale that tastes much better than it sounds—as well as Thomas Kemper Lagers.

★ **Redhook Brewery** (✉ 14300 NE 145th St., Woodinville ☎ 425/483–3232) is a large complex with a pub, a beer garden, a gift shop, and brewing facilities. Tours ($1) run several times daily—enter sober, sample the half-dozen beers (with refills!), and totter your way back down to the bar.

Six Arms (✉ 300 E. Pike St., Capitol Hill ☎ 206/223–1698), named for its six-armed Indian dancer logo, is a spacious, popular, two-story brewpub with 17 house and craft beers on tap. Two that stand out are the medium-bodied Hammerhead, and the dark Terminator Stout. As you head back to the rest rooms, note the fermenting tanks painted with amusing murals.

Coffeehouses

Unlike the city's brewpubs, Seattle's coffeehouses are defined as much by who they serve (and how) as by the beverages they pour. You can linger for hours over a latte or get a cup-to-go at a drive-through espresso stand. Every neighborhood has its own distinctive coffee culture.

B&O Espresso (✉ 204 Belmont Ave. E, Capitol Hill ☎ 206/322–5028) is a cute, cozy neighborhood favorite—with one of the city's last indoor smoking sections. This was one of Seattle's earliest purveyors of the magical elixir known as the latte, and the drinks are still sheer perfection. The on-site bakery turns out gorgeous desserts.

Bauhaus (✉ 301 E. Pine St., Capitol Hill ☎ 206/625–1600) is a smart café in the heart of the Pike–Pine corridor where you can mingle with intellectuals on the rise. The bookshelf-lined walls are full of art and architecture books; the tables are full of punks and nerds.

Habitat Espresso (✉ 202 Broadway E, Capitol Hill ☎ 206/329–3087), a coffee collective, serves organic coffees and teas, baked goods, sandwiches, and soups. Profits from these food and beverage sales go to charities as do those from the souvenir shirts, mugs, and stickers that are also available.

Septième (⊠ 214 Broadway E, Capitol Hill ☎ 206/860–8858) is like a French bistro, with its red-walled dining room, its banquettes, and tables draped in white cloths. But you won't find a supersize bowl of mocha (generously topped with whipped cream) in France. On summer nights you can sip your java to rumba and salsa music by the light of tiki torches.

FodorśChoice ★ **Vivace Roasteria** (⊠ 901 E. Denny Way, Capitol Hill ☎ 206/860–5869), with its curving bar and checkerboard floor, is considered by many as the home of Seattle's finest espresso. Carefully trained *baristas* "pull" espresso drinks made with the café's own blend. The neighboring **Espresso Vivace Sidewalk Bar** (⊠ 321 Broadway Ave. E., Capitol Hill ☎ No phone) has quick-as-a-flash service for take-away drinks. **Wit's End** (⊠ 4642 Fremont Ave. N, Fremont ☎ 206/547–2330) bookstore has a tearoom where you can sip warming, world blends while perusing your purchases. What's more, the event stage brings international folk-music jams (Friday), poetry readings (Sunday), acoustic gatherings (Tuesday), and open-mike literary readings (first and third Wednesdays).

Comedy Clubs

Comedy Underground (⊠ 222 S. Main St., Pioneer Square ☎ 206/628–0303) is literally underground, beneath Swannie's Sports Bar & Grill. Stand-up comedy, open-mike sessions, and comedy competitions are scheduled nightly at 8:30.

Giggles (⊠ 5220 Roosevelt Way NE, University District ☎ 206/526–5653) hosts local comedians and open-mike events starting at 9 PM on Thursday and Sunday (free admission before 8:30). Nationally known comedians perform on Friday and Saturday at 8 and 10.

Jet City Improv (⊠ Ethnic Cultural Center, 3940 Brooklyn Ave. E, University District ☎ 206/781–3879) fuses quick wit with music and games. The audience often provides input on what the improvisational skits should be. On Friday and Saturday nights, catch the **Train of Thought** (⊠ Historic University Theater, 5510 University Way, University District ☎ 206/781–3879) show, in which performers create hilarious scenes, monologues, and music that let audiences see the actual "train of thought" used as inspiration for the sketch.

Market Theater (⊠ 1428 Post Alley, Downtown ☎ 206/781–9273), near Pike Place Market, hosts "Market Fresh Theater" Friday and Saturday at 8:30, followed at 10:30 by the competitive "Theater Sports," a long-running improv event that appeals to the 30-and-under crowd. The latter show is also performed Sunday at 7.

Gay & Lesbian Spots

Most bars are male-oriented, though they welcome mixed crowds who respect the clubs and their patrons. Many establishments are in Capitol Hill, east of Downtown.

aro.space (⊠ 925 E. Pike St., Capitol Hill ☎ 206/320–0424), a sprawling club, brought DJ culture to Seattle. Its turntable masters spin in a space that's reminiscent of the spaceship in Stanley Kubrick's *2001*. The mood is tongue-in-cheek at the weekly drag events, but when the music starts to pump, the dance floor gets serious.

Changes (⊠ 2103 N. 45th St., Wallingford ☎ 206/545–8363) is one of the few gay bars *not* on Capitol Hill. Locals make a night of it on karaoke Monday and Wednesday.

Cuff Complex (⊠ 1533 13th Ave., Capitol Hill ☎ 206/323–1525) strives to be a manly leather bar but attracts all shapes, sizes, and styles. The loud crowded dance floor is tucked away downstairs; the main-floor bar, with its patio, is the place to be on warm nights.

Man Ray (⊠ 514 E. Pine St., Capitol Hill ☎ 206/568–0750) takes you through a time portal to a sparkling-white future world with multiple video monitors bejeweling the circular bar. Try more than a couple of the 30-plus martinis. In summer, the upscale crowd likes to relax on the lanai, which is complete with a fountain.

Neighbors (⊠ 1509 Broadway, Capitol Hill ☎ 206/324–5358), with an entrance in an alley between Pike and Pine streets, isn't easy to find. But keep looking as this bar and dance club is a gay institution thanks in part to its drag shows, theme nights, and relaxed atmosphere.

Re–Bar (⊠ 1114 Howell St., Capitol Hill ☎ 206/233–9873) is a veteran gay bar with a loyal following that enjoys the cabaret shows and week-end stage performances. It's a great place to dance, and everyone has fun at the legendary Queer Disco party on Thursday—just dress the part.

Timberline Tavern (⊠ 2015 Boren Ave., Capitol Hill ☎ 206/622–6220), *the* place for honky-tonkin' and Seattle's only country and western dance club for gays and lesbians, is beloved. Come early Tuesday through Thursday evenings for beginning and advanced dancing lessons.

The Wildrose (⊠ 1021 E. Pike St., Capitol Hill ☎ 206/324–9210) is one of Seattle's few lesbian bars, so expect a mob nearly every night. The crowd at weeknight karaoke is fun and good-natured, cheering for pretty much anyone. Weekends are raucous, so grab a window table early and settle in for perpetual ladies' night.

Sports Bars & Billiards

All-American Sports Bar & Grill (⊠ 4333 University Way NE, University District ☎ 206/545–7771), a memorabilia-filled bar with 24 TVs, is the top gathering spot for University of Washington (UW) Husky fans.

Ballroom in Fremont (⊠ 456 N. 36th St., Fremont ☎ 206/634–2575) is a former warehouse with 15 well-kept pool tables. It serves beer and wine, and has good music, a small dance floor, and people-watching, making the weekend wait for a table pass quickly.

Belltown Billiards (⊠ 90 Blanchard St., Belltown ☎ 206/448–6779) is a spacious neighborhood restaurant with a speakeasylike entrance, tasty southern Italian cuisine, and live music. For the attractive, e-chic clientele mingling around the 12 regulation-size tables, a cue stick risks becoming just another fashion accessory.

F. X. McRory's (⊠ 419 Occidental Ave. S, Pioneer Square ☎ 206/623–4800), an enormous beer hall with soaring ceilings and marble-top tables, has top-grade microbrews, craft beers, imports, and megabrews on 30 taps. Single-malt whiskeys, bourbons, and fresh oysters are also in style here. On stadium sports events nights and St. Patrick's Day, it's a madhouse.

★ **Garage** (⊠ 1130 E. Broadway, Capitol Hill ☎ 206/322–2296), built in 1928 as an auto-repair shop, is now a large, happening, chrome-and-vinyl pool hall, restaurant, and bar. The large garage doors are thrown wide open on warm evenings, making this a pleasurable alternative to other cramped smoky places. There are 18 tournament pool tables; rates are $14 an hour on weekends. Women play free on Sunday; on Monday, anyone can play all night for just $5; and there's a $5-per-hour special daily from 3 to 7.

Jillian's (⊠ 731 Westlake Ave. N, Downtown ☎ 206/223–0300) is part of a nightclub chain that likes to spiff up vintage spaces with retro design schemes and details that seem straight from the Restoration Hardware catalogue. This branch—in a two-story structure that was once a marble company—is no exception. To say the place is popular is an understatement; expect two-hour waits for tables on weekends. Warm up your elbow at downstairs at the bar or upstairs with darts, Ping-Pong, or video games.

Temple Billiards (✉ 126 S. Jackson St., Pioneer Square ☎ 206/682–3242) is the classic snooker joint you've seen a hundred times in the movies—you know, the one with the plaster-chipped walls and low-wattage lighting. People truly tend to focus on the action at the 11 tables. There's even a private balcony with a lone table where you can live out your Minnesota Fats fantasy. Pool fees Friday and Saturday night are $12 or $14 per hour, depending on the number of players; on Sunday and Wednesday prices drop by half and women play free.

Tommy's (✉ 4552 University Way NE, University District ☎ 206/634–3144) is on The Ave, and its college-age crowd really appreciates the microbrews, the live music, and the 15 big-screen TVs always tuned to sporting events. The billiard tables, pinball machines, video games, and dance floor all hum after 7 PM.

Music Clubs

The Northwest's rock and roll heritage extending from the early '60s garage rock of The Kingsmen (who hit the big time with "Louie, Louie") to the legendary Jimi Hendrix to the grunge phenomenon of Pearl Jam and Nirvana. Although rock music is king in this town, a thriving drum-and-bass DJ scene proves that Seattle is evolving. Folk, jazz, blues, and Celtic music are also popular with the microbrew set, and pubs regularly host acoustic performances.

Dance

★ **The Baltic Room** (✉ 1207 E. Pine St., Capitol Hill ☎ 206/625–4444), a classy piano bar turned art deco cocktail club, has quietly become the favorite haunt of a sophisticated clientele. Dress up, but try to keep it comfortable. Top-quality, lesser-known rock, acid jazz, blues, and folk artists attract in-the-know music crowds as well as some celebs to a compact stage area.

Bohemian Reggae Club (✉ 111 Yesler Way, Pioneer Square ☎ 206/447–1514), considered by many to be the city's best dance club, is where the hip-hop and reggae crowds chill to the sounds of Nelly, Ja Rule, Eve, and others. National acts perform at the adjacent Bohemian Backstage, and two DJs spin a groove on weekends. Don't be put off by the metal detectors and brawny security guys—in Seattle, they're pretty much just for show.

Catwalk (✉ 172 S. Washington St., Pioneer Square ☎ 206/622–1863), an ultrafashionable three-room haunt, is where *everyone* dresses as if they're out to strut the runway rather than simply to dance. Theme nights include costume balls, lesbian parties, and the monthly Utopia bash with trapeze artists, jugglers, fire-walkers, and other carnival acts. Stay for the after-hours party if you can't get enough.

★ **Century Ballroom** (✉ 915 E. Pine St., 2nd fl., Capitol Hill ☎ 206/324–7263) is an elegant place for dinner and dancing, with a trendy restaurant and a polished, 2,000-square-foot dance floor. Salsa and swing events often include lessons in the cover charge. There's no smoking, it's 21 and over, and only leather-soled shoes are allowed on the floor.

The Last Supper Club (✉ 124 S. Washington St., Pioneer Square ☎ 206/748–9975), a festive club in a hard-partying district, attracts the young and the trendy. House music and disco rock the walls, and the spacious dance floor is jammed on weekend drag nights.

Pampas Room (✉ 2505 1st Ave., Belltown ☎ 206/728–1337), hidden beneath the top-rated El Gaucho restaurant, is a first-class, 1950s-style club. House band plays a mix of jazz, swing, and salsa into the wee hours. Weekends pack in the professional dancers; if you can't keep up, try blending into the mellower weeknight crowd. Dress way up, check your confidence, and step onto the dance floor.

Polly Esthers & Culture Club (✉ 332 5th Ave. N, Queen Anne ☎ 206/279–1977) is a two-story retro dance club spinning '70s and '80s favorites beneath a disco ball. Bare walls, strobe lights, and worn carpet surround the post-college crowd (and at least two bachelorette parties a night). Weekends are a crush.

700 Club (✉ 700 Virginia Ave., Downtown ☎ 206/343–7518) draws twentysomething singles to its dark basement rooms. Soft red light falls onto card tables surrounded by stackable chairs; patrons sit, smoke, drink, and listen to live or DJ-spun hip-hop, funk, and acid jazz. The dance floor undulates with highly individual moves.

The Vogue (✉ 1516 11th Ave., Capitol Hill ☎ 206/324–5778), a spacious club on the Pike–Pine corridor, gets cozy fast as crowds squeeze in and groove to the latest alternative and industrial beats. Artful hair and piercings are all the rage on Saturday's New Wave night; bring your leather and props for Fetish Night on Sunday.

Washington Dance Club (✉ 1017 Stewart St., Capitol Hill ☎ 206/628–8939) invites everyone to swoosh about the refurbished 1930s Avalon Ballroom, whose 3,000-square-foot maple wood dance floor is polished to perfection. Learn tango, swing, salsa, and ballroom moves with professional dancers, or drop in for a theme party.

Folk & World Music

Fiddler's Inn (✉ 9219 35th Ave. NE, University District ☎ 206/525–0752) is a low-key (and smoke-free) neighborhood pub where you can hear fiddles and other instruments in the nightly mix of folk, Celtic, and blues shows. Excellent Northwest microbrews and wines are on tap—perfect for gathering courage on open-mike Monday.

Gordon Biersch (✉ 600 Pine St., Downtown ☎ 206/405–4205), in the upscale Pacific Place mall, presents singer-songwriters nightly in the bar adjacent to its noted restaurant. There's never a cover charge, and there are always outstanding ales, stouts, and porters.

Hopvine Pub (✉ 507 15th Ave. E, Capitol Hill ☎ 206/328–3120) puts the spotlight on singer-songwriters and acoustic folk artists. The musicians, many of them local, perform before a cheerful neighborhood crowd.

Murphy's Pub (✉ 2110 45th St. NE, Wallingford ☎ 206/634–2110) is a spacious watering hole with a dart pit. It also happens to have small stage that hosts Irish or folk performances on weekends.

Owl n' Thistle Irish Pub (✉ 808 Post Ave., Downtown ☎ 206/621–7777) presents acoustic folk music on a small stage in a cavernous room. It's an affable pub near Pike Place Market, and it's often loaded with regulars who appreciate both the well-drawn pints of Guinness and the troubadours.

Tir Na Nog (✉ 801 1st Ave., Downtown ☎ 206/264–2700) means "land of youth" in Gaelic, but young and old alike enjoy this comfortable pub. It's full of Irish bric-a-brac and expatriates from the Emerald Isle; Irish bands play several nights a week.

Tractor Tavern (✉ 5213 Ballard Ave. NW, Ballard ☎ 206/789–3599) is Seattle's top spot to catch local and national acts that specialize in roots music and alternative country. The large, dimly lit hall has all the right touches—wagon-wheel fixtures, exposed brick walls, and a cheery staff. The sound system is outstanding.

Jazz, Blues & R&B

Ballard Firehouse (✉ 5429 Russell St. NW, Ballard ☎ 206/784–3516), a Seattle music institution, books local and national blues, rock, and oldies bands nightly.

Fodor's Choice ★ **Dimitriou's Jazz Alley** (✉ 2037 6th Ave., Downtown ☎ 206/441–9729) is where Seattle's hip and groovy dress up to see nationally known jazz artists. The cabaret-style theater, where intimate tables for two surround the stage, runs smoke-free shows nightly except Monday. Those with reservations for cocktails or dinner, served during the first set, receive priority seating and $2 off the combined meal-and-show ticket.

★ **The Fenix** (✉ 109 S. Washington St., Pioneer Square ☎ 206/405–4323), Seattle's legendary club, was demolished by a 2001 earthquake but re-opened hotter than ever. The three-story behemoth has five circular neon-lit bars, three dance floors, a café, a pool room, and a stage. It's *the* place to jam with top local DJs and rockers.

J & M Café (✉ 201 1st Ave. S, Pioneer Square ☎ 206/292–0663) crowds singles together at family-style tables. Blues bands jam here most weekends. Expect to party.

Latona Pub (✉ 6423 Latona Ave. NE, Green Lake ☎ 206/525–2238), at the south end of Green Lake, is a funky, friendly, no-smoking neighborhood bar that presents local folk, blues, or jazz musicians nightly.

Scarlet Tree (✉ 6521 Roosevelt Way NE, Ravenna ☎ 206/523–7153), north of UW in Ravenna, serves up great burgers and live rhythm and blues most nights.

Rock

The Breakroom (✉ 1325 E. Madison, Capitol Hill ☎ 206/860–5155) is *the* place to catch Seattle's alternative rock bands. There are pool and air-hockey tables in an area at the back of the space.

Crocodile Café (✉ 2200 2nd Ave., Belltown ☎ 206/441–5611) books alternative music acts—many of them nationally known—nightly except Monday. The main room is usually packed; the back bar is something of a getaway. Nonconcert nights still draw throngs to munch on Mexican and American fare.

Graceland (✉ 109 Eastlake E, Capitol Hill ☎ 206/381–3094) is a dimly lit club that specializes in alternative rock. The low-ceiling performance area has the cramped feel of a ship's hold, but the raised seating at the rear offers excellent views of the rockin' on stage and the stompin' on the dance floor. All-ages events are also held here regularly.

Showbox (✉ 1426 1st Ave., Downtown ☎ 206/628–3151), near Pike Place Market, presents locally and nationally acclaimed artists. Rave nights and guest DJ appearances are also popular in this one-time ballroom. The lounge area near the entrance is a quieter spot to enjoy the show.

The Sit & Spin (✉ 2219 4th Ave., Belltown ☎ 206/441–9484) laundromat—which also houses a bar, nightclub, greasy spoon, and art gallery—is a fun neighborhood dive with nightly live music. It's the perfect spot for the multitasker.

THE ARTS

The high-tech boom provided an enthusiastic and philanthropic audience for Seattle's blossoming arts community. Benaroya Hall is now a national benchmark for acoustic design. Its main tenant is the Seattle Symphony, led by conductor Gerard Schwarz. At the Seattle Center, the ethereal Marion Oliver McCaw Hall combines Northwest hues and hanging screens in colorful light shows accompanying performances by the Seattle Opera and the Pacific Northwest Ballet.

The Seattle Repertory Theater, also at Seattle Center, hosts new and classical works, as well as preview runs of plays bound for Broadway. The celebrated Seattle Children's Theatre presents plays and musicals written for youths but polished and sophisticated enough for adults. Events for Bumbershoot, Seattle's Labor Day weekend arts festival, are held throughout the Seattle Center grounds.

Tickets for high-profile performances range from $11 to $125; fringe theater plays and performance art events range from $5 to $25. Many alternative theaters host "pay-what-you-can" evenings. The Seattle Symphony offers half-price tickets to seniors and students one hour before scheduled performances. Movie tickets run from $8.50 for first-run films to $2 at the value-priced suburban cinemas; tickets are often free at outdoor movie nights in summer.

For complete music and theater listings, check the city's two free arts weeklies, *The Stranger* and the *Seattle Weekly,* both published on Thursday, and the Friday editions of the daily papers the *Seattle Times* and the *Seattle Post-Intelligencer.*

Dance

Meany Hall for the Performing Arts (⊠ 15th Ave. NE and 41st Ave. NE, University District ☎ 206/685–2742 ⊕ www.meany.org), on the UW campus, hosts important national and international companies September through May. The emphasis is on modern and jazz dance.

On the Boards (⊠ 100 W. Roy St., Queen Anne ☎ 206/217–9888 ⊕ www.ontheboards.org) presents contemporary dance performances, as well as theater, music, and multimedia events. The main subscription series runs from October through May, but events are scheduled nearly every weekend year-round.

Pacific Northwest Ballet (⊠ McCaw Hall at the Seattle Center, Mercer St. at 3rd Ave., Queen Anne ☎ 206/441–2424 ⊕ www.pnb.org), the resident Seattle company and school, has an elegant home at the Seattle Center. The season, which runs September through June, always includes a mix of classic and international productions (think *Swan Lake* and *Carmina Burana*). *The Nutcracker,* with choreography by Kent Stowell and sets by Maurice Sendak, is a Christmastime tradition.

Film

Broadway Market Cinemas (⊠ 425 Broadway E., at Harrison St., Capitol Hill ☎ 206/323–0231), in an upscale neighborhood minimall, shows mainstream movies and art-house films on four screens.

★ **Cinerama** (⊠ 2100 4th Ave., Belltown ☎ 206/441–3080 ⊕ www.cinerama.com), a 1963 cinema scooped up and restored by billionaire Paul Allen, seamlessly blends the luxury of the theater with state-of-the-art technology. Behind the main, standard-size movie screen sits an enormous, 30-foot by 90-foot restored curved panel—one of only three in the world—used to screen old three-strip films like *How the West Was Won,* as well as 70-millimeter presentations of *2001: Space Odyssey.* The sight lines throughout are amazing. Rear-window captioning, assistive listening devices, audio narration, wheelchair access, and other amenities ensure that everyone has an outstanding experience.

Egyptian Theater (⊠ 801 E. Pine St., at Broadway, Capitol Hill ☎ 206/323–4978 to theater, 206/324–9996 for Seattle International Film Festival), an art deco movie palace that was formerly a Masonic temple, screens first-run films. It's also the prime venue of the wildly popular Seattle International Film Festival.

Grand Illusion Cinema (⊠ 1403 NE 50th St., at University Way, University District ☎ 206/523–3935), Seattle's longest-running independent movie house, was a tiny screening room in the 1930s. Now it's an outstanding home for independent and art films, one whose cozy, 70-seat space feels as comfortable as a home theater—albeit one without a bathroom (you can use the facilities at the coffee shop next door).

SIGHTS & SOUNDS OF SUMMER

WHEN THE CLEAR, WARM Northwest summer days finally arrive, Seattle-area nightlife and arts quickly spill into the great outdoors. Look for free events everywhere: parks host weekly concerts on the grass, and regional amphitheaters tweak their sound systems for the big acts. People hit the streets for art walks and festivals.

Weekdays at noon you'll hear the sounds of Seattle's free **Out to Lunch** (☎ 206/623–0340) concerts. From mid-June to early September, well-known music and dance groups perform outdoors in various places around Downtown while locals munch brownbag lunches.

Although the **First Thursday Gallery Walk** (☎ 206/587–0260) takes place monthly all year, in summer Seattle's talents show off their skills to even larger crowds. This artsy Downtown stroll, which centers on the galleries of Pioneer Square, runs from 6 to 9 PM. Street performances and espresso carts dot the sidewalks in between.

A cinderblock wall, a parking lot, and a projector set up on scaffolding entice throngs to drag their lawn chairs out for movies under the stars at the **Fremont Outdoor Cinema** (✉ N. 35th St. and Phinney Ave., Fremont ☎ 206/781–4230). Some movies are mainstream (The Matrix), some are classics (Casablanca), and some are hilarious, twisted flick (e.g., The Blob) with comedians from Jet City Improv dubbing the sound. There's a suggested $5 donation.

Casual, rocking concerts take place at **Pier 62 & 63** (✉ 200 Alaskan Way, Downtown ☎ 206/281–8111). The backdrop of Elliott Bay on a warm night can't be beat. Catch the sounds for free while on a waterfront stroll or from the edge of a sailboat cruising by the docks.

In Marymoor Park, you can enjoy a weekly dose of well-known performers whose music stars in the **Concerts at Marymoor** (✉ 6046 West Lake Sammamish Pkwy. NE, Redmond ☎ 206/205–3661). Reserved seats and general admission lawn areas are available for catching eclectic acts that run from Norah Jones and the Irish Tenors to Meatloaf and Willie Nelson.

At the **Chateau Ste. Michelle** (✉ 14111 NE 145th St., Woodinville ☎ 425/415–3300 ⊕ www.ste-michelle.com) winery you can catch top international entertainers June through August during the Summer Festival on the Green. You can take a winery tour, have a picnic on the grounds, and then stroll by the vineyards, ponds, and gardens to the amphitheater.

On the stunning Columbia River bluffs about three hours east of Seattle, **The Gorge** (✉ 754 Silica Rd. NW, George ☎ 206/464–2000) is still the major outdoor summer venue—even though White River Amphitheater in southern Auburn provides major competition. It's a hard-rocking place that can host more than 20,000 fans for the likes of ZZ Top, the Dave Matthews Band, and Steely Dan.

The **White River Amphitheater** (✉ 40601 Auburn Enumclaw Rd., Auburn ☎ 360/825–6200) opens to a gorgeous backdrop of snowy Mt. Rainier. Carved Native American decorations on the buildings suit the beautiful location on the Muckleshoot Indian Reservation. Sit below the triangular roof or on the lawn (chair rentals are available) to listen to such well-known acts as Aerosmith, Beck, Fleetwood Mac, and Neil Young.

There's no better way to spend a romantic summer evening than at the **Pink Door** (✉ 1919 Post Alley, Downtown ☎ 206/443–3241). Hidden away in Post Alley, steps from Pike Place Market, this cozy bar tops off its stunning Puget Sound and Olympic Mountains views with tantalizing drinks. Sip a violet martini on the covered deck, and you will know true bliss.

Harvard Exit (✉ 807 E. Roy St., Capitol Hill ☎ 206/323–8986), a first-run and art-film house, is in the former home of the Women's Century Club, hence the quaint, antiques-filled lobby. The small theater is at the north end of Capitol Hill.

Little Theater (✉ 608 19th Ave., Capitol Hill ☎ 206/675–2055), a former woodworking studio, is a hodgepodge of leftovers: the projector, sound system, 49 seats, and popcorn machine were donated by other neighborhood cinemas. The compact space shows offbeat art-house films, locally produced documentaries, and shorts. Look for special events (free chicken and mashed potatoes at the 7 PM Friday screenings in July) or hilarious stage productions that totally involve the audience.

Varsity Theater (✉ 4329 University Way NE, University District ☎ 206/632–3131) showcases a mix of first-run, classic, and cult movies.

Museums & Galleries

Frye Art Museum (✉ 704 Terry Ave., First Hill ☎ 206/622–9250 ⊕ www.fryeart.org) has the collection of art maven and meat-packing mogul Charles Frye, exhibits representational art illuminated solely by natural light. Shows are as charming and unusual as the space they inhabit.

★ **Greg Kucera Gallery** (✉ 212 3rd Ave. S, Pioneer Square ☎ 206/624–0770 ⊕ www.gregkucera.com), widely regarded as Seattle's finest modern gallery, shows work from top Northwest artists as well as nationally celebrated painters, photographers, and sculptors. The gallery's sculpture deck is a pleasant place not only to experience art but also city views.

Grover/Thurston Gallery (✉ 309 Occidental Ave. S, Pioneer Square ☎ 206/223–0816 ⊕ www.groverthurston.com) is a spacious congenial haven for contemporary art. It has Seattle's largest collection of paintings by Northwest artists.

Henry Art Gallery (✉ NE 41st St., at 50th Ave. NE, University of Washington, University District ☎ 206/543–2280 ⊕ www.henryart.org) displays contemporary visual art in a sleek, airy space. Multimedia productions are capably presented; solo shows are curated wisely.

Howard House (✉ 2017 2nd Ave., Belltown ☎ 206/256–6399 ⊕ www.howardhouse.net) hosts some of Seattle's most avant-garde painters and sculptors and their trend-setting digital, mixed media, and installation art.

★ **Seattle Art Museum** (✉ 100 University St., Downtown ☎ 206/654–3100 ⊕ www.seattleartmuseum.org), in Robert Venturi's boldly designed building, has collections ranging from Northwest Native American art to modern paintings and Asian textiles. Out front, the gigantic "Hammering Man" sculpture, moving in slow, perpetual motion, acts as a landmark for visitors.

Seattle Asian Art Museum (✉ 1400 Prospect St., Capitol Hill ☎ 206/654–3100 ⊕ www.seattleartmuseum.org), in Volunteer Park, has a beautiful, tree-lined setting overlooking the city. The serene galleries, in the art deco building that once housed the Seattle Art Museum, display Asian art, sculpture, and photography.

Music

Northwest Chamber Orchestra (✉ 1305 4th Ave., Suite 522, Downtown ☎ 206/343–0445 ⊕ www.nwco.org) performs everything from baroque to modern at the Illsley Nordstrom Recital Hall in Benaroya Hall and outdoors at the Seattle Asian Art Museum.

Seattle Opera (✉ McCaw Hall at Seattle Center, Mercer St. at 3rd Ave., Queen Anne ☎ 206/389–7676 ⊕ www.seattleopera.org), whose home is the beautiful Marion Oliver McCaw Hall, stages such productions as *Carmine, Ariadne auf Naxos,* and *The Girl of the Golden West* from August through May. Evening event guests are treated to a light show from 30-foot hanging scrims above an outdoor piazza. Extra women's bathrooms and a soundproof baby "crying room" make the programs comfortable and family-friendly.

Fodor's Choice ★ **Seattle Symphony** (✉ Benaroya Hall, 1203 2nd Ave., at University St., Downtown ☎ 206/215–4747 ⊕ www.seattlesymphony.org) performs under the direction of Gerard Schwartz from September through June in stunning, acoustically superior Benaroya Hall. This exciting symphony has been nominated for numerous Grammy Awards and is well-regarded nationally and internationally.

Performance Venues

Benaroya Hall (✉ 200 University St., Downtown ☎ 206/215–4800) is so state of the art that the acoustics are pure in every one of the main hall's 2,500 seats. This makes seeing the Seattle Symphony, which is based here, a requisite. The four-story lobby has a curved glass facade that makes intermissions almost as impressive as performances.

Cornish College of the Arts (✉ 710 E. Roy St., Capitol Hill ☎ 206/323–1400 ⊕ www.cornish.edu/events) serves as headquarters for distinguished jazz, dance, and other groups. It also hosts superior student productions.

King Kat Theater (✉ 2130 6th Ave., Belltown ☎ 206/269–7444) is a large concert venue that books national folk, blues, and alternative rock acts. A former cinema, it affords great views from every seat, and the all-ages policy let families to enjoy a concert together.

Kirkland Performance Center (✉ 350 Kirkland Ave., Kirkland ☎ 425/893–9900 ⊕ www.kpcenter.org) brings experiential performance art to the stage. Many of the productions are multicultural music, dance, or theater events, some of which involve mixed media.

Fodor's Choice ★ **Marion Oliver McCaw Hall** (✉ Mercer St. at 3rd Ave., Queen Anne ☎ 206/389–7676 or 206/441–2424 ⊕ www.seattlecenter.org), home of the Seattle Opera and the Pacific Northwest Ballet, is an opulent, glass-enclosed structure reflecting the Northwest skies. Inside, walls are painted in the hues of Northwest sunsets and northern lights; outside, on the piazza, occasional evening light shows are projected onto 30-foot banners dangling above a pond. (Hint: If you're not here for a performance, head atop the parking garage across the street and catch the light show for free.)

Meydenbauer Center (✉ 11100 NE 6th St., Bellevue ☎ 425/637–1020 ⊕ www.meydenbauer.com) has state-of-the-art equipment and excellent acoustics. It hosts performances by children's theater troupes, the Ballet Bellevue, the Bellevue Civic Theater, and other groups.

Moore Theater (✉ 1932 2nd Ave., Downtown ☎ 206/443–1744 ⊕ www.themoore.com), built in 1907, is Seattle's oldest theater and still hosts off-Broadway performances and music events. A quick peek at the prominent marquee clues you in to what's happening: jazz concerts, instrumental duets, hard-rock bookings, pop-music shows. The venerable hall was featured in Pearl Jam's video, *Evenflow,* and many of the big grunge music acts of Seattle's early '90s rock heyday performed here.

Paradox Theater (✉ 1510 University Way NE, University District ☎ 206/524–7677) has a mix of all-ages punk, pop, and spoken word performances.

Paramount Theatre (✉ 907 Pine St., Downtown ☎ 206/682–1414 ⊕ www.theparamount.com), opened in 1928 as a vaudeville and silent film venue. Today its 2,800 cushy seats and opulent details make it a great place to see popular music acts, top comedians, and international dance troupes. Monday night brings silent movies accompanied by the original Publix organ.

Seattle Center (✉ 305 Harrison St., Queen Anne ☎ 206/684–8582 ⊕ www.seattlecenter.org) has several halls that present theater, opera, dance, music, and performance art. Live music, theme dances, and festivals are staged monthly in the Center House. The Seattle Center is also the site of Labor Day weekend's Bumbershoot Festival, which celebrates the arts.

Readings

★ **Elliot Bay Book Co.** (⊠ 101 S. Main St., Pioneer Square ☎ 206/624–6600 ⊕ www.elliottbaybook.com) presents a popular series of author readings in a cozy, basement room next to a café. Events are free, but tickets are often required.

Kane Hall (⊠ University of Washington, NE 41st St. and 15th Ave. NE, University District ☎ 206/543–2985) hosts hundreds of cultural events, concerts, lectures, and readings by internationally renowned artists, poets, authors. Many events are free, but tickets are required.

Richard Hugo House (⊠ 1634 11th Ave., Capitol Hill ☎ 206/322–7030 ⊕ www.hugohouse.org) is a haven for writers, with classes, private work areas, and readings by Northwest luminaries and authors on their way up. As it's in a Victorian building that was once a residence, it's a warm, homey place.

University Book Store (⊠ 4326 University Way NE, University District ☎ 206/634–3400 ⊕ www.bookstore.washington.edu), near the UW campus, schedules free readings by best-selling authors and academics. The second-floor space sets you right amid the book stacks, perfect for browsing afterward. Tickets are required—and they usually go quickly.

Theaters

A Contemporary Theater (⊠ 700 Union St., Downtown ☎ 206/292–7676) launches exciting works by emerging dramatists. Four staging areas include a theater-in-the-round and an intimate downstairs space for small shows. The April to November season highlight is *Late Night Catechism,* the long-running play dubbed the *Cats* of Seattle.

Crepe de Paris (⊠ Rainier Tower, 1333 5th Ave., Downtown ☎ 206/623–4111), an unassuming business-lunch restaurant with '70s-style leather and Plexiglas details, hosts dinner theater—specifically sidesplitting cabarets and musicals. On show nights, you choose from a set, prix-fixe selection; other nights there's a full menu.

Empty Space Theater (⊠ 3509 Fremont Ave., Fremont ☎ 206/547–7500) stages maverick productions November through June. The cozy theater has 150 tightly packed seats for viewing works by new writers and, occasionally, such famous names as David Mamet or Sam Shephard.

FodorśChoice ★ **5th Avenue Theater** (⊠ 1308 5th Ave., Downtown ☎ 206/625–1418 ⊕ www.5thavenuetheatre.org) opened in 1926 as a silent movie house and vaudeville stage, complete with a giant pipe organ and ushers who dressed up as cowboys and pirates. Today the chinoiserie landmark has its own theater company, which stages lavish productions October through May. At other times the theater hosts concerts, lectures, and films.

Intiman Theater (⊠ 201 Mercer St., Queen Anne ☎ 206/269–1901 ⊕ www.intiman.org/), at the Seattle Center, presents important contemporary works and classics of the world stage from May through November in its 485-seat space.

Nippon Kan Theater (⊠ 409 7th Ave. S, International District ☎ 206/841–2521), a national historic landmark built in 1909, was once the gathering place for Japanese-Americans in Seattle. The building was boarded up in 1942, when all Japanese were moved to internment camps during World War II, but the beautiful interior was still intact when the theater reopened in 1981. Today, as a venue for concerts, plays, neighborhood events, and touring international performers, it's an integral part of Seattle's Asian-American community.

★ **Northwest Actors Studio** (✉ 1100 E. Pike St., Capitol Hill ☎ 206/324–6328), Seattle's oldest theater arts center, has a second-floor main stage and a third-floor cabaret space with an open bar. There's always something unique on the schedule, as the studio is home to such locally beloved troupes as the circus-style Bare; the UW student improvisational Collective; the free-form duo Improsia; the hilarious Jet City Improv comedy team; and Seattle's oldest improv group, Unexpected Productions.

Northwest Asian American Theater (✉ 628 S. Washington St., International District ☎ 206/340–1445), below the Wing Luke Asian Museum, embraces innovative performances by artists in Seattle's Asian and Pacific Islander communities. Their Black Box season focuses on diverse, non-Asian productions, and the on-site RAW gallery exhibits Asian-American visual art. Catch international flicks here each fall here as part of the Seattle Asian-American Film Festival.

Northwest Puppet Center (✉ 9125 15th Ave. NE, University District ☎ 206/523–2579) encourages kids to sprawl on the floor while folktales are told by marionettes. The troupe, which has trained in several countries, keeps the lively stories brief (45 minutes). Puppet workshops are available.

Open Circle Theater (✉ 429 Boren Ave. N, Capitol Hill ☎ 206/382–4250) produces cutting-edge, very physical ensemble theater and one-person shows that address humanity through magical mythical stories.

Seattle Children's Theatre (✉ Charlotte Martin Theatre at Seattle Center, 2nd Ave. N and Thomas St., Queen Anne ☎ 206/441–3322 ⊕ www.sct.org), stages top-notch productions of new works as well as adaptations from classic children's literature. After the show, actors come out from behind the scenes to answer questions and explain how the tricks are done.

Seattle Repertory Theater (✉ 155 Mercer St., Queen Anne ☎ 206/443–2222 ⊕ www.seattlerep.org) brings nine new and classic plays to life split among Seattle Center's Bagley Wright and Leo K. theaters during its September through April season. Adoring fans flock to new takes on choice classics as well as those fresh from the New York stage. You can pre-order a boxed dinner from the Café at the Rep before the show, or linger afterward over coffee and dessert.

SPORTS &
THE OUTDOORS

5

FODOR'S CHOICE

Alki Beach, *West Seattle*

Center for Wooden Boats, *Lake Union*

Harbour Pointe Golf Club, *Mukilteo*

Sand Point Magnuson Park, *Sand Point beach*

Whistler, *British Columbia, Canada, ski area*

HIGHLY RECOMMENDED

Matthews Beach Park, *Sand Point*

Schurman Rock, *West Seattle climbing rock*

The Summit at Snoqualmie, *Snoqualmie Pass ski area*

Wild Waves/Enchanted Village, *Federal Way*

Updated by
Shelley Arenas

THE QUESTION IN SEATTLE ISN'T "DO YOU EXERCISE?" Rather it's "What do you do for exercise?" Athleticism is a regular part of most people's lives here, whether it's an afternoon mountaineering trek, a sunrise rowing session, a lunch-hour bike ride, or an evening game of Frisbee. The Cascade Mountains, a 60-minute drive east, have trails and peaks for alpinists of all skill levels. Snoqualmie Pass attracts downhill skiers and snowboarders. The cross-country skiing and snowshoeing are excellent at Snoqualmie Pass or across Stevens Pass. To the west of the city is Puget Sound, where sailors, kayakers, scuba divers, jet skiers, and anglers practice their sports. Farther west the Olympic Mountains beckon adventure-seeking souls to still more sweat-inducing activity amid scenic wilderness.

Spectator sports are also appreciated here. To see how excited Seattle citizens can get about crew racing, stop by the Montlake Cut on the official opening day of the unofficial boating season. The University of Washington (UW) has been a rowing powerhouse since the 1930s, and tickets to Husky football games have been hot items for years. Attendance at Mariners games is at an all-time high, and the Seahawks are gaining steam as well.

Given a choice, though, most Seattleites would rather *do* than watch. More than one visitor has commented that it seems as if most Seattleites are exercising all the time. Visit Green Lake on a sunny weekend day, and you'll probably agree. Fitness is definitely a virtue in these parts, but the motivation isn't so much to look good as it is to *feel* good. And you thought it was just about the coffee.

Amusement Parks

Years ago, Seattle had a number of amusement parks, many at area beaches: Luna Park at Alki Beach was the "Coney Island of the West," Playland at Bitter Lake brought folks from around the state, and trolley lines transported fun-loving Seattle folks to Madison Beach's amusement park. Today Seattle Center's Fun Forest is the only one of these that remains.

Fun Forest Amusement Park. Traditional rides, dating from 1962, when the park was built for the World's Fair, include a roller coaster and a Ferris wheel; other rides reflect the city's aerodynamic legacy with such names as Orbiter (an elevated, green spinning machine) and Jetspin (an inverted spinning ride). There's also a large kiddy-ride area. Rides require tickets, with the most desirable ones requiring the most tickets. About four tickets per ride is common, and they cost $1 each; purchase an all-day wristband to get the most bang for your buck. Outdoor rides are open seasonally, but you can play laser tag and video games year-round in the Entertainment Pavilion. ⊠ *Seattle Center, 5th Ave. and Broad St., Queen Anne* ☎ *206/728–1585* ⊕ *www.funforest.com* ✉ *Free* ☉ *Amusement park: June–Labor Day, daily noon–11; early Sept.–May, Fri. 6 PM–10 PM, Sat. noon–10, Sun. noon–7. Entertainment Pavilion: year-round, Sun.–Thurs. 11–6, Fri. and Sat. 11–11.*

★ **Wild Waves/Enchanted Village.** Western Washington's only theme park is owned by the Six Flags chain and is actually an amusement park and a water park; one ticket gets you into both. Enchanted Village has about two dozen rides, including the large wooden Timberhawk–Ride of Prey roller coaster. Tamer trips include a train ride or a spin on an antique carousel. The Wild Waves park has water rides, slides, and a 24,000-square-foot wave pool. You can't bring your own food and drink into the parks, but there's little need for you to do so with more than a dozen on-site concessions. To get here drive south on I–5 south

HOW TO PLAY

King County Parks and Recreation (☎ 206/296–4232 for information and reservations, 206/296–4171 for interpretive programs ⊕ www.metrokc. gov/parks) manages many of the parks outside of city limits. To find out whether a given in-town park baseball diamond or tennis court is available, contact the **Seattle Parks and Recreation Department** (☎ 206/684–4075 ⊕ www.cityofseattle.net/parks), which is responsible for most of the parks, piers, beaches, playgrounds, and courts within city limits. The department issues permits for events, arranges reservations for facilities, and staffs visitors centers and naturalist programs. **Ticketmaster** (☎ 206/622–4487) sells tickets to many local sporting events. The state manages several parks and campgrounds in greater Seattle. For more information contact **Washington State Parks** (☎ 800/233–0321 for general information, 800/452–5687 for campsite reservations ⊕ www.parks.wa.gov/parkpage.asp).

for about 27 mi from Downtown. ⊠ 36201 Enchanted Pkwy. S (Exit 142B off I–5), Federal Way ☎ 253/661–8000 ⊕ www.wildwaves.com ☞ $24.99 ⊙ Mid-May–mid-June, weekdays 9:30–4, weekends 10–6. Mid-June–July 3, daily 10–7. July 4–Labor Day, daily 10–8.

Baseball

Despite the crippling departure of all-stars Ken Griffey, Jr., Randy Johnson, and Alex Rodriguez, the Seattle Mariners keep coming back stronger every season. The team plays in the West Division of the American League, and their home is Safeco Field, a retractable-roof stadium. Even if nothing's happening on the field, the walkways have plenty of stunning viewpoints that overlook the port's giraffelike cranes and the Olympic Mountains.

If you're in the mood for minor-league play, take I–5 roughly 30 mi either north or south of town. To the north, the Everett Aqua Sox play short-season Class A ball in the Northwest League. Keep an eye out for Harold the Pig, who delivers balls to the pitching mound. Admission is $5–$12. Parking in the South Lot and on the street north of the stadium is free, but arrive about an hour early to get a space. For AAA Pacific Coast League action and a fabulous view of Mt. Rainier, head south to see the Tacoma Rainiers. Both teams are Mariners farm clubs and offer an up-close, family-oriented baseball experience.

Basketball

The men's NBA season runs from November to April. The Seattle SuperSonics play at Key Arena in the Seattle Center. You can buy tickets at the box office or by calling the NBA toll-free number.

After the demise of the Seattle Reign, the city's first pro women's team, hopes were immediately pinned on the WNBA to pick Seattle for an expansion team. The coach dribbled through Downtown for an entire day once to win supporters to the cause. Prayers were answered with the formation of the Seattle Storm, which plays its home games at Key Arena. The season is from mid-June to August.

The UW Huskies represent Seattle basketball in the Pac-10 Conference. The team has had less than its share of success. The tough women's team—which enjoys a very loyal (and loud) fan base—has, however, advanced to the NCAA tournament several times in recent years.

Beaches

With the Puget Sound to the west and 25-mi-long Lake Washington to the east, Seattle has miles and miles of waterfront, much of it speckled with beaches. In addition smaller lakes, products of ancient glacial movements, spring forth throughout the city and the suburbs. You're never far from some body of water or another. Most Lake Washington beaches in Seattle, Kirkland, and Bellevue have lifeguards on duty in summer. Free swimming lessons are given at several Seattle beaches for ages 6 and up.

Fodor's Choice **Alki Beach** (✉ 1702 Alki Ave. SW, West Seattle ☎ 206/684–4075). In summer, cars inch along Alki Avenue, seeking a coveted parking space, all the passengers heading for this 2½-mi stretch of sand. It's something of a California beach scene (except for the water temperature), with in-line skaters, joggers, and cyclists sharing the walkway and sun-loving singles playing volleyball and flirting. Year-round, families come to build sand castles, beachcomb, and fly kites; in winter, storm-watchers come to see the crashing waves. Facilities include drinking water, grills, picnic tables, phones, and rest rooms; restaurants line the street across from the beach. To get here from Downtown, take either I–5 south or Highway 99 south to the West Seattle Bridge and exit onto Harbor Avenue Southwest, turning right at the stoplight.

Golden Gardens Park (✉ 8498 Seaview Pl. NW (near NW 85th St.), Ballard ☎ 206/684–4075). Puget Sound waters are bone-chilling cold, but that doesn't stop folks from jumping in to cool off. Besides brave swimmers, the park is packed with sunbathers in summer. In other seasons, beachcombers explore during low tide, and groups gather around bonfires to socialize and watch the sun go down. The park has drinking water, grills, picnic tables, phones, and rest rooms. It also has two wetlands, a short loop trail, and a rugged coast with breathtaking views. From Downtown, take Elliott Avenue North, which becomes 15th Avenue West, and cross the Ballard Bridge. Turn left to head west on Market Street and follow signs to the Ballard Locks; continue about another mile to the park.

Houghton Beach Park (✉ 5811 Lake Washington Blvd., Kirkland ☎ 425/828–1217). On hot days, sun-worshipers and swimmers flock to this beach south of downtown Kirkland on the Lake Washington waterfront. The rest of the year, the playground attracts families, and the fishing pier stays busy with anglers. Facilities include drinking water, picnic tables, phones, and rest rooms.

Juanita Beach Park (✉ 9703 Juanita Dr. NE, Kirkland ☎ 425/828–1217). Directly across Juanita Bay from peaceful wetlands, this beach hops: children playing in the sand, sunbathers on the dock, swimmers in the closed-in swimming area, and picnickers in the park. There are grills, picnic tables, phones, rest rooms, drinking water, and a snack bar (seasonal).

Madison Park (✉ 2300 43rd Ave. E, Madison Park ☎ 206/684–4075). The sandy Lake Washington beach, with easy access to the water, the sloping lawn, the playgrounds, and the tennis courts fill quickly on warm days. There are coffee shops and other amenities nearby; the beach has drinking water, picnic tables, phones, rest rooms, and showers. From Downtown, go east on Madison Street for about 3 mi, turn right on East Howe Street and then turn left to head north on 43rd Avenue.

Madrona Park (✉ 853 Lake Washington Blvd., Madrona ☎ 206/684–4075). Several beach parks and green spaces front the lake along Lake Washington Boulevard; Madrona Park is one of the largest. Young swimmers stay in the roped-in area while teens and adults swim out to

CloseUp

WHERE THEY PLAY

Bank of America Arena at Hec Edmundson Pavilion. What's known locally as "Hec Ed" is where the UW's men's and women's basketball teams play. ⊠ 3870 Montlake Blvd. NE, University District ☎ 206/543–2200 ⊕ gohuskies.ocsn. com.

Cheney Stadium. For some AAA Pacific Coast League baseball action and a fabulous view of Mt. Rainier, head south to this stadium, which is home to the Tacoma Rainiers, a Mariners' affiliate team. If you're totally broke, there's a grassy knoll outside of left field from which you can watch the entire game, but you didn't hear that here. Take I–5 south to Exit 132, follow Highway 16 west for 2 mi, get off at the South 19th Street East exit; take first right (Cheyenne St.), and follow the road to stadium parking lots. ⊠ 2502 S. Tyler, Tacoma ☎ 253/752–7707 ⊕ www.tacomarainiers.com.

Everett Memorial Stadium. The Everett Aquasox, an affiliate of the Seattle Mariners, play their games at this open ballpark, which is also a favorite of aficionados of old-fashioned baseball. ⊠ 3900 Broadway Ave. (Exit 192 off I–5), Everett ☎ 425/258–3673 ⊕ www. aquasox.com.

Husky Stadium. This U-shaped stadium overlooks Lake Washington, so you can arrive by boat as well as by bike, bus, or car. The notoriously loud UW Husky fans are, however, noted for their ability to cause traffic jams on home game days. ⊠ University of Washington, 3800 Montlake Blvd. NE, University District ☎ 206/543–2200 ⊕ gohuskies.ocsn.com.

Key Arena. Seattle Center has its hands full not only with the Seattle SuperSonics (NBA) and the Seattle Storm (WNBA) but also with the Seattle Thunderbirds (a minor-league hockey club) and all the major concerts. The surrounding area has plenty to offer post-game, with restaurants to the north and south. Traffic is a major problem on game nights. ⊠ Seattle Center, 1st Ave. N and Mercer St., Queen Anne ☎ 206/283–3865, or 800/ 4NBA–TIX for Supersonics tickets, 206/

217–9622 Seattle Storm information, 425/869–7825 or 206/448–7825 Seattle Thunderbirds information ⊕ www. seattlecenter.com.

Safeco Field. It may sound cliché but there really isn't a bad seat in the house. When it rains, the retractable roof deflects most of the drops. When it's sunny, you can watch the sun set over the Olympics (the mountains!) from behind the Mariners' second base. One local sports columnist refers to the venue—the most expensive stadium in recorded history and $100 million over budget—as "the guilty pleasure." ⊠ 1st Ave. S and Atlantic St., Sodo ☎ 206/346–4000 ⊕ seattle. mariners.mlb.com.

Seahawks Stadium. On the site of the former Kingdome and just a block away from Safeco Field, this state-of-the-art stadium is home base for the Seattle Sounders soccer team as well as the Seahawks. The public paid $300 million of the facility's $430 million construction tab; Seahawks owner Paul Allen picked up the rest of the tab. ⊠ 800 Occidental Ave., Sodo ☎ 425/827–9777 ⊕ www. seahawks.com/stadium.

a floating raft with a diving board. Runners and in-line skaters follow the mile-long trail along the shore. Kids clamber about the sculpted-sand garden and climb on rocks and logs. Grassy areas encourage picnicking; there are grills, picnic tables, phones, rest rooms, and showers. A barbecue stand is open seasonally. From Downtown, go east on Yesler Way about 2 mi to 32nd Avenue. Turn left onto Lake Dell Avenue and then right; go to Lake Washington Boulevard and take a left.

★ **Matthews Beach Park** (✉ Sand Point Way NE and NE 93rd St., Sand Point ☎ 206/684–4075). On warm summer days, the parking lot and nearby streets overflow with people visiting Seattle's largest freshwater swimming beach. The Burke-Gilman Trail, popular with cyclists and runners, travels through the park. Picnic areas, basketball hoops, and a big playground round out the amenities. From Downtown, take I–5 north and get off at the Lake City Way Northeast exit. Stay on Lake City Way for about 1½ mi. Turn right on to Northeast 95th Street, right onto Sand Point Way Northeast, and left onto Northeast 93rd Street.

Newcastle Beach Park (✉ 4400 Lake Washington Blvd. SE, off 112th SE Exit from I–405, Bellevue ☎ 425/452–6881 ⊕ www.ci.bellevue.wa. us/parks). On Lake Washington in Bellevue, this large park has a big swimming beach, a fishing dock, nature trails, volleyball nets, drinking water, phones, rest rooms, and a large grassy area with picnic tables. The playground is a favorite thanks to a train that tots can sit in and older kids can climb on and hop from car to car.

Fodor'sChoice **Sand Point Magnuson Park** (✉ Bordered by NE 65th and 74th Sts., Sand
★ Point Way NE and Lake Washington [entrances at 65th St. and 74th St.], Sand Point ☎ 206/684–4946). As it was once an airport, it's not surprising that this 200-acre park northeast of the University District is flat and open. The paved trails are wonderful for cycling, in-line skating, and pushing a stroller. Many kids have learned to ride their two-wheelers here; quite a few more have spent time on the large playground. Leashed dogs are welcome on the trails; a large off-leash area includes one of the few public beaches where pooches can swim. Farther south, on the mile-long shore, there's a swimming beach, a seasonal wading pool, and a boat launch. The park also has tennis courts, sports fields, and a terrific kite-flying hill. Be sure to look for the unique public art: *The Fin Project: From Swords to Plowshares* uses submarine fins to depict a pod of orca whales. *No Appointment Necessary* has two bright red chairs extended into the sky. *The Sound Garden* (at the neighboring National Oceanic and Atmospheric Administration campus) has steel pipes that give off sounds when the wind blows for an art display that you can hear as well as see. From Downtown, take I–5 north to the Northeast 65th Street exit, turn right and continue east to Sand Point Way Northeast.

Bicycling

The Seattle Parks Department sponsors Bicycle Saturdays and Sundays on different weekends May through September. On these days, a 4-mi stretch of Lake Washington Boulevard—from Mt. Baker Beach to Seward Park—is closed to motor vehicles. Many riders continue around the 2-mi loop at Seward Park and back to Mt. Baker Beach to complete a 10-mi, car-free ride.

The trail that circles Green Lake is popular with cyclists, though runners and walkers can impede fast travel. The city-maintained Burke-Gilman Trail, a much less congested path, follows an abandoned railroad line 12 mi along Seattle's waterfront from Lake Washington almost to Salmon Bay. Myrtle Edwards Park, north of Pier 70, has a two-lane path for bicycling and running.

King County has more than 100 mi of paved and nearly 70 mi of unpaved routes including the Sammamish River, Interurban, Green River, Cedar River, Snoqualmie Valley, and Soos Creek trails. For more information contact the King County Parks and Recreation office.

The **Bicycle Alliance of Washington** (☎ 206/224–9252 ⊕ www.bicyclealliance.org), the state's largest cycling advocacy group, is a great source for information. The **Cascade Bicycle Club** (☎ 206/522–2453 ⊕ www.cascade.org) has more than 4,500 members and organizes more than 1,000 rides annually for recreational and hard-core bikers. Of its major events the most famous is the Seattle-to-Portland Bicycle Classic. The **Seattle Bicycle Program** (☎ 206/684–7583 ⊕ www.seattle.gov/transportation/bikeprogram.htm) was responsible for the creation of the city's multiuse trails (a.k.a. bike routes) as well as pedestrian paths and roads with wide shoulders—things, in other words, that benefit bicyclists. The agency's Web site has route maps.

Gregg's Greenlake Cycle (✉ 7007 Woodlawn Ave. NE, Green Lake ☎ 206/523–1822 ⊕ www.greggscycles.com). On Green Lake's northern end, this Seattle institution has been in business since 1932. It sells and rents mountain bikes, standard road touring bikes, and hybrids; helmets and locks are included with each rental. Gregg's is close to the Burke-Gilman Trail and across the street from the Green Lake Trail. Rental fees range from $15 to $30 for the day, $20 to $35 overnight, and $60 to $120 per week. Gregg's also rents in-line skates, jogging strollers, snowboarding equipment, and snowshoes.

Marymoor Velodrome (✉ 6046 W. Lake Sammamish Pkwy. NE, Redmond ⊕ www.marymoorvelodrome.org). When not used for competitive racing—National Championship meets, regional Olympic trials, the Goodwill Games—the banked oval here is open to the public. Granted, it's a bit of a haul from Seattle to Redmond, but for serious speedsters, there's no substitute. Since the Burke-Gilman Trail links up in Bothell with the Sammamish River Trail (which is connected to Marymoor Park), you can ride from Seattle to Marymoor, though you may not have anything left for the track once you get here. A free junior program for ages 5–8 introduces children to track cycling, with track bikes provided for free during classes and races.

Boating & Sailing

The **Unlimited Hydroplane Races** (☎ 206/728–0123) are a highlight of Seattle's Seafair festivities from mid-July through the first Sunday in August. Races are held on Lake Washington near Seward Park. Tickets cost $15–$25. In summer, weekly sailing regattas take place on Lakes Union and Washington. Contact the **Seattle Yacht Club** (☎ 206/325–1000 ⊕ www.seattleyachtclub.org) for schedules.

Agua Verde Paddle Club and Cafe (✉ 1303 NE Boat St., University District ☎ 206/545–8570 ⊕ www.aguaverde.com). If you hate to choose between your Mexican food and your kayaking, consider checking out Agua Verde. Start out by renting a kayak and paddling along either the Lake Union shoreline, with its hodgepodge of funky-to-fabulous houseboats and dramatic Downtown vistas, or Union Bay on Lake Washington, with its marshes and cattails. Afterward, take in the lakefront as you wash down a bite with a margarita. Kayaks are available March through October and are rented by the hour—$12 for singles, $16 for doubles, and $18 for triples. The third and fourth hours are free weekdays; fourth hours are free on weekends.

Fodor'sChoice
★ **Center for Wooden Boats** (✉ 1010 Valley St., Lake Union ☎ 206/382–2628 ⊕ www.cwb.org). Seattle's free maritime heritage museum also

rents classic wooden rowboats and sailboats. Rowboats are $12.50 or $15 an hour (depending on whether there's one person or two) on weekdays and $18 or $20 an hour on weekends. Sloops and catboats cost $15.75–$46 an hour, depending on the type and size of the vessel. There's a $5 skills-check fee. Free half-hour guided sails and steamboat rides are offered on Sunday from 2 to 3 (arrive an hour early).

Green Lake Boat Rental (✉ 7351 W. Green Lake Way N, Green Lake ☎ 206/527–0171) is the source for canoes, paddleboats, sailboats, kayaks, sailboards, and rowboats to ply Green Lake's calm waters. On beautiful summer afternoons, however, be prepared to spend most of your time negotiating other traffic on the water as well as in the parking lot. Fees are $10 an hour for paddleboats, single kayaks, and rowboats; $12 an hour for double kayaks; and $14 an hour for sailboats and sailboards.

Moss Bay Rowing and Kayak Center (✉ 1001 Fairview Ave. N, Lake Union ☎ 206/682–2031 ⊕ www.mossbay.net). Moss Bay rents a variety of rowing craft—including Whitehall pulling boats, wherries, and sliding-seat rowboats—for $15 per hour. You can also rent a rowing shell or a sailboat. After a skills check (which costs $35), another $35 gets you an hour in a recreational or racing shell (single or double) or a sailboat. Single kayaks rent for $10 per hour, doubles go for $15. Also growing in popularity are dragon boats for up to 25 people and war canoes for up to 10 people. The cost is $10 per person per hour, and reservations are advised.

Northwest Outdoor Center (✉ 2100 Westlake Ave. N, Lake Union ☎ 206/281–9694). This center on Lake Union's west side, rents one- or two-person kayaks (it also has a few triples) by the hour or day, including equipment and basic or advanced instruction. The hourly rate is $10 for a single and $15 for a double, with daily maximums of $50 and $70, respectively. Third and fourth hours are free during the week; a fourth hour is free weekends. If you want to find your own water, NWOC offers "to go" kayaks; the rate for a single is $50 first day, plus $25 each additional day. Doubles cost $70 the first day and $35 for each day thereafter. In summer, reserve least three days ahead. NWOC also runs guided sunset ($35 per person) and moonlight ($25 per person) trips. Day excursions are also possible, and every May, there are two overnight whale-watching trips to the San Juan Islands.

Waterfront Activities Center (✉ 3800 Montlake Blvd. NE, University District ☎ 206/543–9433). This center behind UW's Husky Stadium rents three-person canoes and four-person rowboats for $7.50 an hour February through October. You can tour the Lake Washington shoreline or take the Montlake Cut portion of the ship canal and explore Lake Union. You can also row to nearby Foster Island and visit the Washington Park Arboretum.

Wind Works Sailing Center (✉ 7001 Seaview Ave. NW, Ballard ☎ 206/784–9386 ⊕ www.windworkssailing.com). Although members are given first picks at Wind Works, which is on Shilshole Bay, nonmembers can arrange rentals. Experienced sailors are allowed to skipper their own boats after a brief qualifying process. Sailing a 25-foot Catalina will cost you $125 on weekdays and $167 on weekends; rates for a 43-foot Hunter are $321 on weekdays and $428 on weekends. In summer as many as 30 people can spring for a sunset cruise on a 61-foot, 1930s-era racing yacht, although only Wind Works staff can skipper it. The cruise runs 6 PM–10 PM and costs $935 weekdays, $1,080 weekends.

Yarrow Bay Marina (✉ 5207 Lake Washington Blvd. NE, Kirkland ☎ 425/822–6066 ⊕ www.yarrowbaymarina.com/rentals.htm). The marina rents 19- and 22-foot runabouts for $60 an hour on weekdays and $65 an hour on weekends. There's a two-hour minimum; weekly rentals are also an option.

Fishing

Green Lake is stocked with more than 10,000 legal-size rainbow trout each year. Anglers can also vie for brown trout, largemouth bass, yellow perch, and brown bullhead catfish. The parks department maintains three fishing piers along the lake's shores: East Green Lake Drive at Latona Avenue Northeast; West Green Lake Drive North and Stone Avenue North; and West Green Lake Way North, just north of the shellhouse. You can't deny the bizarre combination of hooking one in while North Face–clad moms jog by with their toddlers in sports utility strollers.

Lake Washington has its share of parks department piers as well. You can fish year-round for rainbow trout, cutthroat trout, and large- and smallmouth bass. Chinook, coho, and steelhead salmon are also available, but often subject to restrictions. Check regulations in the "Sport Fishing Rules" pamphlet (available at most sporting goods stores) when you buy your license. A two-day license costs about $7; annual licenses range $20–$42 for residents, depending on the type of fishing, and about double that for nonresidents.

For saltwater fishing, Seattle has public piers along Shilshole Bay in Golden Gardens Park. Elliott Bay has public piers at Waterfront Park. Shilshole Bay charter-fishing companies offer trips to fish for salmon, rockfish, cod, flounder, and sea bass.

Adventure Charters (✉ 7001 Seaview Ave. NW, Ballard ☎ 206/789–8245 ⊕ www.seattlesalmoncharters.com) takes private groups out on six-person troll boats to fish for salmon, bottom fish, and crab—depending on the season. The guided trips last for six or seven hours. The price per person is $125 October–May and $135 June–September; a license, tackle, and bait are included, and your fish will be cleaned or filleted and bagged for free.

Fish Finders Private Charters (✉ 6019 Seaview Ave. NW, Ballard ☎ 206/632–2611 ⊕ www.fishingseattle.com) takes groups of four or more out on Puget Sound for guided salmon fishing trips. The cost is $135 per person plus $6 for a fishing license. Morning trips last about six hours; afternoon trips are about five hours. All gear, bait, cleaning, and bagging are included in the fee.

Fitness Clubs

Most large Downtown hotels have workout facilities, but there are other options. Gateway Athletic, Seattle Athletic, and Vault are members of the IHRSA reciprocal membership Passport program. If you belong to an IHRSA club in another city, you're eligible for special daily or short-term guest rates. Check with your local club before you leave.

All Star Fitness (✉ 330 2nd Ave. W, Queen Anne ☎ 206/282–5901 ⊕ www.allstarfitness.org). It's usually packed with 20- to 30-year-old urban professionals—maybe because it's one of the few gyms that has an indoor pool, plenty of Cybex machines, and a full schedule of classes (some only for women) that includes yoga, kickboxing, and step. There are lockers, towels, a sauna, a steam room, and a co-ed Jacuzzi. A day pass runs $10–$15, depending on the services you use, and includes classes. All Star Fitness has branches Downtown, in West Seattle, and in Woodinville, and it's affiliated with the Gateway Athletic Club.

Ballard Health Club (✉ 2208 NW Market St., Ballard ☎ 206/706–4882). Ballard is an anomaly among clubs. It's incredibly low-key and reasonably priced, with everything you need and nothing more: weights, cardio machines, many classes (including three kinds of yoga), a stretching room, and day care facility. Locker rooms have saunas; towels are available. A day pass costs $8 and includes access to classes.

Gateway Athletic Club (✉ 700 5th Ave., 14th fl., Downtown ☎ 206/343–4692 ⊕ www.allstarfitness.org). This member of the All Star Fitness chain is designed to impress with its striking views, tidy facilities, and attentive service. In addition to the usual lineup of free weights, weight machines, and cardio equipment, there are lots of classes, some of them unusual (ski conditioning, for example), as well as a squash court and a swimming pool. Day passes are $10–$15.

Pure Fitness (✉ 808 2nd Ave., Downtown ☎ 206/224–9000 ⊕ www.vaultfitness.com). This club, which is in a former bank, combines lots of equipment and classes with some unusual architectural features. The main floor has free weights; treadmills; and Cybex, Hammer Strength, and rowing machines. The loftlike second level contains a large aerobic studio and rows and rows of cardio machines facing a phalanx of TV monitors. Downstairs are saunas, steam rooms, and locker rooms. An enormous old vault door opens to the spa pool, which has an 8-foot waterfall that seems to flow from the corner of the ceiling. Classes on Qi Gong, an exercise combining movement with intellectual and emotional focus, are offered. Massage therapy costs $40–$90. The club also has tanning beds, nutrition counseling, personal trainers, and chiropractic services. Guest passes cost $10 a day. There are four other Pure Fitness clubs—one in Westlake, another in Lynnwood, and two more in Tacoma.

Seattle Athletic Club (✉ 2020 Western Ave., Downtown ☎ 206/443–1111 ⊕ www.sacdt.com). Beyond this club's deceptively modest entrance, one block north of Pike Place Market, are more than 60,000-square-feet of free weights, Cybex machines, treadmills, Stairmasters, rowing machines, recumbent cycling machines, an indoor track, a full-size basketball court, racquetball and squash courts, and a pool. The club also offers a full slate of classes, from power cycling, step, and cardio to toning, Pilates, tai chi, and yoga. Massage therapy starts at $55 for a half-session for guests of affiliate hotels.

Washington Athletic Club (✉ 1325 6th Ave., at Union St., Downtown ☎ 206/622–7900 ⊕ www.wac.net). It may no longer be a men's club, but this five-floor facility is still where a lot of hobnobbing goes on. You can also lift weights, take fitness classes, train in martial arts, and participate in wellness programs. The spa has massage, body scrubs, facials, hair and nail services. You can only work out here if you're the guest of a member or are a member of an affiliated club (call or see the list on the Web site), in which case you don't have to pay for a pass and you qualify for reduced rates at the Inn at the WAC.

Football

Since 2002, the Seattle Seahawks have been playing in their $430 million stadium (which also hosts soccer matches), a tremendous improvement over the decrepit Kingdome that was imploded several years ago. The stadium is a civic project kick-started by Microsoft cofounder and billionaire Paul Allen, the Seahawks owner, who also built the Experience Music Project and saved the Cinerama movie theater from destruction.

Frankly, people get more excited about the Huskies than the Seahawks, perhaps because so many UW students stay in town after graduating. Despite the endless litany of player scandals and the termination of Rick Neuheisel as coach in 2003 due to NCAA rules violations, the team has stayed strong, making it to the Rose Bowl (or close) several times in recent years.

Golf

Bellevue Municipal Golf Course (⊠ 5500 140th Ave. NE, Bellevue ☎ 425/452–7250). Bellevue has a driving range and a short par-71 course with generous greens and few hazards. It's a very busy course; reservations are recommended, especially for weekends. Call on Monday for tee times. Greens fees are $29.50 Friday–Sunday and $25.50 Monday–Thursday; carts rent for $27.

Crossroads Par 3 Golf Course (⊠ 15801 NE 8th St., Bellevue ☎ 425/452–4873). This course consists of 9 par-3 holes with small, flat greens throughout. Amenities are limited to a soda-vending machine and a putting green. Greens fees are $7 weekends and $6 weekdays, and tee times are first-come, first-served. You can play the course in about 90 minutes, and it's a great option for beginners.

Green Lake Pitch and Putt (⊠ 5701 W. Green Lake Way N, at N. 57th St., Green Lake ☎ 206/632–2280). This 9-hole, par-3, pitch-and-putt course plays extremely short and easy. The cost is $4, and it's open 9 AM–dusk, March–October.

Fodor'sChoice
★ **Harbour Pointe Golf Club** (⊠ 11817 Harbour Pointe Blvd., Mukilteo ☎ 800/233–3128 ⊕ www.harbourpt.com). If you're willing to spend some time and money, drive about 30 minutes north of Seattle to the town of Mukilteo and this club. Its challenging 18-hole championship layout—with 6,800 yards of hilly terrain and wonderful Puget Sound views—is one of Washington's best. Greens fees are $59 Friday through Sunday and $47 the rest of the week. Carts cost $15 per person. There's also a driving range where you can get 65 balls for $5. Reserve your tee time online, up to 21 days in advance. Inquire about early-bird, twilight, off-season, and junior discounts.

Interbay Family Golf Center (⊠ 2501 15th Ave. W, Magnolia ☎ 206/285–2200 ⊕ www.interbaygolf.com). Interbay has a driving range ($5.50 for 50 balls, $9 for 100, $12 for 150), a 9-hole executive course ($15 weekends, $12.50 weekdays), and a miniature golf course ($7). The range and miniature golf course are open daily 7 AM–11 PM March–October and 7 AM–10 PM November–February; the executive course is open dawn to dusk year-round.

Jackson Park (⊠ 1000 NE 135th St., Olympic Hills ☎ 206/363–4747 ⊕ www.seattlegolf.com). There's an 18-hole course and a 9-hole executive course. Weekdays, greens fees are $25 and $12, respectively; on weekends expect to pay $30 and $12. Carts at the larger course cost $22; those on the smaller course are $14.

Jefferson Park (⊠ 4101 Beacon Ave. S, Beacon Hill ☎ 206/762–4513 ⊕ www.seattlegolf.com). The 18-hole course has views of the city skyline *and* Mt. Rainier. The par-27, 9-hole course has a lit driving range with heated stalls that's open from dusk until midnight. Greens fees are $30 on weekends and $25 weekdays for the 18-hole course; you can play the 9-hole course for $12 daily. Carts are $22 and $14, and $2 buys you a bucket of 30 balls at the driving range.

West Seattle Golf Course (⊠ 4470 35th Ave. SW, West Seattle ☎ 206/935–5187 ⊕ www.seattlegolf.com) This 18-hole course has a reputation for being tough but fair. Greens fees are $25 weekdays, $30 weekends. It's $22 for a cart.

Willows Run Golf Course (⊠ 10402 Willows Rd. NE, Redmond ☎ 425/883–1200 ⊕ www.willowsrun.com). Willows has it all: an 18-hole, links-style course; a 9-hole, par-27 course; and a lit, 18-hole putting course that's open until 11 PM. Thanks to an improved drainage system, Willows plays reasonably dry even in typically moist Seattle-area weather. Greens fees for 9 holes are $11 weekdays, $13 Friday through Sunday; those for 18 holes are $41 or $55. Carts cost $18.50 per rider. There are also two pro shops and a driving range (75 balls cost $7, 35 balls cost $4).

Hockey & Ice Skating

The Seattle Thunderbirds, a major junior (class A) team, play in the Western League. It's a strong team that finished first in the United States in the 2003 season and fourth in 2002. The best regular season finish was back in the 1989–90 season, when the Birds posted a 52-17-3 record, including a 33-2-1 mark at home. (Eight players were selected in the first round of the NHL draft in the 1990s, with two of those, Peter Nedved in 1990 and Patrick Marleau in 1997, going number two overall.) You can catch a game from late September through the end of March in Seattle Center's Key Arena.

If you've got your heart set on playing hockey or just gliding across the ice, you'll have to drive to satisfy your dreams: there's not a single public rink within the city limits.

Highland Ice Arena (✉ 18005 Aurora Ave. N, Shoreline ☎ 206/546–2431 ⊕ www.highlandice.com). Pick-up matches are held here several times a week ($10 per person), and there are adult and youth league teams. There's public skating daily; session times vary, so call ahead. The cost is $8, including skates. Free sessions (skate rental extra) are held several times a year.

Kingsgate Ice Arena (✉ 14326 124th Ave. NE, Kirkland ☎ 425/823–1242). Adult hockey drop-in sessions take place monthly. The arena also organizes youth and adult league teams and is home base to the Sno-King Amateur Hockey Association. Schedules for public skating vary from month to month; admission is $6 plus $2 for rentals. Drop-in hockey matches cost $10.

Lynnwood Ice Center (✉ 19803 68th Ave. W [between 196th and 200th Sts. NW], Lynnwood ☎ 425/640–9999). The area's only NHL–size rink is just over the Snohomish County line. League games, pick-up games, and hockey classes are all offered. Cheap Skate Night is on Wednesday, when admission is cut to $4.50 for an hour; other times admission is $6.50 plus $2.50 for skate rental.

The Horses

Take in Thoroughbred racing from April through September 15 at **Emerald Downs** (✉ 2300 Emerald Downs Dr., Auburn ☎ 253/288–7000 or 888/931–8400 ⊕ www.emeralddowns.com), a 166-acre track about 15 mi south of Downtown, east of I–5. Admission is $4. A few horseback-riding outfitters have guided treks through the surrounding hills. For most of the horses, you must weigh less than 250 pounds. Be sure to call ahead to schedule your ride.

Ez Times Outfitters (✉ 18703 Hwy. 706, Elbe ☎ 360/569–2449). EZ Times has one- to three-hour guided horseback-riding trips on 20,000 acres of state forest trails near Mt. Rainier. Rates are $25 an hour. For a less strenuous outing, you can take a carriage ride, which will run you $50 an hour for two people and $10 per hour for each additional rider.

Skyland Ranch (✉ 43100 Reiter Rd., Gold Bar ☎ 360/793–2611). Skyland, which is popular with area youth groups, offers guided tours along the Skykomish River that cost $20 an hour weekdays and $30 an hour weekends; deduct $5 an hour if you ride without a guide. Night rides on Fridays and Saturdays before the full moon cost $75 including a meal served by the light of a bonfire. The ranch is also home to a voluntary residential alcohol and drug treatment program for men ages 18 and older.

Tiger Mountain Outfitters (✉ 24508 SE 133rd St., Issaquah ☎ 425/392–5090). This Eastside outfitter leads three-hour, 10-mi rides to a lookout point on Tiger Mountain. The cost is $50 per person, and rides set out at 10 AM and 3 PM in summer and 1 PM in winter.

In-line Skating

In-line skating, or rollerblading, has been an integral part of the city's fitness scene for the past two decades, especially on the 3-mi trail around Green Lake. That's where experienced skaters show off their moves and buff bodies, while beginners skate gingerly on the crowded route, hoping not to take a spill. The trails along Alki Beach, Myrtle Edwards Park, and Sand Point Magnuson Park, as well as the Burke-Gilman Trail, offer long smooth surfaces for more leisurely 'blading.

Rain City Skate Park (✉ 801 Holgate Ave. S, Sodo ☎ 206/749–5511 ⊕ www.raincityskatepark.com). Indoor rinks are a great place to be on a drizzly Seattle day. At Rain City, in-line skaters share the floor with skateboarders. Admission is $6 weekdays for a five-hour session; $8 weekends for about three hours. You can rent pads and helmets (required) for $5.
Urban Surf (✉ 2100 N. Northlake Way, Wallingford ☎ 206/545–9463 ⊕ www.urbansurf.com). Across from Gas Works Park and adjacent to the Burke-Gilman Trail, Urban Surf rents in-line skates, pads, and helmets for $5 an hour or $16 for 24 hours. The company sells and rents gear for surfboarding, windsurfing, and kiteboarding, too.

Running

The roughly 3-mi trail that rings picturesque Green Lake seems custom-made for running—and walking, bicycling, rollerblading, fishing, lounging on the grass, and feeding the waterfowl. Seward Park has a more secluded, less used 3-mi loop where the park juts out into Lake Washington in southeast Seattle. At least one pair of bald eagles is known to nest in the park, so it's not unusual for a trip around the loop to include spotting an eagle *and* Mt. Rainier.

Other good running locales are the Burke-Gilman Trail, the reservoir at Capitol Hill's Volunteer Park, and at Myrtle Edwards Park, north of Pier 70 downtown. Discovery Park in Fremont has a 3-mi trail that takes you "off-roading" through patches of woods, meadows, and bluffs—just be sure to consult a map to avoid having to backtrack.

Club Northwest (⊕ www.cnw.org) has been around since 1972 and helped start many of the area's well-known annual races, including the Seattle Marathon, the Jingle Bell Run, the Seafair Torch Run, and others. **Eastside Runners** (⊕ www.eastsiderunners.com) has been welcoming runners of all ages and abilities in East King County since 1980. The club sponsors weekly runs and the annual Mt. Si Relay. **Seattle Frontrunners** (⊕ www.seattlefrontrunners.org) is a gay and lesbian running and walking club that sponsors several weekly runs/walks and welcomes all participants regardless of sexual orientation or athletic ability.

Rock Climbing

The mountains of Washington have cut the teeth (among other body parts) of many a world-class climber. So it's only natural that there are several places to get in some practice.

Recreational Equipment, Inc. (✉ 222 Yale Ave. N, Downtown ☎ 206/223–1944 Ext. 4086). Every day around 200 people have a go at REI's Pinnacle, a 65-foot indoor climbing rock. Climbing hours are Monday 10–6,

Wednesday–Friday 10–9, Saturday and Sunday 10–7. The cost is $15 including equipment. Although reservations are a good idea, you can also schedule a climb in person. The wait can be anywhere from 30 minutes to four hours, but it's rare that you don't get to climb on the very day you sign up.

★ **Schurman Rock** (✉ Camp Long, 5200 35th Ave. SW, West Seattle ☎ 206/684–7434 ⊕ www.ci.seattle.wa.us/parks/environment/camplong.htm). The nation's first man-made climbing rock was designed in the 1930s by local climbing expert Clark Schurman. Generations of climbers have practiced here, from beginners to rescue teams to such legendary mountaineers as Jim Whittaker, the first American to conquer Mt. Everest. Years of use took their toll on Schurman Rock, and in 1999 it was closed. Fund-raising led by the Seattle Parks Foundation secured money to pay for restoration, and the rock was reopened in 2003. Rappelling classes for kids ($150 for 15 kids for two hours) are offered year-round at Camp Long, which is also the site of Seattle's only in-city campground, whose cabins rent for $35 a night.

Stone Gardens Rock Gym (✉ 2839 NW Market St., Ballard ☎ 206/781–9828 ⊕ www.stonegardens.com). Beyond the trying-it-out phase? Head here and take a stab at the bouldering routes and top-rope faces. Although there's plenty to challenge the advanced climber, the mellow vibe is a big plus for families, part-timers, and the aspiring novice-to-intermediate crowd. The cost is $14.

Vertical World (✉ 2123 W. Elmore St., Magnolia ☎ 206/283–4497). It opened in 1987 and claims to be nation's first indoor climbing gym. There are 14,000 square feet of climbable surface as well as a bouldering area and weight-lifting equipment. The top-rope routes max out at 32 feet, which can seem pretty darn high when you scramble up under your own power. Tuesday and Thursday nights are busiest, though rainy weekend days also breed lines. The cost is $15 a day, not including equipment rental. Vertical World has locations in Redmond and Bremerton, too.

Skiing

Snow sports may be one of the few reasons to look forward to winter in Seattle. Here the rain becomes a boon for skiers and snowboarders, although a few years ago the rain was so heavy it shut down all the area resorts. Ski season usually lasts from November until April. A one-day adult lift ticket averages about $40, and most resorts rent equipment and have restaurants.

Cross-country trails range from undisturbed backcountry routes to groomed resort tracks. To ski on state park trails you must purchase a Sno-Park Pass, available at most sporting goods stores, ski shops, and forest service district offices. Always call ahead for road conditions, which might prevent trail access.

Call for Snoqualmie Pass ski reports and news about **weather conditions** (☎ 206/634–0200 or 206/634–2754) in the more distant White Pass, Crystal Mountain, and Stevens Pass. You can also do online research or listen to recorded messages about **road conditions** (☎ 800/695–7623 ⊕ wsdot.wa.gov/traffic/road/mnts/mntbas.htm). For information on cross-country trails and trail conditions, contact the **State Parks Information Center** (☎ 800/233–0321 ⊕ www.parks.wa.gov/winter).

Alpental at the Summit (✉ Exit 52 off I–90, Snoqualmie Pass ☎ 425/434–7669 ⊕ www.summit-at-snoqualmie.com). Alpental, part of the Summit at Snoqualmie complex, attracts advanced skiers to its many long steep runs. (Giant Slalom gold medalist Debbie Armstrong trained here for the 1984 Olympics.) A one-day lift ticket will run you $45 weekends, $37 weekdays; equipment is another $30. The resort is 50 mi from Seattle, but it's right off the highway so you avoid icy mountain roads. **Crystal Mountain** (✉ 33914 Crystal Mountain Blvd. ☎ 360/663–2265 🌐 www.crystalmt.com). Serious skiers and boarders don't mind the 2½-hour drive here (it's about 75 mi from the city). The slopes are challenging, the snow conditions are usually good, and the views of Mt. Rainier are amazing. A one-day lift ticket costs about $45; full rental packages run $27–$33. There are only three lodging options on or near the mountain (Crystal Mountain Hotels, Crystal Mountain Lodging Suites, and Alta Crystal Resort). They tend to fill up on busy winter weekends, so book ahead if you want to stay the night.

Hurricane Ridge (✉ Olympic National Park, 17 mi south of Port Angeles ☎ 360/452–0330 or 360/565–3131 for road reports). The cross-country trails here, in Olympic National Park, begin at the lodge and have great views of Mt. Olympus. A small downhill ski and snowboarding area is open weekends and holidays; lift tickets are $6–$18. There's also a tubing/sledding hill. The Hurricane Ridge Visitor Center has a small restaurant, an interpretive center, and rest rooms. Admission to the park is $10. Call ahead for road conditions before taking the two-hour drive from Seattle.

★ **The Summit at Snoqualmie** (✉ Exit 52 off I–90, Snoqualmie Pass ☎ 425/434–7669 or 206/236–7277 Ext. 3372 for Nordic center 🌐 www.summit-at-snoqualmie.com). Chances are good that a local skier took his or her first run at Snoqualmie, the resort closest to the city. With three ski areas—Summit West, Summit Central, and Summit East—gentle slopes, rope tows, moseying chairlifts, a snowboard park, and dozens of educational programs, it's the obvious choice for an introduction to the slopes. One-day lift tickets cost $45 weekends, $37 weekdays; equipment packages are about $30 a day. The Nordic Center at Summit East is the starting point for 50 km of cross-country trails. Guided snowshoe hikes are offered here on weekends. The $12 trail pass includes two rides on the chairlifts.

Fodor's Choice
★ **Whistler** (✉ Hwy 99, Whistler, B.C., Canada ☎ 800/766–0449 🌐 www.whistler-blackcomb.com). Whistler, 200 mi north of Seattle, is best done as a three-day weekend trip. And you really can't call yourself a skier here and not go to Whistler at least once. (Just make sure your car has chains or snow tires.) The massive resort is renowned for its nightlife, which is just at the foot of the slopes. You abandon your car outside the village upon arrival and negotiate the entire hotel/dining/ski area on foot. A one-day lift ticket costs about $70 (Canadian), and rental packages are about $32 (Canadian). The area includes more than 28 km of cross-country trails, usually open November–March. For die-hard skiers and boarders who want an extended season, there's summer skiing on Blackcomb Glacier through July. Expect continued improvements to both the facilities here and to the Sea-to-Sky Highway, as Whistler ramps up for the 2010 Winter Olympics.

Soccer

The nation's fastest growing sport is almost as popular in Seattle as it is everywhere else outside the United States. For outdoor soccer, catch the A-League Seattle Sounders at Seahawks Stadium. Tickets are $12 for reserved seating. The Seattle Sounders Select women's league team plays at the stadium, too. The **Greater Seattle Soccer League** (✉ 9750 Greenwood Ave. N, Greenwood ☎ 206/782–6831 🌐 www.gssl.org), the country's leading nonprofit adult soccer association, has 20 skill divisions in four age groups. Matches are played year-round.

Swimming

Seattle Parks and Recreation maintains eight indoor pools (Queen Anne, Ballard, Evans, Rainier Beach, Southwest, Medgar Evers, Helene Madison, and Meadowbrook) year-round and two outdoor pools (Colman and Mounger). Entrance to most is $1.75–$3.25. All have lifeguards, lockers, changing rooms, showers, and classes and special events.

Ballard Pool (✉ 1471 NW 67th St., Ballard ☎ 206/684–4094 ⊕ www.cityofseattle.net/parks/aquatics). Ballard, one of Seattle's older pools, has classes and public swims, including daily lap swims, adults-only swims, and water-exercise programs. Schedules change seasonally; check the parks department Web site.

Mounger Pool (✉ 2535 32nd Ave. W, Magnolia ☎ 206/684–4708 ⊕ www.cityofseattle.net/parks/aquatics). Mounger is actually two pools. The "big" one is 25 yards long and has a 50-foot corkscrew slide and five lanes. The little pool is 40 feet long, warmer, and less than 4-feet deep.

Queen Anne Pool (✉ 1920 1st Ave. W, Queen Anne ☎ 206/386–4282 ⊕ www.cityofseattle.net/parks/aquatics). This 25-yard-long indoor pool is a 10-minute drive from Downtown. There are early morning and evening lap times, adult swim sessions, family swims, and water exercise programs.

Tennis

There are 151 public tennis courts in Seattle's parks. To schedule an outdoor court, call the **Citywide Athletics Office** (☎ 206/684–4077).

The **Amy Yee Tennis Center** (✉ 2000 Martin Luther King Jr. Way S, Mt. Baker ☎ 206/684–4764). All ages are welcome at this facility, which has 10 indoor courts, 4 outdoor courts, and many programs and lessons. You pay $18 (for 1¼ hours) to reserve a court for singles play and $24 for doubles. The center is open weekdays 6 AM–10:30 PM and weekends 7 AM–7:30 PM July–September and 7 AM to 9:30 PM October–June. Also known as the Seattle Tennis Center, it's about 3 mi southeast of Downtown, near I–90.

Yoga

The city has many yoga studios that can accommodate you, whether you're a Hatha, Ashtanga, or Kundalini devotee.

8 Limbs Yoga Center (✉ 500 E. Pike St., Capitol Hill ☎ 206/325–1511 ⊕ www.eightlimbsyoga.com). This center welcomes drop-ins and manages to challenge intermediate students without alienating novices. Hatha, Ashtanga, Satsang, and Viniyoga are offered. Classes cost $10 for one hour and $18 for two hours.

Samadhi Yoga (✉ 1205 E. Pike St., Capitol Hill ☎ 206/329–4070 ⊕ www.samadhi-yoga.com). Samadhi combines yoga with an aerobic workout surrounded by statues of Hindu deities. Classes have an Ashtanga focus. Classes are $10–$15, less if you buy a multiclass card.

Yoga Life Studio (✉ 7200 Woodlawn Ave. NE, Green Lake ☎ 206/529–0581 ⊕ www.yogalifeseattle.com). This relaxing studio offers various types of yoga classes throughout the day and welcomes both beginners and experienced practitioners. Prenatal yoga, Reiki, and a monthly "TranceDance" combining yoga and music are also on the schedule, and massage and yoga therapy is available. As a drop-in you pay $14 a class; multiclass cards are available.

SHOPPING

FODOR'S CHOICE

Elliott Bay Book Company, *Pioneer Square*

Recreational Equipment, Inc., *Downtown*

Sur La Table, *Downtown*

Stonington Gallery, *Pioneer Square*

Uwajimaya, *International District*

HIGHLY RECOMMENDED

Bellevue Square, *Bellevue*

Elliott Bay Antiques, *Pioneer Square*

Great Jones Home, *Downtown*

J. Gilbert Footwear, *Belltown*

Les Amis, *Fremont*

Lola Pop, *Fremont*

Mario's of Seattle, *Downtown*

Opus 204, *Belltown*

Peter Miller Details, *Downtown*

University Village, *University District*

Updated by
Vanessa Lazo
Greaves

SEATTLE HAS PERSONALITY—SEVERAL OF THEM IN FACT, each with its own shopping preference. Downtown is polished and professional; Belltown and Capitol Hill hum with urban cool. Pike Place Market is earthy with local crafts and farm-fresh produce; arts and antiques repose amid the Victorian charms of Pioneer Square. The International District is full of pan-Asian languages and cultures; Fremont revels in tongue-in-cheek, counterculture chic. The University District is alive with collegiate youth; Queen Anne and the Eastside (Bellevue, Redmond, and others) are enclaves of relaxed gentility.

Much of Seattle is accessible on foot, though you need transportation to hilltop and outlying regions. The Metro buses offer free rides in the Downtown area, including Pioneer Square and most of Belltown, and can take you almost anywhere else you'd care to shop, including Bellevue and Kirkland on Lake Washington's east side. Pick up a free copy of *Browse By Bus,* available at hotels and visitor information kiosks. To find all the free parking spots, as well as the cheapest lots, and for a rundown of the meter rules, grab the brochure *How to Park in Downtown Seattle,* available at most Seattle information displays in major stores.

Many shops are open daily, though some specialty establishments keep shorter evening and Sunday hours. Mall hours are generally 9:30 AM–9 PM except on Sunday, when stores are usually open from 11 to 6. If you arrive too early, just hang out in a café and practice ordering lattes like a local.

Belltown

Urban hipsters flock to Belltown to eat, drink, and shop among their peers, creating a potent concentration of ultracool in a district that stretches north from Virginia Street to Denny Way between Western Avenue and Westlake Avenue North. Many places are closed on Sunday and Monday. *Best shopping: Along 1st Ave. between Virginia and Bell Sts.*

Antiques & Collectibles
Pacific Galleries (⌧ 2121 3rd Ave., Belltown ☎ 206/441–9990) handles such an immense volume of Asian, European, and American antiques that the company holds auctions in this showroom *and* one in Greenlake. (Here they're held every five weeks, but you're welcome to drop in to browse or leave an absentee bid.) To shop for antiques head to the store or the emporium, both in Downtown.

Clothing
Darbury Stenderu (⌧ 2121 1st Ave., Belltown ☎ 206/448–2625) dazzles with groovy, hand-printed, natural-fiber creations for men and women. **Endless Knot** (⌧ 2300 1st Ave., Belltown ☎ 206/448–0355) fashions batik cloth into free-flowing women's apparel.
Gian Decaro Sartoria (⌧ 2025 1st Ave., Belltown ☎ 206/448–2812) tailors professional and casual wardrobes for many well-heeled businessmen—including Microsoft's Bill Gates. Just remember, though, you don't have to be a billionaire to dress like one.
Karan Dannenberg Clothier (⌧ 2232 1st Ave., Belltown ☎ 206/441–3442) clothes women in opulent fabrics, many of which are wrinkle resistant.
Kuhlman (⌧ 2419 1st Ave., Belltown ☎ 206/441–1999) dresses both sexes in sophisticated urban designs often made with superb European and Japanese fabrics.
Margaret O'Leary (⌧ 2025 1st Ave., Belltown ☎ 206/441–6691) designs gorgeous hand-loomed cashmere knits for women, as well as fine cotton and linen apparel.

BLITZ TOURS

IT'S BEST TO SET ASIDE an afternoon for each of the tours, as antiques dealers and art gallery owners tend to open their establishments late in the morning. Note, too, that many shops and galleries are closed Sunday and/or Monday.

On the first Thursday of each month—called "First Thursday" around town—art galleries premiere new shows and stay open until 8 PM or later. Pick up a free copy of Art Guide Northwest or Art Access, available in most galleries, for maps and a current overview of shows.

Antiques

Asian. Seattle is such a prime source for fine Asian antiques that you could spend days browsing and still not see it all. This tour gets you to a few of the highlights. Start at Honeychurch Antiques, on Capitol Hill's southwestern edge, near James Street and Boren Avenue, where you can get an education by browsing the museumlike displays. Then it's a quick ride by cab or bus to Pioneer Square, to Elliott Bay Antiques on South Jackson Street, just west of Second Avenue South. Go one block west to Occidental Avenue South and head for the brick-paved Occidental Mall and into Carolyn Staley Fine Japanese Prints. One more block west on South Jackson Street brings you to Chidori Asian Antiques. Walk one and one-half blocks south along First Avenue South and visit Kagedo Japanese Art and Antiques. Just a short way south is Azuma Gallery. Take a cab or drive 10 minutes' north to the base of Queen Anne, where the Crane Gallery and Galen Lowe Art & Antiques are side-by-side on West Roy Street.

Mid-Century Modern. In 1962, while the local Boeing plant built jet airplanes, Seattle built the Space Needle to welcome the World's Fair. Small wonder that Seattle—nicknamed "The Jet City"—embraced the era's futuristic furnishings, designed by such international luminaries as Charles and Ray Eames, Herman Miller, Russel Wright, and Isamu Noguchi.

Start your quest for martini-chic by perusing vintage furniture on Capitol Hill at Standard Home, near the corner of Pike Street and Boren Avenue. Afterward head six blocks uphill to Chartreuse International, near the corner of Pike Street and Boylston Avenue. Just a few more steps east brings you to Martin-Zambito Fine Art, where you can find period art to go with the furniture. Cross the street and walk one block north to Pine Street, turn left on Pine Street, and saunter down to Bellevue Avenue and Area 51. A short cab or bus ride takes you to Laguna in Pioneer Square on Washington Street between First Avenue South and Second Avenue South, where there's tableware to match that vintage Hans Wegner furniture you just bought.

Traditional. Seattle is a relatively young city but it does respect its elders. Start your day at David Weatherford Antiques and Interiors in Capitol Hill at Fourteenth Avenue East and East John Street. Your next stop is Downtown at Walker-Poinsett Antiques, which is on the arcade level of the Fairmont Olympic Hotel, at Fourth Avenue and University Street. Walk three blocks west to Porter Davis Antiques, on the corner of First Avenue and University Street. Hop on a free Metro bus and head south on First Avenue to Pioneer Square and Jean Williams Antiques, just a few steps east of First Avenue South on South Jackson Street.

Arts

Galleries Galore. Pioneer Square is the hub of Seattle's dynamic art scene, with other galleries peppered throughout the city, especially along First Avenue near the Seattle Art Museum. Start in Pioneer Square at Linda Hodges Gallery on First Avenue South, north of South Jackson Street. Continue one block east on South Jackson Street to Foster/White Gallery, on the corner of Occidental Avenue South. Cross to the north side of the street where there's a concentration of fine galleries that includes Davidson Galleries and Grover/Thurston Gallery.

At the north end of Occidental Avenue South walk east on South Main Street a few steps to Bryan Ohno Gallery, then continue east to Third Avenue South and the must-see Greg Kucera Gallery. From First Avenue in Pioneer Square, you can walk, take a free Metro bus, or hop a taxi to William Traver Gallery, about seven blocks north on the south edge of Pike Place Market, at the corner of First Avenue and Union Street. If you take in the Seattle Art Museum along the way on First Avenue, be sure to walk east one block up the hill to Kimzey Miller Gallery, on the corner of Second Avenue and Seneca Street.

Native American Artistry. Woven into the fabric of Seattle's aesthetic are the traditional arts and artifacts of Northwest Coast Native Americans. Several fine galleries showcase traditional and contemporary works by native artists. Excellent pieces also are produced by nonnative artists in the "native style." Be an informed buyer: ask about the artist, his or her tribal affiliation, and the work's oral history. If it's a contemporary piece, look for superior craftsmanship.

Start in Pioneer Square with a visit to Stonington Gallery, near the corner of Occidental Avenue South and South Jackson Street. Flury & Company is just west, on First Avenue South. From Flury, walk or take a free Metro bus to the Legacy Ltd., at the corner of First Avenue and Madison Street. The Seattle Art Museum and its outstanding Native American collection is just three blocks north on First Avenue and University Street. Ride a Metro bus or take a taxi to the University of Washington campus, northeast of Downtown, to peruse the collection at the Burke Museum of Natural History and Culture, and browse in the museum store. Snow Goose Associates is a few minutes' drive north of the university on Roosevelt Way Northeast.

★ **Opus 204** (✉ 2000 1st Ave., Belltown ☎ 206/728–7707) is a must-shop destination for locally designed women's clothes in luxurious fabrics and artistic silhouettes. The shop also has great raincoats.

Patagonia (✉ 2100 1st Ave., Belltown ☎ 206/622–9700) sells functional outdoor wear—made with earth-friendly materials such as hemp and organic cotton—for the whole family. The line of whimsically patterned fleecewear for children is particularly charming.

Eyewear

Ottica Seattle (✉ 2025 1st Ave., Belltown ☎ 206/443–0320) makes shopping for glasses a sensory treat in a swank space with rich red walls, swooping gold curtains, and oversize mirrors—all the better to check out your new, fashion-forward eyewear.

Footwear

★ **J. Gilbert Footwear** (✉ 2025 1st Ave., Belltown ☎ 206/441–1182) wraps your feet in fashion and comfort with Taryn Rose designs. The shop also sells sportswear, accessories, and the Terra Plana line of men's shoes with styles named after famous architects.

Gifts & Home Decor

Egbert's (✉ 2231 1st Ave., Belltown ☎ 206/728–5682) carries contemporary Italian and Scandinavian designs and is the U.S. headquarters for Erik Jørgensen furniture. Look for vases by Alvar Aalto, Murano glass signed by artist Carlo Moretti, and jubilant African art.

Riflessi (✉ 2302 1st Ave., Belltown ☎ 206/728–5840) fills this vivid gallery with hand-painted majolica, glassware, and framed art from studios all over Italy.

Urban Ease (✉ 2512 2nd Ave., Belltown ☎ 206/443–9546) showcases regionally designed contemporary furniture and housewares and is the exclusive Northwest source for high-style Italian modular kitchen, bedroom, and wall systems by Poliform.

Waterworks (✉ 2030 1st Ave., Belltown ☎ 206/441–9300) makes your bath time sublime with its collection of first-class fixtures, lavatories, tubs, tiles, and bath accessories.

Paper Goods

Paperhaus (✉ 2008 1st Ave., Belltown ☎ 206/374–8566) takes a minimalist approach in displaying its notebooks, portfolios, and pens.

Capitol Hill

College students come to this hilly neighborhood to shop for cheap, funky, and vintage clothing. Urbanites are drawn here for styles that are way ahead of the curve. And everyone makes a run to the excellent used bookstores. Broadway Market is the neighborhood shopping center, but a gathering of small stores runs for about a mile along Broadway Avenue and along Pike and Pine Streets. This buzzing district is also the hub of Seattle's gay community, which flocks to the ever-so-hip restaurants, shops, and clubs. *Best shopping: E. Pike and E. Pine Sts. between Boren Ave. and Broadway Ave. E, E. Olive Way between Bellevue and Broadway Aves. E, and Broadway Ave. E between E. Olive Way and E. Roy St.*

Antiques & Collectibles

Area 51 (✉ 401 E. Pine St., Capitol Hill ☎ 206/568–4782) is a 6,000-square-foot industrial space where anything of good modern design might materialize, especially if it's from the 1960s and '70s. Check out the Dwell bed linens with retro prints.

Chartreuse International (✉ 711 E. Pike St., Capitol Hill ☎ 206/328–4844) is a dependable source for authentic mid-century modern furniture and wares by Harry Bertoia, Arne Jacobsen, Isamu Noguchi, and others.

David Weatherford Antiques and Interiors (✉ 133 14th Ave. E, Capitol Hill ☎ 206/329–6533) sells handsome, 18th-century French and English furniture, artwork, and accessories in an 1894 mansion.

Honeychurch Antiques (✉ 1008 James St., Capitol Hill ☎ 206/622–1225), on the neighborhood's southwestern edge, has fine 19th-century Japanese and Chinese furniture. Read the informational tags as you wander through this serene shop to improve your Asian antiques IQ.

Standard Home (✉ 1108 Pike St., near Boren Ave., Capitol Hill ☎ 206/464–0850) is packed with mid-century modern furniture and housewares by such luminaries as George Nelson, Charles and Ray Eames, Russel Wright, and Hans Wegner. You can also find a few licensed reproductions in the mix.

Art Galleries

G. Gibson Gallery (✉ 514 E. Pike St., Capitol Hill ☎ 206/587–4033) focuses on vintage and contemporary photography and mixed-media works.

Martin - Zambito Fine Art (✉ 721 E. Pike St., Capitol Hill ☎ 206/726–9509) specializes in regional American artists, with an emphasis on WPA and Depression-era paintings and studio ceramics.

Books, Printed Materials & Music

Bailey/Coy Books (✉ 414 Broadway Ave. E, Capitol Hill ☎ 206/323–8842) is well-stocked with volumes on many topics. There's a substantial gay and lesbian section.

Confounded Books (✉ 315 E. Pine St., Capitol Hill ☎ 206/441–9880) specializes in underground, alternative, and European comics, independent 'zines, and small-press books.

Fillipi Book & Record Shop (✉ 1351 E. Olive Way, Capitol Hill ☎ 206/682–4266) stocks secondhand books and magazines plus collectible sheet music and 78-, 45-, and 33-rpm records.

Horizon Books (✉ 425 15th Ave. E, Capitol Hill ☎ 206/329–3586) has seven rooms of used, neatly organized books on all topics.

J & S Broadway News (✉ 204 Broadway Ave. E, Capitol Hill ☎ 206/324–7323) carries more than 1,500 international periodicals.

Twice Sold Tales (✉ 905 E. John St., Capitol Hill ☎ 206/324–2421) is an excellent source for gently used books. It stays open late on weekends—a bonus if you're ever sleepless in Seattle. Other locations in Fremont and the University District don't keep such late hours.

Wall of Sound (✉ 315 E. Pine St., Capitol Hill ☎ 206/441–9880) has world music, jazz, blues, and experimental works.

Clothing

Broadway Boutique (✉ 113 Broadway St. E, Capitol Hill ☎ 206/325–0430) is the place to shop for something funky and cheap. Look for tropical-pattern halter tops, wide-leg pants, and platform shoes. Dress it all up with a zebra backpack or a feather boa.

Dumb Clothing (✉ 413 E. Pine St., Capitol Hill ☎ 206/322–6630) is the brainchild of Paula Fletcher, who uses wild fabrics to create one-of-a-kind designs. She often gives her clothes quirky embellishments, too. Finish your look with jewelry made by local artists.

Le Frock (✉ 317 E. Pine St., Capitol Hill ☎ 206/623–5339) sells a mix of good-quality men's and women's vintage clothing and gently used contemporary designer labels. Shop to the inspiring music of Billie Holiday and Sarah Vaughan.

Panache (✉ 225 Broadway St. E, Capitol Hill ☎ 206/726–3300) carries floral slip dresses with slanted, ruffled edges; batik sarong skirts; and chic silk separates. It stocks the requisite accessories, too. The extensive men's section has dress clothes and shoes.

Red Light (✉ 312 Broadway Ave. E, Capitol Hill ☎ 206/329–2200) lets you mix and match the decades with its miniskirts, feather boas, handbags, designer jeans, camp shirts, and darling tops. Time-warp toys, lunch boxes, underwear sets, and other cool kitsch are also available. If you're in the University District visit the sister store.

Vintage Chick (✉ 303 E. Pine St., Capitol Hill ☎ 206/625–9800) carries men's and women's clothing and jewelry from the 1920s to the '70s—most of it funky and cute. Vintage bridal and evening wear is especially popular; expert alterations are available.

Footwear

Edie's (✉ 319 E. Pine St., Capitol Hill ☎ 206/839–1111) caters to men and women who like to trek up and down Capitol Hill in trendy, sporty shoes. Lounge on the big purple couch while you try on something in your size.

Goods (✉ 1112 Pike St., Capitol Hill ☎ 206/622–0459) has a wall full of high-end, limited-edition sneakers not available through retail chains. The locally designed Manik skateboards double as cool wall art. You may wish the tiny Japanese toys in the display cases were for sale, too.

Seattle Retro Shoe Store (✉ 1524 E. Olive Way, Capitol Hill ☎ 206/322–2305) is a hopping, high-tech store that attracts sports-shoe junkies. Savvy "sneakerheads" line up to buy limited edition Nikes and reissued styles from the 1980s. Vintage shoes are also on sale at premium prices.

Gifts & Home Decor

Kobo (✉ 814 E. Roy St., Capitol Hill ☎ 206/726–0704) carries hand-loomed textiles, studio ceramics, and figurines by Japanese and Northwest artisans.

Ragen & Associates (✉ 517 E. Pike St., Capitol Hill ☎ 206/329–4737) imports dramatic garden accessories from Italy and Asia.

Mall

Broadway Market (✉ 401 Broadway Ave. E, Capitol Hill ☎ 206/322–1610 ⊕ www.thebroadwaymarket.com) caters to the neighborhood's alternative aesthetic with cafés, hip clothing merchants, and art-house cinemas. Pick up an international newspaper at the Bulldog News kiosk and pretend to read it while you people-watch.

Downtown

Seattle's retail core might feel business-crisp by day, but it's casual and arts-centered by night, and the shopping scene reflects both these moods. Within a few square blocks—between First Avenue on the west and Boren Avenue on the east, and from University Street to Olive Way—you'll find department store flagships, a trio of high-gloss vertical malls, dozens of upper-echelon boutiques, and elite retail chains. The streets buzz seven days a week. Development south of Pike Place Market, along First Avenue from University Street to Pioneer Square—especially around Harbor Steps at First Avenue and Union Street—has attracted a string of exceptional shops. One block closer to Elliott Bay, on Western Avenue, several high-end home furnishings showrooms make up an informal "Furniture Row." The Waterfront, with its small, kitschy stores and open-air restaurants is a great place to dawdle. *Best shopping: 4th, 5th, and 6th Aves. between Pine and Spring Sts., and 1st Ave. between Virginia and Madison Sts.*

Antiques & Collectibles

Antiques at Pike Place (✉ 92 Stewart St., Downtown ☎ 206/441–9643) is well stocked with vintage objects, many in nicely organized cases.

Big People Toys (✉ 90 Madison St., Downtown ☎ 206/749–9016) offers 18th- and 19th-century antiques from China, Mongolia, and Tibet.

The lacquered trunks and small boxes are lovely, but what may arrest your attention is the stunning collection of insects under glass.

Glenn Richards (✉ Price–Asher Building, 964 Denny Way, Downtown ☎ 206/287–1877) gathers contemporary and antique tables, chests, screens, lamps, and other furnishings from all over Asia. Perhaps a handsome, carved-stone Japanese lantern is just what your garden needs.

★ **Great Jones Home** (✉ 1921 2nd Ave., Downtown ☎ 206/448–9405) takes inspirations from current fashion trends, filling this spacious skylit store with an eclectic mix of antiques, linens, and ornaments for your home. One wall is devoted to delectable imported textiles.

Pacific Galleries (✉ 2244 1st Ave. S, Downtown ☎ 206/264–9422 ✉ 241 S. Lander St., Downtown ☎ 206/292–3999) offers entirely different shopping experiences at its Downtown branches. The First Avenue store of the gallery with locations in Belltown and Greenlake sells high-end European antiques. The South Lander Street emporium has more than 200 reputable antiques dealers.

Porter Davis Antiques (✉ 103 University St., Downtown ☎ 206/622–5310) has 18th- and 19th-century European and American furniture accessorized with deluxe porcelain, silver, and Asian decorative arts.

Two Angels Antiques (✉ 1527 Western Ave., Downtown ☎ 206/340–6005) has European antiques from the 17th through the 20th centuries. There's also a 4,000-square-foot warehouse—chock-full of goodies—that's open by appointment.

Walker-Poinsett Antiques (✉ 411 University St., Downtown ☎ 206/624–4973) sells high-quality 17th- to 19th-century furniture, 16th-century brass candlesticks, and early-19th-century Sheffield plate.

Weatherford Gallery (✉ 1200 2nd Ave., Downtown ☎ 206/324–6514) specializes in 18th- and 19th-century European furniture and fine Asian porcelains. Note that Saturday, Sunday, and Monday are by appointment only. The main store on Capitol Hill has more goods on display.

Art Galleries

Foster/White Gallery (✉ 1331 5th Ave., Downtown ☎ 206/583–0100), in Rainier Square, is Washington's exclusive representative for glass artist Dale Chihuly, and exhibits works by Northwest masters such as Kenneth Callahan, Mark Tobey, and George Tsutakawa. There are also branches in Pioneer Square and Kirkland.

Kimzey Miller Gallery (✉ 1225 2nd Ave., Downtown ☎ 206/682–2339) has paintings, glass, and sculpture by contemporary Northwest and international artists.

The Legacy Ltd. (✉ 1003 1st Ave., Downtown ☎ 206/624–6340) is renowned for its stunning contemporary works and historic pieces by Northwest Coast Indian and Alaskan Eskimo artists, as well as for its friendly, knowledgeable staff.

Lisa Harris Gallery (✉ 1922 Pike Pl., Downtown ☎ 206/443–3315), in the Pike Place Market, represents Northwest and West Coast painters, sculptors, photographers, and printmakers.

Seattle Art Museum (✉ 100 University St., Downtown ☎ 206/654–3100) has a store that's packed with books, cards, and gifts relating to or complementing its superb permanent collection of art and artifacts from Asia, Africa, and the Pacific Northwest or its changing exhibits.

Vetri (✉ 1404 1st Ave., Downtown ☎ 206/667–9608), dedicated to the art of studio glass, has innovative pieces from emerging young artists, many from Washington's famous Pilchuck Glass School.

William Traver Gallery (✉ 110 Union St., Downtown ☎ 206/587–6501), mounts stunning exhibitions of contemporary glass works, ceramics, paintings, and mixed-media installations in a vast, theatrical, light-drenched space.

Woodside/Braseth Gallery (✉ 1533 9th Ave., Downtown ☎ 206/622–7243) specializes in works by such Northwest masters as Mark Tobey, William Ivey, George Tsutakawa, and William Cumming.

Books & Printed Material

Arundel Books (✉ 1113 1st Ave., Downtown ☎ 206/624–4442) carries new, used, and rare titles on architecture, the arts, and history.

Left Bank Books (✉ 92 Pike St., Downtown ☎ 206/622–0195) specializes in poetry and in titles on progressive politics and gay and lesbian issues.

M. Coy Books (✉ 117 Pine St., Downtown ☎ 206/623–5354) is not only pet-friendly, it's also beloved by those who enjoy contemporary literature. Grab something to peruse before taking a seat at the espresso bar.

Peter Miller Architecture and Design Books (✉ 1930 1st Ave., Downtown ☎ 206/441–4114) attracts Seattle's architects to a well-stocked bookstore that's every bit as cool and urbane as its owner. Portfolios and drawing tools are on hand for the discerning designer.

Read All About It International Newsstand (✉ 93 Pike St., Downtown ☎ 206/624–0140), in the Pike Place Market, carries more than 1,500 magazines and newspapers from around the world.

Clothing

Alexandra's (✉ 412 Olive Way, Downtown ☎ 206/623–1214) has thousands of women's designer-label pieces on consignment. Most seem to have hardly been worn. Look for Giorgio Armani, Calvin Klein, Donna Karan, and Richard Tyler, among others.

Alhambra (✉ 101 Pine St., Downtown ☎ 206/621–9571) is an exquisite women's clothing boutique. Look for fine fabrics and detailing.

Anthropologie (✉ 1509 5th Ave., Downtown ☎ 206/381–5900) favors bright, trendy women's apparel and stylish household accessories—modern and reproduction vintage. Visit its sister store in University Village.

Baby and Co. (✉ 1936 1st Ave., Downtown ☎ 206/448–4077), known for its dreamy window displays, dresses women in esoteric creations by Comme des Garçon and Yojhi Yamamoto.

Banana Republic (✉ 500 Pike St., Downtown ☎ 206/622–2303) sells its polished urban clothing in the opulent, 1914 Coliseum Theater. The men's department is just a few steps north on Fifth Avenue. There are also branches in Bellevue Square and University Village.

Betsey Johnson (✉ 1429 5th Ave., Downtown ☎ 206/624–2887) spotlights fanciful fashions (faux fur, wild prints, bell sleeves, etc.) priced just over $100.

Butch Blum (✉ 1408 5th Ave., Downtown ☎ 206/622–5760) dresses men in high-end apparel from Zegna, Barbera, Issey Miyake, and others. It's also the region's exclusive source for Armani's Black label. For women there are Schumacher—a youthful German sportswear line—and Armani jeans. A smaller store in University Village carries upscale casual wear for both sexes.

Eddie Bauer (✉ 1330 5th Ave., Downtown ☎ 206/622–2766) built this flagship store, replete with waterfalls and handmade wooden canoes, to properly show off its outdoorsy men's and women's clothing and its signature bed and bath wares. Similar goods are available at branches in Bellevue Square, Redmond Town Center, and University Village—minus the waterfalls.

Eileen Fisher (✉ 525 Pine St., Downtown ☎ 206/748–0770) is an airy gallery that's the perfect place to display the designer's signature line of unstructured yet elegant women's clothing.

Escada (✉ 1302 5th Ave., Downtown ☎ 206/223–9433) offers classy, designer, ready-to-wear outfits, evening attire, sportswear, footwear, fragrances, and accessories in an ultrachic boutique.

Fini (⊠ 86 Pine St., Downtown ☎ 206/443–0563) carries stylish jewelry, handbags, scarves, hats, and gloves—everything you need to help you finish your look.

Flora and Henri (⊠ 717 Pine St., Downtown ☎ 206/749–9698) fashions muted cottons, linens, and silks into extraordinary children's garments. The lines are classic and the details hand stitched, yet nothing is too precious to play in. There's a second location in Capitol Hill.

The Gap (⊠ 1530 5th Ave., Downtown ☎ 206/254–8000) is loaded with trendy, affordable play clothes for the whole family. The huge Downtown store carries the full line of Gap apparel, including Gap Baby, Body, and Maternity. There are branches in Bellevue Square, Northgate Mall, Redmond Town Center, Southcenter Mall, and University Village.

Ian (⊠ 1907 2nd Ave., Downtown ☎ 206/441–4055) is a fabulous place to shop if you're a trendy young man or woman with a healthy bank account. There's high-end street wear by Juicy Couture, Stüssy, and G-Star.

Isadora's Antique Clothing (⊠ 1915 1st St., Downtown ☎ 206/441–7711) has elegant men's and women's garments that date from the 1900s to the 1950s.

Jeri Rice (⊠ 421 University St., Downtown ☎ 206/624–4000) carries women's apparel by Lora Piana, Vera Wang, and Jean Paul Gaultier.

Kenneth Cole (⊠ 520 Pike St., Downtown ☎ 206/382–1680) sells its sleek signature clothing, footwear, luggage, and accessories for men and women.

★ **Mario's of Seattle** (⊠ 1513 6th Ave., Downtown ☎ 206/223–1461) has creations by Armani, Zegna, and Dolce & Gabbana. Ascend the ornate staircase to shop for women's designers. A free-standing Hugo Boss boutique sells suits, sportswear, and tuxedos.

Nancy Meyer (⊠ 1318 5th Ave., Downtown ☎ 206/625–9200) has sexy European lingerie by Fernando Sanchez, La Perla, and others. The staff is adept at recommending styles and sizes for the best fit.

Northwest Pendleton (⊠ 1313 4th Ave., Downtown ☎ 206/682–4430), a Northwest tradition since 1909, sells plaid clothing and blanket designs by Native American artists. If you're in Bellevue Square, stop at the branch store.

Old Navy (⊠ 601 Pine St., Downtown ☎ 206/264–9341) is everywhere. This one has a lively line of dancing legs suspended from the ceiling and three floors of clothes for the young and young-at-heart.

Olive (⊠ 1633 6th Ave., Downtown ☎ 206/254–1310) is a boutique department store with bright trendy clothing and accessories for women; a wine merchant; a room dedicated to cosmetics and spa and bath products; and a café that sells Vietnamese spring rolls, French coffee, and bubble tea.

Quicksilver (⊠ 409 Pike St., Downtown ☎ 206/625–9670) outfits young board riders—skate, surf, and snow—with cool fashions and seasonal hardware.

Sway and Cake (⊠ 1631 6th Ave., Downtown ☎ 206/624–2699), where clothes are the Sway and shoes are the Cake, you can dress your girly self in the hottest styles from New York and Los Angeles.

Tulip (⊠ 1201 1st Ave., Downtown ☎ 206/223–1791) is a high-end boutique with a "boyfriend couch," where your other half can cool his heels while you try on ethereal dresses or denim by Seven, Habitual, and Citizens of Humanity.

Urban Outfitters (⊠ 1509 5th Ave., Downtown ☎ 206/381–3777) provides one-stop shopping for urbanites who have more fashion-savvy than cash. The street clothes are fun, and the home accessories are quirky. There's a sister store in the Broadway Market.

Zebraclub (⊠ 1901 1st Ave., Downtown ☎ 206/448–8452), at Pike Place Market, has loads of fashion denim for men and women, including Diesel and Levi's vintage collection.

Department Stores

Bon-Macy's (⊠ 3rd Ave. and Pine St., Downtown ☎ 206/506–6000), a Seattle landmark for 100+ years and the last of the true Downtown department stores, is a reliable source for clothing, housewares, cosmetics, furniture, and toys. Branch locations include Bellevue Square, Southcenter Mall, and Northgate Mall.

Nordstrom (⊠ 500 Pine St., Downtown ☎ 206/628–2111), the local retail giant, sells clothing, accessories, cosmetics, jewelry, and lots of shoes—true to its roots in footwear—including many hard-to-find sizes. There are branches at Bellevue Square, Northgate Mall, and Southcenter Mall.

Footwear

Furla (⊠ 1420 5th Ave., Downtown ☎ 206/749–5555) sells affordable, finely crafted Italian footwear for women, plus gorgeous handbags, belts, wraps, and scarves in this streamlined boutique.

John Fluevog (⊠ 1611 1st Ave., Downtown ☎ 206/441–1065) carries its own brand of fun, funky boots, chunky leather shoes, and urbanized wooden sandals.

Maggie's Shoes (⊠ 1927 1st Ave., Downtown ☎ 206/728–5837) is a good place to buy fashionable men's and women's shoes in fine Italian leather. It also sells a few select pieces of women's Italian sportswear.

Ped (⊠ 1115 1st Ave., Downtown ☎ 206/292–1767) sees shoes as art for your feet, gathering unique and unusual designs from all over the world for men and women who appreciate the exclusivity of a small boutique.

Gifts & Home Decor

Current (⊠ 629 Western Ave., Downtown ☎ 206/622–2433) has European furniture and home accessories that are so enticing that design-conscious, bargain-hunting Seattleites live for the annual September sale.

Diva (⊠ 1300 Western Ave., Downtown ☎ 206/287–9992), whose elegantly minimalist showroom is designed by Antonio Citterio, is the exclusive Northwest source for streamlined Italian furniture by B&B Italia, also designed by Citterio.

Found Objects (⊠ 1406 1st Ave., Downtown ☎ 206/682–4324) combines contemporary jewelry, ceramics, and textiles—many handmade by local artisans—with good quality vintage housewares.

Inform (⊠ 1220 Western Ave., Downtown ☎ 206/622–1608) sells sleek spare furniture in a modern, gallerylike setting.

Ligne Roset (⊠ 55 University St., Downtown ☎ 206/341–9990) offers the complete line of its signature French contemporary furniture.

McKinnon Furniture (⊠ 1015 Western Ave., Downtown ☎ 206/622–6474) sells hand-crafted, made-to-order furniture made from non-threatened U.S. hardwoods.

★ **Peter Miller Details** (⊠ 1924 1st Ave., Downtown ☎ 206/448–3436), carries a well-edited stock of indispensable *objets* for home and office. The emphasis is on contemporary Scandinavian design.

Fodor'sChoice
★ **Sur La Table** (⊠ 84 Pine St., Downtown ☎ 206/448–2244), in the Pike Place Market, has been a culinary aficionado's haven since 1972. It's packed to the rafters with kitchen stuff—some 12,500 items, give or take, including an exclusive line of copper cookware. Check the schedule of in-store demonstrations. There's another branch is in Kirkland.

Twist (⊠ 1503 5th Ave., Downtown ☎ 206/315–8080) carries theatrical and whimsical jewelry, crafts, and furnishings—all handmade in America.

Watson Kennedy Fine Living (⊠ 86 Pine St., Downtown ☎ 206/443–6281) is a jewel box of a shop that sells luxurious bath products. The sister store on First Avenue has tableware, fine food products, and fine linens.

Jewelry

Turgeon Raine (⊠ 1407 5th Ave., Downtown ☎ 206/447–9488) sells gems and jewelry in a spacious contemporary gallery. It's Washington's exclusive representative for Patek Philip watches.

Luggage

Louis Vuitton (⊠ 416 University St., Downtown ☎ 206/749–0711) offers the full line of its famous luggage and handbags, as well as smaller accessories.

Malls

City Centre (⊠ 1420 5th Ave., Downtown ☎ 206/624–8800 ⊕ www. shopcitycentre.com) houses more than 20 retailers in a sleek structure adorned with spectacular art glass. Find the latest in upscale, urban fashion at Barneys New York. Discover why architects and design professionals love the wares at Design Concern. Romp through two floors of toys at FAO Schwarz.

Pacific Place (⊠ 600 Pine St., Downtown ☎ 206/405–2655 ⊕ www. pacificplaceseattle.com) is an elegant atrium with about 30 retailers as well as a couple of restaurants and a top-notch cinema complex. Wow your sweetheart with jewelry from Cartier and Tiffany & Co. Find sexy sophisticated fashions from Bebe, MaxMara, Nicole Miller, and Club Monaco. Add to your domestic comforts at Pottery Barn, Restoration Hardware, and Williams-Sonoma Grande Cuisine. Or ponder the meaning of the "J" as you shop for casual clothing at J. Crew and J. Jill. A third-floor skybridge provides a sheltered route to Nordstrom.

Westlake Center (⊠ 1601 5th Ave., Downtown ☎ 206/467–1600 ⊕ www. westlakecenter.com) is a busy place. Roughly 60 stores and food vendors draw crowds to a four-story glass pavilion that's also the Downtown link for the Monorail to Seattle Center. Fill a basket with locally produced specialty foods and crafts at Made in Washington, splurge on a fabulous writing instrument from Montblanc, or find quirky gifts and jewelry at Fireworks.

Market

Pike Place Market (⊠ Pike Pl. at Pike St., west of 1st Ave., Downtown ☎ 206/682–7453 ⊕ www.pikeplacemarket.org) hums from the break of day, when the fish and produce arrive, until late at night, when the restaurants close. This exhilarating open-air market is where Seattleites shop for seasonal cut flowers; fruits and vegetables; wild salmon; and superb cheeses, breads, meats, wines, and pastries. Crafts vendors line the walkways, and singular stores are tucked into alleys, halls, and staircases. You could spend a whole day exploring and still not see it all. The market is open Monday–Saturday 9–6 and Sunday 11–5.

Outdoor Clothing & Equipment

Adidas (⊠ 1501 5th Ave., Downtown ☎ 206/382–4317), the German sporting-goods giant, has two high-tech floors of athletic shoes, clothing, and accessories.

NikeTown (⊠ 1500 6th Ave., Downtown ☎ 206/447–6453) does its part to promote shopping-as-theater with a cavernous space packed to the rafters with athletic shoes and sports apparel.

The North Face (⊠ 1023 1st Ave., Downtown ☎ 206/622–4111) is a premium source for outdoor equipment, apparel, and footwear.

Fodor'sChoice
★ **Recreational Equipment, Inc.** (⊠ 222 Yale Ave. N, Downtown ☎ 206/223–1944), which everybody calls REI, has an incredible selection of outdoor gear at its enormous flagship store. You can try things out along the mountain-bike test trail, in the simulated rain booth, or on the 65-foot climbing wall. Branch locations are at Redmond Town Center and Southcenter Mall.

CloseUp

SEATTLE SOUVENIRS

THE SPACE NEEDLE IS TO *Seattle what the Eiffel Tower is to Paris. The* **Space Base Gift Shop** (⊠ *400 Broad St., Queen Anne* ☎ *800/809– 0902) has the city's ultimate icon rendered in endless ways. Among the officially licensed goods are bags of Space Needle Noodles, towering wooden pepper grinders, and a cache of foot-long vintage wooden pens ordered for the 1962 World's Fair, but delivered after it had ended and only recently unearthed. If none of these items appeals to you—and you have time and patience—you can construct a 40-inch-tall paper model of the awesome edifice.*

Are you experienced? Answer in the affirmative as you strut your psychedelic stuff in groovy tees, caps, and more bearing the graphic likeness of Seattle's home-grown guitar genius, Jimi Hendrix. Experience Music Project's **EMP Store** (⊠ *2901 Broad St., Queen Anne* ☎ *206/ 262–3192) has all this paraphernalia and the music to go with it.*

If one food could be called this region's specialty it just might be salmon. But how can you share this perishable delicacy with the folks at home? No, don't stuff one into your luggage. Instead go to **Pike Place Fish Market** (⊠ *86 Pike Place, Downtown* ☎ *206/682–7181). The friendly, fish-flinging experts here will not only wrap up your purchase but will also ship it across the country for you. (Don't forget to ask them if they work for scale.)*

Hikers and gardeners in the cool, damp Pacific Northwest are all too familiar with banana slugs, creepy gastropods that can grow to more than 10 inches long. At **Simply Seattle** (⊠ *1600 1st Ave., Downtown* ☎ *206/448–2207) you can lick this monster mollusk in the form of a Slug Sucker—a chocolate lollipop shaped and colored to resemble a slug. One version has "salt" sprinkled on its back. Ugh.*

You may want a Seattle Seahawks football jersey or a UW Huskies T-shirt, but it's the Ichiro Suzuki bobble head doll that sets many a Seattle baseball fan's heart aflutter. At the **Seattle Mariners Team Store** (⊠ *21250 1st Ave. S, Downtown* ☎ *206/346–4287) in Safeco Field you can stock up on whatever hits your ball out of the park. And bring your camera and pose for a picture in front of the oversize murals that run along First Avenue South bearing portraits of this year's players. There are also Mariners Team Stores Downtown at Fourth Avenue and Stewart Street and at the Bellevue Square and Southcenter malls.*

Wine & Specialty Foods

Delaurenti Specialty Food Markets (⊠ 1435 1st Ave., Downtown ☎ 206/ 622–0141) is *the* place to shop for a Mediterranean picnic. Imported meats and cheeses crowd the deli cases, and packaged delicacies pack the aisles. Try the truffle-infused olive oil for a gastronomic treat. The wine shop upstairs has excellent Italian vintages.

Pike & Western Wine Shop (⊠ 1934 Pike Pl., Downtown ☎ 206/441– 1307) has a comprehensive stock of wines from the Pacific Northwest, California, Italy, and France—and expert advice to guide your choice.

Three Dog Bakery (⊠ 1408 1st Ave., Downtown ☎ 206/364–9999) inspires your canine pals to sit up and beg for all natural, fresh-baked treats with names like Beagle Bagels and Snickerpoodles.

Fremont

Full of things inspiring and outrageous, this openly creative community—the self-proclaimed "center of the universe"—has a collection of colorful shops across from the Fremont Bridge. The two main roads, Fremont Place North and the busier Fremont Avenue North, merge at this conglomeration of quirky clothing, vintage, and housewares shops, but there's plenty of parking along the side streets. If you want originals by Seattle designers and artists, the finds here are top-quality and reasonably priced. To get a taste of what's available, don't miss the weekly summer Sunday Market along the waterfront (with free parking nearby). *Best shopping: The blocks bound by Fremont Pl. N and Evanston Ave. N to N. 34th St. and Aurora Ave. N.*

Antiques & Collectibles

Deluxe Junk (✉ 3518 Fremont Pl. N, Fremont ☎ 206/634–2733) brings back the past with things that are flamboyant, retro, or chic. Some objects fall into all three categories.

Fremont Antique Mall (✉ 3419 Fremont Pl. N, Fremont ☎ 206/548–9140) is an underground complex of 50 dealers who sell vintage clothing and items from popular American culture.

Books, Printed Materials & Music

Dusty Strings (✉ 3406 Fremont Ave. N, Fremont ☎ 206/634–1662) has acoustic guitars, fiddles, lutes, banjos, and more exotic stringed instruments, such as citterns and bouzoukis. If you're looking for folk music CDs this place has hundreds of them.

J & S Fremont News (✉ 3416 Fremont Ave. N, Fremont ☎ 206/633–0731) is well stocked with newspapers and magazines, and has a row of clocks that tell the time in Tokyo, Paris, New York, and—wouldn't you know it—Fremont. While browsing the foreign press, pick up a free copy of *The Walking Guide to Fremont.*

Sonic Boom (✉ 3414 Fremont Ave. N, Fremont ☎ 206/547–2666) is in touch with the current music scene, especially the Northwest and independent labels. Browse for new and used records and CDs here and at the Capitol Hill and Ballard stores. Check local schedules for in-store performances and release parties.

Twice Sold Tales of Fremont (✉ 3504 Fremont Ave. N, Fremont ☎ 206/632–3759) is a general-interest used bookstore with a soft spot for cats.

Clothing

Bellefleur (✉ 720 N. 35th St., Fremont ☎ 206/545–0222) is a sensuous little shop fluttering with sexy European undies. It also has lotions and potions.

Enexile (✉ 611 N. 35th St., Fremont ☎ 206/633–5771) outfits men and women in modern streetwear by Anna Sui, French Connection, and others.

Fritzi Ritz Vintage Clothing (✉ 750 N. 34th St., Fremont ☎ 206/633–0929) is crammed with cool vintage apparel. Staffers label everything so it's easy to find clothes by era.

★ **Les Amis** (✉ 3420 Evanston Ave. N, Fremont ☎ 206/632–2877) is all about luscious fabrics. Look for ultra-feminine dresses, gorgeous knits, and frothy lingerie from the best up-and-coming lines.

Private Screening (✉ 3504 Fremont Pl. N, Fremont ☎ 206/548–0751) has classic clothing from the 1920s to the 1960s. Let the vintage Western wear bring out your inner cowpoke.

Gifts & Home Decor

Bitters Co. (✉ 513 N. 36th St., Fremont ☎ 206/632–0886) is a general store with unusual textiles, linens, tableware, and jewelry. Look for hand-crafted furniture from Guatemala, Indonesia, and the Philippines as well as an in-house line of tables made from reclaimed Douglas fir.

Burnt Sugar (⊠ 601 N. 35th St., Fremont ☎ 206/545–0699), the store on the corner with the rocket on the roof, carries whimsical vintage furniture, hand-crafted photo albums, soaps, candles, jewelry, and other delights. Spend some quality time at the cosmetic bar sampling products by Susan Posnick, Body & Soul, and Somme Institute.

Dandelion Botanical Company (⊠ 708 N. 34th St., Fremont ☎ 206/545–8892) creates custom-scented candles and body products in a charming space that feels like an old-fashioned apothecary shop.

Essenza (⊠ 615 N. 35th St., Fremont ☎ 206/547–4895) is a refreshing, light-filled boutique that sells Italian bath items by Santa Maria Novella, the complete line of Fresh products, handmade bed linens, women's loungewear, delicate jewelry, and exquisite children's clothing.

Frank & Dunya (⊠ 3418 Fremont Ave. N, Fremont ☎ 206/547–6760), a shop named after the owners' dogs, sells colorful, locally crafted, functional art.

Portage Bay Goods (⊠ 706 N. 34th St., Fremont ☎ 206/547–5221) is a great source for crafts produced by local artisans using environmentally friendly methods.

Footwear

Frankie (⊠ 617 N. 36th St., Fremont ☎ 206/547–1030) lets you slip your feet into comfy shoes from Donald J. Pliner, Camper, and Fornarina. There are styles for men and women.

★ **Lola Pop** (⊠ 711 N. 35th St., Fremont ☎ 206/547–2071) indulges feminine cravings for high fashion footwear, handbags, and accessories from Italy and France. Look for Cynthia Rowley, Nancy Nancy, and L'autre Chose.

International District

Uwajimaya—the megamarket, bookstore, and eatery—is the major shopping attraction of the International District (referred to locally as "the I.D."). The rest of the neighborhood warrants browsing, too, though, since it's filled with small tea houses, groceries, and mom-and-pop shops that underscore the city's strong Asian character. Here you can pick up Chinese pastries, jade and gold jewelry, Asian produce, and Eastern herbs and tinctures. Little souvenir shops, dusty and deep, sell Japanese kites, Vietnamese bowls, Chinese slippers, Korean art, and tea or dish sets. *Best shopping: S. King St., between 5th and 8th Aves. S.*

Antiques & Collectibles

Eileen of China (⊠ 624 S. Dearborn St., International District ☎ 206/624–0816) is the neighborhood's best-known antiques shop. The selection ranges from rosewood dining and living room sets, armoires, and cabinets to stone carvings and fine art.

Market

Fodor'sChoice ★ **Uwajimaya** (⊠ 600 5th Ave. S, International District ☎ 206/624–6248 ⊕ www.uwajimaya.com) is one of West Coast's largest Japanese grocery and gift markets, though it also sells items from many other places in Asia. A 30-foot-long red Chinese dragon stretches above its piles of produce and aisles of packaged goods from Korea, Indonesia, the Philippines, India, Thailand, and more. Glass tanks teem with fish, crabs, lobster, prawns, and geoducks; the frozen-foods cases contain even more delicacies. A busy food court serves sushi, Japanese bento-box meals, Chinese stir-fry combos, Korean barbecue, Hawaiian dishes, Vietnamese spring rolls, and an assortment of jellied milk drinks and teas. The housewares section is well stocked with dishes, appliances, and decorations. There's also a card section, a Hello Kitty corner, a bank, and Yuriko's cosmetics, where you can find Shiseido products that are usually available only in Japan. Plan an extra hour to browse the attached Kinokuniya bookstore. The large parking lot is free for one hour with a minimum $5 purchase or two hours with a minimum $10 purchase (don't forget to have your ticket validated). The market is open Monday through Saturday 9 AM–11 PM and Sunday 9 AM–10 PM.

Pioneer Square

Stand under the iron-and-glass Pioneer Square Pergola at First Avenue and Yesler Street and give silent thanks to the citizens who fought to keep high-rise development out of this turn-of-the-20th-century district. As you browse your way south on First Avenue—exploring side-street boutiques as well—you'll understand why art galleries, antiques stores, and one-of-a-kind merchants prefer this neighborhood. Graceful brick facades, high ceilings, and wood floors seem custom-built for these shops. Pick up a free copy of *Seattle's Pioneer Square Map & Guide* available at most area merchants. In the evenings the square is given over to live music and young revelers. *Best shopping: 1st Ave. S, between Yesler Way and S. Jackson St., and Occidental Ave. S between S. Main and Jackson Sts.*

Antiques & Collectibles

Azuma Gallery (⊠ 530 1st Ave. S, Pioneer Square ☎ 206/622–5599) specializes in traditional and contemporary Japanese prints, screens, baskets, and art objects.

Carolyn Staley Fine Japanese Prints (⊠ 314 Occidental Ave. S, Pioneer Square ☎ 206/621–1888) deals in fine antique *ukiyo-e* (17th- to 19th-century paintings and prints depicting scenes from everyday life) and modern Japanese woodblock prints.

Chidori Asian Antiques (⊠ 108 S. Jackson St., Pioneer Square ☎ 206/343–7736) sells high-quality Asian antiques; pre-Columbian and primitive art; and antiquities from all over the world.

★ **Elliott Bay Antiques** (⊠ 165 S. Jackson St., Pioneer Square ☎ 206/340–0770) is a premier source for top-quality Chinese antique furniture and Buddhist sculptures.

Flury & Company (⊠ 322 1st Ave. S, Pioneer Square ☎ 206/587–0260) has a fascinating vintage photographs by Edward Curtis, along with Native-American antiques, traditional carvings, baskets, jewelry, and tools.

Jean Williams Antiques (⊠ 115 S. Jackson St., Pioneer Square ☎ 206/622–1110) stocks fine 18th- and 19th-century English, French, and Biedermeier furniture.

Kagedo Japanese Art and Antiques (⊠ 520 1st Ave. S, Pioneer Square ☎ 206/467–9077) has Japanese antiques and works by modern masters. Among the treasures are intricately carved *okimono* (miniature figures rendered in wood, ivory, or bronze), stone garden ornaments, basketry, and textiles.

Laguna (⊠ 116 S. Washington St., Pioneer Square ☎ 206/682–6162) carries collectible 20th-century American dinnerware, art pottery, vintage linens, tiles, and tile-topped tables.

Art Galleries

Bryan Ohno Gallery (⊠ 115 S. Main St., Pioneer Square ☎ 206/667–9572) carries contemporary sculpture and Asian art and represents Northwest artists.

Davidson Galleries (⊠ 313 Occidental Ave. S, Pioneer Square ☎ 206/624–7684) specializes in contemporary painting, sculpture, prints, and drawings as well as antique prints.

Foster/White Gallery (✉ 123 S. Jackson St., Pioneer Square ☎ 206/622–2833) showcases paintings and sculpture by Northwest masters and spectacular glass works by Dale Chihuly.

Greg Kucera Gallery (✉ 212 3rd Ave. S, Pioneer Square ☎ 206/624–0770) is a top venue for national and regional artists, with more than 4,000 square feet of exhibition space that include an outdoor sculpture deck.

Grover/Thurston Gallery (✉ 309 Occidental Ave. S, Pioneer Square ☎ 206/223–0816) specializes in contemporary figurative and narrative works, many by Northwest artists.

Kibo Galerie (✉ 323 Occidental Ave. S, Pioneer Square ☎ 206/442–2100) has a stunning collection of tribal masks and statuary from all over Africa.

Linda Hodges Gallery (✉ 316 1st Ave. S, Pioneer Square ☎ 206/624–3034) specializes in works by contemporary Northwest artists.

Fodor'sChoice ★ **Stonington Gallery** (✉ 119 S. Jackson St., Pioneer Square ☎ 206/405–4040) has contemporary masterworks by Northwest Coast tribal members as well as artists working in the native style.

Books, Printed Materials & Music

Bud's Jazz Records (✉ 102 S. Jackson St., Pioneer Square ☎ 206/628–0045) is a tightly packed underground store that sells all jazz and lots of it, including hard-to-find recordings.

David Ishii Bookseller (✉ 212 1st Ave. S, Pioneer Square ☎ 206/622–4719) is a small but mighty shop filled with a highly selective stock of used, out-of-print, and rare books. Many of the titles are dedicated to the owner's off-duty passions—baseball and fly-fishing.

Fodor'sChoice ★ **Elliott Bay Book Company** (✉ 101 S. Main St., Pioneer Square ☎ 206/624–6600), an enormous independent bookstore often held as Seattle's literary heart, stocks 150,000+ titles arranged on rustic wooden shelves in a labyrinth of rooms. The store hosts popular lectures and readings by local and international authors. A side room contains used books—about 22,000 of them—on all subjects; some are signed first editions.

Flora & Fauna Books (✉ 121 1st Ave. S, Pioneer Square ☎ 206/623–4727) attends to the natural world with new, used, and rare books on horticulture and birding.

Metsker Maps (✉ 702 1st Ave., Pioneer Square ☎ 206/623–8747) has the cartographical goods to guide you to where in the world you need go.

Seattle Mystery Bookshop (✉ 117 Cherry St., Pioneer Square ☎ 206/587–5737) thrills you with new, used, and collectible suspense novels.

Wessel & Lieberman (✉ 208 1st Ave. S, Pioneer Square ☎ 206/682–3545) specializes in first editions, Americana, book arts, and fine letterpress in a tidy shop with dark green walls and handsome wooden shelves. An extensive annex is on the underground level of Grand Central Arcade.

Clothing

Ebbets Field Flannels (✉ 404 Occidental Ave. S, Pioneer Square ☎ 206/262–0260) sells bits of baseball history with faithful reproduction team jackets, jerseys, and caps from the 1920s to '60s, focusing on the Negro Leagues, minor leagues, and the Pacific Coast League.

Ragazzi's Flying Shuttle (✉ 607 1st Ave., Pioneer Square ☎ 206/343–9762) sells exquisite, hand-woven clothing, textiles, and throws.

Footwear

Clog Factory (✉ 217 1st Ave. S, Pioneer Square ☎ 206/682–2564) has shelves with clogs of all sizes, lined up like jelly beans between the high, exposed-brick walls. There's a good selection of comfy Dansko and Bastad shoes.

Gifts & Home Decor

Fireworks Fine Crafts Gallery (✉ 210 1st Ave. S, Pioneer Square ☎ 206/682–8707) sells whimsical hand-crafted jewelry, ceramics, and small items of furniture. It's just as fun to shop in the Bellevue Square, University Village, and Westlake Center branches.

Glass House Studio (⊠ 311 Occidental Ave. S, Pioneer Square ☎ 206/682–9939), Seattle's oldest glassblowing studio and gallery, lets you watch fearless artisans at work in the "hot shop." Studio pieces and other works on display are for sale.

Northwest Fine Woodworking (⊠ 101 S. Jackson St., Pioneer Square ☎ 206/625–0542) represents the work of more than 30 artist owner-members who value furniture craftsmanship and design. You can find almost anything in the showroom or have it handmade for you. Shipping is available.

Mall

Grand Central Arcade (⊠ 214 1st Ave. S, Pioneer Square ☎ 206/623–7417) has an exposed-brick interior courtyard and an underground cache of fascinating shops. Locals linger at tables near a fireplace on damp Northwest days, sipping espresso and munching treats from Grand Central Bakery. You can sort through hundreds of rubber stamps at Paper Cat and peruse antiquarian books and images at David Ishii Books and Michael Maslin Historic Photographs. Go downstairs to see the wares at the Pottery School, sigh over the Japanese paper art at Tai Designs, or get an expert opinion at Grand Central Wine Merchant.

Toys

Magic Mouse Toys (⊠ 603 1st Ave., Pioneer Square ☎ 206/682–8097) proves that it's never too late to have a happy childhood. The two floors of top-notch playthings here include collectible Steiff animals, Brio trains, dozens of games and puzzles, books, and more than 100 kinds of teddy bears.

Seattle Magic Shop (⊠ 106 1st Ave. S, Pioneer Square ☎ 206/622–2757) is full of tricks, jokes, novelties, and collectibles. If you play your cards right you might be allowed into the secret, magicians-only backroom.

Queen Anne

There are actually two shopping areas in this hillside neighborhood—around the Seattle Center at the bottom of the slopes and along Queen Anne Avenue North at the top. East from the Seattle Center along Queen Anne and Mercer avenues are tiny cafés, bookstores, antiques and consignment shops, and bike stores. The cluster of businesses at the top of the hill includes crafts shops and coffeehouses. *Best shopping: Along Queen Ave. N between W. Harrison and Roy Sts. and between W. Galer and McGraw Sts.*

Antiques & Collectibles

Crane Gallery (⊠ 104 W. Roy St., Queen Anne ☎ 206/298–9425), at the foot of Queen Anne Hill, offers top-notch Japanese, Chinese, Korean, Tibetan, and Southeast Asian antiques and art objects, including bronzes, lacquer items, and porcelain pieces.

Galen Lowe Art & Antiques (⊠ 102 W. Roy St., Queen Anne ☎ 206/270–8888), at the foot of Queen Anne Hill, assembles a highly individualized and esoteric collection of Japanese art, furniture, textiles, outsider art and objets d'art in a small but stunning gallery.

Books, Printed Materials & Music

Easy Street Records (⊠ 20 Mercer St., Queen Anne ☎ 206/691–3279), at the base of Queen Anne, is a large, lively independent music store with a terrific reputation for its cache of new releases, imports, and rare finds.

Queen Anne Avenue Books (⊠ 1811 Queen Anne Ave. N, Queen Anne ☎ 206/283–5624) is a friendly neighborhood bookstore with a fine selection of children's literature.

Clothing

Adelita (✉ 1422 Queen Anne Ave. N, Queen Anne ☎ 206/285–0707), a boutique furnished like a romantic boudoir, caters to "the revolutionary fashionista" with strong yet feminine apparel as well as spa products and unique accessories. The fitting room is cushy.

Hilltop Yarn and Needlepoint Shop (✉ 2224 Queen Anne Ave. N, Queen Anne ☎ 206/282–1332) fills the lower rooms of a 1914 craftsman bungalow from floor to ceiling with colorful yarns both plain and fancy. The upstairs bedrooms are cozy classrooms for knitting, crocheting, needlepoint, and felting lessons.

La Femme (✉ 1622 Queene Ave. N, Queen Anne ☎ 206/285–2443) is a chic little shop that carries sexy, flirty, sophisticated clothing along with jeans from Paper Denim & Cloth, Lovetanjane lingerie, handmade shoes, and jewelry by local artists.

Nancy's Sewing Basket (✉ 2221 Queen Anne Ave. N, Queen Anne ☎ 206/282–9112) stocks bolts of fine fabrics, including imported linens and silks. Don't miss the back room filled with exquisite vintage ribbons and millinery supplies.

Queen Anne Mail & Dispatch / Undies & Outies (✉ 2212 Queen Anne Ave. N, Queen Anne ☎ 206/286–1024) feels like an old-fashioned general store. One side of the place has delectable Italian lingerie by Cosabella, an eclectic mix of women's casual clothing, and comfy, stylish shoes. The other side has a dandy mailing service with a long wooden counter and floor-to-ceiling wooden mail cubicles.

Gifts & Home Decor

Four Winds (✉ 1517 Queen Anne Ave. N, Queen Anne ☎ 206/282–0472) enchants you with exotic Tibetan, Nepali, and Indonesian crafts, jewelry, textiles, furniture, and candles. There are also more than 50 varieties of incense.

The Homing Instinct (✉ 1622 Queen Anne Ave. N, Queen Anne ☎ 206/281–9260) is a cottagelike boutique filled with such household items as fine linens, elegant tableware, and sumptuous bath products. The baby gifts are sweet as well.

Ravenna Gardens (✉ 2201 Queen Anne Ave. N, Queen Anne ☎ 206/283–7091) displays gear and gifts for genteel gardeners in a light, airy, corner store. You can find many more plants at the larger University Village location.

Stuhlbergs Fine Home Accessories (✉ 1805 Queen Anne Ave. N, Queen Anne ☎ 206/352–2351), in a cottage with a lovely shade garden in front, sells such things as fine Italian pewter and Petit Bateau baby clothes.

Wines & Specialty Foods

McCarthy & Schiering Wine Merchants (✉ 2401 Queen Anne Ave. N, Queen Anne ☎ 206/282–8500) is a great place for oenophiles, with a large selection of Northwest wines and a knowledgeable staff.

Teacup (✉ 2207 Queen Anne Ave. N, Queen Anne ☎ 206/283–5931), which has custom-blended tea for an expedition to Mt. Everest, sells more than 150 varieties of the stuff. Don't leave without sampling a refreshing cup.

University District

The U-District's parallel shopping corridors are along Roosevelt Way Northeast and University Way Northeast. Each has a line of worn-looking but well-stocked book, clothing, and accessories stores. University Way NE has more shops and small, inexpensive ethnic restaurants, as well as the venerable main branch of the University Bookstore. Students have kept the prices low and the merchandise playful, and many merchants can give you tokens good for up to two hours of parking at validated lots. For crafts and produce check out the University District Farmers Market held on Saturday from May through November. *Best shopping: University Way NE between NE 42nd and 47th Sts., and University Village at 25th Ave. NE and NE 45th St.*

Books, Printed Materials & Music

Bulldog News and Fast Espresso (✉ 4208 University Way NE, University District ☎ 206/632–6397) has nearly 3,000 newspapers and magazines, both domestic and foreign. Just dash in, pick up a paper, a shot of espresso, and go. You can also hop on-line. The first five minutes are free with a coffee purchase; after that it's 50¢ per 10 minutes. The store also maintains a small but well-stocked kiosk at Broadway Market on Capitol Hill.

Cellophane Square (✉ 4538 University Way NE, University District ☎ 206/634–2280), a store with an affinity for indie rock, punk, and garage bands, will buy, sell, and trade used CDs and vinyl. It also carries new releases, and it has classical and jazz sections on the second floor. From time to time there are in-store performances.

Cinema Books (✉ 4753 Roosevelt Way NE, University District ☎ 206/547–7667) caters to film fans, TV junkies, and theater buffs with new and rare books, posters, and ephemera.

Half Price Books Records Magazines (✉ 4709 Roosevelt Way NE, University District ☎ 206/547–7859) has such great deals that you might well walk out with twice as much as you planned. The children's and history book sections are particularly notable.

University Book Store (✉ 4326 University Way NE, University District ☎ 206/634–3400), on the UW campus, is the nation's second-largest independent college bookstore. There's a well-stocked general book department, lots of university souvenirs, and author events all year long. The Downtown branch sells business and professional books.

Clothing

Buffalo Exchange (✉ 4530 University Way NE, University District ☎ 206/545–0175), a big, bright shop of new and recycled fashions, is always crowded—even on Saturday night—with UW girls looking for bargains. It takes time to browse the stuffed racks, but the trendy rewards are great: sequined jeans, leather jackets, vintage-style dresses.

Moksha (✉ 4542 University Way NE, University District ☎ 206/632–1190) sells hip little skirts and dresses fashioned out of old Indian saris and embellished with gossamer overlays and intricate beading. Or maybe you'd prefer cute girly T-shirts and trendy denim. It's all unique and affordable.

Red Light Clothing Exchange (✉ 4560 University Way NE, University District ☎ 206/545–4044) is filled with well-organized, good-quality vintage clothing from the 1940s to the '80s. Sample outfits from each era—complete with accessories—adorn the dressing rooms. There's plenty of denim, leather, and disco threads alongside cowboy boots and evening wear. There's also an equally well-stocked branch in Capitol Hill.

Pitaya (✉ 4520 University Way NE, University District ☎ 206/548–1001) is an unexpectedly chic boutique that's on top of the trends. The clothes are not only stylish and fun but also priced just right for college girls.

Footwear

5 Doors Up (✉ 4309 University Way NE, University District ☎ 206/547–3192) is a destination for fashion forward sports shoe fans of both sexes. Look for limited editions of Puma's Mihara line, totally cool Fly London for men, and ultra-high-top Converse sneakers usually available only in Japan.

M. J. Feet (✉ 4334 University Way NE, University District ☎ 206/632–5353) has Birkenstock shoes in every configuration—from sandals to almost dressy—and colorful socks, hats, and bags. There's a second store in Bellevue.

Woolly Mammoth (✉ 4303 University Way NE, University District ☎ 206/632–3254) sells comfortable, high-quality casual shoes—from rugged mud-brown sandals to funky, seafoam-green flip-flops. It's what staffers like to call "Euro comfort." Look for Dansko, Naot, Josef Seibel, Merrell, and more.

Gifts & Home Decor

Burke Museum of Natural History and Culture (✉ 17th Ave. NE and NE 45th St., University District ☎ 206/543–5590), on the UW campus, displays historic Northwest coast Native American works, and sells contemporary masks, plaques, rattles, and prints in its store.

La Tienda Folk Art Gallery (✉ 4138 University Way NE, University District ☎ 206/632–1796) has a colorful melange of handblown glass, pottery, jewelry, clothing, masks, toys, musical instruments, CDs, books, and games from different cultures. The sister store in Ballard is definitely worth a visit.

Snow Goose Associates (✉ 8806 Roosevelt Way NE, University District ☎ 206/523–6223), just north of UW, represents Alaskan Eskimo, Canadian Inuit, and Northwest Coast Native American artists.

Shopping Center

★ **University Village** (✉ NE 45th St. and 25th Ave. NE, University District ☎ 206/523–0622), northeast of the campus, is a pleasant outdoor shopping plaza with trees, fountains, whimsical sculptures, and other good-life adornments. Among the more than 80 upscale shops and restaurants are branches of Pottery Barn, Williams-Sonoma, Banana Republic, Smith & Hawken, Crate & Barrel, and Restoration Hardware. You can redo your kid's room at the Land of Nod, schedule your own makeover at Sephora, and sample divine delicacies from Fran's Chocolates. The whole place is kid-friendly, and there's ample free parking.

The Eastside

Bellevue

The shopping scene here rivals that of Seattle. Sleek, glass-encased high-rises show that this is a powerful sister metropolis in the making. Its core is Bellevue Square mall and the attractive cluster of upscale shops and restaurants on the mall's southwest corner. Bellevue Galleria and Bellevue Place are two smaller malls that also have upscale shops, restaurants, movies, and parking. The community's retail strip stretches from Bellevue Square between Northeast 4th and 8th streets to the enormous, department store–anchored Crossroads Shopping Center several miles to the east. *Best shopping: Bellevue Square—it really does seem to have it all.*

CENTERS & MALLS **Bellevue Galleria** (✉ 550 106th Ave. NE, Bellevue ☎ 425/452–1934). Although small as malls go, it's a convenient satellite to the bigger Bellevue Square mall. Stores include Habits for the Home, Men's Warehouse, Sahara Fine Arts, and Tower Records, but it's best to come for a day of spa pampering at Gene Juarez rather than for a whole day of shopping. There's plenty of evening entertainment, too, with four restaurants, the Rock Bottom Brewery, and the Regal Cinemas.

★ **Bellevue Square** (✉ Bellevue Way, Bellevue ☎ 425/454–8096 ⊕ www.bellevuesquare.com). More than 200 stores fill Seattle's favorite outskirts mall. Notables include Nordstrom, the Bon Marché, Pottery Barn, and Crate & Barrel, Aveda, Banana Republic, Coach, Esprit, and Swatch. The wide walkways and benches, the many children's clothing stores, the first-floor play area, and the third-floor children's museum make this a great place for kids. All this and you can park for free in the attached garage. **Crossroads Shopping Center** (✉ 15600 NE 8th St., Bellevue ☎ 425/644–1111 ⊕ www.crossroadsbellevue.com). Sixty shops—including Bed Bath & Beyond, Gottschalks, and Old Navy—surround the open Public Market Stage where there's free live music 7:30–10 PM on Saturday, and an open mike on Friday 6:30–10 PM. A giant chessboard and playground are nearby, and the Crossroads Cinema anchors the southeast corner. If you're hungry, there are more than 20 restaurants.

Kirkland

Kirkland has a stretch of boutiques, elegant restaurants, and patio bars along Lake Street South, which is where wealthy Eastsiders take their business when they want to get back to a small-town environment. It's not hard to see why: you can't beat the beauty of the waterfront Waverly and Marina parks. If you want a mall-type experience, there are several within five minutes' drive. *Best shopping: Lake St. S between Central Way NE and 3rd Ave. S.*

MALLS **Carillon Point** (✉ 2000 Carillon Point, Kirkland ☎ 425/822–1700 ⊕ www.carillon-point.com). In the scoop of Yarrow Bay, this attractive mall is fronted by a western view of Lake Washington and the forested hills of the opposite shores. Wander along the waterfront, where white sailboats skim the waves and ducks and muskrats paddle right up into the lily pads. It's a hot spot for sunset dining at the Yarrow Bay Grill or Cucina! Cucina!, but you can stop in at other times for a spa treatment at the Woodmark Hotel or a cut at Michael David Salon. The parking lot is free after 7 PM.

Kirkland Parkplace (✉ 600 Central Way, Kirkland ☎ 425/827–7789 ⊕ www.kirklandparkplace.net). This big outdoor mall has a bit of everything, from supermarkets to drugstores to restaurants. With several salons, a 24-hour fitness center, a yoga facility, and a movie theater, it's more of an event site than a shopping spot—hence its popularity with local youth on weekend evenings. There's free valet parking on weekdays near the Parkplace Office Supply (no gratuities accepted).

Elsewhere on the Eastside

Redmond Town Center is the main mall where the big names reside, many of them Northwest giants: Eddie Bauer, REI, and Gene Juarez, among others. There are also many little strip malls, filled with small clothing shops, fast-food restaurants, and chain stores, along the main roads that link Redmond with Bellevue, Issaquah, and Woodinville.

CENTERS & **Factory Stores at North Bend** (✉ I–90 at Exit 31, North Bend ☎ 425/888–
MALLS 4505). About one hour east of Seattle, this outlet center has discounts at 30+ brand-name stores including The Gap, Nike, and Osh Kosh B'Gosh. Parking is ample and free. And the view of nearby Mt. Si is spectacular. **Gilman Village** (✉ 317 Gilman Blvd., Issaquah ☎ 425/392–6802 ⊕ www. gilmanvillage.com). The look of this outdoor mall is upscale country, and the garden stores, gift shops, and art galleries—often carrying locally made items—lend a real sense of place. There are also several small restaurants and three free parking lots.

Redmond Town Center (✉ 16495 NE 74th St., Redmond ☎ 425/867–0808 ⊕ www.shopredmondtowncenter.com). There's an REI with a climbing rock here, as well as a Borders Books, Pier 1 Imports, and Victoria's Secret. The complex is laid out like a village and interspersed with fountains and play areas. The Gap, the Limited, Garden Botanika, and others join the roster of shops. There are also a Loews Cineplex, several large ethnic chain restaurants (Amigos, Cucina! Cucina!, Thai Ginger), and lots of free parking.

SIDE TRIPS FROM SEATTLE

7

FODOR'S CHOICE

Christina's, *Eastsound restaurant*
Colette's Bed & Breakfast, *near Port Angeles*
Crystal Mountain Ski Area, *Crystal Mountain*
Duck Soup Inn, *San Juan Island restaurant*
Hoh Valley Trail, *Olympic National Park*
Inn at Langley, *Langley*
Wonderland Trail, *Mt. Rainier National Park*

HIGHLY RECOMMENDED

HOTELS Alexander's Country Inn, *Ashford*
BJ's Garden Gate, *Port Angeles*
National Park Inn, *Longmire*
Panacea Bed and Breakfast, *Friday Harbor*
Paradise Inn, *Paradise*
Wellspring, *Ashford*

RESTAURANTS C'est Si Bon, *near Port Angeles*
Dupuis Restaurant, *Port Angeles*

SIGHTS Bloedel Reserve, *Bainbridge Island*
Grove of the Patriarchs, *Mt. Rainier National Park*
Johnston Ridge Observatory, *Mt. St. Helens*
Longmire Museum, *Mt. Rainier National Park*
San Juan Center for Art & Nature, *San Juan Island*
San Juan Island National Historic Park, *Friday Harbor*
Sol Duc Trail, *Olympic National Park*
Trail of the Cedars, *North Cascades National Park*
Weyerhauser/Hoffstadt Bluff Visitors Center, *Mt. St. Helens*

Revised and
expanded by
Gina Bacon,
John Doerper,
Holly S. Smith

THE WATERS OF THE SALISH SEA SURROUND PEACEFUL, rural Whidbey Island, a one-hour ferry ride from Seattle. The northern Puget Sound area is brimming with quaint historical towns that offer shopping, dining, and plenty of natural beauty. Plan on more than a day trip to fully appreciate the remote San Juan Islands.

If you head west to Olympic National Park, north to North Cascades National Park, or east to the Cascade Range, you can hike, bike, or ski. Two-and-a-half hours southeast of Seattle is majestic Mt. Rainier, the fifth-highest mountain in the contiguous United States. Mt. Rainier National Park offers 400 square mi of wilderness. Two hours beyond Rainier, close to the Oregon border, is the Mt. St. Helens National Volcanic Monument. The state-of-the-art visitor centers here show breathtaking views of the crater and lava dome and the spectacular recovery of the areas surrounding the 1980 blast.

About the Restaurants

Washington's abundant seafood shows up on menus throughout the state, and spicy yet subtle flavors testify to strong Asian influences. Tender halibut, sweet Dungeness crab, plump oysters, and delicate mussels are as popular as the ubiquitous salmon. Coastal forests are rich in wild mushrooms, and the inland valleys are famed for their beef and lamb, as well as their wines. In autumn, the mountains produce a bountiful harvest of wild berries; in fact, almost every region of the state grows great berries, as well as vegetables and apples. This bounty translates, in the hands of the state's many skilled chefs, into some of the west's finest cuisine.

About the Hotels

There's a good mix of expensive and moderately priced properties throughout the state. Some of Washington's best lodgings are in bed-and-breakfasts (B&Bs) or small inns surrounded by breathtaking natural beauty. They're often equipped with hot tubs and in-room fireplaces that take the edge off the crisp wintry inland air. A vast B&B network is operated by the state tourism board, and you can request a brochure or research your options on-line.

WHAT IT COSTS					
	$$$$	**$$$**	**$$**	**$**	**¢**
RESTAURANTS	over $32	$24–$32	$16–$24	$8–$16	under $8
HOTELS	over $250	$200–$250	$150–$200	$100–$150	under $100

Restaurant prices are per person, for a main course at dinner. Hotel prices are for two people in a standard double room in high season, excluding tax.

THE ISLANDS

The 35-minute ferry ride in Puget Sound to Bainbridge Island from downtown Seattle provides superb views of the city skyline and surrounding hills. On a nice day a pleasant excursion is a ferry trip across Possession Sound to Whidbey Island, 30 miles northwest of Seattle. It's a great way to watch gulls, terns, sailboats, and the occasional orca or bald eagle—not to mention the surrounding scenery, which takes in Camano Island and the North Cascades. Or you can drive across from the mainland on Route 20 at the island's northern end. From the air, Whidbey Island looks like a languid dragon, with Fidalgo Island to the north as its head. The Deception Pass Bridge links Whidbey to Fidalgo Island. From the bridge it's just a short drive to Anacortes, Fidalgo's main town and the terminus for ferries to the San Juan Islands.

There are 176 named islands in the San Juan archipelago, although these and large rocks around them amount to 743 at low tide and 428 at high tide. Sixty are populated (though most have only a house or two) and 10 are state marine parks, some of which are accessible only to kayakers navigating the Cascadia Marine Trail. The three largest islands, Lopez, Orcas, and San Juan, are served regularly by ferries and seaplanes. These islands support a little fishing and farming, but tourism generates by far the largest revenues.

Serene, well-appointed inns cater to visitors, and creative chefs operate small restaurants, serving food as contemporary as anything in Seattle. Each of the San Juans maintains a distinct character, though all share in the archipelago's blessings of serene farmlands, unspoiled coves, blue-green or gray tidal waters, and radiant light. The area receives approximately 250 days of sunshine a year. Nevertheless, the San Juans stay cool in summer (around 70°F) and get outright cold in winter, when temperatures can hover at the freezing point.

Bainbridge Island

① *9 mi northwest of Seattle by ferry.*

Bainbridge's small-town vibe and scenic countryside tempt visitors to stay a while. From the ferry terminal, take a walking tour of Winslow along its compact main street, Winslow Way, where it's easy to wander away an afternoon among the antiques shops, art galleries, bookstores, and cafés. You're free to use the yellow bicycles around the ferry docks.

Pass the Winslow Way turnoff and head about ¼ mi north on Olympic to the **Bainbridge Island Vineyard and Winery** (✉ 682 Hwy. 305 ☎ 206/842–9463), open for tastings and tours Wednesday–Sunday noon–5. If you first grab lunch provisions, you can picnic on the pretty grounds.

★ The 150-acre **Bloedel Reserve** has fine Japanese gardens, a bird refuge, a moss garden, and other gardens planted with island flora. A French Renaissance–style mansion, the estate's showpiece, is surrounded by 2 mi of trails and ponds dotted with trumpeter swans. Dazzling rhododendrons and azaleas bloom in spring, and Japanese maples colorfully signal autumn's arrival. Reservations are essential, and picnicking is not permitted. ✉ *7571 NE Dolphin Dr., 6 mi west of Winslow, via Hwy. 305* ☎ *206/842–7631* ⊕ *www.bloedelreserve.org* ✉ *$6* ⊙ *Wed.–Sun. 10–4.*

Where to Eat

$–$$$ ✕ **Ruby's on Bainbridge.** Dark wood accents, antique paintings, and a fireplace in this old Tudor manor surround candlelit, linen-cloaked tables with views of Rich Passage. Brie with warm mango chutney or roasted beet salad precede such mouth-watering entrées as *Amatriciana* (sautéed bacon and kalamata olive sauce over angel-hair pasta) and chicken-stuffed ravioli in Riesling cream sauce. Vegetarians will be pleased with the eggplant layered with mozzarella and tomatoes, or the mushrooms in marsala cream sauce. ✉ *4738 Lynnwood Center Rd., Winslow* ☎ *206/780–9303* ▤ *AE, MC, V.*

$–$$ ✕ **Bistro Pleasant Beach.** The simple restaurant focuses on flavorful, beautifully presented cuisine. Fine choices are the roasted lamb with cabernet glaze or the linguine with crisp prawns, fresh spinach and feta; yet, even the straightforward seafood chowder has gourmet aspirations. The seasonal Vintner Series set dinners, limited to 60 guests, pair exquisite appetizers and entrées with traditional but versatile wines. ✉ *241 Winslow Way W, Winslow* ☎ *206/842–4347* ▤ *AE, MC, V* ⊙ *Closed Mon.*

$ ✕ **Harbor Public House.** An 1881 estate home overlooking Eagle Harbor was renovated to create this casual restaurant at Winslow's pub-

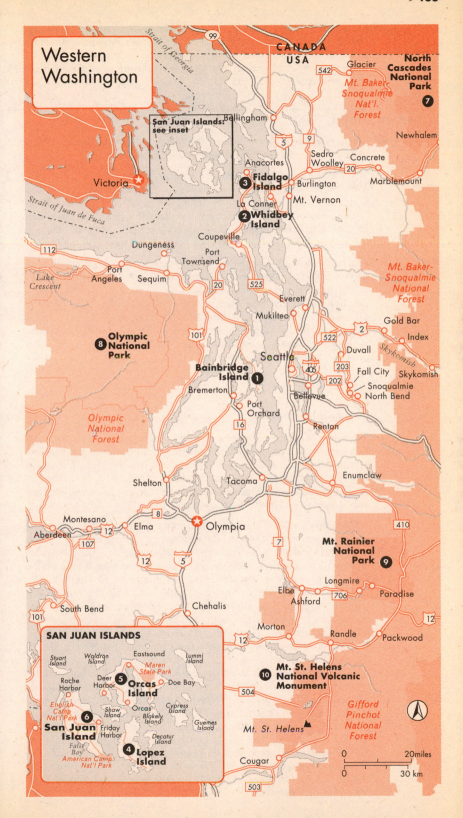

Western Washington

San Juan Islands: see inset

CANADA
USA

Strait of Georgia

99

542 Glacier

North Cascades National Park 7

Mt. Baker Snoqualmie Nat'l. Forest

Newhalem

Bellingham

5

9

Sedro Woolley

Concrete

20 Marblemount

Anacortes

Victoria

Strait of Juan de Fuca

Fidalgo Island 3

Burlington

Mt. Vernon

La Conner

Whidbey Island 2

Coupeville

Dungeness

112

Port Townsend

Lake Crescent

Port Angeles

Sequim

20

525

Mt. Baker-Snoqualmie National Forest

Everett

Mukilteo

Gold Bar

2

Index

522

Duvall

Skykomish

Skykomish

Olympic National Park 8

101

Seattle

Bainbridge Island 1

405

203

Fall City

202

Snoqualmie
North Bend

Bremerton

Bellevue

Olympic National Forest

Port Orchard

16

Renton

Enumclaw

Shelton

Tacoma

410

Montesano

12

Elma

Aberdeen

107

8

Olympia

5

7

Mt. Rainier National Park 9

12

12

5

Longmire

Paradise

South Bend

Chehalis

Elbe
Ashford

706

Packwood

101

Morton

12

Randle

12

504

Mt. St. Helens National Volcanic Monument 10

Gifford Pinchot National Forest

Mt. St. Helens

Cougar

503

SAN JUAN ISLANDS

Stuart Island

Waldron Island

Eastsound

Maren State Park

Lummi Island

Roche Harbor

Deer Harbor

Orcas Island 5

Doe Bay

English Camp Nat'l Park

San Juan Island 6

Shaw Island

Orcas

Cypress Island

Blakely Island

Guemes Island

Friday Harbor

False Bay

American Camp Nat'l Park

Decatur Island

Lopez Island 4

0   20 miles

0   30 km

lic marina. Seafood tacos, pub burgers, and grilled flatiron steak sandwiches are typical fare, as are key lime pie and root beer floats. This is where the pleasure-boating and kayaking crowds come to dine in a relaxed, waterfront setting. Things get raucous during Tuesday-night open-mike sessions. ⊠ *231 Parfitt Way, Winslow* ☎ *206/842–0969* 🖃 *AE, DC, MC, V.*

Whidbey Island

❷ *The ferry makes a 3-mi trip from Mukilteo (5 mi south of Everett) across Possession Sound to Clinton, on Whidbey Island.*

Whidbey is a blend of low pastoral hills, evergreen and oak forests, meadows of wildflower (including some endemic species), sandy beaches, and dramatic (though unstable) bluffs. It's a great place for taking slow drives or bicycle rides down country lanes, for viewing sunsets over the water, and for boating or kayaking along the protected shorelines of Saratoga Passage, Holmes Harbor, Penn Cove, and Skagit Bay.

The best beaches are on the west side, where wooded and wildflower-bedecked bluffs drop steeply to sand or surf—which can cover the beaches at high tide and can be unexpectedly rough on this exposed shore. Both beaches and bluffs have great views of the shipping lanes and the Olympic Mountains. Maxwelton Beach, with its sand, driftwood, and great views across Admiralty Inlet to the Olympic Mountains, is popular with the locals. Possession Point includes a park, a beach, and a boat launch. West of Coupeville, Ft. Ebey State Park has a sandy spread; West Beach is a stormy patch north of the fort with mounds of driftwood.

Langley
7 mi north of Clinton.

The village of Langley is above a 50-foot-high bluff overlooking Saratoga Passage, which separates Whidbey from Camano Island. A grassy terrace just above the beach is a great place for viewing birds that are on the water or in the air. On a clear day, you can see Mt. Baker in the distance. Upscale boutiques selling art, glass, jewelry, and clothing line First and Second streets in the heart of town.

WHERE TO
STAY & EAT
$–$$$

✕ **Star Bistro.** This 1980s-vintage bistro atop the Star Store feels like someone's comfortable dining room. The seasonal menu changes weekly. Lunch might include duck confit with wild mushroom salad, grilled figs, and seasonal greens. Dinner might bring cioppino; penne pasta with grilled eggplant, goat cheese, rosemary, and warm herb vinaigrette; a house-smoked pork chop with fire-roasted peppers and corn relish; or risotto with king salmon. Less adventurous eaters can opt for fish-and-chips or a burger. Popular for lunch, the dining room remains crowded well into late afternoon and evening. ⊠ *201½ 1st St.* ☎ *360/221–2627* ⊕ *www.star-bistro.com* ⚓ *Reservations not accepted* 🖃 *AE, MC, V* ☾ *No dinner Mon.*

$–$$

✕ **Garibyan Brothers Café Langley.** Terra-cotta tile floors, antique oak tables, and the aroma of garlic, basil, and oregano set the mood at this Mediterranean restaurant with Northwest touches. The tables are small but not too close together. Exotic dishes include rich hummus and baba ghanoush, eggplant moussaka, stuffed grape leaves, Mediterranean seafood stew, and lamb or chicken shish kabob. For Northwest fare, try the Dungeness crab cakes, Penn Cove mussels, or a seafood salad. Green or Greek salads accompany all entrées. The staff is friendly, professional, and helpful. ⊠ *113 1st St.* ☎ *360/221–3090* 🖃 *MC, V* ☾ *Closed Tues. Jan.–Mar. No lunch Tues.*

¢–$ ✕ **Dog House Backdoor Restaurant.** A friendly and relaxed waterfront tavern and family restaurant, the Dog House is filled with collectibles that include a 1923 nickelodeon. This is the town's most popular restaurant, both for the quality and for the low prices of its tacos, burritos, juicy burgers, creative pizzas, and homemade chili. For vegetarians there are tempura vegetables, a fresh vegetable platter, and sweet-potato fries. Listed on the National Register of Historic Places, the restaurant has a fine view of the Langley waterfront and Saratoga Passage and, on a clear day, the snow-capped volcanic cone of distant Mount Baker. ⊠ *230 1st St.* ☎ *360/221–9996* ⚓ *Reservations not accepted* ▭ *No credit cards.*

$$$–$$$$ ✕⊞ **Inn at Langley.** Langley's most elegant inn, the concrete-and-wood
Fodor'sChoice Frank Lloyd Wright–inspired structure perches on a bluff above the beach.
★ Asian-style guest rooms, all with fireplaces and balconies, have dramatic marine and mountain views. Stark yet comfortable rooms contrast beautifully with the lush landscape, which might be overpowering against a more baroque backdrop. Island Thyme Restaurant ($$$$; reservations essential) serves innovative prix-fixe, five-course seasonal dinners Friday and Saturday nights only, and Sunday supper in summer. For guests, the complimentary Continental breakfast includes the chef's own muesli, seasonal fruit, and fresh muffins. ⊠ *400 1st St., 98260* ☎ *360/221–3033* ⊕ *www.innatlangley.com* ↪ *24 rooms* ↻ *Restaurant, in-room hot tubs, spa* ▭ *MC, V* ⊺⊙⊺ *CP.*

$–$$ ⊞ **Saratoga Inn.** This inn is at the edge of Langley, a short walk from the town's shops and restaurants. Wood-shingle siding, gabled roofs, and wraparound porches lend the inn a Pacific Northwest authenticity. This theme extends to the interior, with wood floors and fireplaces. The carriage house, which has a deck as well as a bedroom with a king-size bed, a bathroom with a claw-foot tub, and a sitting area with a sleep sofa, offers more privacy. Included in the price is afternoon tea with hors d'oeuvres. ⊠ *201 Cascade Ave., 98260* ☎ *360/221–5801 or 800/698–2910* ⊟ *360/221–5804* ⊕ *www.foursisters.com* ↪ *15 rooms, 1 carriage house* ↻ *Cable TV, business services, meeting room; no a/c, no smoking* ▭ *AE, D, MC, V* ⊺⊙⊺ *BP.*

¢–$ ⊞ **Eagle's Nest.** Views of the Saratoga Passage and Cascade Mountains abound at this hilltop inn. The octagonal shape of the contemporary building allows for maximum privacy in the rooms, each of which has a private balcony. The living room's enormous brick fireplace is flanked by elongated octagonal windows in clear and peach-color glass. ⊠ *4680 Saratoga Rd., 98260* ☎ *360/221–5331* ⊕ *www.eaglesnestinn.com* ↪ *4 rooms, 1 cottage* ↻ *Cable TV, in-room VCRs, hot tub, hiking; no room phones, no kids under 12, no smoking* ▭ *D, MC, V* ⊺⊙⊺ *BP.*

SHOPPING At **Blackfish Gallerio** (⊠ 5075 S. Langley Rd. ☎ 360/221–1274) you can see pieces by Kathleen Miller, who produces enamel jewelry and hand-painted clothing and accessories; and Donald Miller, whose photographs depict the land and people of the Northwest; as well as works by other regional artists. The **Cottage** (⊠ 210 1st St. ☎ 360/221–4747) stocks vintage and imported men's and women's clothing. **Gaskill/Olson Gallery** (⊠ 302 1st St. ☎ 360/221–2978) exhibits and sells paintings, jewelry, pottery, and sculpture by established and emerging artists in a variety of media. Exhibits change on the first Saturday of the month.

Meet glass and jewelry artist Gwenn Knight at her gallery, the **Glass Knight** (⊠ 214 1st St. ☎ 360/221–6283), which also exhibits work by other Northwest artists. The **Museo** (⊠ 215 1st St. ☎ 360/221–7737), a gallery and gift shop, carries contemporary art by recognized and emerging artists.

Greenbank

14 mi northwest of Langely.

About halfway up Whidbey Island is the hamlet of Greenbank, home to the 125-acre **Greenbank Farm,** a loganberry farm and former winery that Island County purchased in late 1997. Volunteers now farm the berries, but the winery has closed. Local wines are, however, sold in a small wine shop, which also sells richly flavored jam. A small café next door sells pies. The 1904 barn, which once housed the winery, now serves as a community center.

The farm has a pond and walking trails with panoramic views of Admiralty Inlet, Saratoga Passage, and the Olympic and Cascade Mountains. A herd of alpacas is being raised on the farm by the Whidbey Island Alpacas company for their soft, spinnable hair and for sale as pets. The farm is also the site of several community events, including a Loganberry Festival each July, and a Sunday farmers' market held in summer. Picnic tables are scattered throughout the farm. ⊠ *657 Wonn Rd.* ☎ *360/678–7700* ⊕ *www.greenbankfarm.com* ⊡ *Free* ☉ *Daily 10–5.*

The 53-acre **Meerkerk Rhododendron Gardens** contain 1,500 native and hybrid species of rhododendrons and more than 100,000 spring bulbs on 10 acres of display gardens with numerous walking trails and ponds. The flowers are in full bloom in April and May. Summer flowers and fall color provide interest later in the year. The 43 remaining acres are kept wild as a nature preserve. ⊠ *Resort Rd.* ☎ *360/678–1912* ⊕ *www. meerkerkgardens.org* ⊡ *$3* ☉ *Daily 9–4.*

Coupeville

On the south shore of Penn Cove, 15 mi north of Greenbank.

Restored Victorian houses grace many of the streets in quiet Coupeville, Washington's second oldest city. It also has one of the largest national historic districts in the state, and has been used for filming movies depicting 19th-century New England villages. Stores above the waterfront have maintained their old-fashioned character. Captain Thomas Coupe founded the town in 1852. His house was built the following year, and other houses and commercial buildings were built in the late 1800s. Even though Coupeville is the Island County seat, the town has a laid-back, almost 19th-century air.

☾ The **Island County Historical Museum** has exhibits on Whidbey's fishing, timber, and agricultural industries, and conducts tours and walks. The square-timber **Alexander Blockhouse** outside dates from the Puget Sound Indian War of 1855. Note the squared logs and dove-tailed joints of the corners—no overlapping log ends. This construction technique was favored by many western Washington pioneers. Several old-time canoes are exhibited in an open, roofed shelter. ⊠ *908 NW Alexander St.* ☎ *360/678–3310* ⊡ *$2* ☉ *May–Oct., daily 10–5; Nov.–Apr., Fri.–Mon. 11–4.*

☾ **Ebey's Landing National Historic Reserve** encompasses a sand and cobble beach, bluffs with dramatic views down the Strait of Juan de Fuca, two state parks, and several (privately held) pioneer farms homesteaded in the early 1850s. The reserve, the first and largest of its kind, holds nearly 100 nationally registered historic structures, most of them from the 19th century. Miles of trails lead along the beach and through the woods. Cedar Gulch, south of the main entrance to Ft. Ebey, has a lovely picnic area in a wooded ravine above the beach.

Ft. Casey State Park, on a bluff overlooking the Strait of Juan de Fuca and the Port Townsend ferry landing, was one of three forts built after

1890 to protect the entrance to Admiralty Inlet. Look for the concrete gun emplacement and a couple of 8-inch "disappearing" guns. The Admiralty Head Lighthouse Interpretive Center is north of the gunnery emplacements. There are also grassy picnic sites, rocky fishing spots, and a boat launch. ⊠ *2 mi west of Rte. 20* ☎ *360/678–4519 or 800/233–0321* ⊕ *www.parks.wa.gov* ⊟ *Free. Parking $5* ⊙ *Daily 8 AM–sunset.*

In late May **Ft. Ebey State Park** blazes with native rhododendrons. West of Coupeville on Point Partridge, it has 22 acres of beach, campsites in the woods, trails to the headlands, World War II gun emplacements, wildflower meadows, spectacular views down Juan de Fuca Strait, and a boggy pond. ⊠ *3 mi west of Rte. 20* ☎ *360/678–4636 or 800/233–0321* ⊕ *www.parks.wa.gov* ⊟ *Free. Parking $5* ⊙ *Daily sunrise–sunset.*

WHERE TO STAY & EAT

$$$ ✗ **Rosi's.** Within a Victorian home, this restaurant has three candlelit dining rooms serving a combination of Italian and Pacific Northwest cuisine. Among the entrées are chicken *mascarpone* (cream cheese), osso buco, lamb chops, and Penn Cove mussels. Lunch is much less expensive than dinner. ⊠ *602 N. Main St.* ☎ *360/678–3989* ⊟ *AE, MC, V* ⊙ *No lunch weekends.*

$–$$ ✗ **Christopher's Front Street Cafe.** This eclectically furnished restaurant—whose tables are set with linens, fresh flowers, and candles—is warm and casual. The new American menu features local oysters and mussels, and such flavorful fare as raspberry barbecued salmon, bacon-wrapped pork tenderloin with mushrooms, lamb stew, and grilled ahi tuna—all prepared with a light touch. The wine list is extensive. ⊠ *23 Front St.* ☎ *360/678–5480* ⊟ *AE, MC, V.*

¢–$$$ ⊞ **Captain Whidbey Inn.** Almost a century old, this venerable madrona lodge on a wooded promontory offers a special kind of hospitality and charm now rarely found. The lodge rooms, furnished with antiques, tend to be small, but they are well appointed with modern amenities; rooms on the north side have splendid views of Penn Cove. There are additional rooms in a separate modern motel building overlooking a quiet saltwater lagoon. Gracefully aged, surrounded by native shrubs and trees, the Captain Whidbey is the perfect hideout for those who want to escape the stress of the modern age. ⊠ *2073 Captain Whidbey Inn Rd. (off Madrona Way), 98239* ☎ *360/678–4097 or 800/366–4097* ⊕ *www.captainwhidbey.com* ⇗ *25 rooms* ⚲ *Restaurant, bar, library* ⊟ *AE, MC, V.*

¢–$ ⊞ **Ft. Casey Inn.** The inn comprises nine Georgian revival duplexes built in 1907 to house U.S. Army artillery officers and their families. Stationed here until the 1940s, the officers manned coastal batteries designed to defend Puget Sound and the U.S. naval base at Bremerton. The duplexes stand on a hillside overlooking the former parade grounds. Each has a fireplace, two bedrooms, a living room, and a kitchen (with breakfast fixings on hand). Owners Gordon and Victoria Hoenig restored the tin ceilings and decorated the units with rag rugs, old quilts, hand-painted furniture, and sundry Colonial touches. ⊠ *1124 S. Engle Rd., 98239* ☎ *360/678–8792 and 866/661–6604* ⊕ *www.fortcaseyinn.com* ⇗ *9 units* ⚲ *Kitchens, bicycles* ⊟ *AE, MC, V.*

¢ ⊞ **Compass Rose Bed and Breakfast.** Inside this 1890 Queen Anne Victorian, a veritable museum of art, artifacts, and antiques awaits you. The proprietor's naval career carried him and his wife to all corners of the globe, from which they have collected the inn's unique adornments. The innkeepers' friendliness will make your stay all the more enjoyable and interesting. ⊠ *508 S. Main St., 98239* ☎☎ *360/678–5318* ☎ *800/237–3881* ⊕ *www.compassroseandb.com* ⇗ *2 rooms* ⚲ *Cable TV; no smoking* ⊟ *No credit cards* ⊠⦿ *BP.*

Oak Harbor

10 mi north of Coupeville.

Oak Harbor gets its name from the majestic Oregon oaks that grow above the bay. Dutch and Irish immigrants settled the town in the mid-1800s; several windmills in town were built by descendants of the Dutch as symbols of their heritage. The marina, at the east side of the bay, has a picnic area with views of Saratoga Passage and the entrance of Penn Cove.

Deception Pass State Park has 19 mi of rocky shore and beaches, three freshwater lakes, and more than 38 mi of forest and meadow trails. The park occupies the northernmost point of Whidbey Island and the southernmost tip of Fidalgo Island, on both sides of the Deception Pass Bridge. Park on Canoe Island and walk across the bridge for views of two dramatic saltwater gorges, whose tidal whirlpools have been known to swallow large logs. ✉ *Rte. 20, 7 mi north of Oak Harbor* ☎ *360/675–2417* ✉ *Park free; campsite fees vary* ☉ *Apr.–Sept., daily 6:30 AM–dusk; Oct.–Mar., daily 8 AM–dusk.*

WHERE TO EAT
$–$$

✗ **Island Grill.** This friendly roadside café in the woods south of Deception Pass serves fresh and flavorful American fare such as salads, burgers, and fish-and-chips. You can enjoy your meal in the comfortable dining room, or pick up food from the take-out window for a picnic on the waterfront at adjacent Deception Pass State Park. ✉ *41020 Rte. 20* ☎ *360/679–3194* ▭ *MC, V.*

Fidalgo Island

❸ *15 mi north of Oak Harbor.*

Anacortes has some well-preserved brick buildings along the waterfront, several well-maintained old commercial edifices downtown, and many beautiful older homes off the main drag.

The frequently changing exhibits at the **Anacortes Historical Museum** (✉ 1305 8th St., Anacortes ☎ 360/293–1915) focus on the cultural heritage of Fidalgo and nearby Guemes Island.

West of Anacortes, near the ferry landing, **Washington Park** has dense forests, sunny meadows, trails, and a boat launch. A narrow loop road winds through woods to overlooks with views of islands and saltwater. You can picnic or camp under tall trees near the shore. ✉ *12th St. and Oakes Ave.* ☎ *360/293–1927* ✉ *Free; camping $12–$15* ☉ *Daily sunrise–sunset.*

Where to Eat

$–$$$

✗ **Randy's Pier 61.** The dining room's nautical theme is in keeping with the waterfront setting. From here you can see across the channel to Guemes Island and the San Juans; don't be surprised if a sea lion looks up from the tide rips or if a bald eagle cruises by. Specialties include seafood gumbo, crab cakes, salmon Wellington, crab-stuffed prawns, and a beautifully flavored (and expertly cooked) apples-and-almond salmon. The staff is professional and friendly. ✉ *209 T Ave., Anacortes* ☎ *360/293–5108* ▭ *AE, D, MC, V.*

¢–$$

✗ **Rockfish Grill.** It's a comfortable family restaurant that's affiliated with the Anacortes Brewery. Both establishments are in a restored 1929 building that has seen many uses, including saloon, ice cream parlor, and plumbing shop. Note the mahogany back bar; it was crafted in Pennsylvania and once graced the Skagit Saloon. The food is simple but tasty pub fare: wood-fired pizzas and salmon, grilled steak, and pasta dishes as well as sandwiches, burgers, and fish-and-chips. Beers range from pilsner to amber ale, porter, stout, and seasonal brews. ✉ *320 Commercial Ave., Anacortes* ☎ *360/588–1720* 🖃 *MC, V.*

Shopping

Compass Wines (✉ 1405 Commercial Ave., Anacortes ☎ 360/293–6500) is one of the state's premier wine shops, with lots of hard-to-find vintages from small wineries whose annual releases sell out quickly. Besides wines, Compass purveys artisan cheeses, provisions yachts and charter boats, and assembles delectable lunch baskets.

Lopez Island

4 *45 minutes by ferry from Anacortes.*

Quiet and relatively flat Lopez, the island closest to the mainland, has gentle, sloping roads, pebbly beaches, and peaceful trails through the woods. Of the three San Juan islands with facilities to accommodate overnight visitors, Lopez has the smallest population (approximately 1,800), and with its old orchards, weathered barns, and rolling green pastures, it's the most rustic. Lopez Village, the only settlement, has a market, a few shops and galleries, a couple of restaurants, and a post office.

The **Lopez Island Historical Museum** has relics from the region's Native American tribes and early settlers, including some impressive ship and small-boat models and maps of local landmarks. ✉ *28 Washburn Pl., Lopez Village* ☎*360/468–2049* 🖃*Donations accepted* ⏱ *July and Aug., Wed.–Sun. noon–4; May, June, and Sept., Fri.–Sun. noon–4.*

Odlin County Park has a mile of sandy shoreline—a rarity on the shores of the Salish Sea. The park also has a pier, a floating dock, mooring buoys, ballparks, a covered cooking shack, and 30 campsites on 80 wooded acres. ✉ *Off Ferry Rd., 1 mi south of the ferry landing* ☎ *360/468–2496* 🖃*Free* ⏱ *Daily.*

A quiet forest trail along beautiful **Shark Reef** leads to an isolated headland jutting out above the bay. The sounds of raucous barks and squeals mean you're nearly there, and eventually you may see throngs of seals and seagulls on the rocky islets across from the point. Bring binoculars to spot bald eagles in the trees as you walk, and to view sea otters frolicking in the waves near the shore. The trail starts at the Shark Reef Road parking lot south of Lopez Village, and it's a 15-minute walk to the headland. ✉ *Off Shark Reef Rd., 2 mi south of Lopez Island Airport* ☎ *360/856–3500 or 800/527–3305* 🖃 *Free* ⏱ *Daily.*

Lopez Island Vineyard is spread over 6 acres about 1 mi north of Lopez Village. The winery produces chardonnay, merlot, and cabernet sauvignon–merlot blends, as well as sweeter wines, such as those made from raspberries, blackberries, and other local fruits. The tasting room is open Memorial Day through Labor Day, Wednesday through Sunday, from noon to 5 PM or by appointment in other seasons. ✉ *Fisherman Bay Rd., north of Cross Rd.* ☎ *360/468–3644* ⊕ *www.lopezislandvineyards. com* 🖃 *Free* ⏱ *Daily.*

Where to Stay & Eat

$$–$$$ ✕ **Bay Café.** Boats dock right outside this pretty waterside mansion at the entrance to Fisherman Bay. In winter sunlight streams into the window-framed dining room; in summer you can relax on the wraparound porch before a gorgeous sunset panorama. Seafood tapas, such as basil-and goat-cheese-stuffed prawns with saffron rice, or sea scallops with sun-dried tomatoes, delightfully tickle the palate. Homemade sorbet and a fine crème caramel are among the desserts. Weekend breakfasts draw huge crowds. ⊠ *Lopez Village* ☎ *360/468–3700* ▭ *MC, V* ☉ *No lunch. Closed Sun.–Thurs. Oct.–May.*

$–$$ 🏠 **Edenwild.** This large Victorian-style farmhouse, surrounded by gardens and framed by Fisherman's Bay, looks as if it's at least a century old, but it actually dates from 1988. Large rooms, each painted or papered in different pastel shades, are furnished with simple antiques; some have clawfoot tubs and brick fireplaces. The sunny dining room is a cheery breakfast spot. In summer you can sip tea on the wraparound ground-floor veranda or relax with a book on the garden patio. ⊠ *132 Lopez Village Rd., Lopez Village 98261* ☎ *360/468–3238 or 800/606–0662* 🖷 *360/468–4080* ⊕ *www.edenwildinn.com* ⇝ *6 rooms, 2 suites* ⌂ *Dining room; no kids under 13* ▭ *AE, D, MC, V* ⫶⊙⫶ *BP.*

Sports & the Outdoors

BICYCLING **Cycle San Juans** (⊠ Rte. 1 ☎ 360/468–3251) offers rentals and tours under the slogan "Cycle with bald Lopezian to discover island curiosities." **Lopez Bicycle Works** (⊠ 2847 Fisherman Bay Rd. ☎ 360/468–2847 ⊕ www.lopezbicycleworks.com) can bring bicycles to your door or the ferry.

BOATING & **Harmony Charters** (☎ 360/468–3310 ⊕ www.interisland.net/countess)
SAILING maintains a 63-foot, two-cabin motorboat, for lunch ($65) and dinner ($75) cruises, as well as for trips to British Columbia and Alaska ($200 per person per day). Prices include crew, food, sports equipment, utensils, and linens. **Kismet Sailing Charters** (☎ 360/468–2435 ⊕ www.rockisland.com/~sailkismet) makes eight-hour cruises ($450 per person), three-day cruises ($145 per person per day), and custom charter trips in a skippered 36-foot yacht.

SEA KAYAKING **Elakah! Expeditions** (☎ 360/734–7270 or 800/434–7270 ⊕ www.elakah.com), a family-run sea-kayaking company, leads kayaking clinics on Lopez and two- to five-day trips ($225 to $495) around the San Juans. Specialty trips, such as those for women only, are also organized. **Lopez Kayaks** (☎ 360/468–2847 ⊕ www.lopezkayaks.com), open May to October at Fisherman Bay, offers a four-hour tour of the southern end of Lopez for $75 and a two-hour sunset tour for $35. Kayak rentals start at $12 an hour or $40 per day, and the company can deliver kayaks to any point on the island.

Shopping

The **Chimera Gallery** (⊠ Village Rd. ☎ 360/468–3265), a local artists' cooperative, exhibits and sells crafts, jewelry, and fine art. **Fish Bay Mercantile** (⊠ Lopez Rd. ☎ 360/468–2126) is a fun, quirky gallery full of handcarved wooden masks and furnishings, handwoven shawls and blankets, handmade jewelry, and scenic paintings by island artists—plus quirky international stuff like the Hindu lunchbox collection. **Grayling Gallery** (⊠ 3630 Hummel Lake Rd. ☎ 360/468–2779) displays the paintings, prints, sculptures, and pottery works of nearly a dozen Lopez Island artists. **Islehaven Books** (⊠ Village Rd. ☎ 360/468–2132), which is supervised in part by the owner's pack of five Russian wolfhounds, is stocked with publications on San Juan Islands history and activities, as well as books about the Pacific Northwest. There's also a good selection of mysteries, literary novels, children's books, and craft kits, plus greeting cards, art prints, and maps. Many of the items sold here are the works of local writers, artists, and photographers.

Orcas Island

⑤ *75 minutes by ferry from Anacortes.*

Roads on flower-blossom–shape Orcas Island, the largest of the San Juans, sweep through wide valleys and rise to gorgeous hilltop views. Spanish explorers set foot here in 1791, and the island is named for their ship—not for the black-and-white whales that frolic in the surrounding waters. The island was also the home of Native American tribes, whose history is reflected in such places as Pole Pass, where the Lummi people used kelp and cedar-bark nets to catch ducks, and Massacre Bay, where in 1858 a tribe from southeast Alaska attacked a Lummi fishing village.

Today, farmers, fishermen, artists, retirees, and summer-home owners make up the population of about 4,000. Houses are spaced far apart, and towns typically have just one major road running through them. Resorts dotting the island's edges are evidence of the thriving local tourism industry. Orcas is a favorite place for weekend getaways from the Seattle area any time of the year, as well as one of the state's top settings for summer weddings.

Eastsound, the main town, lies at the head of the East Sound channel, which nearly divides the island in two. Small shops here sell jewelry, pottery, and crafts by local artisans. Along Prune Alley are a handful of stores and restaurants.

The Funhouse is a huge, nonprofit activity center and museum for families. Interactive exhibits on age, hearing, kinetics, video production, among other subjects, are all educational. Kids can explore an arts and crafts yurt, a climbing wall, a library, Internet stations, and a big metal "Jupiter" tree fort. Sports activities include indoor pitching cages and games, as well as an outdoor playground. Kids and adults can also take classes on music, theater, digital film, and poetry. There are free programs for pre-teens and teenagers on Friday and Saturday nights (hint to mom and dad, who might want to enjoy dinner alone on this romantic island). ⊠ *30 Pea Patch La., Eastsound* ☎ *360/376–7177* ⊕ *www.thefunhouse.org* ⊠ *$5* ⊙ *Sept.–June, weekdays 3–5:30, Sat. 11–3; July and Aug., Mon.–Sat. 11–5.*

Moran State Park comprises 5,000 acres of hilly, old-growth forests dotted with sparkling lakes, in the middle of which rises 2,400-foot-high Mt. Constitution, the tallest peak in the San Juans. A drive to the summit affords exhilarating views of the islands, the Cascades, the Olympics, and Vancouver Island. You can explore the terrain along 14 hiking trails and choose from among 151 campsites if you'd like to stay longer. ⊠ *Star Rte. 22, Head northeast from Eastsound on Horseshoe Hwy. and follow signs* ⊕ *Box 22, Eastsound 98245* ☎ *360/376–2326, 800/452–5678 for reservations* ⊠ *Camping $11 fee, plus $6 per night.*

Where to Stay & Eat

$$$–$$$$ ✕ **Christina's.** Copper-top tables and paintings by island artists enhance
Fodor's Choice this cozy bayside spot. The seasonal menu focuses on local seafood, pre-
★ pared with fresh herbs and served with vegetables. Look for delicacies like spring greens with fennel and Samish Bay cheese; roast chicken with mushroom bread pudding; and curry coconut fish stew. Fine views of the East Sound make for a romantic dinner on the rooftop terrace or the enclosed porch. An excellent wine list and a bevy of rich desserts complement every meal. This is a place to propose. ⊠ *310 N. Beach Rd., Eastsound* ☎ *360/376–4904* ⊟ *AE, DC, MC, V* ⊙ *Closed Tues. Oct.–mid-June. No lunch.*

¢–$ ✕ **Bilbo's Festivo.** Stucco walls, colorful tiles, and wood benches reflect this restaurant's Tex-Mex inclinations. And believe it or not, the food here is healthy. The fresh, delectable burritos, enchiladas, and chalupas are lard-free. There's also fabulous homemade guacamole and locally-grown organic salad greens. Margaritas are served in the courtyard in summer, and you can warm your hands around the patio firepit on cool autumn evenings. Kids dash immediately to the outdoor play area. ✉ *N. Beach Rd. and A St., Eastsound* ☎ *360/376–4728* ⌖ *Reservations not accepted* 🖃 *AE, MC, V* ⊘ *No lunch Oct.–May.*

$$$–$$$$ ▨ **Rosario Spa & Resort.** Shipbuilding magnate Robert Moran built this Mediterranean-style mansion on Cascade Bay in 1906. It's now on the National Register of Historic Places and worth a visit even if you're not staying here. The house has retained its original Mission-style furniture and numerous antiques; its centerpiece, an Aeolian organ with 1,972 pipes, is used for summer concerts in the ballroom. Some of the rooms are compact and basic; others are luxurious suites with outdoor decks, Jacuzzis, gas fireplaces, and kitchens. You can hike, kayak, and scuba dive nearby or stay in for a day of pampering in the downstairs Avanyu Spa. From your room you can watch seaplanes splash down in the bay and fishing and sailboat charters come into the marina. With prior notice, a Rosario shuttle will meet you at the ferry dock and take you to the hotel. ✉ *1 Rosario Way, Eastsound 98245* ☎ *360/376–2222 or 800/562–8820* ⊕ *www.rosario.rockresorts.com* ⟿ *111 rooms, 4 suites* ⌃ *2 restaurants, cable TV, some in-room hot tubs, some kitchens, 2 tennis courts, 3 pools (1 indoor), fitness classes, gym, hot tub, sauna, spa, dock, boating, fishing, boccie, croquet, hiking, horseshoes, shuffleboard, volleyball, lounge, concert hall, shop, children's program (ages 5–13), concierge, Internet, business services, meeting rooms* 🖃 *AE, DC, MC, V.*

¢–$$$ ▨ **Turtleback Farm Inn.** Eighty acres of meadow, forest, and farmland in the shadow of Turtleback Mountain surround this forest-green inn. Rooms are divided between the carefully restored late-19th-century green-clapboard farmhouse and the newer cedar Orchard House. All are well-lit, with hardwood floors, wood trim, and colorful curtains and quilts, some of which are made from the fleece of resident sheep. The inn is a favorite place for local weddings. Breakfast is in the dining room or on the deck overlooking the valley. The Elopement package includes a minister, flowers, champagne, photos, and more. ✉ *1981 Crow Valley Rd., Eastsound 98245* ☎ *360/376–3914 or 800/376–4914* 🖷 *360/376–5329* ⊕ *www.turtlebackinn.com* ⟿ *11 rooms* ⌃ *Dining room, bar* 🖃 *MC, V* ⊺⊙⌁ *BP.*

¢–$ ▨ **Doe Bay Village Resort & Retreat.** Neohippies and outdoorsy types flock to this commune and hostel, formerly a nudist colony, at the eastern tip of Orcas. Patchwork accommodations include tent and RV sites, yurts and geodomes, and cabins. The hostel has one private room for couples and another room with six beds. The window-lined, wood-floored Café Doe Bay, which faces the ocean, is open daily for self-serve breakfasts at $1 per item; dinners are served two or three times per week, depending on the number of resort guests and the cook's whim. The small beach is perfect for kayak launches. Cabin guests have free access to the resort's mineral baths and sauna ($4 for others). ✉ *Star Rte. 86 off Pt. Lawrence Rd. near Olga* ⌂ *Box 437, Olga 98279* ☎ *360/376–2291* 🖷 *360/376–4755* ⊕ *www.doebay.com* ⟿ *30 cabins, 7 yurts, 3 geodomes, 15 campsites, 2 RV sites, 1 house, 2 rooms, 1 6-bed dorm* ⌃ *Café, hot tub, massage, sauna, beach, volleyball, mineral bath* 🖃 *AE, MC, V.*

Sports & the Outdoors

BICYCLES &   **The Boardwalk** (✉ Orcas Village ☎ 360/376–2791 ⊕ www.
MOPEDS   orcasislandboardwalk.com), at the ferry landing, rents road and mountain bikes. **Key Moped Rental** (✉ Eastsound ☎ 360/376–2474) rents mopeds May through October. **Susie's Mopeds** (✉ Eastsound ☎ 360/376–5266 or 800/532–0087) rents mopeds June through September.

BOATING &   **Amante Sail Tours** (✉ Deer Harbor ☎ 360/376–4231) offers half-day sail-
SAILING   ing trips for up to six people for $35 per person. **Deer Harbor Charters**

(✉ Deer Harbor ☎ 360/376–5989 ⊕ www.deerharborcharters.com) has several small sailboats making half-day cruises around the San Juans for $45 to $75 per person. Outboards and skiffs are also available, as is fishing gear. **Orcas Boat Rentals** (✉ Deer Harbor ☎ 360/376–7616 ⊕ www.orcasboats.com) has sailboats, outboards, and skiffs for full and half-day trips. **West Beach Resort** (⊕ 3 mi west of Eastsound ☎ 360/376–2240 or 800/937–8224 ⊕ www.westbeachresort.com) rents motorized boats, kayaks and canoes, and fishing gear.

SEA KAYAKING   **Crescent Beach Kayaks** (✉ Eastsound ☎ 360/376–2464) caters to families with free instruction and kayak rentals. **Orcas Outdoors Sea Kayak Tours** (✉ Orcas Village ☎ 360/376–2222 ⊕ www.orcasoutdoors.com) has one- and three-hour journeys, as well as day trips and rentals; a second branch is based at the Outlook Inn in Eastsound. **Osprey Tours** (✉ Eastsound ☎ 360/376–3677 or 800/529–2567 ⊕ www.fidalgo.net/~kayak) uses handcrafted wooden Aleutian-style kayaks for half-day, full-day, and overnight tours of the islands.

SCUBA DIVING   **Island Dive & Water Sports** (✉ Rosario Resort, Eastsound ☎ 360/376–7615 ⊕ www.divesanjuan.com) has a dive shop with rentals and offers a complete program of services, including instruction, airfills, and charter trips. Two custom dive boats make two-tank dives for $75 with gear; resort packages are available. **West Beach Resort** (✉ West Beach ☎ 360/376–2240 or 877/937–8224) is a popular dive spot where you can fill your own tanks.

WHALE-WATCHING   **Deer Harbor Charters** (☎ 360/376–5989 or 800/544–5758) has whale-watching cruises around the island straits. **Eclipse Charters** (☎ 360/376–4663 or 800/376–6566 ⊕ www.orcasislandwhales.com) searches around Orcas Island for whale pods and other wildlife. **Whale Spirit Adventures** (✉ West Sound Marina ☎ 360/376–5052 or 800/376–8018 ⊕ www.whalespirit.com) offers whale-sighting tours to the accompaniment of new-age chanting or flutes.

Shopping

Crow Valley Pottery (✉ 2274 Orcas Rd., Eastsound ☎ 360/376–2351 or 800/684–4297 ⊕ www.crowvalley.com) carries ceramics, metalworks, blown glass, and sculptures. **Darvill's Rare Print Shop** (✉ Eastsound ☎ 360/376–2351) specializes in maps and unique bird and floral prints. **Orcas Island Artworks** (✉ Main St., Olga ☎ 360/376–4408 ⊕ www.orcasisland.com/artworks) displays pottery, sculpture, jewelry, art glass, paintings, and quilts by resident artists.

San Juan Island

❻   *45 minutes by ferry from Orcas Island, 75 minutes by ferry from Anacortes.*

Lummi Indians were the first settlers on San Juan, with encampments along the north end of the island. North-end beaches were especially busy during the annual salmon migration, when hundreds of tribal members would gather along the shoreline to fish, cook, and exchange news. Many of the Lummi tribe were killed by smallpox and other imported diseases in the 18th and 19th centuries. Smallpox Bay was where tribal members plunged into the icy water to cool the fevers that came with the disease.

The 18th century brought explorers from England and Spain, but the island remained sparsely populated until the mid-1800s. From the 1880s Friday Harbor and its newspaper were controlled by lime-company owner and Republican bigwig John S. McMillin, who virtually ran San

Juan Island as a personal fiefdom from 1886 until his death in 1936. The town's main street, rising from the harbor and ferry landing up the slopes of a modest hill, hasn't changed much in the past few decades, though the cafés and shops are snazzier now than they were in the 1960s and '70s. San Juan is the most convenient Pacific Northwest island to visit, since you can take the ferry here and explore the entire island by public transportation or bicycle.

You'll recognize the **Whale Museum** by the mural painted on its exterior. Models of whales and whale skeletons, recordings of whale sounds, and videos of whales are the attractions. Workshops survey marine-mammal life and San Juan ecology. ⊠ *62 1st St. N* ☎ *360/378–4710* ⊕ *www.whale-museum.org* ✉ *$6* ✆ *June–Sept., daily 10–5; Oct.–May, daily 11–4.*

The **San Juan Historical Museum**, in an old farmhouse, presents island life at the turn of the 20th century through historic photography, documents, and buildings. ⊠ *405 Price St.* ☎ *360/378–405* ⊕ *www.sjmuseum.org* ✉ *$3* ✆ *Oct.–Apr., Tues. and Thurs. 10–2; May–Sept., Thurs.–Sat. 1–4.*

To watch whales cavorting in Haro Strait, head to **Lime Kiln Point State Park,** on San Juan's western side just 6 mi from Friday Harbor. The little white 1914 lighthouse is a landmark for boats cruising these waters. The best period for sighting whales is from the end of April through August, but a resident pod of orcas regularly cruises past the point. ⊠ *6158 Lighthouse Rd.* ☎ *360/378–2044* ✉ *Free* ✆ *Daily 8 AM–10 PM.*

★ ☾ **San Juan Island National Historic Park** commemorates the Pig War, in which the United States and Great Britain nearly went to war over their respective claims on the San Juan Islands. The dispute began in 1859 when an American settler killed a British soldier's pig, and escalated until roughly 500 American soldiers and 2,200 British soldiers with five warships were poised for battle. Fortunately, no blood was spilled and the disagreement was finally settled in 1872 in the Americans' favor, with Emperor William I of Germany as arbitrator.

The park comprises two separate areas on opposite sides of the island. English Camp, in a sheltered cove of Garrison Bay on the northern end, includes a blockhouse, a commissary, and barracks. American Camp, on the southern end, has a visitor center and the remains of fortifications. From June to August you can take guided hikes and see reenactments of 1860s-era military life. ⊠ *American Camp 6 mi southeast of Friday Harbor; English Camp 9 mi northwest of Friday Harbor; Park Headquarters, 125 Spring St., Friday Harbor* ☎ *360/468–3663* ⊕ *www. nps.gov/sajh.*

★ ☾ The **San Juan Center for Art & Nature** is essentially a 19-acre open-air art gallery within the spectacular Westcott Bay Reserve. You can stroll along winding trails to view more than 80 sculptures spread amid freshwater and saltwater wetlands, open woods, blossoming fields, and rugged terrain. The park is also a haven for birds; more than 120 species nest and breed here. Art workshops and events are scheduled throughout the year in the tented area. ⊠ *Westcott Dr., off Roche Harbor Rd.,* ☎ *360/370–5050* ⊕ *www.wbay.org.*

It's hard to believe that fashionable **Roche Harbor** at the northern end of San Juan Island was once the most important producer of builder's lime on the West Coast. In 1882 John S. McMillin gained control of the lime company and expanded production. But even in its heyday as a limestone quarrying village, Roche Harbor was known for abundant flowers and welcoming accommodations. McMillin transformed a bunkhouse into private lodgings for his invited guests, who included such notables as Teddy Roosevelt. The guest house is now the Hotel de Haro, which displays period photographs and artifacts in its lobby. The staff has maps of the old quarry, kilns, and the Mausoleum, an eerie Greek-inspired memorial to McMillin.

McMillin's heirs operated the quarries and plant until 1956, when they sold the company to the Tarte family. Although the old lime kilns still stand below the bluff, the company town has become a resort. Locals say it took two years for the limestone dust to wash off the trees around the harbor. McMillin's former home is now a restaurant, and workers' cottages have been transformed into comfortable visitors' lodgings. With its rose gardens, cobblestone waterfront, and well-manicured lawns, Roche Harbor retains the flavor of its days as a hangout for McMillin's powerful friends—especially since the sheltered harbor is very popular with well-to-do pleasure boaters.

Where to Stay & Eat

$$-$$$ ✗ **Duck Soup Inn.** Blossoming vines thread over the cedar-shingled walls
Fodor'sChoice of this restaurant. Inside, island-inspired paintings and a flagstone fire-
★ place are the background for creative meals served at comfortable booths. Everything is made from scratch daily, including sourdough bruschetta and ice cream. You might start with Thai-style prawn roll-ups, made with peanuts, scallions, coconut, hot chilies, lime, and fresh mint; or perhaps applewood-smoked Westcott Bay oysters. For a second course, you might have grilled quail or chili rellenos. Vegetarian options and child portions are available. Northwest, California, and European wines are also on hand. ⊠ *50 Duck Soup La.* ☎ *360/378–4878* ▭ *MC, V* ⊘ *Closed Nov.–Mar. and Mon.–Tues. No lunch.*

¢–$ ✗ **Front Street Ale House.** This dark, woodsy English-style ale house serves traditional pub fare: bangers and mash (sausages and mashed potatoes), bubble and squeak (grilled cabbage and mashed potatoes), and a terrific shepherd's pie. A draught from the adjacent San Juan Brewing Company is the perfect accompaniment—try the Pig War Stout or Royal Marine Pale Ale. If you can't decide what to drink, choose the beer sampler, which comes with five types of draughts served in shot glasses. On Thursdays in winter, the bar hosts adults-only trivia tournaments, during which local contestants win kooky, white elephant–style prizes. The second-floor Top Side area has a dance floor and great harbor views. ⊠ *1 Front St., Friday Harbor* ☎ *360/378–2337* ⚓ *Reservations not accepted* ▭ *AE, MC, V.*

$$$–$$$$ 🏨 **Friday Harbor House.** This contemporary hotel takes advantage of its bluff-top location with floor-to-ceiling windows that overlook the marina, ferry landing, and San Juan Channel below. Sleek, modern, wood furnishings and fabrics in beige hues fill the rooms, all of which have fireplaces, deep jetted tubs, and at least partial views of the water. The elegant restaurant serves seasonal meals and special wine-tasting dinners, often to a backdrop of glowing sunsets in summer. ⊠ *130 West St., Friday Harbor 98250* ☎ *360/378–8455* 🖷 *360/378–8453* ⊕ *www.fridayharborhouse.com* 🛏 *20 rooms* ⚒ *Restaurant, in-room data ports, in-room hot tubs, refrigerators, cable TV; no smoking* ▭ *MC, V* ⎮◯⎮ *CP.*

★ $$ 🏨 **Panacea Bed and Breakfast.** Steel magnate Peter Kirk had this Craftsman bungalow built as a summer home in 1907. Rooms are all differently decorated: the Garden Room has a botanical motif, the sunny Trellis Room is done in peach hues, and the Arbor Room has French doors leading out to the garden. You may take breakfast in the parlor—or have it in bed, served on antique Limoges china. Bountiful wicker-basket picnics, with all the trimmings, can be prepared for a day's excursion. ⊠ *595 Park St., Friday Harbor 98250* ☎ *360/378–3757 or 800/639–2762*

☎ 360/378–8543 ⊕ www.panacea-inn.com ⇆ 4 rooms ⚘ Dining room, picnic area, some in-room hot tubs, cable TV, airport shuttle; no a/c, no room phones, no kids, no smoking ⊟ MC, V �{○} BP.

¢ ⊞ **Roche Harbor Resort.** First a log trading post built in 1845, and later an 1880s lime-industry complex, including hotel, homes, and offices, this sprawling resort is still centered around the lime deposits that made John S. McMillan his fortune in the late 19th century. Rooms are filled with notable antiques, like the clawfoot tub where actor John Wayne used to soak. Luxury suites in the separate McMillan House have fireplaces, heated bathroom floors, and panoramic water views from a private veranda. The beachside Company Town Cottages, once the homes of lime company employees, have rustic exteriors but modern interiors. Elsewhere are contemporary condos with fireplaces; some have lofts and water views. Walking trails thread through the resplendent gardens and the old lime quarries. The resort is a very popular boating base, as it's an official entry point to Canada, just 15 mi to the north. ⊠ *4950 Reuben Memorial Dr., Roche Harbor 98250, 10 mi northwest of Friday Harbor off Roche Harbor Rd.* ☎ *360/378–2155 or 800/451–8910* ⊟ *360/ 378–6809* ⊕ *www.rocheharbor.com* ⇆ *16 rooms without bath, 14 suites, 9 cottages, 20 condos* ⚘ *Restaurant, café, coffee shop, grill, grocery, some kitchens, some minibars, some microwaves, some refrigerators, cable TV in some rooms, some in-room VCRs, tennis court, pool, dock, boating, marina, shops, playground, airstrip, travel services; no TVs in some rooms* ⊟ *AE, MC, V.*

Sports & the Outdoors

BOATING & SAILING
Amante Sail Tours (☎ 360/376–4321) leads morning and afternoon sails for two to six guests. **Charters Northwest** (☎ 360/378–7196) offers three-day and week-long full-service sailboat and powerboat charters. **Harmony Sailing Charters** (☎ 360/468–3310) conducts day-long and multi-day sailboat charters throughout the San Juan Islands and the Pacific Northwest. **Kismet Sailing Charters** (☎ 360/468–2435) leads overnight excursions through the San Juans and southwest Canada on a 36-foot-long customized yacht. **Snug Harbor Resort Marina** (☎ 360/378–4762) provides marina services and van service to and from Friday Harbor, including ferry and airport shuttle service, and rents small powerboats.

SCUBA DIVING
Island Dive & Water Sports (⊠ Friday Harbor ☎ 360/378–2772), at the waterfront, is a full-service dive shop with classes, equipment, airfills, and charters. Single-tank dives cost $55 and two-tank dives cost $75, with gear included. Overnight adventure packages with two days of diving start at $200.

SEA KAYAKING
Crystal Seas Kayaking (☎ 360/378–7899 or 888/625–7245) combines sea kayaking and sailing trips. **A Leisure Kayak Rentals** (☎ 360/378–5992 or 800/836–8224) will shuttle you from the ferry to the start of your kayaking class; hourly, daily, and overnight tours are also scheduled. **San Juan Kayak Expeditions** (☎ 360/378–4436) runs kayaking and camping tours in two-person kayaks.

WHALE-WATCHING
Salish Sea Charters (☎ 360/378–8555 or 877/560–5711) has three tours per day from April through September that get you right up next to the orcas. **Western Prince Cruises** (☎ 360/378–5315 or 800/757–6722) operates a four-hour narrated whale-watching tour.

Shopping

Rainshadow Arts (⊠ 20 1st St., Friday Harbor ☎ 360/378–0988 ⊕ www. rainshadow-arts.com) displays Pacific Northwest arts and crafts: baskets, pottery, watercolors, sculpture, photographs, and clocks. **Waterworks Gallery** (⊠ 315 Argyle St., Friday Harbor ☎ 360/378–3060) represents eclectic, contemporary artists.

Near Friday Harbor, the **San Juan Vineyards** (✉ 2000 Roche Harbor Rd. ☎ 360/378–9463 or 888/983–9463), 3 mi north of Friday Harbor, has a winery, tasting room, and gift shop, and organizes such special events as May barrel tastings, "Bottling Day" in July, volunteer grape-harvesting in October, and winter wine classes and tastings. Visit **Westcott Bay Sea Farms** (✉ 904 Westcott Dr., off Roche Harbor Rd. ☎ 360/378–2489), a rustic oyster farm tucked into a small bay 2 mi south of Roche Harbor, for some of the tasty oysters, especially from November through April.

The Islands A to Z

To research prices, get advice from other travelers, and book travel arrangements, visit www.fodors.com.

BOAT & FERRY TRAVEL

Washington State Ferries ply Puget Sound, including from Seattle to Bainbridge Island; between Mukilteo and Clinton, on Whidbey Island; and between Port Townsend and Keystone, also on Whidbey. You can get updated ferry information on the Web site.

Washington State ferries depart from Anacortes, about 76 mi north of Seattle, to the San Juan Islands. Sunny weekends and summer months mean long lines of cars at ferry terminals all around the San Juan Islands. No reservations are accepted (except for the Sidney–Anacortes run from mid-May through September). Passengers and bicycles load first, and loading stops two minutes before sailing time.

The Mosquito Fleet connects Everett to Friday Harbor daily from early July through Labor Day, Thursday through Sunday in September, and weekends in October for $39.50. The *San Juan Island Commuter* has daily scheduled service for $35 one-way to 16 islands in the San Juans, including four islands that are state parks. The ferry also carries kayaks, bicycles, and camping equipment. April through October, the *P.S. Express* passenger-only ferry cruises daily from Port Townsend to Friday Harbor for $53 one-way.

🚢 **Boat & Ferry Information Mosquito Fleet** ☎ 425/252–6800 or 800/325–6722 🌐 www.whalewatching.com. **P.S. Express** ☎ 360/385–5288 🌐 www.pugetsoundexpress. com. **San Juan Island Commuter** ✉ Bellingham Cruise Terminal, 355 Harris Ave., No. 104, Bellingham ☎ 360/734–8180 or 888/734–8180. **Washington State Ferries** ☎ 206/464–6400, 888/808–7977, or 800/843–3779 (automated line) in WA and BC 🌐 www.wsdot.wa.gov/ferries.

CAR TRAVEL

You can reach Whidbey Island by heading north from Seattle or south from the Canadian border on I–5, west on Route 20 onto Fidalgo Island, and south across Deception Pass Bridge. A traffic hazard unique to western Washington is called a "sun-slowdown." A motorist slows way down when faced by the spectacle of the heavenly orb popping into his or her line of vision. These peculiar events are even mentioned on regional radio road reports.

To reach the San Juan Islands from Seattle, drive north on I–5 to Exit 230. From here, head west on Route 20 and follow signs to Anacortes, the mainland terminal for ferry travel to the islands. You may have to wait in long lines to take your car on the ferry. You can avoid the lines by leaving your car on the mainland and arranging for pick-up service at the island ferry terminal. Most B&B owners provide this service with prior arrangement.

Island roads have one or two lanes, and all carry two-way traffic. Slow down and hug the shoulder when passing another car on a one-lane road.

Expect rough patches, potholes, fallen branches, wildlife, and other hazards—plus the distractions of sweeping water views. Carry food and water, since you may want to stop frequently to explore.

VISITOR INFORMATION

Tourist Information Anacortes Chamber of Commerce ⌧ 819 Commercial Ave., Suite G, Anacortes ☎ 360/293-7911. **Bainbridge Island Chamber of Commerce** ⌧ 590 Winslow Way ☎ 206/842-3700 ⊕ www.bainbridgechamber.com. **Central Whidbey Chamber of Commerce** ⌧ 5 S. Main St., Coupeville ☎ 360/678-5434 ⊕ www.centralcoupevillechamber.com. **Greater Oak Harbor Chamber of Commerce** ⌧ 32630 Hwy. 20, Oak Harbor ☎ 360/675-3535 ⊕ www.oakharborchamber.org. **Langley Chamber of Commerce** ⌧ 124½ 2nd St., Langley ☎ 360/221-6765. **San Juan Islands Visitors Bureau** ⌧ Box 98, Friday Harbor 98250 ☎ 360/468-3748 ⊕ www.sanjuanislander.com.

THE PARKS

Countless snow-clad mountain spires dwarf glacial valleys and lowland, old-growth forests in North Cascades National Park. Considered by some the most spectacular mountain scenery in the lower 48 states, the untrammeled expanse covers 505,000 acres of rugged mountain land. Only Route 20 (North Cascades Highway) traverses the park, and it's closed by snow at Diablo Lake half the year. Furthermore, it's within the Ross Lake National Recreation Area and Okanogan National Forest and never touches the park itself, which is almost entirely roadless.

Area towns include La Connor (68 mi north of Seattle), where Morris Graves, Kenneth Callahan, and other painters set up shop in the 1940s; Mount Vernon, an attractive riverfront community 11 mi northwest of La Connor; and Sedro-Woolley, a former mill and logging town that's 9 mi northeast of Mount Vernon and is a gateway to park. Note that you're better off making Mount Vernon or even La Connor a hub for park exploration: Sedro-Woolley's hotels and restaurants reflect the fact that the town is in something of a slump.

Wilderness covers much of the rugged Olympic Peninsula, the westernmost corner of the continental United States. Its heart of craggy mountains and a 60-mi strech of its ocean shore are safeguarded in Olympic National Park, 95% of which is designated wilderness land. Several thousand acres more are protected in Olympic National Forest, five wilderness areas, and seven Indian reservations.

With a population of about 19,000, Port Angeles (84 mi northwest of Seattle) is the Olympic Peninsula's largest town and a major gateway to Olympic National Park. Sprawling along the hills above the Strait of San Juan de Fuca, Port Angeles is also a main sea-transport link for car and passenger ferries sailing to Victoria, British Columbia. The former logging town of Forks, 56 mi southwest of Port Angeles, is a small, quiet gateway town for Olympic National Park's Hoh River valley unit.

Mt. Rainier is so massive that its summit is often obscured by its own shoulders. When the summit *is* visible—from up-close vantage points—the views are breathtaking. The impressive volcanic peak stands at an elevation of 14,411 feet, making it the fifth highest in the lower 48 states. More than 2 million visitors a year return home with a lifelong memory of its image. Its 235,612 acres were preserved by President McKinley in 1899, when he made it the nation's fifth national park. Douglas fir, western hemlock, and western red-cedar—some more than 1,000 years old—stand in cathedral-like groves. Dozens of thundering waterfalls are accessible from the road or by a short hike.

The town of Ashford (80 mi south of Seattle) sits astride an ancient trans-Cascades trail used by the Yakama Indians to trade with the natives of western Washington. The town began as a logging railway terminal; today, the village provides access to Nisqually (Longmire) entrance to Mt. Rainier National Park, and caters to 2 million annual visitors with lodges, restaurants, groceries, and gift shops along Route 706.

Packwood, 13 mi southwest of Mt. Rainier National Park's Steven's Canyon entrance, is a pretty village on Route 12, below White Pass. It's a great base for exploring wilderness areas as it's between Mt. Rainier and Mt. St. Helens. From Randle to the west, a road runs through national forest land to the east side of Mt. St. Helens and the Windy Ridge Viewpoint, the best place from which to observe the destruction wrought by the 1980 eruption and the dramatic renewal of the natural landscape.

North Cascades National Park

❼ *Park's west entrance, on Rte. 20 (North Cascades Hwy.), is 65 mi from I–5.*

Grizzly bears and wolves are believed to inhabit the North Cascades, along with other endemic wildlife. Bald eagles are present year-round along the Skagit River and the various lakes. In December, they flock by the hundreds to the Skagit to feed on a rare winter salmon run, remaining through January. Black bears are often seen in spring and early summer along the road in the high country, feeding on new green growth. Deer and elk are often seen in early morning and late evening, grazing and browsing at forest's edge.

The park never closes, though access is limited by winter snows. Summer is peak season—and up here, summer begins in July and ends around Labor Day—especially along the alpine stretches of the North Cascades Highway. Wildflowers paint the mountain meadows, hummingbirds and songbirds pepper the forest air, and even the high ridges are pleasantly warm. Although the views are best this time of year—when the usual spate of Pacific storms moderates—valleys can still start the day shrouded in fog.

Autumn brings crisp nights and many cool, sunny days. The North Cascades Highway is a popular drive in September and October, when the changing leaves—on larch, the only conifer that sheds its leaves, as well as aspen, vine maple, huckleberry, and cottonwood—make a colorful show. Snow closes the North Cascades Highway by November, and the road doesn't fully reopen until late April.

Visitors centers—with pay phones, bathrooms, park information, nature walks, lectures, and children's programs—are found along the North Cascades Highway in Sedro-Woolley, in Marblemount, Newhalem, and Winthrop, and in Stehekin (accessible only by boat, plane, or on foot) at the head of Lake Chelan. Several trails are also accessible along this route, including Sterling Munro, River Loop, and Rock Shelter, three short trails into lowland old-growth forest, all at Mile 120 near Newhalem; and the Happy Creek Forest Trail at Mile 134. Campgrounds aside, there are no lodging facilities in the park; for a hotel or restaurant you'll have to head to a nearby town.

A Northwest Forest Pass, $5 per day or $30 per annum, is required for hiking in North Cascades National Park, Ross Lake National Recreation Area, and most of Mt. Baker-Snoqualmie National Forest. A free wilderness permit is required for overnight backcountry activities; you can acquire one—in person only—at the Wilderness Information Center in Marblemount or at park ranger stations.

From Sedro-Woolley, **North Cascades Highway** (Route 20) winds through the green pastures and woods of the slowly narrowing upper Skagit Valley. As the mountains close in on the river and the highway, the road climbs only imperceptibly. Skagit Valley, like other valleys of the North Cascades, was cut below sea level by the glaciers of the last ice age, some 15,000 years ago. Close to sea level, the largely flat valley floor was created when the gash was filled in with alluvial deposit carried down from the mountains by the rivers. Beyond Concrete, a former cement-manufacturing town, the road begins to climb into the mountains, to Ross and Diablo dams.

East of Ross Lake, several turnouts offer great views of the lake and the snow-capped peaks surrounding it. The whitish rocks in the road cuts are limestone and marble. Meadows along this stretch of the highway are covered with wildflowers from June to September; nearby slopes are golden and red with fall foliage from late September through October. The pinnacle point of this stretch is 5,477-foot-high Washington Pass, east of which the road drops down along Early Winters Creek to the Methow Valley in a series of dramatic switchbacks (with vista turnouts).

From the Methow Valley, Route 153 takes the scenic route down the Methow River, with its apple, nectarine, and peach orchards, to Pateros on the Columbia River. From here, you can continue east to Grand Coulee or south to Lake Chelan.

North Cascades National Park Headquarters, the major administrative center, is a good place to pick up passes and permits, as well as to obtain information about current conditions. ✉ *810 Rte. 20, Sedro-Woolley* ☎ *360/856–5700* ⊕ *www.nps.gov/noca* ☾ *Mid-Oct.–mid-May, weekdays 8–4:30; late May–mid-Oct., daily 8–4:30.*

The **North Cascades Institute** (NCI) offers classes, field trips, and wilderness adventures such as backpack trips to hot springs within the Cascades. Contact them for information about these events or for a comprehensive catalog of books, guides, maps, and other materials. Especially popular are hiking guides such as *Best Easy Day Hikes in the North Cascades* and *100 Hikes in the North Cascades.* ✉ *810 Rte. 20, Sedro-Woolley* ☎ *360/856–5700 Ext. 209, 291, or 515* ⊕ *www. ncascades.org or www.nwpubliclands.com.*

The **North Cascades Visitor Center** has an extensive series of displays on the natural features of the surrounding landscape. You can learn about the history and value of old-growth trees, the many creatures that depend on the temperate rain-forest ecology, and the effects of human activity. Park rangers frequently conduct programs; check bulletin boards for schedules. ✉ *Rte. 20, Newhalem* ☎ *206/386–4495 Ext. 11* ☾ *Memorial Day–Labor Day, daily 9–4:30; Labor Day–Memorial Day, weekends 9–4:30.*

Where to Stay & Eat

$–$$$ ✗ **Kerstin's.** The intimate dining room overlooks the channel. The menu, which changes seasonally, includes portobello mushrooms roasted with pesto, pan-braised fresh king salmon, pork tenderloin, rib eye steak with Indonesian spices, halibut, and lamb shank with port wine sauce. The oysters baked in garlic-cilantro butter and finished with Parmesan are particularly popular. ✉ *505 S. 1st St., La Conner* ☎ *360/466–9111* ▭ *AE, DC, MC, V* ☾ *Closed Tues.*

¢–$ ✗ **Calico Cupboard.** This storefront bakery–café turns out some of the best pastries in Skagit County. It's very popular for breakfast and lunch and can become uncomfortably crowded on summer weekends (in which case you can buy the goodies at the take-out counter for a picnic in the park). ✉ *720 S. 1st St., La Conner* ☎ *360/466–4451* ⊟ *No credit cards* ⊘ *No dinner.*

¢–$ ✕ **Skagit River Brewing Company.** A former produce warehouse now houses one of western Washington's best microbreweries, along with a pub serving better-than-average food. Highlights include wood-fired pizzas, a half-pound pub burger, and a big bean burrito. Hewn-wood tables and comfortable couches make lounging inviting. There's a barbecue grill right outside, where the chef will prepare your ribs or chicken wings. ✉ *404 S. 3rd St., Mount Vernon* ☎ *360/336–2884* ⊟ *AE, MC, V.*

$–$$ ✕▥ **Wild Iris.** Right next to the sligtly less expensive Heron, this B&B is a large, sprawling, modern (1992) Victorian-style inn. Most of the rooms are suites, and these have CD players, robes, fireplaces, whirlpool spa tubs, and private decks or balconies. The small (24-seat) restaurant, Le Jardin ($$–$$$), serves dinners made with local ingredients. Dishes include wild salmon with seasonal herbs, seared beef fillet with a black-currant demi-glace, and wild mushroom polenta. There's a six-course tasting menu for $69 ($49 without wine). ✉ *121 Maple Ave., La Conner 98257* ☎ *360/466–1400* ⊕ *www.wildiris.com* ⇥ *4 rooms, 12 suites* ♿ *Restaurant, cable TV, in-room data ports; no a/c* ⊟ *AE, MC, V* ⊠ *BP.*

$–$$$ ▥ **La Conner Channel Lodge.** La Conner's only waterfront hotel is an understated modern facility overlooking the narrow Swinomish Channel. Each room has a private balcony and a gas fireplace and is decorated in subdued gray tones with wooden trim; 12 rooms have whirlpool baths. ✉ *205 N. 1st St., La Conner 98257* ☎ *360/466–1500* ⊟ *360/466–5902* ⊕ *www.laconnerlodging.com* ⇥ *29 rooms, 12 suites* ♿ *Business services, meeting room* ⊟ *AE, D, DC, MC, V* ⊠ *CP.*

¢–$ ▥ **Heron.** This B&B, in a Victorian house, has a stone fireplace in the parlor. The rooms are spacious, and the homemade breads and muffins served with breakfast in the formal dining room are scrumptious. The on-site Watergrass Day Spa offers organic skin-care treatments and massage therapies that are simultanously simple and luxurious. ✉ *117 Maple Ave., La Conner 98257* ☎ *360/466–4626* ⊟ *360/466–3254* ⊕ *www.theheron.com* ⇥ *9 rooms, 3 suites* ♿ *Hot tub, spa, some pets allowed (fee); no a/c* ⊟ *AE, MC, V* ⊠ *BP.*

¢–$ ▥ **Hotel Planter.** This renovated hotel, the oldest in La Conner, is on the National Register of Historic Places. Homey rooms, which have fine views of the hill or the waterfront, are furnished with handmade country-style furniture; the TVs are hidden in armoires. A shaded courtyard enhanced by garden sculptures is the place to linger in serenity. ✉ *715 1st St., La Conner 98257* ☎ *360/466–4710 or 800/488–5409* ⊟ *360/466–1320* ⊕ *www.hotelplanter.com* ⇥ *12 rooms* ♿ *Hot tub; no smoking* ⊟ *AE, MC, V* ⊠ *EP.*

¢ ▥ **White Swan Guest House.** This B&B is in an 1898 Queen Anne farm house on Fir Island in the Skagit River delta (near the tulip fields). Although built in the late 19th century, it's been thoroughly renovated and brought up to modern standards. The house is surrounded by lovely English-style gardens which have been featured in national garden magazines. ✉ *15872 Moore Rd., Mount Vernon 98723* ☎ *360/445–6805* ⊕ *www.thewhiteswan.com* ⇥ *3 rooms without bath, 1 cottage* ♿ *Kitchenettes; no a/c, no room phones, no smoking* ⊟ *MC, V* ⊠ *CP.*

CAMPING FACILITIES ⚠ **Newhalem Creek Campground.** With three loops, a small amphitheater, a playground, and a regular slate of ranger programs in summer, Newhalem Creek is the main North Cascades campground. Above the Skagit River in old-growth forest, it is adjacent to the visitor center, and close to several trails that access the river and the surrounding second-growth forest. ♿ *Flush toilets, dump station, drinking water, fire* *grates, picnic tables, public telephone, ranger station ⇌ 111 RV sites ⊠ Rte. 20, along the access road to the park's main visitor center ☎ 360/ 873–4590 Ext. 17, or Ext. 16 for Marblemount Ranger Station ⊕ www. nps.gov/noca/pphtml/camping.html ⊠ $12 ▭ No credit cards ☉ Mid-Oct.–mid-Apr.*

Sports & the Outdoors

HIKING **Cascade Pass.** Perhaps the most popular park hike, this much-traveled, moderate, switchbacked, 3⅔-mi trail leads to a divide from which dozens of peaks can be seen. The meadows here are covered with alpine wild-flowers in July and early August. A Northwest Forest Pass is needed. On sunny summer weekends and holidays, the trailhead parking lot can fill up; it's best to arrive before noon. The trip up and back will take the average hiker less than four hours, but allow plenty of extra time at the summit for admiring the wildflowers and gawking at the sur-rounding peaks. ⊠ *End of Cascade River Rd., 14 mi from Marblemount.*

Rainy Pass. An easy and accessible 1-mi paved trail leads to Rainy Lake, a waterfall, and glacier-view platform. ⊠ *Rte. 20, 38 mi east of visitor center at Newhalem.*

Skagit River Loop. One of the most notable hikes in the park, this 1⅕-mile handicapped-accessible trail loops through stands of huge, old-growth firs and cedars, dipping down to the Skagit River and out onto a river-side gravel bar. ⊠ *Near North Cascades visitor center.*

Thornton Lakes Trail. A 5-mi climb into an alpine basin with two pretty lakes, this steep and strenuous hike takes about 5–6 hours round-trip. Northwest Forest Pass needed. ⊠ *Rte. 20, 3 mi west of Newhalem.*

★ **Trail of the Cedars.** Only ½ mi long, this trail winds its way through one of the finest surviving stands of old-growth Western red cedar in Wash-ington. Some of the trees on the path are more than 1,000 years old. ⊠ *Near North Cascades visitor center.*

Olympic National Park

❽ *U.S. 101, 89 mi west of I–5 at Exit 88 or 121 mi north of I–5 at Exit 104.*

One of the largest, most remote, and least-developed protected areas in the United States, Olympic National Park preserves 922,651 acres of the peninsula's magnificent, mountainous interior and wave-stung shore-line. South and east of U.S. 101, the interior's thick forests of spruce, fir, and cedar spread out, supporting a thriving population of black bears, cougars, deer, elk, and numerous small animals. In the center rises a crown of glacier-topped peaks, almost as difficult to traverse now as it was a century ago. West of U.S. 101 the park claims 65 mi of wild coastline, where bald eagles, osprey, blue herons, and hawks soar the skies, and migrating whales, sea lions, sea otters, and seals swim off-shore.

Olympic's most popular panoramas, such as the view from atop Hur-ricane Ridge north to Vancouver Island, or the seascape at Ruby Beach, are best viewed during the clear-sky, sunny months of July, August, and September. Misty, rain-splashed days, however, add indelible atmo-sphere to the rain forest valleys and the Pacific coastline; and they are truer representations of the area's character, even if they obscure dis-tant views. Rain is possible any time of year, but it's most common from November through April.

U.S. 101 encircles most of the park's interior, and numerous smaller roads branch inward toward the mountains and outward toward the beaches. Even though few roads penetrate very far into the park, you can still see many of Olympic's larger wild animals by roadsides and at meadow edges at dawn and dusk. Bears are most commonly seen in May and June, and in fall when they prowl berry patches. Elk spend the summer in the high country and return to lowland valleys in autumn. Keep in mind that all wild animals are just that—wild—and both people and animals benefit by keeping their distance.

The park's six entrances are open 24 hours year-round, and most gate stations are staffed daily from 9 to 4. The vehicle admission fee is $5. Parking at Ozette, the trailhead for one of the park's most popular hikes, is $1 per day. June through September are peak months, when the park receives 75% of its annual visitors. Its most popular sites, such as Hurricane Ridge, can approach capacity by 10 AM. May and October are much less crowded and have generally favorable weather. Winter brings persistent cloudiness, frequent rain, and chilly temperatures; crowds are almost nonexistent from Thanksgiving to Easter. When it snows the slopes draw skiers and snowshoers, although Hurricane Ridge Road is closed from Monday to Thursday, November through March.

At the **Olympic National Park Visitor Center,** park rangers provide advice on where to go and how to maximize your time, as well as information on campgrounds, wildlife movement in the park, programs, weather forecasts, and almost anything else you might want to know. You can pick up free road and trail maps, information pamphlets, and the park's newspaper, the *Bugler,* as well as buy books, postcards, and souvenirs. Ranger talks, guest programs, children's events, and other activities are scheduled throughout the year. ✉ *600 E. Park Ave., Port Angeles 98362* ☎ *360/565-3130* ⊕ *www.nps.gov/olym.*

The park's premier scenic drive is from the Port Angeles visitor center to **Hurricane Ridge.** The road climbs steeply to 5,242 feet, from the thick fir forest in the foothills to alpine meadow at the top of the ridge. As you drive upward, you may notice marmots and goats ambling along the roadsides. Meanwhile, ever-larger panoramas reveal spectacular views on all sides. From the Hurricane Ridge visitor center at the top, you can see the heart of the mountains to the south and Canada to the north, across the Strait of Juan de Fuca. Trails on Hurricane Ridge take you through alpine meadows covered with wildflowers in spring and summer. In winter, the area has miles of cross-country ski and snowshoeing routes, and even a modest downhill-ski operation. ✉ *Hurricane Ridge Rd., 17 mi south of Port Angeles* ☎ *360/565-3130, 360/452-0329 for snow conditions* ⊙ *Visitor centers daily 10–5.* **Lake Crescent.** Almost everyone who visits the park sees Lake Crescent, as U.S. 101 winds along its southern shore, giving way to gorgeous views of azure waters rippling in a basin formed by Tuscan-like hills. In the evening, low bands of clouds caught between the surrounding mountains often linger over its reflective surface. Along the lake's 12-mi perimeter are campgrounds, resorts, trails, and places to canoe and fish. ✉ *U.S. 101, 16 mi west of Port Angeles and 28 mi east of Forks* ☎ *360/928–3380.*

The Sol Duc Valley is one of those magical, serene places where all the Northwest's virtues seem at hand—lush lowland forest, a sparkling river, salmon runs, and quiet hiking trails. Native Americans dipped into the soothing waters of **Sol Duc Hot Springs** for generations. Today visitors come from all areas to soak in the three hot sulfuric pools, ranging in temperature from 98°F to 104°F. Sol Duc Hot Springs Resort, built in 1910, has simple cabins for overnight visitors, plus a restaurant and hamburger stand. You need not patronize the resort to use the hot springs. ✉ *Soleduck Rd., on Lake Crescent, 12 mi south of Fairholm* ☎ *360/327–3583* ✉ *$10* ⊙ *Apr.–mid-May and Oct., daily 9–5; mid-May–Sept., daily 9–9.*

Lake Ozette, the third largest glacial impoundment in Washington, anchors the coastal strip of Olympic National Park at its north end. The small town of Ozette, home of a coastal tribe, is the trailhead for two of the park's better one-day hikes. Three-mile trails lead over boardwalks through swampy wetland and coastal old-growth forest to the ocean shore and uncrowded beach. The northernmost trail reaches shore at Cape Alava, westernmost point in the continental United States. Wet weather makes the boardwalks slippery, so watch your step. ⊠ *At the end of Hoko-Ozette Rd., 26 mi southwest of Rte. 112 near Sekiu* ☎ *360/963–2725.*

An 18-mi spur road winds from U.S. 101 to the **Hoh River Rain Forest,** where spruce and hemlock trees soar to heights of more than 200 feet. Alders and big-leaf maples are so densely covered with mosses they look more like shaggy prehistoric animals than trees. Look for elk browsing in shaded glens. And be prepared for rain: the region receives 140 inches or more a year (that's 12 feet and up). The Hoh Visitor Center, near the campground and the trailheads, has maps and information. The 18-mi Hoh River Trail, one of the most popular in the park, follows the Hoh River to the base of Mt. Olympus, which rises 7,965 feet above the forest floor. Two other much shorter trails lead through the forestland around the visitor center. Naturalist-led campfire programs and walks are conducted almost daily in July and August. ⊠ *From U.S. 101 (about 20 mi north of Kalaloch) take Upper Hoh Rd. 18 mi east to Hoh Rain Forest Visitor Center* ☎ *360/374–6925.*

Lake Quinault, 4½ mi long and 300 feet deep, is partly in Olympic National Park, partly in Olympic National Forest, and partly on the Quinault reservation. The glimmering lake is the first landmark you reach when driving the west-side loop of U.S. 101. The rain forest is at its densest and wettest here, with moss-draped maples and alders, and towering spruces, firs, and hemlocks. Enchanted Valley, high up near the Quinault River's source, is a deeply glaciated valley that's closer to the Hood Canal than to the Pacific Ocean. A scenic loop drive circles the lake and travels around a section of the Quinault River. Quinault Lodge is on the southeast side of the lake, while several public and private campgrounds border the northwest side. ⊠ *U.S. 101, 38 mi north of Hoquiam* ☎ *360/288–2444* ☉ *Ranger station May–Sept., daily 8–5.*

Where to Stay & Eat

★ $$–$$$ ✗ **C'est Si Bon.** Far more formal and more French than is typical on the Olympic Peninsula, this first-rate restaurant stands out for its setting. Tables cloaked in white linen are set above views of a rose garden, and ornate chandeliers illuminate European oil paintings on bold red walls. The menu—think onion soup, Cornish hen, filet mignon, and lobster tail—is written by the French expatriate owners. The wine list is superb, with French, Australian, and American choices, including Washington wines. ⊠ *2300 U.S. 101E (4 mi east of Port Angeles)* ☎ *360/452–8888* ♤ *Reservations essential* ☐ *AE, DC, MC, V* ☉ *Closed Mon. No lunch.*

$$–$$$ ✗ **Toga's International.** The European-inspired cuisine at this classy restaurant, in a former home, melds world flavors and cooking styles with the best local ingredients. Mountain views from the dining room and patio harken images of the chef-owner's former home in Germany's Black Forest. For an unusual treat, have your meal cooked on a *Jagerstein* (hunting stone) right at your table. This is one of the few places west of Seattle where you can order cheese, meat, or seafood fondue (with a day's notice). ⊠ *122 W. Lauridsen Blvd., Port Angeles* ☎ *360/452–1952* ♤ *Reservations essential* ☐ *MC, V* ☉ *Closed Sun. and Mon. and Sept. and Jan.*

$–$$ ✕ **The Bushwhacker.** More than two decades of excellent steaks keep the locals coming back to this surf-and-turf restaurant. It's a big, friendly place where families gather to dig into huge, perfect cuts of meat or seafood dishes. It's tempting to fill up at the massive salad and soup bar, which comes with every meal, but save room for your main course—and the amazing desserts. ⊠ *115 E. Railroad Ave., Port Angeles* ☎ *360/457–6768* ▭ *AE, MC, V.*

$–$$ ✕ **Crab House.** This first-class waterfront restaurant, linked to the Red Lion Inn in front of the Port Angeles Pier, is one of the region's most famous spots for fresh local seafood. Crab is the specialty, of course, and it shows up in a tasty variety of dishes, including crab hash, crab bisque, crab cakes, and crab-stuffed fish specials. Windows surrounding the elegant dining room let you view the serene gray waters where much of what's on the menu is caught daily. This is where well-to-do locals splurge on black-tie events. ⊠ *221 N. Lincoln St., Port Angeles* ☎ *360/457–0424* ▭ *AE, D, DC, MC, V.*

★ **$–$$** ✕ **Dupuis Restaurant.** Flower-filled gardens surround this old-time seafood spot on U.S. 101 between Port Angeles and Sequim. One of the dining rooms was a tavern in the 1920s. Close-set tables in the elegant main dining room are lit by small chandeliers overhead. Windows frame views of the well-tended gardens. Grilled local fish, steamed crabs and oysters, seafood sautés, and a selection of Continental choices, like cheese-topped French onion soup, round out the menu. ⊠ *256861 U.S. 101, Port Angeles* ☎ *360/457–8033* ▭ *AE, MC, V* ⊘ *No lunch.*

$–$$ ✕ **Smoke House Restaurant.** Rough-panel walls give a rustic appeal to the dining room of this two-story Forks favorite. Successful surf-and-turf specials remain unchanged since the place opened as a smokehouse in 1975. Smoked salmon is a top-seller, but the steaks and prime rib are also delicious. Burgers, fries, and milk shakes are sure to please the kids. ⊠ *193161 U.S. 101, Forks* ☎ *360/374–6258* ▭ *D, MC, V* ⊘ *No lunch weekends.*

$ ✕ **Forks Coffee Shop.** This modest restaurant on the highway in downtown Forks serves terrific, home-style, classic American fare. From 5 AM onward you can dig into giant pancakes and Sol Duc scrambles (eggs, sausage, hash browns, and veggies all scrambled together). At lunch, there's a choice of soups, salads, and hot and cold sandwiches. Dinner specials come with free trips to the salad bar and may include entrées like baked ham, baby-back ribs, grilled Hood Canal oysters, and spaghetti. ⊠ *U.S. 101, Forks* ☎ *360/374–6769* ▭ *MC, V.*

$–$$$ ✕▥ **Kalaloch Lodge.** A two-story cedar lodge overlooking the Pacific, Kalaloch has 20 cabins and five lodge rooms with sea views. Log cabins have either fireplaces or woodstoves, knotty pine furnishings, earth-tone fabrics, and kitchenettes; the ones on the waterfront also have deep couches looking seaward out of a picture window. To suit the rustic ambience, no phones or TVs are in the rooms, but there's a common area where guests gather for entertainment. The restaurant's menu ($–$$) changes seasonally, but usually includes local oysters, crab, and salmon. Dinner is served in the main dining room and in the upstairs cocktail lounge—which, like the restaurant, has unobstructed ocean views. ⊠ *157151 U.S. 101* ✉ *HC 80, Box 1100, Forks 98331* ☎ *360/962–2271 or 866/525–2562* 🖷 *360/962–3391* ⊕ *www.visitkalaloch.com* ⤴ *10 rooms, 44 cabins* ♨ *Restaurant, grocery, kitchenettes, bar, shop, library, some pets allowed (fee); no room phones, no room TVs* ▭ *AE, MC, V.*

$–$$ ✕▥ **Lake Quinault Lodge.** On a lovely glacial lake in Olympic National Forest, this beautiful early-20th-century lodge complex is within walking distance of the lakeshore and hiking trails in the spectacular old-growth forest. A towering brick fireplace is the centerpiece of the great room, where antique wicker furnishings sit beneath ceiling beams painted with Native American designs. In the rooms, modern gadgets are traded in for old-fashioned comforts, such as clawfoot tubs and fireplaces. The lively bar is a good place to unwind after a day spent outdoors. The restaurant ($–$$) serves upscale seafood entrées like baked salmon with capers and onions. ✉ *S. Shore Rd.* ✉ *Box 7, Quinault 98575* ☎ *360/288–2900 or 800/562–6672* 🖨 *360/288–2901* ⊕ *www.visitlakequinault.com* ⇨ *92 rooms* ⌂ *Restaurant, some in-room VCRs, putting green, indoor pool, lake, hot tub, sauna, dock, boating, fishing, hiking, bar, recreation room, some pets allowed (fee), no-smoking rooms; no room phones, no TV in some rooms* ➦ *MC, V.*

$ ✕▣ **Sol Duc Hot Springs Resort.** Deep in the brooding forest along the Sol Duc River, this remote 1910 resort is surrounded by 5,000-foot-tall mountains. Bubbling, steaming sulfur springs fill the three large outdoor pools, and the swimming pool is filled with slightly warmed glacial runoff. Some forest cabins have kitchens, but all are spartan; however, after a day's hike, a dip, and dinner at The Spring restaurant ($–$$), you'll hardly notice. The attractive fir-and-cedar-paneled dining room serves unpretentious meals all day, drawing on top Northwest seafood and produce. ✉ *Soleduck Rd.* ✉ *Box 2169, Port Angeles 98362* ☎ *360/327–3583* 🖨 *360/327–3593* ⊕ *www.solduchotsprings.com* ⇨ *32 rooms, 6 cabins* ⌂ *Restaurant, grocery, some kitchenettes, pool, hot springs, hiking, bar, shop* ➦ *MC, V* ⊘ *Closed mid-Oct.–mid-May.*

¢–$ ✕▣ **Lake Crescent Lodge.** Deep in the forest at the foot of Mt. Storm King, this comfortable farmhouse-style lodge, built in 1916, has a wraparound veranda and picture windows framing the lake's sapphire waters. Rooms in the rustic Roosevelt Cottage have polished wood floors, stone fireplaces, and lake views, while Tavern Cottage quarters resemble modern motel rooms. Second-floor rooms in the historic lodge, a former pub, have shared baths. The lodge's fir-paneled dining room ($–$$$) overlooks the lake, and the adjacent lounge is often crowded with campers. Seafood dishes like grilled salmon or steamed Quilcene oysters, as well as classic American fare, highlight the restaurant menu. ✉ *416 Lake Crescent Rd., Port Angeles 98363* ☎ *360/928–3211* 🖨 *360/928–3253* ⊕ *www.lakecrescentlodge.com* ⇨ *30 motel rooms, 17 cabins, 5 lodge rooms with shared bath* ⌂ *Restaurant, dining room, lake, dock, boating, fishing, hiking, lounge; no room phones, no room TVs* ➦ *AE, DC, MC, V* ⊘ *Closed Nov.–Apr.*

$$–$$$ ▣ **Colette's Bed & Breakfast.** A contemporary mansion curving around

Fodor'sChoice 10 acres of gorgeous waterfront property, this B&B offers space, ser-
★ vice, and luxury equaled by no other property in the area. Leather sofas and chairs and a river-rock fireplace make the great front room a lovely spot to watch the water through expansive 20-foot windows. The suites—with names like Iris, Azalea, and Cedar—also overlook the water and have fireplaces, balconies, CD and DVD players, and two-person Jacuzzis. A specially made outdoor fireplace means you can enjoy the deck even in winter. Multi-course breakfasts include espresso-based drinks and fresh fruit. ✉ *339 Finn Hall Rd., 10 mi east of Port Angeles, 98362* ☎ *360/457–9197 or 888/457–9777* 🖨 *360/452–0711* ⊕ *www.colettes.com* ⇨ *5 suites* ⌂ *Dining room, in-room data ports, in-room hot tubs, refrigerators, cable TV, in-room VCRs; no kids under 18, no smoking* ➦ *MC, V* ❐ *BP.*

$$–$$$ ▣ **Domaine Madeleine.** The owners of this luxury B&B on a bluff above the Strait of Juan de Fuca love to pamper their guests. Rooms, which have private entrances, are decorated with either Impressionist or Asian accents and overlook water and mountain views. Gas fireplaces, designer robes, two-person whirlpool tubs, CD players, and VCRs are more ensuite bonuses. The living room, set aside for private use with bookings

of the Renoir Room, has a 14-foot-tall basalt fireplace, antique Asian furnishings, and a harpsichord. For breakfast expect a five-course gourmet affair with fresh baguettes, chicken crepes, and seafood omelets. ⊠ *146 Wildflower La., 8 mi east of Port Angeles, 98362* ☎ *360/457–4174 or 888/811–8376* 🖷 *360/457–3037* ⊕ *www.domainemadeleine. com* 🗢 *4 rooms* ⟁ *Dining room, some refrigerators, in-room VCRs, library, meeting rooms; no kids under 12, no smoking* ▤ *AE, D, DC, MC, V* ¶⟨ *BP.*

★ **$–$$$** ⊡ **BJ's Garden Gate.** A gingerbread-style porch fronts this waterfront Victorian home on three acres of landscaped grounds. Exquisitely appointed guest rooms include Victoria's Repose, which has a finely carved half-tester English oak bed and a balcony with a private two-person hot tub. All rooms have fireplaces, Jacuzzis, CD players and VCRs, plus panoramic water views. Antiques are artfully arranged throughout the living and dining rooms, which have expansive views of the strait. Gorgeous flower gardens, which have been featured in national commercials, help make this an ideal romantic getaway. ⊠ *397 Monterra Dr., Port Angeles 98362* ☎ *360/452–2322 or 800/880–1332* ⊕ *www. bjgarden.com* 🗢 *5 rooms* ⟁ *Dining room, in-room data ports, in-room hot tubs, cable TV, in-room VCRs; no kids, no smoking* ▤ *AE, MC, V* ¶⟨ *BP.*

¢–$$ ⊡ **Miller Tree Inn Bed and Breakfast.** Built as a farmhouse in 1916, this pale yellow B&B is still bordered on two sides by pastures. Numerous windows make the rooms bright, cheerful places to relax amid antiques, knick-knacks, and quilts. Premier rooms have king-size beds, gas fireplaces, hot tubs for two, and VCRs. A separate apartment has a private entrance and kitchenette. One parlor has a library and piano, the other has games. In summer, lemonade and cookies are served on the lawn or the wide front porch. From October through April, nearby rivers offer prime salmon and steelhead fishing. ⊠ *654 E. Division St., Forks 98331* ☎ *360/374–6806 or 800/943–6563* 🖷 *360/374–6807* ⊕ *www. millertreeinn.com* 🗢 *6 rooms, 1 apartment* ⟁ *Dining room, some in-room hot tubs, some in-room VCRs, kitchenette, hot tub, fishing, recreation room, library, some pets allowed (fee); no a/c, no room phones, no TV in some rooms, no kids under 7, no smoking* ▤ *MC, V* ¶⟨ *BP.*

¢–$ ⊡ **Five Sea Suns Bed & Breakfast.** The clever name of this cozy 1926 inn refers to its rooms, each elegantly appointed in the theme of a time of year: the four seasons plus an Indian summer. If you stay in Lente (spring), you can enjoy a breezy balcony. Na Zomer (Indian summer) is in a separate carriage house. The B&B overlooks the mountains and the bay, which you can view from the pondside pergola and landscaped gardens. When you arrive, coffee is served in a silver tea set in your room. ⊠ *1006 S. Lincoln, Port Angeles 98362* ☎ *360/452–8248 or 800/708–0777* 🖷 *360/417–0465* ⊕ *www.seasuns.com* 🗢 *5 rooms* ⟁ *Dining room, picnic area, pond, travel services, airport shuttle; no a/c, no room phones, no kids under 12, no smoking* ▤ *AE, MC, V* ¶⟨ *BP.*

¢–$ ⊡ **Tudor Inn.** This 1910 Tudor-style B&B stands behind a white picket fence in a residential neighborhood. Several gathering spots throughout the house—a piano parlor, an antiques-filled sitting room, a front porch, and a back deck—encourage mingling. Guest rooms, all with views of the water or Hurricane Ridge, have themes like Country, Wedgewood, and Oriental. Yours might have a fireplace, balcony, or clawfoot bathtub. Candlelight breakfast and afternoon tea are included. ⊠ *1108 S. Oak St., Port Angeles 98362* ☎ *360/452–3138 or 866/286–2224* ⊕ *www.tudorinn.com* 🗢 *5 rooms* ⟁ *Dining room, piano, library; no kids under 12, no smoking* ▤ *MC, V* ¶⟨ *BP.*

¢–$ ⊡ **Forks Motel.** The town's largest motel has been around since 1955, offering friendly service and pleasant, simple accommodations, from small rooms with showers to two-bedroom suites with kitchens and Jacuzzis. The well-kept pool is open from May through September. ⊠ *351 S. Forks Ave., Forks 98331* ☎ *360/374–6243 or 800/544–3416* ᗊ *360/374– 6760* ⊕ *www.forksmotel.com* ᗒ *61 rooms, 12 suites* ᗢ *Some kitchens, cable TV, pool, wading pool, laundry facilities, business services, no-smoking rooms, some pets allowed (fee); no a/c in some rooms* ⊟ *AE, D, DC, MC, V.*

¢ 🔲 **Eagle Point Inn.** Beside the Soleduck River and surrounded by forest land, this beautiful log lodge is the picture of a peaceful country retreat. Inside, exposed-log walls are the background for antique and reproduction finery, including polished-wood furnishings, crocheted white table-cloths, and Tiffany lamps. Spare, elegant bedrooms have antique fringed lamps; one bath has a black clawfoot tub. Downstairs, a great stone fire-place makes the living room an inviting spot to spend the evening. In summer, you can cook in the outdoor kitchen by the river, or gather round a bonfire on crisp autumn nights. The B&B is about 10 mi north of Forks off U.S. 101. ⊠ *202 Stormin' Norman Rd., Beaver 98305* ☎ *360/327– 3236* ⊕ *www.eaglepointinn.com* ᗒ *3 rooms* ᗢ *Dining room, kitchen, outdoor hot tub, fishing, hiking; no room phones, no room TVs, no kids under 12, no smoking* ⊟ *No credit cards* ⁝◯⁝ *BP.*

¢ 🔲 **Hoh Humm Ranch Bed and Breakfast.** This 200-acre former ranch is surrounded by rolling fields where tame llamas, deer, goats, and other animals roam. Simple, comfortable rooms overlook the valley and river below, where you can cast for salmon, trout, and steelhead. Hikers can head 6 mi south to Ruby Beach or 7 mi north to the Hoh River rain forest. The ranch is 20 mi south of Forks. ⊠ *171763 U.S. 101, near milepost 172, Forks 98331* ☎ *360/374–5337* ᗊ *360/374–5344* ⊕ *www. olypen.com/hohhumm* ᗒ *4 rooms without bath* ᗢ *Dining room, fish-ing, some pets allowed; no a/c, no room phones, no room TVs, no smok-ing* ⊟ *No credit cards* ⁝◯⁝ *BP.*

¢ 🔲 **Port Angeles Inn.** Blue-and-white-striped awnings and lattice wood-work give this simple motel a cheerful look. The inn is in the middle of town, and some rooms on the upper floor have good views of the har-bor. Rooms are done in warm colors; the four King Rooms have bal-conies and two also have kitchenettes. ⊠ *111 E. Second St., Port Angeles 98362* ☎ *360/452–9285 or 800/421–0706* ᗊ *360/452–7935* ⊕ *www.portangelesinn.com* ᗒ *22 rooms, 2 suites* ᗢ *In-room data ports, some kitchenettes, some microwaves, some refrigerators, cable TV* ⊟ *D, MC, V* ⁝◯⁝ *CP.*

CAMPING
FACILITIES   Campgrounds in Olympic National Park range from primitive back-country sites to paved trailer parks with nightly naturalist programs. Each designated site usually has a picnic table and grill or fire pit, and most campgrounds have water, toilets, and garbage containers. Park camp-grounds have no hook-ups, showers, or laundry facilities. Firewood is available from camp concessions, but if there's no store you can collect dead wood within 1 mi of your campsite. Dogs are allowed in camp-grounds but not on trails or in the backcountry. Trailers should be 21 feet long or less (15 feet or less at Queets Campground). There's a camping limit of two weeks.

Intrepid hikers can camp virtually anywhere along the park's shoreline or in its forested areas. The required overnight wilderness-use permit costs $5, plus $2 per person per night. Passes are available at visitor cen-ters and ranger stations. Note that when you camp in the backcountry, you must choose a site at least ½ mi inside the park boundary.

🔺 **Altaire Campground.** This small campground sits amid an old-growth forest by the river in the narrow Elwha River valley. A popular trail leads downstream from the campground. ✉ *Elwha River Rd., 8 mi south of U.S. 101, Olympic National Park* ☎ *No phone* 🏕 *30 sites* ⚐ *Flush toilets, drinking water, fire grates* 🎫 *$10* 🖃 *No credit cards* ⊘ *Closed Nov.–Mar.*

⚠ **Cycle Campground.** Designed for bicyclists, this camp is set in the Sol Duc valley between Forks and La Push. Firewood, coffee, and apple cider are free. The fee includes one support vehicle per site. There's a group fire ring and a hot tub. ✉ *101 Mora Rd., Forks* ☎ *360/374–8665* 🏕 *10 tent sites, 4 tent cabins, 3 tepees* ⚐ *Flush toilets, full hook-ups, drinking water, grills, picnic tables, electricity, public telephone* 🎫 *Tents $10, tepee or tent cabin (2 people) $40* 🖃 *MC, V* ⊘ *Closed Nov.–Apr.*

⚠ **Conestoga Quarters RV Park Campground.** Off U.S. 101, partly surrounded by a fir forest, this compact RV park provides a shuttle van to take you into Port Angeles and to the ferry dock. All of the sites have full hook-ups; eight sites have phones. ✉ *40 Sieberts Creek Rd.* ☎ *360/452–4637 or 800/808–4637* 🏕 *8 tent sites, 34 RV sites* ⚐ *Flush toilets, full hook-ups, drinking water, showers, grills, picnic tables, electricity, public telephone, play area* 🎫 *Tents $14, RVs $21* 🖃 *D, MC, V* ⊘ *Closed Nov.–Mar.*

⚠ **Dosewallips Campground.** Popular with hikers, and hunters in the fall, this small, remote campground lies beneath Mt. Constance, one of the most conspicuous peaks in the park. The campground is in old-growth forest along the river. The long gravel access road is not suitable for RVs. ✉ *Dosewallips River Rd., 15 mi west of Brinnon, Olympic National Park* ☎ *No phone* 🏕 *30 sites* ⚐ *Pit toilets, drinking water, fire grates* 🎫 *$10* 🖃 *MC, V* ⊘ *Closed Nov.–Apr.*

⚠ **Elwha Campground.** The larger of the Elwha Valley's two campgrounds, this is one of Olympic's year-round facilities, with two campsite loops in an old-growth forest. ✉ *Elwha River Rd., 7 mi south of U.S. 101, Olympic National Park* ☎ *No phone* 🏕 *41 sites* ⚐ *Flush toilets, drinking water, fire grates, public telephone, ranger station* 🎫 *$10* 🖃 *MC, V.*

⚠ **Heart O' the Hills Campground.** At the foot of Hurricane Ridge in a grove of tall firs, this popular, sometimes crowded campground offers a regular slate of programs in summer. The price is a distinct lack of the peace and calm most people expect in a national park. ✉ *Hurricane Ridge Rd., Olympic National Park* ☎ *No phone* 🏕 *105 sites* ⚐ *Flush toilets, drinking water, fire grates, public telephone, ranger station* 🎫 *$10* 🖃 *MC, V.*

⚠ **Hoh Campground.** Crowds flock to this rain forest campground under a canopy of moss-draped maples, towering spruce trees, and morning mist. ✉ *Hoh River Rd., 17 mi east of U.S. 101, Olympic National Park* ☎ *No phone* 🏕 *89 sites* ⚐ *Flush toilets, dump station, drinking water, fire grates, public telephone, ranger station* 🎫 *$10* 🖃 *MC, V.*

⚠ **Hoh River Resort Campground.** Spruce trees shade this all-around sportsman's hangout along the Hoh River. Fishing and hiking are nearby. ✉ *175443 U.S. 101, 20 mi south of Forks* ☎ *360/374–5566* 🏕 *13 sites with hook-ups, 7 tent sites* ⚐ *Flush toilets, full hook-ups, drinking water, showers, grills, picnic tables, electricity, public telephone, general store* 🎫 *RVs and tents $10* 🖃 *MC, V.*

⚠ **Kalaloch Campground.** Kalaloch is the biggest and most popular Olympic campground. Its vantage of the Pacific is duplicated nowhere on the park's coastal stretch, although the campsites themselves are set back in the spruce fringe. ✉ *U.S. 101, ½ mi north of the Kalaloch Information Station, Olympic National Park* ☎ *No phone* 🏕 *177 sites* ⚐ *Flush toilets, dump station, drinking water, fire grates, public telephone, ranger station* 🎫 *$12* 🖃 *MC, V.*

Lake Quinault Rain Forest Resort Village Campground. Sprawled on the south shore of Lake Quinault, this campground has ample recreation facilities, including beaches, canoes, ball fields, and horseshoes. ⊠ *3½ mi east of U.S. 101, S. Shore Rd., Lake Quinault* ☎ *360/288–2535* ⌗ *30 sites ⚹ Flush toilets, full hook-ups, drinking water, showers, grills, picnic tables, electricity, public telephone, general store* ⊠ *RVs and tents $16* ▭ *MC, V* ☯ *Closed Nov.–Mar.*

Lonesome Creek RV Park. A mile of sandy beach abuts this shoreside park in La Push. The on-site store sells Native American arts. ⊠ *490 Ocean Dr., La Push* ☎ *360/374–4338* ⌗ *41 sites, 40 with full hookups ⚹ Flush toilets, drinking water, showers, grills, picnic tables, electricity, public telephone, general store* ⊠ *Tents $15, RVs $20–$30* ▭ *MC, V.*

Ozette Campground. Hikers heading to Cape Alava, a scenic promontory that's the westernmost point in the lower 48 states, use this lakeshore campground as a jumping-off point. There's a boat launch and a small beach. ⊠ *Hoko-Ozette Rd., 26 mi south of Rte. 112, Olympic National Park* ☎ *No phone* ⌗ *15 sites ⚹ Pit toilets, fire grates, ranger station* ⊠ *$10* ▭ *MC, V.*

Queets Campground. Amid lush old-growth forests in the southwestern corner of the park, near the park's largest Douglas fir tree, this campground is not suitable for trailers or RVs. There's no water. ⊠ *Queets River Rd., 12 mi east of U.S. 101, Olympic National Park* ☎ *No phone* ⌗ *20 sites ⚹ Pit toilets, fire grates, ranger station* ⊠ *$8* ▭ *No credit cards.*

Salt Creek RV Park. Adjacent to a golf course, this large park offers every conceivable campground amenity, including nightly security patrols and an on-site store. Quiet hours are 10 PM to 8 AM, and fireworks and firearms are strictly prohibited. ⊠ *53802 Rte. 122 W* ☎ *360/928–2488* ⌗ *51 sites ⚹ Flush toilets, full hook-ups, drinking water, guest laundry, showers, grills, picnic tables, electricity, public telephone, play area* ⊠ *$20 RVs* ▭ *AE, MC, V.*

Salt Creek and Tongue Point Recreation Area. Swimming in fresh and salt water, fishing, hiking, and beachcombing provide bountiful activity at this Clallam County park along a creek. There are no hook-ups. ⊠ *13 mi west of Port Angeles on Rte. 112, 3 mi north on Hayden Creek Rd.* ☎ *360/928–3441* ⌗ *90 sites ⚹ Flush toilets, drinking water, showers, grills, picnic tables, public telephone, play area, swimming (river, ocean)* ⊠ *$10* ▭ *No credit cards* ☯ *Closed Nov.–Mar.*

Sol Duc Campground. Sol Duc resembles virtually all Olympic campgrounds except for one distinguishing feature—the famed hot springs are a short walk away. The nearby Sol Duc River has several spots where visitors can watch spawning salmon work their way upstream. ⊠ *Sol Duc Rd., 11 mi south of U.S. 101, Olympic National Park* ☎ *No phone* ⌗ *80 sites ⚹ Flush toilets, dump station, drinking water, fire grates, public telephone, ranger station, swimming (hot springs)* ⊠ *$12* ▭ *No credit cards* ☯ *Closed Nov.–Mar.*

South Beach Campground. The first campground travelers reach as they enter the park's coastal stretch from the south, this is basically an overflow campground for the more popular and better-equipped Kalaloch a few miles north. Campsites are set in the spruce fringe, just back from the beach. There is no water. ⊠ *2 mi south of the Kalaloch information station at the southern boundary of the park, U.S. 101* ☎ *No phone* ⌗ *50 sites ⚹ Pit toilets, fire grates* ⊠ *$8* ▭ *No credit cards* ☯ *Closed Nov.–Mar.*

Sports & the Outdoors

BOATING Serene **Lake Crescent,** surrounded by the Olympic mountain forests, is one of the park's most popular places to boat. Besides canoeing and kayaking, you can drive motorboats and waterski here. Speedboats are not permitted around the designated swimming area at the west end of the lake. Rangers lead 75-minute tours of the lake aboard the *Storm King,* in cooperation with **Mosquito Fleet Enterprises** (☎ 425/252–6800 or 800/325–6722 ⊕ www.whalewatching.com), from late May through September. You can buy tickets at the Olympic National Park Visitor Center in Port Angeles.

Fairholm General Store (⊠ U.S. 101, Fairholm ☎ 360/928–3020) rents rowboats and canoes for $10 to $45 on Lake Crescent. The store is at the west end of the lake, 27 mi west of Port Angeles. It's open May through September, daily 9 to 6. **Lake Crescent Lodge** (⊠ 416 Lake Crescent Rd. ☎ 360/928–3211) rents rowboats for $8.50 per hour and $35 per day.

CLIMBING Mt. Olympus and other peaks in the park are very popular with climbers, partly because they are rugged and quite challenging, but not overly high. Olympus, the tallest, tops out at 7,965 feet. Get expert advice from rangers before setting out. The mountains are steep, the landscape is broken up by escarpments and ridges, and there are bridgeless creeks and rivers to cross. It's easy to take a fall or to get lost (which happens every year to inexperienced hikers and climbers). All climbers are asked to register with park officials and purchase wilderness permits before setting out.

Olympic Mountain Outdoors (⊠ Box 1468, Port Townsend ☎ 360/379–5336 ⊕ www.olympicguides.com) offers guided hiking, camping, skiing, snowshoeing, and wildlife-watching trips. **Olympic Mountaineering** (⊠ 140 W. Front St., Port Angeles ☎ 360/452–0240 ⊕ www.olymtn.com) organizes climbs and hikes in Olympic National Park. Climbing classes at an indoor gym and outdoor adventure clinics are also offered.

FISHING Rainbow and cutthroat trout are found in the park's streams and lakes, and salmon ply the rivers and shores. You don't need a state fishing license to fish in the park; however, anglers must acquire a salmon–steelhead punch card when fishing for those species. The Bogachiel, Hoh, Quinault, Skokomish, and Dosewallips rivers are world-famous steelhead streams. Ocean fishing and shellfish and seaweed harvesting require licenses, which are available at sporting goods and outdoor supply stores. Fishing regulations vary throughout the park; check regulations for each location.

Diamond Back Guide Service (⊠ 140 Dolan Ave., Port Angeles ☎ 360/452–9966) leads fishing trips and scenic boat excursions around the peninsula. **Jim Leons Outdoor Adventures** (⊠ 382 Elk Valley Rd., Forks ☎ 360/374–3157 ⊕ www.fishingnorthwest.com/jimleons) conducts fishing and hunting trips around the Olympic Peninsula. **Mike Schmitz Olympic Peninsula Fishing Guides** (⊠ Box 2688, Forks ☎ 360/364–2602 or 888/577–4656 ⊕ www.forks-web.com/mschmitz) runs fishing trips on the Hoh, Sol Duc, and other rivers. The **Quillayute River Guide Service** (⊠ Box 71, La Push ☎ 360/374–2660 ⊕ www.forks-web.com/jim) focuses on steelhead fishing on the Quillayute and Hoh rivers.

HIKING Wilderness beaches provide the park's most unusual hiking experience: an opportunity to explore an essentially unaltered Pacific coastline. Entry points are at La Push, Rialto Beach, and Cape Alava. Be sure to read the tide tables before starting out on beach trails. Plan your route carefully or you risk being trapped by the ocean. Park rangers and volunteers at the visitor centers can show you how to read the tide tables and warn you of any dangerous areas.

In the interior, trails embedded in forested river valleys provide perfect warm-ups for the intense climbs into alpine country. The Elwha, Dosewallips, Skokomish, Quinault, Hoh, and Sol Duc valleys all have developed trails that wend upstream, finally climbing into high passes and a glacier-rimmed alpine basin where they link up with each other.

Boulder Creek Trail. The 5-mi round-trip walk up Boulder Creek leads to the Olympic hot springs, a half-dozen pools of varying temperatures; some are clothing-optional. ⊠ *End of the Elwha River Rd., 4 mi south of Altaire Campground.*

Cape Alva Trail. Beginning at Ozette, this 3-mi trail leads from forest to wave-tossed headlands. Be careful on the often-slippery boardwalks. ⊠ *End of the Hoko-Ozette Rd., 26 mi south of Rte. 112, west of Sekiu.*

Fodor's Choice **★** **Hoh Valley Trail.** Leaving from the Hoh Visitor Center, this rain forest jaunt takes you into the Hoh Valley, wending its way alongside the river, through moss-draped maple and alder trees, and past open meadows where elk roam in winter. ⊠ *Hoh Visitor Center, 18 mi east of U.S. 101.*

Hurricane Ridge Trail. A ¼-mi alpine loop, most of it wheelchair-accessible, leads through wildflower meadows overlooking numerous vistas of the interior Olympic peaks to the south and the Strait of Juan de Fuca panorama to the north. ⊠ *Hurricane Ridge visitor center, Hurricane Ridge Rd., 17 mi south of Port Angeles.*

★ **Sol Duc Trail.** This easy, 1½-mi gravel path off Sol Duc Road winds through thick Douglas fir forests toward the thundering, three-chute Sol Duc Falls. Just ¹⁄₁₀ mi from the road, below a wooden platform over the Sol Duc River, you come across the 70-foot Salmon Cascades. In late summer and autumn, thousands of salmon negotiate 50 mi or more of treacherous waters to reach the cascades and the tamer pools near Sol Duc Hot Springs. The popular 6-mi **Lovers Lane loop Trail** links the Sol Duc falls with the hot springs. You can continue up from the falls 5 mi to the **Appleton Pass Trail**, at 3,100 feet. From there you can hike on to the 8½-mi mark, where views at the High Divide are from 5,050 feet. ⊠ *Sol Duc Rd., 11 mi south of U.S. 101.*

SKIING & **SNOWSHOEING** Snow is most likely to fall from mid-December through late March on the Olympic Peninsula. For recorded road and weather information from November through April, call 360/565–3131. **Hurricane Ridge** is the area to head to for downhill and cross-country skiing. The most popular route for day mushers is the 1½-mi Hurricane Hill Road, west of the visitor center parking area. A marked snow-play area with trails and gentle hills has been set aside near the visitor center for cross-country skiers, snowshoers, and inner tubers. There's a weekend and holiday ski lift that runs from 10 to 4, plus two rope tows and a ski school. Cross-country trails start next to the downhill area and Hurricane Ridge Lodge. Free guided snowshoe walks take place Friday through Sunday at 2, with signups at the lodge an hour beforehand. There's also a supervised tubing area, open Friday through Sunday, ¼ mi before the parking area on the right side of the road, as well as a children's tubing area across from the lodge. Ski and snowshoe rentals cost $12 to $35 at the Hurricane Ridge visitor center.

Mt. Rainier National Park

❾ *Nisqually (Longmire) entrance: Rte. 706, 14 mi east of Rte. 7. Ohanapecosh (Stevens Canyon) entrance: Rte. 123, 5 mi north of U.S. 12. White River entrance: Rte. 410, 3 mi north of Chinook and Cayuse passes.*

Rainier is an episodically active volcano, showing off every thousand years or so, and steam vents are still active at its summit. With more than two dozen major glaciers, the mountain holds the largest glacial system in continental United States. The winter tempests that bring the snow so much resemble those of the Himalayas that Everest expeditions train here. But that's on the mountain's face above 10,000 feet; most visitors see a much more benign place with an unmatched spirit.

Wildflower season in the meadows at and above the timberline is mid-July through August, depending on the exposure (southern earlier, northern later) and the preceding winter's snowfall. Most of the park's higher-elevation trails aren't snow-free until late June. You're not as likely to see Rainier's wildlife—deer, elk, black bears, cougars, and other creatures—as often as you might at other parks, such as Olympic. As always, the best times are at dawn and dusk, when animals can often be spotted at forest's edge. Fawns are born to the park's does in May, and the bugling of bull elk on the high ridges can be heard in late September and October, especially on the park's eastern side.

The major roads to Mt. Rainier National Park—Routes 410, 706, and 123—are paved and well-maintained state highways. They eventually, however, become mountain roads and wind up and down many steep slopes. Drive with caution. Vehicles hauling large loads should gear down, especially on downhill sections. Even drivers of passenger cars should take care not to overheat brakes by constant use. Storms can cause delays at any time of year, and you can expect to encounter road-work several times if you are circumnavigating the mountain in summer. Side roads that wind into the park's western slope are all narrow, unpaved, and subject to frequent flooding and washouts.

All but Carbon River Road and Route 706 to Paradise are closed by snow in winter. During this time, however, Carbon River Road is subject to frequent flooding near the park boundary. (Route 410 is open to the Crystal Mountain access road entrance.) Cayuse Pass usually opens in late April; the Westside Road, Paradise Valley Road, and Stevens Canyon Road usually open in May; Chinook Pass, Mowich Lake Road, and White River Road, late May; and Sunrise Road, late June. All these dates are subject to weather fluctuations.

Crowds are heaviest in July, August, and September, when the parking lots often fill before noon. For this period campsites are reserved several months in advance, and other lodgings are reserved as much as a year ahead. Washington's rare periods of clear winter weather bring lots of residents up for cross-country skiing.

Mt. Rainier is open 24 hours a day but with limited access in winter. Gates at Nisqually (Longmire) are staffed in daylight hours year-round. Facilities at Paradise and Ohanapecosh are open daily from late May to mid-October, and Sunrise is open July to early October. Access to the park in winter is limited to the Nisqually entrance. The Jackson Memorial Visitor Center at Paradise is open on weekends and holidays in winter.

During off-hours you can buy passes at the gates from machines that accept credit and debit cards. The entrance fee is $10 per vehicle, which covers everyone in the vehicle for seven days. Motorcycles and bicycles pay $5. Annual passes are available for $30. Climbing permits are $30 per person per climb or glacier trek. Wilderness camping permits, which must be obtained for all backcountry trips, are free, but advance reservations are highly recommended and cost $20 per party.

There are public phones and rest rooms at all park visitor centers (Sunrise, Ohanapecosh, and the Jackson Memorial Visitor Center at Paradise) as well as at the National Park Inn in Longmire and the Paradise Inn at Paradise. The only fully accessible trail in the park is Kautz Creek Trail, a ½-mi boardwalk that leads to a splendid view of the mountain. Parts of the Trail of the Shadows at Longmire and the Grove of the Patriarchs at Ohanapecosh are accessible. The campgrounds at Cougar Rock, Ohanapecosh, and Sunshine Point have several accessible sites. All off-road vehicle use—4X4 vehicles, ATVs, motorcycles, snowmobiles—is prohibited in the park.

★ ☺ The town of Longmire, east of the Nisqually entrance, is the main southern gateway to Mt. Rainier National Park. Glass cases in the **Long-mire Museum** contain plants and animals from the park, including a large, friendly looking stuffed cougar. Photographs and geographical displays provide an overview of the park's history. The visitor center, next to the museum, has some perfunctory exhibits on the surrounding forest and its inhabitants, as well as information about park activities. ⊠ *Rte. 706, 17 mi east of Ashford and 6 mi east of Nisqually entrance* ☎ *360/569–2211 Ext. 3314* ☒ *Free with park admission* ☺ *July–Labor Day, daily 9–5; Labor Day–June, daily 9–4:15.*

Fantastic mountain views, alpine meadows crisscrossed by nature trails, a welcoming lodge and restaurant, and an excellent visitor center combine to make Paradise the first stop for most visitors to Mount Rainier National Park. There are visitor services, a ranger station, and lodging at 5,400 feet. The **Jackson Memorial Visitor Center at Paradise** has 360-degree views of the park, information, displays, and seasonal programs. The Stevens Canyon Road from Paradise east to Ohanapecosh is truly spectacular, with close-up views of the mountain, wildflowers, and the red and yellow fall foliage of huckleberry, mountain ash, and alpine dwarf willow. It's accessible from the Nisqually entrance at the park's southwest corner and from Stevens Canyon entrance at the park's southeast corner (summer only). ⊠ *Rte. 706, 9 mi east of Longmire.* ☎ *360/569–2211 Ext. 2357* 🖷 *360/569–2170* ⊕ *www.nps.gov/mora* ☒ *Free* ☺ *May–mid-Oct., daily 9–6; mid-Oct.–Apr., weekends 10–5.*

★ ☺ As it's on an island in the Ohanapecosh River, the **Grove of the Patriarchs** is protected from the fires that periodically sweep the area. This small grove of 1,000-year-old trees is one of Mt. Rainier National Park's most memorable attractions. A 1½-mi loop trail heads over a small bridge through old-growth Douglas fir, cedar, and hemlock. ⊠ *Rte. 123, just north of Stevens Canyon entrance, 20 mi east of Paradise on Stevens Canyon Rd., 13 mi north of Packwood via Rte. 123 and U.S. 12.*

At the **Ohanapecosh Visitors Center,** south of the Grove of the Patriarchs, you can learn about the region's dense old-growth forests through interpretive displays and videos. ⊠ *Rte. 123, 11 mi north of Packwood, 1½ mi south of Stevens Canyon entrance* ☎ *360/569–2211 Ext. 6046* ☺ *Late May–Oct., daily 9–6.*

As you head north from the Grove of the Patriarchs you'll reach the White River and the park entrance that's named after it. At the **Sunrise Visitor Center,** to the east, you can watch the alpenglow fade from Rainier's domed summit. You can also view exhibits on this region's alpine and subalpine ecology. Nearby loop trails lead you through alpine meadows and forest to overlooks that afford broad views of the Cascades and Rainier. ⊠ *Sunrise Rd., 15 mi east of White River park entrance* ☎ *360/663–2425* ☺ *July 4–Oct. 1, daily 9–6.*

Where to Stay & Eat

★ **$–$$** ✕⊞ **Alexander's Country Inn.** Serving guests since 1912, Alexander's offers premier lodging just a mile from Mt. Rainier. Antiques and fine linens lend the main building romance. Two adjacent guest houses are also for rent. Rates include a hearty breakfast and evening wine. The cozy restaurant ($–$$; closed weekdays in winter), the best place in town for lunch or dinner, serves fresh fish and pasta dishes; the bread and the desserts are baked on the premises. Box lunches are available for picnics. ✉ *37515 Rte. 706 E (4 mi east of Ashford), Ashford 98304* ☎ *360/569–2300 or 800/654–7615* 🖷 *360/569–2323 or 800/654–7615* ⊕ *www.alexanderscountryinn.com* ⇌ *12 rooms, 2 3-bedroom houses* ⚐ *Restaurant, hot tub* ⊟ *MC, V* ⦿ *BP.*

★ **¢–$** ✕⊞ **National Park Inn.** A large stone fireplace takes pride of place in the common room of this otherwise generic country inn, the only one of the park's two lodgings that's open year-round. Such rustic details as wrought-iron lamps and antique bentwood headboards adorn the rooms. The fare in the restaurant ($–$$) here is simple American. For breakfast, don't miss the home-baked cinnamon rolls. For lunch there are hamburgers, soups, and sandwiches. Dinner entrées include maple hazelnut chicken and grilled red snapper with black bean sauce and corn relish. The inn is operated as a B&B from October through April. ✉ *Longmire Visitor Complex, Hwy. 706, 10 mi east of Nisqually entrance, Longmire 98304* ☎ *360/569–2275* 🖷 *360/569–2770* ⊕ *www.guestservices. com/rainier/* ⇌ *25 rooms, 18 with bath* ⚐ *Restaurant, shop; no a/c, no room phones* ⊟ *MC, V* ⦿ *BP (in winter).*

★ **¢–$** ✕⊞ **Paradise Inn.** With its hand-carved Alaskan cedar logs, burnished parquet floors, stone fireplaces, Indian rugs, and glorious mountain views, this 1917 inn is a sterling example of national park lodge architecture. German architect Hans Fraehnke designed the decorative woodwork. In addition to the full-service dining room, there's a small snack bar and a snug lounge. Lunches are simple and healthful: grilled salmon, salads, and the like. For dinner, you might find the signature bourbon buffalo meatloaf, Mediterranean chicken, and poached salmon with blackberry sauce. Summer sees leisurely Sunday brunches. ✉ *Hwy. 706, Paradise* ⌂ *c/o Mount Rainier Guest Services, Box 108, Star Rte., Ashford 98304* ☎ *360/569–2275* 🖷 *360/569–2770* ⊕ *www.guestservices.com/ rainier/* ⇌ *127 rooms, 96 with bath* ⚐ *Restaurant, bar, snack bar; no room phones, no room TVs* ⊟ *MC, V* ⊘ *Closed Nov.–mid-May.*

$–$$ ⊞ **Mountain Meadows Inn Bed and Breakfast.** Antiques, Native American baskets, and John Muir memorabilia adorn the living room of this homey inn, 6 mi southwest of Mt. Rainier National Park. The modern cottage has three units, each with its own entrance and kitchen. ✉ *28912 State Rte. 706 E, Ashford 98304* ☎ *360/569–2788* ⊕ *www.mt-rainier. net* ⇌ *6 rooms, 3 efficiencies* ⚐ *Some kitchens, pond, hot tub; no a/c, no room phones, no room TVs, no children under 4, no smoking* ⊟ *MC, V* ⦿ *BP.*

¢–$ ⊞ **Inn of Packwood.** Mt. Rainier and the Cascade Mountains tower above this inn surrounded by lawns at the center of Packwood. Pine paneling and furniture lend the rooms rustic charm. You can swim in an indoor heated pool beneath skylights or picnic beneath a weeping willow. ✉ *13032 Hwy. 12, Packwood 98361* ☎ *360/494–5500* 🖷 *360/ 494–5503* ⊕ *www.innofpackwood.com* ⇌ *34 rooms* ⚐ *Picnic area, some kitchenettes, some microwaves, some refrigerators, cable TV, pool, spa* ⊟ *MC, V* ⦿ *CP.*

★ ¢–$ 🏠 **Wellspring.** The accommodations here include tastefully designed log cabins, a tree house, and a room in a greenhouse. All guest quarters are individually decorated. There's a queen-size feather bed suspended by ropes beneath a skylight in the Nest Room; the Tatoosh Room has a huge stone fireplace and can house up to 10 people. Also available are a variety of spa facilities, as befits a property created by a massage therapist. ⊠ *54922 Kernehan Rd., Ashford 98304* ☎ *360/569–2514* 🛏 *9 cabins* ⚒ *Some kitchenettes, some microwaves, some refrigerators, pond, hot tubs, outdoor hot tub, massage, saunas, spa, hiking; no room phones, no room TVs, no smoking* ▤ *MC, V.*

¢–$ 🏠 **Whittaker's Bunkhouse.** This 1912 motel once housed loggers and mill-workers. In those days it was referred to as "the place to stop on the way to the top." In the early 1990s famed climber Lou Whittaker bought and renovated the facility. Today it's a comfortable hostelry, with inexpensive single bunks as well as larger private rooms. ⊠ *30205 SR 706 E, Ashford 98304* ☎ *360/569–2439* ⊕ *www.welcometoashford. com* ⚒ *Restaurant, hot tub* 🛏 *20 rooms* ▤ *MC, V.*

☾ ¢ 🏠 **Cowlitz River Lodge.** You can't beat the location of this comfort-able two-story family motel: it's just off the highway in Packwood, the gateway to Mt. Rainier National Park *and* the Mt. St. Helens National Volcanic Monument. A lodge-like construction and a large stone fire-place in the great room add some character—a good thing as guest rooms have standard motel furniture and bedding. ⊠ *13069 U.S. 12, Pack-wood 98361* ☎ *360/494–4444 or 888/305–2185* 🖨 *360/494–2075* ⊕ *www.escapetothemountains.com* 🛏 *32 rooms* ⚒ *Cable TV, hot tub, conference room, laundry facilities* ▤ *AE, DC, MC, V* ⍾ *CP.*

¢ 🏠 **Nisqually Lodge.** Fires in the grand stone fireplace of this lodge hotel a few miles west of Mt. Rainier National Park lend the Great Room warmth and cheer. Guest rooms are comfortable and have standard motel decor. ⊠ *31609 State Rd., Ashford 98304* ☎ *360/569–8804* 🖨 *360/ 569–2435 or 888/674–3554* ⊕ *www.escapetothemountains.com* 🛏 *24 rooms* ⚒ *Cable TV, hot tub, playground, laundry facilities, business services; no smoking* ▤ *AE, MC, V* ⍾ *CP.*

CAMPING FACILITIES There are five drive-in campgrounds in the park—Cougar Rock, Ipsut Creek, Ohanapecosh, Sunshine Point, and White River—with almost 700 sites for tents and RVs. None of the park campgrounds has hot water or RV hookups; showers are available at Jackson Memorial Visitor Center.

For backcountry camping you must obtain a free wilderness permit at one of the visitor centers. Primitive sites are spaced at 7- or 8-mile in-tervals along the Wonderland Trail. A copy of *Wilderness Trip Planner: A Hiker's Guide to the Wilderness of Mount Rainier National Park,* avail-able from any of the park's visitor centers or through the superinten-dent's office, is an invaluable guide if you're planning backcountry stays. Reservations are available for specific wilderness campsites, from May 1 to September 30, for $20. For more details, call the Wilderness Information Center at 360/569–4453.

⚠ **Cougar Rock Campground.** This secluded, heavily wooded camp-ground with an amphitheater is one of the first to fill up. You can re-serve group sites for $3 per person, per night, with a minimum of 12 people per group. Reservations are accepted for summer only. ⊠ *2½ mi north of Longmire* ☎ *800/365–2267 or 301/722–1257* ⊕ *reservations. nps.gov* 🛏 *173 sites* ⚒ *Flush toilets, dump station, drinking water, fire grates, ranger station* 🎫 *$15* ⊘ *Closed mid-Oct.–late May.*

⚠ **Ipsut Creek Campground.** The quietest park campground is also the most difficult to reach. It's in the park's northwest corner, amid a wet, green, and rugged wilderness; many self-guided trails are nearby. The campground is theoretically open year-round, though the gravel Carbon River Road that leads to it is subject to flooding and potential closure at any time. Reservations aren't accepted here. ✉ *Carbon River Road, 4 mi east of the Carbon River entrance* ☎ *360/569–2211* ⬛ *31 sites* ⬥ *Running water (non-potable), fire grates* 💲 *$9 summer, winter free.*

⚠ **La Wis Wis Campground.** Alongside a small creek in Gifford Pinchot National Forest, this forest service campground is a few miles from the Ohanapecosh gateway to Rainier. ✉ *Off Rte. 12, 7 mi northeast of Packwood then ½ mi west on Forest Service Rd. 1272* ☎ *360/494–5515* ⬛ *100 sites* ⬥ *Drinking water, grills, picnic tables* 💲 *$12* ▭ *No credit cards* ⊘ *Closed Oct.–Apr.*

⚠ **Mowich Lake Campground.** This is Rainier's only lakeside campground. It's at 4,959 feet and is, by national park standards, peaceful and secluded. It's accessible only by 5 mi of convoluted gravel roads, which are subject to weather damage and potential closure at any time. ✉ *Mowich Lake Road, 6 mi east of the park boundary* ☎ *360/568–2211* ⬛ *30 sites* ⬥ *Pit toilets, running water (non-potable), fire grates, picnic tables, ranger station* 💲 *Free* ⬥ *Reservations not accepted* ⊘ *Closed Nov.–mid July.*

⚠ **Mounthaven Resort.** Amid tall firs, this small, RV-only campground resort is just west of the national park boundary. Recreation includes volleyball, badminton, and horseshoes. ✉ *Rte. 706, Ashford 98304* ☎ *800/456–9380* ⊕ *www.mounthaven.com* ⬛ *19 RV sites, 11 cabins* ⬥ *Flush toilets, full hookups, drinking water, laundry facilities, showers, fire pits, grills, picnic tables, electricity, public telephone* 💲 *$25 RV sites; $124–$219 cabins* ▭ *MC, V* ⊘ *Open year-round.*

⚠ **Packwood RV Park.** This large complex in Packwood provides grassy sites in the foothills of Mt. Rainier. ✉ *Rte. 12, Packwood 98361* ☎ *360/494–5145* ⊕ ⬛ *88 sites, 77 with hookups* ⬥ *Flush toilets, full hookups, drinking water, showers, grills, picnic tables, electricity, public telephone* 💲 *$20 RVs* ▭ *MC, V.*

⚠ **Ohanapecosh Campground.** In the park's southeast corner, this lush, green campground has a visitor center, amphitheater, and self-guided trail. It's one of the first campgrounds to open. Reservations are accepted for summer only. ✉ *Ohanapecosh Visitor Center, Rte. 123, 1½ mi north of park boundary* ☎ *800/365–2267 or 301/722–1257* ⊕ *reservations.nps.gov* ⬛ *189 sites* ⬥ *Flush toilets, dump station, drinking water, fire grates, ranger station* 💲 *$12* ⊘ *Closed late-Oct.–May.*

⚠ **Sunshine Point Campground.** This is a pleasant, partly wooded campground near the river, and one of the first to fill up. ✉ *5 mi past the Nisqually entrance* ☎ *360/569–2211* ⬛ *18 sites* ⬥ *Drinking water, fire grates.* 💲 *$10* ⬥ *Reservations not accepted.*

⚠ **White River Campground.** At an elevation of 4,400 feet, White River is one of the park's highest and least-wooded campgrounds. Here you can enjoy campfire programs, self-guided trails, and partial views of Mt. Rainier's summit. ✉ *5 mi past White River entrance* ☎ *360/569-2211* ⬛ *112 sites* ⬥ *Flush toilets, drinking water, fire grates, ranger station* 💲 *$10* ⬥ *Reservations not accepted* ⊘ *Closed mid-Sept.–late June.*

Sports & the Outdoors

HIKING It's almost impossible to experience the blissful beauty of the alpine environment or the hushed serenity of the old-growth forest without getting out of your car and walking. The numerous trails in and around Mt. Rainier range from low-key one-hour strolls to weekslong traverses around the mountain. Although the mountain seems benign on calm summer days, each year dozens of hikers and trekkers lose their way and must be rescued. Weather that approaches cyclonic levels can appear quite suddenly, any month of the year. With the possible exception of the short loop hikes listed below, you should carry day-packs with warm clothing, food, and other emergency supplies on all treks.

Nisqually Vista Trail. This gradually sloping, 1¼-mi round-trip trail is popular with hikers in summer and cross-country skiiers in winter. It heads out through subalpine meadows to point overlooking Nisqually Glacier. In summer, listen for the shrill alarm calls of the area's marmots. ✉ *Jackson Memorial Vsitor Center, Rte. 123, 1 mi north of Ohanapecosh, at the high point of Rte. 706.*

Skyline Trail. This 5-mi loop, one of the park's highest, beckons day-trippers with a cinemagraphic vista of alpine ridges and, in summer, meadows filled with brilliant flowers and birds. At 6,800-feet, Panorama Point, the spine of the Cascade Range, spreads away to the east, and Nisqually Glacier grumbles its way downslope. ✉ *Jackson Memorial Visitor Center, Rte. 123, 1 mi north of Ohanapecosh at the high point of Rte. 706.*

Sourdough Ridge Self-Guiding Trail. The mile-long loop of this easy trail takes you through the delicate subalpine meadows. A gradual climb to the ridge top yields magnificent views of Mt. Rainier and the more distant volcanic cones of Mounts Baker, Adams, Glacier, and Hood. ✉ *Sunrise Visitor Center, Sunrise Rd., 15 mi from the White River park entrance.*

Trail of the Shadows. This ½-mi trek is notable for its glimpses of meadowland ecology, its colorful soda springs (don't drink the water), James Longmire's old homestead cabin, and the foundation of the old Longmire Springs Hotel, which was destroyed around 1900. ✉ *Rte. 706, 10 mi east of Nisqually entrance.*

Van Trump Park Trail. You gain an exhilarating 2,200 feet while hiking through a vast expanse of meadow with views of southern Puget Sound. The 5 mi trail provides good footing, and the average hiker can make it up in three to four hours. ✉ *Rte. 706 at Christine Falls, 4.4 mi east of Longmire.*

Fodor'sChoice
★ **Wonderland Trail.** All other Mt. Rainier hikes pale in comparison to this stunning 93-mi hike, which completely encircles the mountain. The trail passes through everything from the old-growth forests of the lowlands to the wildflower-studded alpine meadows of the highlands. Be sure to pick up a mountain goat sighting card from a ranger station or information center to help in the park's ongoing effort to learn more about the park's goat population. Wonderland is a rugged trail; elevation gains and losses totaling 3,500 feet are common in a day's hike, which averages 8 mi. Most hikers start out from either Longmire or Sunrise and take 10–14 days to cover the 93-mi route. Wilderness permits are required and reservations are strongly recommended. ✉ *Longmire Wilderness Information Center, Rte. 706, 17 mi from Ashford; Sunrise Visitor Center, Sunrise Rd., 15 mi from the White River park entrance.*

MOUNTAIN CLIMBING Climbing Mt. Rainier is not for amateurs. Near-catastrophic weather can occur quite suddenly at any time of the year. That said, if you're experienced in technical, high-elevation snow, rock, and icefield adventuring, climbing Mt. Rainier can be memorable. Experienced climbers can fill out a self-registration climbing card at the Longmire, Paradise, White River, or Carbon River ranger stations and lead their own groups of two or more. In winter, the Paradise Climbing Ranger Station has self-registration available 24 hours a day, 7 days a week; Jackson Visitor Center in Paradise is open 10–5 on weekends and holidays only; and the Longmire Museum is open 9–4 daily. You must register with a ranger before leaving and check out upon return. There's a $30 annual climbing fee no matter how many climbs are made per year. This applies to anyone venturing above 10,000 feet or onto one of Rainier's glaciers.

Rainier Mountaineering Inc., a highly regarded concessionaire, cofounded by Himalayan adventurer Lou Whittaker, makes climbing the Queen of the Cascades an adventure open to anyone in good health and physical condition. The company teaches the fundamentals of mountaineering at one-day classes held during climbing season, from late May through early September. Participants are evaluated on their fitness for the climb; they must be able to withstand a 16-mi round-trip with a 9,000-foot gain in elevation. Winter ski programs are also offered. Costs run $100–$200 for the guide's Glacier Hike, one-day climbing school, and crevasse rescue school. The two-day summit climb package is $771, including classes. ⊠ *Jackson Memorial Visitor Center, Rte. 123, 1 mi north of Ohanapecosh, at the high point of Rte. 706* ☎ *888/892–5462* ⊕ *www.rmguides.com.*

SKIING
Fodor's Choice
★

Crystal Mountain Ski Area. The state's biggest and best-known area is open in summer for chairlift rides ($15) that afford sensational views of Rainier and the Cascades. In winter, daily lift rates are $44. Crystal Mountain has 1,300 acres of serviced lift area and 1,000 acres of backcountry. ⊠ *Crystal Mountain Blvd., off Rte. 410, Crystal Mountain* ☎ *360/663–2265* ⊕ *www.crystalmt.com* ☉ *June–Sept. (summer chairlift), daily 10–4; mid-Nov.–Apr., weekdays 9–4, weekends 8:30–4.*

Longmire Ski Touring Center. Longmire, which is adjacent to the National Park Inn, rents cross-country ski equipment and provides lessons from mid-December through Easter, depending on snow conditions. A set of skis, poles, and boots is $15 per day. Snowshoe rental is $12 per day. Lessons range from $16 for a two-hour group lesson to $20 for a four-hour guided tour. ⊠ *Rte. 706, 10 mi east of Nisqually entrance, Longmire* ☎ *360/569–2411 or 360/569–2271 mid-week* ☉ *Thanksgiving–Easter, daily 9–5.*

Paradise Ski Area. Here you can cross-country ski or, in the Snowplay Area north of the upper parking lot at Paradise, sled using inner tubes and soft platters from December to April. Check with rangers for any restrictions that may apply. Ranger-led snowshoe walks are held from here and several cross-country ski trails, from novice to advanced, lead from Paradise. ⊠ *Accessible from Nisqually entrance at park's southwest corner and from Stevens Canyon entrance at park's southeast corner (summer only)* ☎ *360/569–2211* ⊕ *www.nps.gov/mora* ☉ *May–mid-Oct., daily sunrise–sunset; mid-Oct.–Apr., weekends sunrise–sunset.*

White Pass Village. This ski area has 54 privately owned condominiums and is about 10 mi east of the Stevens Canyon entrance. White Pass summit is about 6,000 feet. There are 18 trails, including a Nordic network. A beginner lift allows novice skiers to stand for the 70-foot ride up the hill. An all-day lift ticket is $37. Nordic passes are $16 per day. ⊠ *On U.S. 12* ☎ *509/672–3101* ⊕ *www.skiwhitepass.com* ☉ *Nov.–Apr.*

Mt. St. Helens

⑩ *51 mi southwest of Packwood.*

It was once a premier camping destination, with a Mt. Fuji–like cone and pristine forest. But the May 18, 1980, eruption blew off its top and stripped its slopes of forest. The 8,365-foot-high mountain, formerly 9,665 feet high, is one of a string of volcanic Cascade Range peaks that runs from British Columbia's Mt. Garibaldi south to California's Mt. Lassen, and including such notable peaks as Mt. Baker and Mt. Rainier to the north, Mt. Adams to the east, Mt. Hood in Oregon, and Mt. Shasta in California. Most people travel to Mt. St. Helens via the Spirit Lake Memorial Highway (Route 504), whose predecessor was destroyed in a matter of minutes in 1980. This highway has unparalleled views of the mountain and the Toutle River Valley.

The U.S. Forest Service operates the Mt. St. Helens National Volcanic Monument. The user fee is $3 per day per visitor center within the monument or $6 per day for a multicenter pass. Monument passes are available at visitor centers, Ape's Headquarters, and Cascade Peaks Restaurant and Gift Shop on Forest Road 99. You'll also need a Northwest Forest Pass to park at trailheads, visitor centers, and other forest facilities. The pass costs $5 per vehicle per day.

Climbing is limited to the south side of the mountain. Permits are required; the fee is $15 per person. On the east side of the mountain are two bare-bones visitor centers, Windy Ridge and Ape Cave. On the south side of the mountain there's a center at Lava Canyon. The three centers along Route 504 on the forest's west side—Mt. St. Helens Visitor Center (at Silver Lake), Coldwater Ridge Visitor Center Complex, and Johnston Ridge Observatory—are open daily in summer. Johnston Ridge closes from October until May; the other centers remain open daily. Silver Lake has hours from 9 to 6, and Coldwater and Johnson Ridge operate from 10 to 6; hours may be slightly different in winter.

Castle Rock's location on I–5 at the Spirit Lake Highway makes it a major point of entry for the Mt. St. Helens National Monument. The site takes its name from a tree-covered knob that once stood on the banks of the Cowlitz River and served as a navigational landmark for Hudson's Bay Company trappers and traders. The landscape changed dramatically when the 1980 eruption filled the Toutle and Cowlitz rivers with hot volcanic mush. A local **visitor center** (⊠ Hwy. 504, Castle Rock ☎ 360/274–2100) has an exhibit hall portraying the history of Castle Rock and Mt. St. Helens. *The Eruption of Mount St. Helens,* a 30-minute giant-screen film, plays every 45 minutes from 9 AM to 6 PM at the **Cinedome Theater** (⊠ Exit 49 off I–5, Castle Rock ☎ 360/274–9844). Admission is $6.

The **Mt. St. Helens Visitors Center** (⊠ Rte. 504, 5 mi east of I–5, Silver Lake ☎ 360/274–2100) doesn't have great views of the mountain, but it has exhibits documenting the eruption and a walk-through volcano.

★ ☾ **Weyerhauser/Hoffstadt Bluff Visitors Center** (⊠ Rte. 504, 27 mi east of I–5 ☎ 360/274–7750), run by Cowlitz County, contains the only full-service restaurant along Route 504. The center also has picnic areas; a helicopter-tour operator; hiking trails; and the Memorial Grove, which honors the 57 people who lost their lives during the 1980 eruption. Admission is free.

Exhibits at the **Coldwater Ridge Visitors Center** (⊠ Rte. 504, 43 mi east of I–5 ☎ 360/274–2131) document the great blast and its effects on the surrounding 150,000 acres—which were devastated but are going through a remarkable recovery. The center has a small concession area,
★ ☾ and a ¼-mi trail that leads to Coldwater Lake. The **Johnston Ridge Observatory** (⊠ Rte. 504, 53 mi east of I–5 ☎ 360/274–2140) in the heart of the blast zone has spectacular views of the crater and lava dome. Exhibits here interpret the geology of Mt. St. Helens and explain how scientists monitor an active volcano.

The Parks A to Z

To research prices, get advice from other travelers, and book travel arrangements, visit www.fodors.com.

BOAT & FERRY TRAVEL

Washington State Ferries charge $9.50 per vehicle from Port Townsend to Keystone; it's $2.08 each way if you walk on.

🚢 Boat & Ferry Information **Washington State Ferries** ⊠ Colman Dock, Pier 52, Downtown, Seattle ☎ 206/464–6400, 888/808–7977, or 800/843–3779 (automated line) in WA and BC 🌐 www.wsdot.wa.gov/ferries.

BUS TRAVEL

Greyhound and Gray Line offer limited service to points along major thoroughfares. Gray Line of Seattle has regular tours to Mt. Rainier National Park. Rainier Shuttle offers daily service from Sea-Tac to Ashford or Paradise from May 3 to October 10. The Ashford Mountain Center offers shuttle service from June through September to and from Sea-Tac and destinations within the park.

🚻 **Bus Information Ashford Mountain Center Shuttle** ☎ 360/569-2604 ⊕ www. ashfordmountaincenter.com. **Gray Line** ☎ 503/285-9845 or 800/422-7042 in Portland, 206/624-5077 or 800/426-7505 in Seattle ⊕ www.grayline.com. **Greyhound** ☎ 800/231-2222 ⊕ www.greyhound.com. **Rainier Shuttle** ☎ 360/569-2604.

CAR TRAVEL

Interstate 5 is the main north–south route through western Whatcom and Skagit counties. Route 20 heads east from Burlington to Sedro-Woolley and continues on through the North Cascades to the Methow and Okanogan valleys, and across the northeastern mountains to the Idaho state line near Newport.

Most routes, even back roads, have two lanes and are paved; the busier ones have occasional passing lanes. A few remote mountain roads have gravel or dirt surfaces, which makes driving them interesting during the November–April rainy season. Rains can be sufficiently heavy in fall, winter, and spring to make driving dangerous, even on the interstate. Snow falls in the mountains from October or November until as late as May and makes driving extremely hazardous. Route 20 is usually closed (because of avalanche danger) from November through April. Stevens Pass faces intermittent winter closures for avalanche control (the avalanches are dislodged with howitzer shells; snow sliding onto the highway is cleared by plows).

Route 101, the main thoroughfare around the Olympic Peninsula, is a two-lane, well-paved highway. Rural backroads are blacktop or gravel, and tend to have potholes and get washed out during rains. In winter, landslides and wet weather frequently close roads.

Most visitors arrive at the Mt. Rainier National Park's Nisqually entrance, the closest entrance to I–5, via Route 706. Route 410 enters the park from the east. Highway 123 enters from the southeast. Routes 410 and 123 are usually closed in winter. Route 165 leads to Ipsut Creek Campground through the Carbon River entrance to Mowich Lake, in the park's northwest corner.

Route 504 is the main road through the Mt. St. Helens National Volcanic Monument. The Castle Rock Exit (No. 49) of I–5 is just outside the monument's western entrance. Follow 504 into the park. You can access the park from the north by taking Forest Service Road 25 south from U.S. 12 at the town of Randle. Forest Service Road 25 connects with Forest Service Road 90, which heads north from the town of Cougar. The two forest-service roads are closed by snow in winter.

VISITOR INFORMATION

🚻 **Destination Packwood Association** ⌂ Box 64, Packwood 98361 ☎ 360/494-2223 ⊕ www.destinationpackwood.com. **Forks Chamber of Commerce** ✉ 1411 S. Forks Ave., Forks 98331 ☎ 800/443-6757 ⊕ www.forkswa.com. **La Conner Chamber of Commerce** ✉ Lime Dock, 109 N. 1st St., La Conner ☎ 360/466-4778. **Mt. Rainier Business Association** ⌂ Box 214, Ashford 98304 ☎ 360/569-0910 or 877/617-9950 ⊕ www.mt-rainier.com. **Mt. Rainier National Park** ✉ Tahoma Woods, Star Rte., Ashford 98304 ☎ 360/569-2211 ⊕ www.nps.gov/mora/. **Mt. St. Helens National Volcanic Monument** ☎ 360/449-7800 ⊕ www.fs.fed.us/gpnf/mshnvm. **Mount Vernon Cham-**

ber of Commerce ⊠ 117 N. 1st St., Mount Vernon ☎ 360/428-8547. **North Cascades National Park** ⊠ 2105 Rte. 20, Sedro-Woolley ☎ 360/856-5700. **North Olympic Peninsula Visitor and Convention Bureau** ☎ Box 670, Port Angeles 98362 ☎ 360/452-8552 or 800/942-4042 ⊕ www.olympicpeninsula.org. **Olympic National Park** ⊠ 1835 Blacklake Blvd., Olympia 98512 ☎ 360/956-4501. **Port Angeles Chamber of Commerce** ⊠ 121 E. Railroad Ave., 98362 ☎ 360/452-2363. **Sedro-Woolley Chamber of Commerce** ⊠ 714-B Metcalf St., Sedro-Woolley ☎ 360/835-1582 or 888/225-8365 ⊕ www.sedro-woolley.com.

INDEX

NOTES

NOTES

NOTES

FODOR'S KEY TO THE GUIDES

America's guidebook leader publishes guides for every kind of traveler. Check out our many series and find your perfect match.

FODOR'S GOLD GUIDES
America's favorite travel-guide series offers the most detailed insider reviews of hotels, restaurants, and attractions in all price ranges, plus great background information, smart tips, and useful maps.

COMPASS AMERICAN GUIDES
Stunning guides from top local writers and photographers, with gorgeous photos, literary excerpts, and colorful anecdotes. A must-have for culture mavens, history buffs, and new residents.

FODOR'S CITYPACKS
Concise city coverage in a guide plus a foldout map. The right choice for urban travelers who want everything under one cover.

FODOR'S EXPLORING GUIDES
Hundreds of color photos bring your destination to life. Lively stories lend insight into the culture, history, and people.

FODOR'S TRAVEL HISTORIC AMERICA
For travelers who want to experience history firsthand, this series gives in-depth coverage of historic sights, plus nearby restaurants and hotels. Themes include the Thirteen Colonies, the Old West, and the Lewis and Clark Trail.

FODOR'S POCKET GUIDES
For travelers who need only the essentials. The best of Fodor's in pocket-size packages for just $9.95.

FODOR'S FLASHMAPS
Every resident's map guide, with dozens of easy-to-follow maps of public transit, restaurants, shopping, museums, and more.

FODOR'S CITYGUIDES
Sourcebooks for living in the city: thousands of in-the-know listings for restaurants, shops, sports, nightlife, and other city resources.

FODOR'S AROUND THE CITY WITH KIDS
Up to 68 great ideas for family days, recommended by resident parents. Perfect for exploring in your own backyard or on the road.

FODOR'S HOW TO GUIDES
Get tips from the pros on planning the perfect trip. Learn how to pack, fly hassle-free, plan a honeymoon or cruise, stay healthy on the road, and travel with your baby.

FODOR'S LANGUAGES FOR TRAVELERS
Practice the local language before you hit the road. Available in phrase books, cassette sets, and CD sets.

KAREN BROWN'S GUIDES
Engaging guides—many with easy-to-follow inn-to-inn itineraries—to the most charming inns and B&Bs in the U.S.A. and Europe.

BAEDEKER'S GUIDES
Comprehensive guides, trusted since 1829, packed with A–Z reviews and star ratings.

OTHER GREAT TITLES FROM FODOR'S
Baseball Vacations, The Complete Guide to the National Parks, Family Vacations, Golf Digest's Places to Play, Great American Drives of the East, Great American Drives of the West, Great American Vacations, Healthy Escapes, National Parks of the West, Skiing USA.